DEATH OF A NATION
OF A

DEATH
OF A
NATION

**PLANTATION POLITICS
AND THE MAKING OF THE
DEMOCRATIC PARTY**

DINESH
D'SOUZA

ALL
POINTS
BOOKS

All Points Books is an imprint of St. Martin's Press.

www.allpointsbooks.com

Designed by Meryl Sussman Levavi

The Library of Congress Cataloging-in-Publication Data is available upon request.

ISBN 978-1-250-16377-6 (hardcover)
ISBN 978-1-250-20030-3 (signed edition)
ISBN 978-1-250-16782-8 (ebook)

Our books may be purchased in bulk for promotional, educational, or
business use. Please contact your local bookseller or the Macmillan
Corporate and Premium Sales Department at 1-800-221-7945, extension
5442, or by email at MacmillanSpecialMarkets@macmillan.com.

First Edition: July 2018

10 9 8 7 6 5 4 3 2 1

[Master Thomas] told me, if I would be happy, I must lay out no plans for the future. He said . . . he would take care of me . . . and taught me to depend solely upon him for happiness.

—FREDERICK DOUGLASS,
Narrative of the Life of Frederick Douglass,
an American Slave

To our Gang of Four, who complete our family:

Brandon, Danielle, Justin and Julienna

CONTENTS

PREFACE

On Gaining and
Losing a Country

To make us love our country,
our country ought to be lovely.

—EDMUND BURKE, *Reflections on
the Revolution in France*[1]

A nation is so much more than its laws, its political system, even its founding documents. When I first came to America as an exchange student in 1978, I knew little of the Constitution or the Bill of Rights. What first struck me about America was its people. To me, they were a sort of tribe. As a tribe, they had their own mannerisms and styles of speech, their own customs and cuisine, their own way of life and of looking at the world.

Anthropologists call these "folkways." The contemporary word for them is "culture." A nation, political scientist Benedict Anderson says, is an "imagined community," by which he means a community of people who have never met each other but are linked through their common mores and mutual acceptance of each other as fellow citizens. Such loyalty, Anderson notes, can run very deep in that nations, like religions, are one of the very few things that people are willing to die for. People will die for America but they won't die for the Democratic Party, the Los Angeles Raiders, or the United Way.[2]

Yet in constituting a tribe and having shared traditions and loyalties, Americans are no different from any other people in the world. I suppose if I went to Japan or France I would, in a similar manner, encounter the Japanese tribe, the French tribe. I myself hail from a tribe at the other end of the world, the East Indian tribe. We too have our folkways and culture, which I experienced in my childhood years through watching Bollywood movies, listening to radio broadcasts of cricket games, hanging out of the overcrowded trains on my way to school, eating street *bhel puri* and jabbering with my friends in that hybrid language of Hindustani and English that can be called Hinglish, and protesting, while submitting to, the corruption that defines the ordinary transactions of Indian life. So we too were a tribe of our own. Yet from my first experience with Americans, I knew they were a unique sort of tribe, a tribe like no other.

In a single year of living with four different families in Arizona—a preacher and his wife; the local postmaster and his wife; a wealthy rancher, his second wife and daughter; and two young schoolteachers with toddlers—I experienced America through a series of distinctive rituals. These included my first Rotary dinner during which I stared wide-eyed at my plate, bearing ingredients—namely, an absurdly large sirloin steak covered with mushrooms—I had neither tasted nor seen before; a raucous tailgate party preceding the Patagonia Union High School homecoming game; the abundance of American grocery stores, which had more types of cheese and more types of ice cream than I knew existed; the Sadie Hawkins dance, which included some of my early life's most memorable embarrassments; and several church potlucks, including one in which a fellow showed me the odd sight of "In God We Trust" imprinted on his twenty-dollar bill. I remember cheering with my host family at a Little League baseball game; going to malls and restaurants and noticing the funny habit that people have of calling each other "sir"; seeing the Grand Canyon on an exchange student trip that included several strange signs that said "Adopt a Highway"; sampling Girl Scout cookies; attending what was at the time described as a "shotgun wedding," featuring, incredibly, two students from my senior class; the Sphinxlike college application process, which involved me taking something called a standardized test and asking bewildered friends and family in India to write over-the-top recommendations comparing me to the greatest figures who had ever lived; and waving the flag at the Fourth of July fireworks and cookout.

This, for me, was America, America as I first discovered and experienced it. And this America was fascinating in and of itself. But through these experiences—and by looking underneath them—I knew there was a deeper side to America. Who, for example, adopts highways? My mom, visiting years later from Mumbai, could scarcely grasp the concept. It implied a notion of civic engagement, of taking responsibility for something unconnected to one's private sphere, that she found incomprehensibly strange. Featuring God on a nation's currency would seem to suggest not merely that trade is expected to be conducted honestly, under God's supervision, so to speak, but also that the political and economic systems of the country are somehow based on transcendental principles, on the presumption of a divine creator.

The Sadie Hawkins dance, with the girls asking the boys, challenged conventional patriarchal sex roles while, at the same time, affirming the heterosexual norm. Many Indians live in extended families and marry through the intervention and arrangement of parents and relatives; Americans live in "nuclear" families founded by couples who choose each other and marry after falling in love. Even the poorest, least-educated, lowliest American considers himself just as good as any other American; no one can deny there is a powerful ethic of social equality in a country where people call their waiter "sir," as if he were a knight.

Going away to college implied a mobility that expressed itself in phrases like "moving up" and "making it," and wrapped up in all that was the powerful idea of the self-made individual and the self-directed life, in which we are the architects of our own destiny. The American dream is partly about success, but what struck me most about this country was not the spectacular Horatio Alger stories but rather the fact that here even the ordinary guy has a pretty comfortable—and by world standards an enviably lavish—life.

Americans are an active people; they are always doing something. In other countries people stand around idle for hours; Americans pursue even recreation with a kind of manic intensity. Americans work hard and play hard. If you pay Americans more they will work more hours; if you pay other people more they will use the money to work less and go on vacation. In other countries it is common to have adults who literally do nothing—they depend on family or friends to take care of them—but ask an American what he does and literally no one will answer, "Nothing." I observed that this is a culture of effort and self-reliance; laziness and dependency have a stigma attached to them.

In other countries, a flag is just a flag. But in America, I discovered, the flag is the symbol of a founding event, emerging out of the Revolutionary War that articulated principles that could only be fully expressed almost ninety years later in the aftermath of one of the bloodiest civil wars in history. Other nations are the product of history and chance; America, while hardly capable of eluding history, was primarily the product of design. It is that design that gave rise to an American dream; I noted in my mind that there is no such thing as a French dream, an Indian dream, a Chinese dream.

Identity in other countries is based on birth and blood; but in America it is based on embracing American ideals and the American way of life. That's why the American tribe is so multiracial and includes white people, black people and brown people like me. Somehow I could come from another place like India and "become American," while it would be reciprocally unthinkable for an American to come to Mumbai and, no matter how long he lived or worked there, "become Indian." This is the America I fell in love with three decades ago. The American dream became my dream. That's why I made the choice to live here, to work here, to make my life here and to go through the naturalization process and become an American citizen, which I did in 1991.

HOW NATIONS DIE

Nations come and nations go, and it is relevant to our purpose to ask how nations die. The Carthaginians, for instance, were one of the most powerful nations in the world; where are they now? Nations are sometimes wiped out through foreign conquest, as the Carthaginians were in the Punic Wars. The Romans, their conquerors, decimated one nation after another, incorporating them in the Roman Empire. Genghis Khan and his marauding Mongols stormed across the plains of Central Asia, reducing kingdoms and communities to rubble. Hitler and Stalin conspired together to obliterate Poland and share the dividends of her conquest and enslavement. This is a depressingly familiar pattern in history.

Sometimes nations are obliterated by domestic implosion. The Romans were not destroyed merely by barbarian invasions from the North; what made Rome vulnerable was its internal rot, caused by despotism, decadence and debauchery. The Ottomans too became the "sick man of Europe," weakened by internal economic collapse and a decayed ruling class, long before the empire itself was decapitated during World War I. In Europe, the fascists and the communists sought to forcibly uproot their ancestral cultures in order to create new societies and, in their view, new types of human beings.

In my wife Debbie's native country of Venezuela, Hugo Chavez and then Nicolas Maduro destroyed the prosperity and political institutions of that oil-rich country and reduced it to its current state of chaos and impoverishment, a place where babies are abandoned on the street, girls become prostitutes to survive, antibiotics and medical supplies are scarce and citizens eat their domestic animals when they run out of food. "The country I was born in is dying," Debbie says, and the desperate look in her face tells me she is speaking quite literally.

Abraham Lincoln predicted in his Lyceum Address that if America ever perished it would be through internal ruin. "Shall we expect some transatlantic military giant to step the Ocean, and crush us at a blow? Never! . . . If destruction be our lot, we must ourselves be its author and finisher. As a nation of freemen, we must live through all time, or die by suicide."[3] I have for a long time now wondered about that word "we." Who in America would want to kill America? Why would a country that has drawn immigrants for most of its history and that continues to be a magnet for the world want to take itself off the map? And what would the death of America look like?

A few years ago, I witnessed a determined, ruthless effort to kill my American dream. Shortly after I released a highly successful film criticizing Barack Obama, the FBI came banging on my door. Soon I discovered that Preet Bharara, the prosecuting attorney for the Southern District of New York, had charged me with violating campaign finance laws. My heinous offense was to give $20,000 of my own money to a longtime college friend of mine running a quixotic campaign for U.S. Senate in New York.

I knew of course that all kinds of people and groups give millions of dollars to candidates and to the Republican and Democratic Parties. Never having donated before, I gave in the wrong way. Had I given through a political action committee (PAC), I could have given much more.

This is not the place to discuss the legitimacy of campaign finance laws. The relevant point is that such laws are never prosecuted absent evidence of corruption. The only Americans who have been indicted are those who deployed campaign contributions for the purpose of getting an appointment or a tax subsidy or in some respect benefiting themselves. In these cases, of course, the "contribution" was not really a contribution but rather the purchase of a political favor or quid pro quo. But in my case no corruption or quid pro quo was involved; the prosecution conceded I was doing this out of what my attorney termed "misguided loyalty" toward a friend.

The friend, I should mention, was one of a small clan of Dartmouth students whom I befriended just a year after coming to America. With my family thousands of miles away, this little platoon of pals constituted my surrogate family. More than anyone else, they taught me about America and showed me what it means to be an American. I still remember the time they took me to buy my first navy blue blazer and showed me how to dress appropriately. "An Ivy League education," one of them solemnly informed me, "is incomplete without learning to make a proper dimple in your tie."

Essentially they were showing me how to assimilate, not just to America but also to the preppie subculture of the northeastern elite campus. My affection for this group was deep and reciprocated. My loyalty to them was not "misguided" in itself; it had been earned through years of devoted friendship.

Still, I found myself standing frightened and vulnerable in a U.S. courtroom and hearing the ominous phrase, *United States of America versus Dinesh D'Souza*. Those are words that no immigrant wants to hear. I knew that there was a whole team of FBI agents assigned to my case: one to go through my bank records, another to review my tax returns, a third to read through all my books. Their objective was clear: find something on this guy so that we can nail him. And the Obama administration sought to lock me away in federal prison for a period between ten and sixteen months.

A PLOT TO KILL A DREAM

A Clinton-appointee judge didn't go along with this, but he did sentence me to eight months of overnight confinement in a halfway house, where I slept on a bunk bed in a dormitory with sixty hardened federal felons. In addition, I paid a fine and got five years of probation and community service, which I am still doing, so that my penance is not complete until October 2019. And absent a presidential pardon I will remain a lifetime felon.

From the first tap on my door, I knew that they were bent on destroying my life, on uprooting my American dream. But as the process got under way I realized that this was not about me. Sure, I had been reckless in giving the Obama administration a pretext to go after me. Didn't I know there was a target on my back? I had just made a movie— the second-highest-grossing political documentary of all time—exposing the leader of the United States as a hypocrite and a fraud. I knew, better than most, what a thin-skinned narcissist he was. Shouldn't I have expected him to use his full power to retaliate? If you strike at the Empire, won't the Empire strike back? I was obviously the dumbest criminal in America.

Then I saw that this wasn't just personal. Obama didn't just despise me; he despised people like me. I was a nonwhite immigrant born in the same year as Obama, an Ivy League graduate as he was, an American success story just like him, and yet I saw America very differently than he did, and fought for a vision of America that he was assiduously trying to obliterate. People like me represented a threat to Obama's project to "remake America," as he put it, and in the name of that project, he had to defeat us, to discredit us, even to put us out of commission if possible. In trying to kill my American dream, Obama and his minions were going after the America that I love and represent.

So I came to see my travails as reflecting a larger enterprise, not the demise of my American dream but the project for the demise of the American dream itself. I realized that the most likely death of America would not involve the disappearance of its people or the erasure of its national boundaries. Rather, it would involve the destruction and dissolution of all the things that make America distinctive. The death of America is the death of American exceptionalism.

Such a death would involve not only the collapse of America's founding principles but also the extinction of its characteristic mores and values and what Lincoln termed its "mystic chords of memory." In effect, we'd still have the American people but they would no longer bear the recognizable American stamp. They—we—would no longer dream American dreams. The America that I and so many of my fellow Americans have come to love would no longer exist.

If that happens, there will have been little point in my emigrating to this country; my life's path would, to a large degree, have been a mistake. I might still love America but that America would be gone. I would simply not feel the same way about the America that remained, for how can one love a country that has ceased to be lovely? I am tempted to compare this catastrophe to a death in the family, but it would more accurately be a death of the family.

What makes this crisis especially acute is who is perpetrating the murder. It is none other than some of our fellow citizens. One may say that there is a revolt in the family by a faction that seeks to destroy the family, to wreck what the family has always stood for and to replace it by something else entirely, a new family in which many members feel like strangers. Some of them may have to be driven out or locked up because they no longer fit in and are perceived as a threat to the new ideological regime.

I realize with horror that there are many people in America who seek this sort of transformation or, as I have been putting it, demise. In this sense, the existential threat to America is genuine. The death of America is a real possibility. There are very powerful people in America who are working overtime to kill America.

DEATH
OF A
NATION

1

INTRODUCTION

Who Is Killing America?

Dependence begets subservience and venality,
suffocates the germ of virtue, and prepares
fit tools for the designs of ambition.

—THOMAS JEFFERSON,
Notes on the State of Virginia[1]

On July 6, 2017, President Donald Trump addressed the issue of the death of America in an address to the Polish people in Warsaw's Krasinski Square. There he spoke not of America but of Western civilization, a civilization arising out of "bonds of history, culture, and memory," now facing "dire threats to our security and to our way of life." At first it seemed Trump was speaking only about the terrorist threat from radical Islamists. But it soon became clear to Poles and to the world that Trump was addressing a much larger issue.

The West, Trump said, is a particular type of civilization. "We write symphonies. We pursue innovation . . . We strive for excellence, and cherish inspiring works of art that honor God. We treasure the rule of law and protect the right to free speech and free expression. We empower women as pillars of our society and of our success. We put faith and family, not government and bureaucracy, at the center of our lives . . . And above all, we value the dignity of every human life, protect the rights of every person, and share the hope of every soul to live in freedom. That is who we are. Those are the priceless ties that bind us together."

These values, Trump said, do not uphold themselves. We must uphold them. "The fundamental question of our time," he said, "is whether the West has the will to survive." Specifically, "Do we have the desire and the courage to preserve our civilization in the face of those who would subvert and destroy it?" Even while suggesting that larger forces posed an existential threat to America and the West, Trump did not clearly enumerate what those forces were. Instead he issued a call to resistance, resoundingly concluding that "our own fight for the West does not begin on the battlefield—it begins with our minds, our wills, and our souls." Trump expressed confidence that in the end "our people will thrive. And our civilization will triumph."[2]

This speech, encapsulating characteristic Trump themes, brought the Polish crowd to its feet in enthusiastic applause. But in America it evoked a reaction that has defined the mainstream media response to Trump since he first declared his candidacy. Vox insisted that Trump's remarks "sounded like an alt-right manifesto," a reference to an allegedly racist faction that Trump has imported into the political right and the Republican Party. The progressive website Common Dreams detected "an ominous current running beneath Trump's words" that evoked the "infamous 1935 Nazi propaganda film 'Triumph of the Will.'" *The Atlantic,* in an article by Peter Beinart, deplored Trump for his "racial and religious paranoia."

Let's stay with Beinart's logic on this. According to Beinart, when Trump uses the term "our civilization," he is speaking in a kind of code. "His white nationalist supporters will understand exactly what he means." Beinart begins with a disarmingly simple question: what is the West? He argues that it cannot be merely a geographic term since "Poland is further east than Morocco. France is further east than Haiti. Australia is further east than Egypt. Yet Poland, France, and Australia are all considered part of 'the West.' Morocco, Haiti, and Egypt are not."

Nor can the West be an ideological term referring to democracy or industrialization, in Beinart's view. After all, "India is the world's largest democracy." Japan is fully industrialized. Yet obviously Trump does not include these nations in his definition of the West. Beinart concludes that for Trump, "The West is a racial and religious term. To be considered Western, a country must be largely Christian . . . and largely white."

That's what Beinart sees Trump as defending: religious and racial exclusivity. From Beinart's perspective, Trump's main target is not an Islamic threat from abroad, but a perceived threat coming from non-white, non-Christian immigrants to the United States. In Beinart's words, "The 'south' and 'east' only threaten the West's 'survival' if you see non-white, non-Christian immigrants as invaders. They only threaten the West's 'survival' if by 'West' you mean white, Christian hegemony."[3]

Something very interesting is going on here and it's slightly camouflaged by Beinart's apparent hostility to every word Trump spoke. When Trump says that America faces an existential threat to its values and way of life, Beinart actually agrees. So the disagreement between Trump and Beinart is not over whether America is vitally threatened but over the nature and source of the threat.

For Beinart and many others in the progressive or leftist camp, the threat does not come from Islamic radicals or immigrants but rather from "racial and religious paranoia," and the source of the threat is Trump and his white Christian supporters—a group we may call the Trumpsters. In other words, from Beinart and the left's point of view, it is Trump's and the Trumpsters' dangerous crusade on behalf of whiteness and Christianity that is killing America.

I am going to dive into these waters more deeply, but first I want to establish that Beinart is hardly alone in considering Trump to be the serial killer of America's most cherished values and institutions, if not of the country itself. Here are some representative articles from recent months.

Also in *The Atlantic,* Jack Goldsmith asks, "Will Donald Trump Destroy the Presidency?" Short answer: Yes. From Salon: "Donald Trump Is Destroying America's Standing in the World and May End Up Destroying the World." Title of a recent column in the *Baltimore Sun:* "Trump Is Killing American Ideals." Writing in the *New York Times,* Yascha Mounk declares on August 1, 2017, "The Past Week Proves That Trump Is Destroying Our Democracy." Not to be outdone, Ryu Spaeth in the *New Republic* offers "Donald Trump Is Killing Us: Notes from the End of the World as We Know It." And on a personal note, Dana Milbank of the *Washington Post* wants us to know that "President Trump Is Killing Me. Really." Evidently Milbank has been suffering from fatigue, headaches, lack of sleep, even chest pain, and since his health was previously good he attributes the deterioration to you-know-who. In sum, Trump and the Trumpsters pose a clear and present danger to the presidency, to American ideals, to democracy and to the planet. As for Dana Milbank, that poor dude is just trying to shake off his anxiety and get some sleep, and Donald Trump won't even let him do that.[4]

TWO TRUMP CARDS

Ordinarily we could dismiss this rhetoric as part of the routine hyperbole of American politics, especially in the aftermath of a hard-fought election. In this case, however, that would be a mistake. The sheer passion, hatred and fear directed toward Trump is widespread and genuine. A year and a half after the 2016 election, it has not gone away and in many places it has hardly abated. In fact, it goes beyond the progressive left and is shared by many independents, and even some Republicans and conservatives. Deep down, they are convinced that Trump poses a fundamental danger to America's survival as a diverse, open, lawful democratic society.

The whole manic resistance to Trump—from mainstream Democrats refusing to attend his inauguration to the violent disruptions of inaugural events; to the aggressive, if unsuccessful, attempt to get Trump's electors to defect away from him and invalidate his electoral majority; to calls for his impeachment from virtually the day he assumed office; to the nonstop blasting of Trump across virtually all media platforms; to the continuing disruptions, blockades and protests against Trump in cities and on campuses; to a grim, continuing project to oust Trump by showing Russia collusion, or obstruction of justice, or sexual harassment, in other words, by any means necessary—would be inexplicable absent this enduring perception of the man and what he represents.

Here are just a couple of examples of this anti-Trump fever. Writing just a few months after Trump's inauguration, progressive legal scholar Laurence Tribe insisted that "Trump must be impeached." Despite numerous ongoing investigations, Tribe argued that "to wait for the results of the multiple investigations underway is to risk tying our nation's fate to the whims of an authoritarian leader." Trump must be removed immediately because "he poses a danger to our system of government."[5]

Around the same time, Noah Millman published an article in *The Week* raising the prospect of a military coup. Millman's real objective was to prod the Republican leadership into ousting Trump. He warned them to "consider what steps might be necessary to take" before the military generals "take whatever steps they deem necessary in defense of their country." Such steps, Millman predicted, would involve "cordoning off the president" from the chain of command and ensuring "that the president of the United States is, in effect, no longer the president."[6]

In early 2018, psychiatrist Bandy Lee called for Trump to be removed from office and subjected to "forcible commitment" on account of mental instability. Lee hadn't examined Trump, yet this did not prevent her from diagnosing from his tweets and actions a psychological condition that could lead to Trump initiating nuclear war and threatening the extinction of the human species. Several Democratic lawmakers met with Lee for briefings on her "findings."[7]

What, then, does Trump represent that legitimizes even the contemplation of such extreme responses? The first and most incendiary charge is that Trump is a racist and a white supremacist. Democratic senator Elizabeth Warren calls him a "racist bully." Joy Reid of MSNBC calls him "blatantly bigoted" and an "unabashed white nationalist." Invoking what he considers Trump's unrelenting hostility to nonwhite immigrants, especially Muslims and Mexicans, Jay Pearson in the *Los Angeles Times* describes him as a "textbook racist." Writing in *New York* magazine, Frank Rich scorns Trump as a bigot who displays empathy for "neo-Nazis." *Rolling Stone* offers a catalog of Trump's misdeeds—"he built a presidential campaign on racial resentment and fear" and has sustained that theme ever since—in an article titled "Trump's Long History of Racism."[8]

It isn't just Trump; the indictment even includes the people who voted for Trump. These are voters for whom "whiteness is the unifying force," according to progressive novelist and Nobel laureate Toni Morrison. Trump's people seek to "restore whiteness to its former status as a marker of national identity," and they are willing to train "their guns on the unarmed, the innocent, the scared," even to "kill small children attending Sunday school," to "set fire to churches" and to "shoot black children in the street."[9]

"There's No Such Thing as a Good Trump Voter," Jamelle Bouie wrote in *Slate*. "People voted for a racist who promised racist outcomes." Based on a survey of Trump's demographic base of support, a headline in the left-wing *Nation* stated, "Economic Anxiety Didn't Make People Vote Trump, Racism Did." Frank Rich accuses "so-called GOP leaders" of being "Vichy collaborators" who enable Trump. According to Chauncey DeVega of Salon, far from being anomalous, "Donald Trump *is* a normal Republican" and "the Republican Party is the country's largest white identity organization: It mobilizes anti-black and anti-brown animus for political gain." A columnist for *The Hill*, Michael Starr Hopkins, insists that as a consequence of representing and promoting white nationalism, "Republicans and their identity politics are destroying America."[10]

The clear proof of Trump's bigotry, as progressives see it, is those indelible images from Charlottesville of Ku Klux Klansmen and neo-Nazis carrying Trump signs and wearing hats that bear Trump's slogan, "Make America Great Again." On MSNBC, Rachel Maddow highlighted white nationalists like Richard Spencer, David Duke and the organizers of Charlottesville and noted that Trump is the champion of this so-called Alt-Right. Trump is rebuilding "something that was a long-standing force for political power and terror in this country for generations and he is now doing what he can to help them come back."[11]

During the campaign, Hillary made commercials seeking to link Trump to the most extreme figures on the so-called Alt-Right. Asked after his election whether Trump was racist, Hillary Clinton responded that she didn't know what was in his heart but, as Trump's "acceptance" of David Duke's endorsement and his behavior following the white supremacist rally in Charlottesville indicated, "I believe that he has given a lot of encouragement and rhetorical support to the Ku Klux Klan." Calling up the ghosts of "racists and Nazis and white supremacists of all stripes," *Rolling Stone* insists that Trump "supports them in the deepest, darkest, most wizened recesses of his heart."[12]

So Trump doesn't just support racists; he also supports Nazis. This brings us to the second, related charge against Trump—one no less explosive than the first—that Trump is also a fascist, perhaps even a

Nazi. This charge is related to the racism one in that the Nazis were anti-Semites and white supremacists. But Nazism goes beyond racism in that it suggests authoritarianism; lawlessness; a willingness to suspend liberty and override the Constitution and the democratic process; extreme violence, including state-sponsored terrorism against minorities; the possibility of death camps and extermination. Progressives insist that even if Trump hasn't gotten there yet, he is moving in Hitler's direction.

"Fascism, American Style" is the title of columnist Paul Krugman's August 28, 2017 column in the *New York Times*. Following Trump's pardon of Joe Arpaio, an Arizona sheriff who sought to round up and deport illegal immigrants, Krugman invokes the memory of Auschwitz. "There's a word for political regimes that round up members of minority groups and send them to concentration camps." In an interview with Isaac Chotiner of *Slate,* historian Richard Evans says that Trump's election shows "echoes" of the Third Reich, notably in its "stigmatization of minorities." Writing in *Time,* historian Timothy Snyder reminds us that just like the early twentieth-century fascists who ran roughshod over normal political processes, "there is little reason to believe" that Trump and his team "support the American constitutional system as it stands."[13]

Even those on the progressive left who concede that Trump isn't a fascist usually end up concluding that, well, he sort of is. This mentality is conveyed in the title of columnist Charles Blow's October 19, 2017, column in the *New York Times,* "Trump Isn't Hitler. But the Lying . . ." Writing in Salon, Andrew O'Hehir grants that Trump is "not exactly Hitler" but goes on to identify him as "an authoritarian political leader with undeniable fascist tendencies." Economist Joseph Stiglitz insists that Trump is a "fascist kind of figure" who displays "fascist tendencies." Historian Ruth Ben-Ghiat, while conceding that "Trump is not aiming to establish a one-party state," proceeds to compare him with Hitler and Mussolini for attacking "the judiciary, the media, the institutions, hollowing them out." Before it's too late, she says, "I've been trying to warn the public . . . about the dangers that these men bring with them."[14]

As with the charge of racism, the Nazi label is applied by progressives not merely to Trump but to conservatives and Republicans. Columnist

Chris Hedges rails against "Trump and the Christian Fascists," whom he describes as "American fascists, clutching Christian crosses, waving American flags, and orchestrating mass recitations of the Pledge of Allegiance," riding the horses of religious and political bigotry to political power. Matthew MacWilliams writes in Politico that, as with the Germans who supported the Nazis, an affinity for authoritarianism is the "statistically significant variable" defining Trump voters. In another column, "The Other Inconvenient Truth," Charles Blow fumes that Trump, the racists and the neo-Nazis are all "a logical extension of a party that has too often refused to rebuke them" and it "is the Republican Party through which Trump burst that has been courting, coddling and accommodating these people for decades."[15]

So Trump and the right are accused of promoting the deadliest strains of both European and American bigotry. We are, according to Kirk Noden in *The Nation*, living through "the darkest moment of America's history," one defined by "fascism, misogyny, and hate."[16] The umbrella term here is white supremacy, which represents an escalation from previous terms like religious prejudice, racism, even institutional racism. Prejudice connotes mere ignorance and can presumably be rectified through exposure and experience. Even institutional racism refers to the disparate impact that facially neutral policies have on minorities; again, these effects may be unintentional.

White supremacy, however, is an entrenched ideology of hatred and discrimination. Historically, it has led to lynching, mass murder and genocide. From the progressive point of view, white supremacy in all its forms is the most dangerous threat facing this country. Trump and the right have revived this deadly bacillus, and it is they—through this epidemic of hate that they have cultivated and mainstreamed—who are poisoning the body politic and killing America.

THE PROGRESSIVE NARRATIVE

As should be obvious by now, the progressive argument for how Trump and the right are killing America through fascism and white supremacy is an argument based on history. By themselves these terms are mere political labels, but through history they acquire an ominous, talismanic significance. History integrates the present with the past, generating a story line that helps us understand what is going on. Through history we know not merely what terms like fascism, racism and white supremacy mean, we also know what they do, the horrors they are capable of. We know because of the havoc that these ideas have already wrought, here in America and in the world.

The iconic images of racism and fascism—of slave plantations, human auctions, brandings and whippings, a cataclysmic civil war, the night-riding Ku Klux Klan, young men strung up on trees, separate black and white water fountains, the goose-stepping Brownshirts, the Night of Broken Glass, Jews rounded up in concentration camps, the carnage of World War II, the full horror of the Holocaust—form the emotional and visual meaning of white supremacy for us. And these emotions still drive American politics. For the young they are the legacy of history; for the old, of memory. This country does not want to go through any of that again; if we did, it would represent an undoing of all that has been accomplished, a restoration of the barbarism of the past.

Now we are in a position to lay out the progressive narrative of American history, a story so familiar that it infuses virtually every textbook, every media account, every Hollywood movie and every dinner-table conversation. It is, in fact, the conventional wisdom about how America came to be what it is today. I call it the meta-story of American politics because it is the "story behind the story," the underlying white supremacy narrative that directs and shapes the innumerable retail theses, news accounts and TV and movie plots flowing from academia, Hollywood and the media. For many Americans, this conventional wisdom about white supremacy seems obvious, irrefutable, the sine qua non of being an educated person; to question it is to reveal either malice or supreme ignorance, indeed to establish oneself as part of the problem.

No one more clearly lays out the progressive narrative than Ta-Nehisi Coates, a young African American writer for *The Atlantic* and author of the best-selling *Between the World and Me*. Coates' writing, elegant, passionate and engaged, is the product of a thorough immersion in the historiographical writings of the left; consequently, it stands out for eloquence rather than originality, and therefore it reliably reflects currents of thinking that go beyond Coates himself and mirror the expression of the progressive conventional wisdom itself. Coates writes with the zeal of a prosecutor, and from his indictment we get a full progressive account of the crime as well as the entire cast of villains, past and present.[17]

Coates goes right to the heart of the matter, diagnosing white supremacy as the ideology of "torture, theft, and enslavement." White supremacy "dislodges brains, blocks airways, rips muscle, extracts organs, cracks bones, breaks teeth." This type of racism, he says, "ascribes bone-deep features to people" in order to "then humiliate, reduce, and destroy them." White supremacy, he makes clear, represents not only the ruin of blacks and other minorities; it represents the death of all that is good and decent in America. It is "an existential danger to the country and the world."

Coates does not hesitate to say that "racism remains, as it has since 1776, at the heart of this country's political life. To be black in America was to be plundered. To be white was to benefit from, and at times directly execute, this plunder." Coates' selection of the year 1776 is not accidental; white supremacy is a crime that in his view began with the founders. They were the ones who unleashed slavery—what Coates terms the plunder of the body, the plunder of the family and the plunder of labor—and also the "power of whiteness," which is our "awful inheritance," America's "bloody heirloom."

Coates is unimpressed by Jefferson's 1776 declaration that "all men are created equal"; what significance can that have, coming from a racist slave-owner who, together with other racist slave-owners, approved slavery in the Constitution and the founding documents, showcasing their vile hypocrisy? The meaning of the founding, for Coates and other progressives, is that "America begins in black plunder and white democracy, two features that are not contradictory but complementary."

If the founders invented white supremacy, Coates promptly traces the migration of that vicious ideology to the American South. "In the 1850s," he writes, "the South was only bested in the scale of its slavery, by Russian serfdom." Thus the South was not one slave society among many but "a moral offender on a grand scale, plying its trade at a point when much of the rest of the world had moved forward."

The trade of course was cotton, the cornerstone of the Industrial Revolution and the American economy, first cultivated on the slave plantation and then through generations of sharecropping extending well into the twentieth century. Coates describes the depredations of the Southern slave patrols, the South's readiness to go to war to protect slavery, the subsequent Southern resistance to Reconstruction, the murderous terrorism of the Ku Klux Klan and the crushing imposition of segregation and state-sponsored discrimination by Southern legislatures and Southern officials. Here Coates identifies white supremacy with such slavery apologists as John C. Calhoun, "South Carolina's senior senator," and later with racist segregationists such as Theodore Bilbo, "a Mississippi senator and proud Klansman."

Coates draws his white supremacy narrative right through the second half of the twentieth century. Coates points out that during the 1930s and 1940s, African Americans were routinely excluded from government benefits like Social Security. In the 1950s, they were largely excluded from the college access that the GI Bill made possible for a whole generation of white veterans. From the 1930s through the 1960s, blacks were mostly excluded from the home-mortgage market. Thus a century after black emancipation, white supremacy "continued even amidst the aims and achievements of New Deal liberals."

For Coates, the civil rights movement represented a modest progressive accomplishment, by at least creating a facially neutral set of laws for all Americans. Yet Coates insists that despite what President Lyndon Johnson and the civil rights movement did, the basic structure of white supremacy remained intact; racism may have migrated underground but it continued to exercise its covert power. More significant was the Obama presidency, whose symbolic power "assaulted the most deeply rooted notions of white supremacy and instilled fear in its adherents and beneficiaries."

Throughout his writings, Coates takes it for granted that Obama's party—the Democratic Party—is, for all its inadequacies, the party of progress and civil rights, and the Republican Party is the party of racism and white supremacy. "Hate and racism," he insists, is "stoked at the party's base." But how did it get there? Coates embraces the progressive narrative, which holds that the two parties switched sides on civil rights. Like others on the left, he blames Nixon's infamous Southern Strategy for courting the racist vote and winning white Southerners—Ku Klux Klansmen and neo-Nazis included—into the ranks of the GOP.

For Coates, the culmination of this national tragedy is the accession of Trump, whom Coates terms America's first white president in the sense that he was elected essentially by a white constituency and "his ideology is white supremacy in all of its truculent and sanctimonious power." For Coates and many progressives, Trump and the Trumpsters represent far more than a continuation of America's racist history; they represent an attempt to revivify its most potent, destructive elements.

Coates claims that "Trump moved racism from the euphemistic and plausibly deniable to the overt and freely claimed." Whiteness, Coates writes, is "the very core of his power." His objectives are to undo "an entire nigger presidency with nigger health care, nigger climate accords, and nigger justice reform . . . thus reifying the idea of being white." And when white supremacists organized a hate rally in Charlottesville to protest the removal of a monument to Robert E. Lee, Coates said it "makes complete sense" that white supremacy, "nakedly activated" by Trump "from the base of the Republican Party," would then "rally around the cause of the Confederacy."

Coates calls for the strongest type of resistance to a regime that is the modern-day descendant of the slave-owners, the segregationists, the fascists and the racial terrorists. Yet even as he joins the fight against Trump—"I would like to see him resigning and leaving the White House"—Coates in his writings and media statements conveys a mood that is dark, foreboding, apocalyptic. America, for him, seems to be slipping away, and so rotted is the body politic that he may not be sorry to see her go.

To sum up, the progressive narrative of American history reflected by Coates is a grand tour of the horrors of racism that exposes three white supremacist villains: the founders, the South and modern-day conservatives and Republicans, with Trump at their helm. Ultimately, these villains turn out to be all in the same camp, stacked on the same side of the aisle, as it were, because the historical villains can all now be mounted on the back of the Republican elephant.

In other words, modern American conservatism is based on conserving the principles of the founders, and moreover the South is today the political base of the Republican Party. So the sins of the founders and of the South become the legacy of modern-day conservatives and

Republicans, and we have a Manichean narrative in which the white supremacist right is arrayed against a progressive antiracist left in a life-and-death struggle for America's survival as a multiracial democracy.

"KNOWING" WHAT ISN'T TRUE

This progressive narrative is so entrenched, so deeply lodged in our brains, so familiar, that it seems almost heresy to ask: is it true? What if it's not? What if this widely taught and widely accepted truth is a lie? If so, we would not be talking about one lie but a series of lies, lies upon lies, all woven together into a grand narrative of falsehood and deception. Could this be the case? Can it be that what Americans "know" to be true is not, and that even educated Americans have been conned about their own country's history and turned into suckers?

I want to say at the outset that, unlike some conservatives, I am not raising these questions to minimize the horrors of history. This book does not seek to vindicate Trump, Republicans or the right through a racism minimization strategy. When progressive historians Michael Omi and Howard Winant describe U.S. history as characterized by "implacable denial of political rights, dehumanization, extreme exploitation, and policies of minority extirpation," I find myself nodding my head in agreement.[18]

Racism is real enough; the crimes of history are real enough; the question is: who perpetrated them and where can racism be located today? My contention is that the progressive narrative is faked—not fake news but fake history—that the accused are not guilty and that the perpetrators of bigotry both past and present can be found, incredibly enough, on the prosecution's team.

America is not to blame, and the South is not exclusively to blame. Some Americans perpetrated these crimes and other Americans stopped them. So it is essential to distinguish good Americans from bad ones. Moreover, while the secession debate was a North-South debate, I will show that the slavery debate was not. The slavery debate was between the pro-slavery Democratic Party and the antislavery Republican Party. Blame-the-South progressives must contend with all sorts of anomalies: only one in four white Southerners owned slaves or belonged to a family that did; more than 100,000 Southern men joined the Union army in the Civil War.[19]

As we will discover in this book, progressive Democrats are in fact the inventors of racism and white supremacy, and the Republican Party fought them all the way. Progressives and Democrats were also the groups that were in bed with fascism and Nazism in the 1920s and 1930s, while Republicans opposed this cozy alliance. All the villains of the civil rights movement—Birmingham sheriff Bull Connor, Selma sheriff Jim Clark, Arkansas governor Orval Faubus, Georgia governor Lester Maddox, Mississippi governor Ross Barnett, Alabama governor and presidential candidate George Wallace—were Democrats.

So we have the remarkable spectacle today of the party of racism, fascism and white supremacy blaming the party of antiracism and resistance to fascism and white supremacy for being racist, fascist and white supremacist.

In my two previous books *Hillary's America* and *The Big Lie,* I explored how big lies about racism and fascism are effectively promulgated. I noted the dominance of the progressive left in academia, the media and Hollywood, the three biggest megaphones of our culture. Big lies typically originate in academia and are then marketed through the media and the entertainment industry. They become conventional wisdom through refraction from one medium to the other, so the various retellings confirm the narrative and make it seem true and even obvious. So this is how one gets away with big lies.

But here I want to raise a deeper question: what are the lies for? By this I do not mean, what is the psychological disposition of the people who tell such lies, but rather, what do they gain by telling them? What is the ultimate game plan of the liars? What ugly truths are they trying to camouflage through the lies that they tell?

My main objective is not merely to expose lies about white supremacy but to tell a new story of the making of the Democratic Party. We all know about the Democratic Party as it is; very few people know how it became this way. My story is a novel genealogy of American politics that exposes the progressive left, together with its political arm, the Democratic Party, as the party of the plantation, the party of enslavement.

The plantation—viewed as a complete ecology involving exploited inhabitants, rented overseers and the plantation boss or "Massa" running things from the Big House—defines the Democrats not merely in the past but also in the present. Part of the interest of this book is to see how this system in modified fashion operates today, with new bosses, new overseers and new types of exploited inhabitants.

In the past, the Democrats sought to enslave only blacks; now they seek to turn all of America into a plantation, with every ethnic group dependent on and controlled from a new Big House, which is the centralized state. In the book, I will show not merely how the Democratic Party originated as the party of the plantation but also how the plantation in various forms and adaptations provides the inspiration and model for the evolution of the Democrats right up to the present.

If the notion of a Democratic plantation stretching across the entire country seems implausible, let's recall that the man who first predicted it was Abraham Lincoln. In his House Divided speech, Lincoln insisted that Americans would either become all free or all enslaved. "Either the opponents of slavery will arrest the further spread of it, and place it where the public mind shall rest in the belief that it is in the course of ultimate extinction, or its advocates will push it forward, till it shall become alike lawful in all the states, old as well as new—North as well as South."[20]

Lincoln explicitly included whites in his prophecy, arguing that to embrace slavery in principle is to condone the captivity of whites no less than blacks. Long before me, Lincoln accused the Democrats of his day—or "The Democracy," as they were then called—of seeking to turn all of America into a plantation.

Lincoln's stark dichotomy—a nation entirely free or completely enslaved—was in part inspired by the Democratic champion of slavery as a positive good, George Fitzhugh. Toward the end of his pro-slavery tract *Sociology for the South,* Fitzhugh predicted that "one set of ideas will govern and control after awhile the civilized world. Slavery will everywhere be abolished, or every where be re-instituted."[21] Fitzhugh, of course, hoped slavery would become universal and Lincoln hoped it would become extinct. Even so, Lincoln studied Fitzhugh carefully and incorporated his fateful prediction into the House Divided speech.

Lincoln's plantation prophecy was not delivered, Nostradamus-style, as a mere speculation. Rather, it was based on close reasoning drawn from the 1857 *Dred Scott* decision permitting slavery in the territories. Chief Justice Roger Taney, an Andrew Jackson protégé and lifelong Democrat, argued that since "the right of property in a slave is distinctly and expressly affirmed in the Constitution," neither Congress nor a territorial legislature could outlaw it.

After making the obvious point that the right of property in a slave is *not* distinctly and expressly affirmed in the Constitution, Lincoln pointed out that, following *Dred Scott,* the Supreme Court might issue a second decision, concluding by its exact same reasoning that no state could outlaw slavery. In this way slavery would become legal nationwide and the way of the plantation would become the American way. It took a mighty war from 1861 to 1865 to prevent this from happening.

But it is happening now. My argument holds that Lincoln's nightmare of a national plantation is now being realized, and once again the culprit is the Democratic Party. If the progressive narrative constitutes the conventional wisdom, I will make my case through a rival narrative; mine will be the unconventional wisdom.

I introduce figures that may be new for many—the pro-slavery apologist George Fitzhugh; the man known as the Little Magician, Martin Van Buren—and also familiar figures like Franklin Roosevelt, Lyndon Johnson and Barack Obama, whom I will reveal in a new light. These are the villains of my story—a very different cast than the villains of the progressive tale—and throughout they are contrasted with the brooding figure of Lincoln, America's first Republican president and her greatest one yet. Lincoln is the hero of my story and, as in the Civil War period, his philosophical statesmanship defines the American experiment and provides the most penetrating critique of as well as the best alternative to the Democratic plantation.

It is worth mentioning at this point that this is not a narrative where I have my facts and the other side has its facts. This is not a matter of my truths versus someone else's truths. Throughout this book I rely on the indisputable evidence of history, drawn from primary sources and from the most reputable scholars of slavery, racism and fascism: Gordon Wood, David Brion Davis, Orlando Patterson, Eugene Genovese, James McPherson, George Fredrickson, A. James Gregor, Ira Katznelson and others. The facts I present can easily be verified thanks to the technological marvels of the internet.

This body of facts and evidence sets the fixed parameters of debate and narrows the scope for big lies, because while progressives are entitled to their own opinions, they are not entitled to their own facts. In the end, everything turns on whose interpretation of the evidence is right, whether their story or mine is true. This is something that you, the reader, must decide for yourself. You are my judge and my jury.

PRISON OF THE MIND

I will admit that at first glance and for those unfamiliar with my previous work, this argument will seem far-fetched, even crazy. The plantation system, after all, was involuntary; it was based on forcibly confining slaves. Today, the Democrats don't have anyone penned up in this way, and they certainly aren't forcing anyone to work.

This objection, however, can be answered by recalling how the antebellum Democrats regarded the old plantation. Democratic senator James Chesnut regarded his slaves as having it so good on his South Carolina plantation that they cost more than the work they produced. Asked if he ever had runaways, he quipped, "Never! It's pretty hard work to keep me from running away from them!"[22]

Chesnut's wife, the spirited Mary Boykin Chesnut, wrote in her diary in 1861, shortly after the outbreak of the Civil War, "Now if slavery is as disagreeable to Negroes as we think it, why don't they all march over the border where they would be received with open arms?"[23] Her point was that the slaves who wanted to leave could have left; the white men were all at the front and there was no one except women and children to stop them.

Her deeper implication was that in reality many slaves preferred the security of the plantation to the shock and responsibilities of freedom. The plantation, she suggested, had become not merely a prison of the body but also a prison of the mind. It held its population in debased psychological confinement even when there was the opportunity to get up and go. I believe this insight is what drives the modern Democratic Party. The Democrats realized that, long after slavery was ended, they could create new types of plantations that would so degrade and imprison the minds of their inhabitants that very few would want to leave.

Still, there are massive differences between the old slave plantation and the political life of today's Democrats. The old plantation was rural; today's Democrats are largely urban. Slavery was largely though not entirely a Southern institution; today's Democrats have their base in the North and on the coasts. The plantation was sustained through an ideology of states' rights; today's Democrats are the party of centralized government that opposes states' rights. If we must draw on analogies from the past, today's Democrats seem closer to Tammany Hall and the urban machines of the North than to the old rural slave plantation. Didn't Franklin D. Roosevelt nationalize those urban machines to create the model of governance for the modern Democratic Party?

Yes, but the urban machines were themselves based on the slave plantation. Historians rightly credit Martin Van Buren as the man who invented the Northern Democratic machine. Yet he was the close ally of and immediate successor to Democratic Party founder and Tennessee slave-owner Andrew Jackson. Based on his observations of the rural plantation—and the similarities he noted between slaves in the South and newly arriving impoverished immigrants in the North—Van Buren adapted the Democrats' plantation model to urban conditions.

Thus he helped create new ethnic plantations based in the cities, populated by immigrants who were dependent on and exploited by the Democratic Party in the North in somewhat the same manner as the slaves were by the Democrats in the South. These urban machines ripped off the taxpayer not only to enrich corrupt machine bosses but also to buy votes in exchange for promises of employment and basic provisions. In sum the urban machines symbolized by New York's Tammany Hall were themselves mini welfare states, precursors to the Leviathan welfare state Democrats would later establish in the twentieth century.

As Van Buren's adaptation of the slave system to create the urban machines suggests, this is a story of how the old plantation was creatively modified to produce the modern progressive plantation. I'm not saying the Democrats are the same as they were two centuries ago; this is a story of change as well as of continuity. Democrats like Van Buren didn't just extend the rural plantation model from the early nineteenth century to the present. Rather, they transformed it to changing conditions, in response to new demographic realities created by immigrant waves, and also in response to the singular catastrophe that left the old plantation model in ruins.

The old plantation was destroyed by the Civil War. Prior to that, the plantation was the model of Democratic governance and Democratic political domination. Democrats had concocted a whole ideology—the positive-good school of slavery—to uphold and defend the plantation. As I will show in the next chapter, this Democratic apologia for slavery as an institution to be cherished and expanded was radically different from the founders' shared understanding of slavery as a necessary evil that should be curbed until it could be eliminated.

The founders hoped that slavery would disappear and they expected it to. In 1782 Jefferson wrote of "a change already perceptible . . . The spirit of the master is abating, that of the slave rising from the dust . . . the way I hope preparing, under the auspices of heaven, for a total emancipation."[24] Nothing could be further from the vision of the Democratic Party, whose most "moderate" faction saw slavery as a matter of moral indifference and an institution that should be continued indefinitely.

Interestingly the Democrats' prime apologist for slavery, George Fitzhugh, was a self-proclaimed socialist who contrasted the happy inhabitants of the Democratic plantation with what he took to be the exploited laboring class of the capitalist Republican Northern states. Fitzhugh's arguments seem chillingly familiar because his beloved plantation still shapes the ideology of his twenty-first-century Democratic successors.

So does the pro-slavery ideology of Democratic presidential candidate Stephen Douglas, Abraham Lincoln's supreme antagonist. Douglas was a Northern Democrat, and contrary to today's conventional wisdom that views the plantation as a purely Southern creation, Democrats both in the North and the South protected it. Douglas and Fitzhugh were also full-blown white supremacists who railed against blacks in a manner unthinkable of the founders.

When Lincoln in his House Divided speech alleged a four-man conspiracy to nationalize slavery, he named just one Southern Democrat, Roger Taney of Maryland, and three Northern Democrats: Stephen Douglas of Illinois, former president Franklin Pierce of New Hampshire and the current president James Buchanan of Pennsylvania. A few years earlier, Buchanan said that at a time when slavery was besieged throughout the country, slaveholders "have no other allies . . .

except the Democracy of the North," meaning the Northern Democratic Party.[25]

"The great support of Slavery in the South," said Whig senator and later Lincoln's secretary of state William Seward, "has been its alliance with the Democratic party of the North."[26] These are the same Northern Democrats that tried to thwart Lincoln during the war. Their goal was to force him to reconcile with the Confederacy and to restore slavery. Lincoln termed them the "fire in the rear," more dangerous to the nation than even the Confederate army. Eventually, through Lincoln's efforts, the ruin of the plantation in 1865 became also the ruin of the national Democratic Party.

So the Democrats had to reconstruct themselves after the war. This reconstruction—very different from the Reconstruction attempted by Republicans to integrate blacks into the economic and political life of the country—involved not an abandonment of the plantation scheme but its reinvention, both in the North and in the South.

The Democratic urban machine, of course, outlasted the war and continued to hold immigrants in its iron clasp. But for the postbellum Democratic Party of the late nineteenth and early twentieth centuries, sharecropping replaced slavery, and segregation and racial terrorism enforced Democratic control in the South, not just of blacks but also poor whites. Essentially the Democrats reinvented the plantation using a new tool of enslavement: white supremacy.

REBUILDING THE PLANTATION

Progressive Democrats led by Woodrow Wilson sought to rebuild a new type of plantation for the twentieth century. They were quite familiar with the old plantation, being just a single generation removed from it. Contrary to the history books, which assiduously camouflage this fact, progressives are the ones who invented white nationalism and white supremacy in their modern and most virulent forms for the purpose of keeping poor whites in thrall to the Democratic Party. Progressives, in other words, were America's original hate group, and their opponents, the conservative Republicans, were the original champions of the notion that "black lives matter."

The other signal contribution of progressivism was to introduce the idea of the centralized state as the Big House, with racial terrorism and eugenics as the macabre mechanisms for controlling the population of their new plantation and maintaining quality control for its labor. Through progressivism, Wilson inaugurated, one might say, the "birth of a nation" that departed radically from the American founding, a new birth represented by the ominous symbol of the night-riding Ku Klux Klan, which served as the domestic terrorist arm of the Democratic Party.

Yet it was not Wilson but his progressive successor, Franklin D. Roosevelt, who in the 1930s and 1940s institutionalized progressivism in the operations of government and thus created the foundation for the modern Democratic Party. FDR began by replacing the Democratic urban machines with the labor union movement and local Democratic Party bosses with a national boss, namely himself. He introduced the idea of a national plantation—Tammany on the Potomac—with a progressive "brain trust" and progressive administrators as its overseers.

FDR also introduced a concept that seems to secretly inspire Democrats to this day: the 100 percent marginal tax rate. In 1941, FDR proposed a 99.5 percent tax rate on anyone earning over $100,000 a year. In 1942, he went even further, signing an executive order taxing all personal income over $25,000 (which is $300,000 in today's money) at 100 percent. Even his Democratic Congress balked and lowered the top rate to 90 percent, though it crept up to a high of 94 percent during World War II.

FDR insisted that Americans who earned enough to live comfortably should not be allowed to keep any more income beyond that point.[27] Why not take everything they earned above this limit? Although presented as an ideal rather than a policy proposal, FDR's vision—gather up everything you've earned above a certain point and turn it in to the government—amounts to nothing less than American serfdom. FDR was the first to seek to implement the Democratic vision of a national plantation. Thus he laid the foundation for what successive generations of Democrats to this day have pursued.

FDR and his team also gave the plantation a fascist facelift—deliberately introducing elements of Mussolini's Italian fascism into the New Deal—while at the same time drawing on models of Nazi conformity, what the Nazis termed *Gleichschaltung*. (Hitler, for his part, created his own plantation, drawing on schemes that he self-consciously lifted from the Democratic Party and from American progressives.) Some of the fascist elements first introduced by FDR, both in policy and in strategy, are also evident in today's Democratic Party.

Moreover, as Democratic presidents did in the antebellum period, FDR relied on Northern Democrats to play the role they played before the Civil War, namely to ally with Southern Democrats to protect the infrastructure of racism that continued to sustain FDR's national Democratic plantation. Thus while FDR didn't share Hitler's form of racism, he was not above making a Faustian pact with the worst racists in America to get his New Deal agenda passed. FDR and the Democrats' shameful complicity with fascism and white supremacy are ignored by progressive historians, and virtually no textbook even mentions them.

By the 1930s, we can see in FDR's version of the plantation the familiar outlines that define the Democratic Party today. Today's Democrats have the same attachment to the centralized state, the new Big House, and they display the same fascist streak when, for example, they use the instruments of the state against their political opponents. But we cannot stop with FDR; our story would be incomplete without showing how Lyndon Johnson again modified the plantation in the 1960s, and how Bill Clinton and Barack Obama further expanded it in recent decades.

CONVERSION STORIES

LBJ was a lifelong bigot who has somehow in progressive historiography been transformed into a convert to the cause of civil rights. From the recently released JFK Files, we have good reason to suppose LBJ was once a Ku Klux Klan member. An internal FBI memo refers to "documented proof" that LBJ was in the Texas Klan during his early political career.[28]

If true, this is hardly surprising, and it means LBJ now joins Woodrow Wilson, Harry Truman and Supreme Court Justice Hugo Black as high-level Democrats who were also Klansmen. Yet we are asked to believe that this leopard magically changed his spots. Apparently a long list of other Democratic bigots, including West Virginia Klansman and Dixiecrat Robert Byrd, who became Obama's and Hillary's mentor, the "conscience of the Senate," were also converts to the cause of black equality and advancement.

Yet where are their conversion stories? One might expect that when someone undergoes a wrenching transformation from being a white supremacist to an enemy of white supremacy, they would have quite a story to tell. Whittaker Chambers certainly did, when he made the traumatic transformation from communist to anti-communist. Chambers records his intellectual *volte face* in his autobiographical magnum opus *Witness*. Yet there are no such Democratic conversion stories.

This is the dog that didn't bark, the clue that tells us that people like LBJ and Robert Byrd never underwent any big transformation. There was no dark night of the soul, no road to Damascus. They merely transitioned from an earlier incarnation of the Democratic plantation to a newer one. LBJ, for instance, remained the priapic plantation boss he was when he started his career. His transformation was purely tactical; he pushed the Civil Rights Act and the Voting Rights Act not so much to combat an upsurge of white racism but rather in response to the need for a new approach in the wake of rapidly declining white racism.

White racism and white supremacy declined dramatically in the aftermath of World War II—Hitler did more to undermine it than even the civil rights movement, which benefited from the discrediting of fascist doctrines of Nordic supremacy—and this meant LBJ could no longer count on a solid South of white racist Democrats. There were quite simply fewer and fewer of them.

Attracted by the message of free markets, anti-communism, patriotism and upward mobility, non-racist whites in the South had started to move rapidly toward the Republican Party. The Democrats were losing their racist hegemony in the region, and LBJ saw that this represented perhaps the greatest catastrophe for the Democratic Party since Lincoln shut down the old Democratic plantation. Something drastic needed to be done.

If the Democrats intended to retain their majority, LBJ saw they needed to get more black votes. This was quite a change for a Democratic Party whose history was largely based on exploiting black labor and suppressing the black vote. But LBJ saw the opportunity to create a new type of plantation in which blacks could be exploited in a different

way. On this plantation they had a different casting role, not as exploited workers who did not vote but rather as exploited voters who did
not work. In other words, LBJ recognized the importance of turning
blacks into a constituency, which Democrats had never before done in
their party's history.

This was LBJ's own Southern Strategy—a strategy that required LBJ
to turn against his former Dixiecrat allies. It goes unmentioned in progressive historiography, in contrast with Nixon's oft-mentioned Southern Strategy, which is largely a myth. Far from campaigning on a racist
platform—no one has ever cited a single explicitly racist campaign appeal made by Nixon—Nixon campaigned for the non-racist vote of the
rapidly urbanizing Peripheral South, leaving the racist vote of the Deep
South to George Wallace, the Democratic segregationist who won it.

The Republican campaign slogan from the Nixon era—which
tagged the Democrats with being the party of "acid, amnesty and
abortion"—was clearly not about race, but referred instead to the hippie drug lifestyle, to the Vietnam War and to the permissive 1973 *Roe
v. Wade* abortion decision. Nixon's voters were, as in Merle Haggard's
famous 1969 song, Okies from Muskogee who refuse to take drugs
or dodge the draft and "like living right and being free." Whatever
this so-called redneck anthem is about, it isn't about racism or white
supremacy.

True, blacks went from being Republican voters to Democratic
voters, and the South went from being solidly Democratic to now
mostly Republican, but I prove these transformations had little to do
with race. Rather, blacks switched during the 1930s for the economic
benefits of the New Deal, and the South became Republican in the
1980s because of the Reaganite appeal of anti-communism, free markets, patriotism and social issues like family values and opposition to
abortion.

Far from the parties switching platforms, as progressives contend
they did, I show that the ideology of the Republican Party today is
essentially the same as it was during the time of Abraham Lincoln.
Lincoln defined slavery as "you work, I eat," and that is the core philosophy of today's Democratic Party, no less than the Democratic Party
of Lincoln's day. By contrast, the core philosophy of today's GOP is

identical with that of Lincoln: "I always thought the man who made the corn should eat the corn."[29]

The landmark immigration law of the mid-1960s, which opened the door to 25 million new immigrants, mostly from Asia, Africa and South America, created the foundation for the Obama plantation, one that encompasses not only blacks but also Latinos and other minorities. Today's Democratic plantation has come a long way from its roots in the rural antebellum South. It's much bigger now and includes African Americans, Hispanics, Native Americans and to some extent even Asian Americans. Today's Democratic plantation is grimly visible in the urban black ghettos, the Latino barrios, the Native American reservations.

Obama presided over the Democrats' move toward a multicultural plantation, complete with a sustaining ideology of identity politics that reconciles each ethnic group to its political captivity, seeking to create the modern equivalent of the contented slave. Of course today's enslaved, while free in principle to leave the plantation, in practice rarely do so. Drawing on the work of psychologist Martin Seligman, I explain this through the concept of "learned helplessness." The Democrats have created learned helplessness among their captive constituencies, and this keeps them bound by invisible cords to the plantation lifestyle.

There is one important difference between the old Democratic plantation and the new one. The old one was based on forced black labor; the new one is based on the dependent black, Latino or Native American voter. This voter ideally does not work but rather lives off welfare and government provision, which becomes, of course, his motive to sustain the providing party in power. Democrats use coalitions of dependent ethnic minorities in order to generate an electoral majority, thus placing progressive Democrats in charge of the Big House. From there they loot the national treasury in the shameless fashion that the old Tammany bosses looted city hall.

Progressive Democrats benefit themselves and live high on the hog—like the Clintons and Obamas, who went from nothing to multimillionaires, from minor overseers to plantation big bosses—all the while declaring as their motive the tireless pursuit of social justice. These Democrats proclaim themselves the benevolent supervisors of needy, impoverished minorities whom in fact they keep needy and impoverished. These minorities, deprived of education and the skills for advancement, rely on the Democrats to provide for them, thus reducing themselves to dependent subordination and sustaining the progressives in power.

Yet despite these differences, the new plantation bears a striking resemblance to its ancient predecessor. In his classic work *The Peculiar Institution,* historian Kenneth Stampp identified the five distinctive features of the old slave plantation: dilapidated housing, which the slave-owners termed slave quarters; broken families, the product of slave rules that abolished the institution of marriage and permitted the sale of family members at the master's whim; a high degree of violence to police the plantation, necessary of course because slavery was based on captive labor; no opportunity for decent education or advancement, notwithstanding the Democrats' insistence on slavery as a "school of civilization"; and finally the plantation's pervasive atmosphere of hopelessness, despair and nihilism.[30]

We can verify the existence of Democratic plantations today by finding these exact five features in inner-city Baltimore, St. Louis, Oakland or Detroit; in the Latino barrios of California and south Texas; and on Native American reservations like the Pine Ridge reservation in South Dakota. Other features of the plantation—a class of people who devoted themselves to idleness, leisure, gambling and duels provoked by petty slights—can also be found in today's ghettos and barrios. In this respect, the inhabitants of these modern ethnic enclaves resemble not so much the old slaves as the old slave-owners.

RACISM'S NEW FACE

In my earlier books I have discussed the racist past of the Democratic Party, but I did not directly answer the question: where is the racism of the Democrats today? Here I show that racism remains the core of the Democratic project, but to see this we must recognize how racism today takes a quite different form than it has in the past. Today's Democrats don't publicly call blacks "niggers," nor do they lynch or segregate them as they used to.

Today's Democrats, however, are just as indifferent to the plight of blacks as their predecessors, and they create black dependency and exploit black suffering with the same casual indifference as in the past. Today, too, the progressive Democrats have generated a "positive good" apologia for minority enslavement. While benefiting both financially and politically from the new plantation, the progressives insist they are doing it entirely for the benefit of its inhabitants.

Yet as I show in the last section of the book, there is one group that the Democrats have not managed to enslave: working-class whites. This is a group that used to be largely in the grip of the progressives. They were part of FDR's labor coalition. But now they have broken loose, and many of them voted for Trump. I call this group "holdouts." Trump is their hero, and this white working class is attracted to his populist American nationalism, both on economic and on cultural grounds.

So the Democrats—desperate to conceal their own racism—now seek to discredit working-class whites as bigots and to portray Trump's American nationalism as a thinly disguised resurrection of white nationalism. This is why the Charlottesville "Unite the Right" rally was so important for them: it confirmed their image of Trump as the apostle of white supremacy and of neo-Nazis and Ku Klux Klansmen in MAGA hats as the new face of the Republican Party. Yet as I will show, the Charlottesville rally was organized by Jason Kessler, a man of the left who used to be an Obama supporter and Occupy Wall Street guy.

My interview with America's leading white nationalist, Richard Spencer, reveals that contrary to his portrait in the progressive media, he is actually no conservative, no Republican, no man of the right. In fact, his positions on ethnic nationalism, white supremacy, immigration and eugenics show him to be a relic of history, a progressive Democrat in the Woodrow Wilson mode. Yet today's Democratic Party has jettisoned the whole eugenic and segregationist agenda of early progressivism in favor of a new plantation model. Spencer is a political activist who has been left behind as his fellow progressive Democrats have evolved into something else.

Yet according to the left-wing media account, Spencer is the second most dangerous man in America, after Trump, and his ideas could not be more relevant. The entire portrait of white nationalists as conservatives—with Trump and the GOP as their exemplar—is a progressive lie and a deflection. White nationalists like Spencer are decoys of the left, valuable in that they corroborate the big lie of racism and fascism being on the right and draw attention away from the left's own racist exploitation of every ethnic minority group.

Still, I do want to explain why some of these white nationalists—insignificant though they may be as a cultural and political force—nevertheless count themselves in the Trump camp. The short answer is that Trump's American nationalism at least makes room for all citizens, while the ethnic nationalism that defines the Democratic plantation today is based on affirming every ethnic group (including minorities who are illegal aliens) except whites.

White nationalists who would ordinarily feel at home in a party based on ethnic nationalism find themselves demonized in today's Democratic Party. They are the one ethnic group that is unwelcome at the multicultural picnic. The only role for them in the progressive morality play is as confessors and self-flagellators, a role that some white progressives willingly perform, but one that many white nationalists consider unseemly and degrading. So these people have nowhere else to go except to a party that at least counts them as fellow Americans.

Yet if they are in Trump's camp, it does not in any way follow that Trump is in theirs. While Trump is interminably accused of white supremacy for his positions on national security and immigration, the lines that he draws are clearly not racial. On immigration Trump distinguishes the legal immigrant from the illegal alien. But most legal immigrants today are nonwhite; they come from Asia, Africa, South America. Trump has said he wants more skilled immigrants, but he has never said he wants more white immigrants from New Zealand and Iceland and fewer from Barbados and Mumbai.

This is confirmed in a telling conversation between Trump and his former adviser Steve Bannon. Discussing the situation of an Asian Indian worker who took his programming skills back to his native country, Trump said, "We've got to be able to keep great people in the country. We have to be careful of that, Steve. I think you agree with that, Steve?" Steve did not necessarily agree.[31] But Trump's position shows that he had no reluctance to go to bat even for a brown-skinned guy who in his view made a contribution to America's economy and prosperity.

Similarly, on national security, Trump's resistance to Muslim terrorists and Mexican criminals seeking to infiltrate this country is on behalf of all Americans, not just whites. All Americans—white, black and brown—are jeopardized when a truck bomb goes off in Times Square or when illegal Mexican gang members go on a crime spree. "I've been greedy," Trump has confessed to his supporters. "I'm a businessman . . . take, take, take. Now I'm going to be greedy for the United States."[32] And this is an excellent summation of the man.

I close by showing what Trump can do to dissipate the residual force of white nationalism in American politics while also beginning the much bigger and more important task of dismantling the Democratic plantation. I argue that Trump's American nationalism, correctly defined, offers a remedy for ethnic nationalisms of all stripes. If constructed on the Lincoln model, it provides a policy framework for replacing the dependency and hopelessness of the plantation with ladders of opportunity for every American. Far from causing the death of the nation, Trump and the conservatives can come together to show the way for America's restoration, revival and hope.

2

DILEMMA OF THE PLANTATION

The Antislavery Founding

We have the wolf by the ear, and we can neither
hold him, nor safely let him go. Justice is in
one scale, and self-preservation in the other.

—Thomas Jefferson on slavery[1]

When San Francisco 49ers quarterback Colin Kaepernick first refused to stand for the national anthem, he was asked by NFL media reporter Steve Wyche to explain. "I am not going to stand up to show pride in a flag for a country that oppresses black people and people of color," he said.[2] Kaepernick, of course, is the inspiration for the nationwide NFL protests in which players take a knee, or lock arms, or just stay in the locker room during the national anthem. Many fans are outraged and some are boycotting NFL games, resulting in a measurable drop in viewership.

Subsequently, some players who back Kaepernick have attempted a revisionist history of the movement he represents. "It baffles me that our protest is still being misconstrued as disrespectful to the country, flag and military personnel," frets 49ers safety Eric Reid.[3] Reid insists that the protests are all about police brutality and the criminal justice system. Yet why aren't NFL players protesting outside police stations? Why choose to spurn the national anthem unless the objection is to what the national anthem represents?

What the anthem represents is patriotism. It was written by Francis Scott Key in a burst of nationalistic fervor after watching the bombardment of the British fleet during the War of 1812. Key's song was a popular tune for Union troops during the Civil War and became the national anthem in 1916, more than a century after it was written. Its words celebrate American exceptionalism and call upon Americans to rally to the cause of "the land of the free and the home of the brave."

Kaepernick's progressive admirers across the country know exactly what he is protesting. Noel Ransome in Vice writes that Kaepernick "took a knee for all of us" in order to expose "the harsh reality of white supremacy."[4] Ransome makes it clear that the problem is not confined to the justice system but is endemic to American history, American institutions and American life.

Leading progressives insist the problem began with the American founding. Speaking on the two hundredth anniversary of the Constitution, former Supreme Court Justice Thurgood Marshall refused to "find the wisdom, foresight and sense of justice exhibited by the Framers particularly profound. To the contrary, the government they devised was defective from the start." Marshall urged that instead of jingoistic celebration, Americans should seek an "understanding of the Constitution's defects," its immoral project to "trade moral principles for self-interest."[5]

Such views are now commonplace. "Jefferson didn't mean it when he wrote that all men are created equal," fumed historian John Hope Franklin. "We've never meant it. The truth is that we're a bigoted people and always have been. We think every other country is trying to copy us now and if they are, God help the world." Franklin argued that by betraying the ideals of freedom, "the Founding Fathers set the stage for every succeeding generation of American to apologize, compromise, and temporize on those principles."[6]

A recent article in Rolling Stone, written in the wake of the Charlottesville controversy, sought to document "The History of White Supremacy in America." In line with the progressive zeitgeist, the article located the roots of the problem in the American founding, noting that "Article 1 of the Constitution says slaves are three-fifths of a person," proving that "the United States was founded on white supremacy."[7]

To examine whether this progressive critique is correct, we have to resolve "the seeming inconsistency, not to say hypocrisy, of slaveholders devoting themselves to freedom," which historian Edmund Morgan terms "the central paradox of American history." Morgan is not the first to notice the paradox; it was the premise of the British Tory writer Samuel Johnson's sarcastic jibe at the American founding. "How is it that we hear the loudest yelps for liberty among the drivers of Negroes?"[8]

The best way to answer this question is to turn to a debate on this very topic between Abraham Lincoln and the leading Democrats of his day. They debated it with a seriousness and rigor that surpasses anything written on the subject today. We can hardly do better than to begin with them.

Were the founders white supremacists? Did they write slavery and white supremacy into the Constitution? These were the specific issues examined by Supreme Court Justice Roger Taney while writing the notorious *Dred Scott* decision upholding slavery in the territories. Taney emphasized that in answering these questions he was not giving his own personal point of view.

True, Taney was a Southerner and a Democrat—a protégé of Andrew Jackson—but many years previously he had freed his own slaves, and he vehemently objected to the portrayal of him in the Republican press as pro-slavery in his personal beliefs. Taney insisted he was merely interpreting the Constitution according to the intentions of its framers. His objective was to discover what they thought.

Taney reasoned as follows. The founders said in the Declaration of Independence that "all men are created equal." But their actions showed that they could not have believed it. After all, some thirty of the fifty-five framers of the Constitution who gathered in Philadelphia were slave-owners. So was Thomas Jefferson, who drafted the Declaration. Moreover, far from outlawing slavery, the founders permitted it and even added a fugitive slave clause that entitled masters to the return of their runaway slaves.

If the founders actually meant to include blacks in the Declaration of Independence, Taney wrote, this would make their actions "utterly and flagrantly inconsistent with the principles they asserted," and they would deserve "universal rebuke and reprobation." Therefore, Taney reasoned, they cannot have meant to do so. "It is too clear for dispute," he concluded, "that the enslaved African race were not intended to be included, and formed no part of the people who framed and adopted this Declaration." Rather, in line with a "fixed and universal" opinion, the framers according to Taney regarded blacks as "beings of an inferior order."

One can see right away that except for a slight difference of emphasis, Taney's reasoning in *Dred Scott* is identical with that of contemporary progressive critics of the founding. Like him, they agree that the framers were white supremacists who had no intention of including blacks in the Declaration of Independence. This is significant because of what came out of Taney's reasoning, namely his disturbing conclusion that the right to own slaves is "expressly affirmed" in the Constitution and that blacks have "no rights which the white man was bound to respect." Moreover, "The Negro might justly and lawfully be reduced to slavery for his benefit."[9]

Was Taney's constitutional reasoning sound? If progressives today are right about the framers and the Constitution, it follows that Taney was also right about them, because his logic is the same as theirs. And if Taney was right, then *Dred Scott* was right in affirming that blacks have no constitutional rights and Congress has no power to restrict slavery in the territories. Slave-owners have the same right to take their slaves into the territories as they do to, say, exercise their free speech or practice their religion there.

Historians are unanimous that *Dred Scott* also set into motion the events that led to the Civil War. In the words of political scientist Harry Jaffa, "It gave an energy, a confidence, and an intransigence to the pro-slavery cause that ended—if it did end—only at Appomattox."[10] Let's recall that the pledge to outlaw slavery in the territories was the main plank of the Republican Party platform in the 1860 election. *Dred Scott* essentially invalidated the winning party's platform by declaring it unconstitutional.

The Supreme Court's conclusion in *Dred Scott*—in effect affirming a constitutional right to own slaves—was widely hailed by Democrats both in the North and the South. It emboldened the Southern Democrats to press their case for secession. Absent *Dred Scott*, the South may not have seceded and the Civil War might have been averted. So if the ruling was legitimate, it seems to follow that the secessionists were right to break away from the union because of their reasonable fear that Lincoln and the Republicans would overturn their basic constitutional rights.

So we are in a remarkable situation today where progressive Democrats agree with Taney that the founders excluded blacks from the Declaration of Independence. They embrace Taney's reasoning for adopting that view. Yet they reject the pro-slavery conclusion Taney drew from that premise. Thus while they pull down Confederate statues—including at least one Taney statue removed in his native Maryland—they find themselves intellectually in bed with Taney and the Confederacy. This is not entirely surprising, however, because Taney was a Democrat. So were Jefferson Davis, Alexander Stephens and the leading men of the Confederacy. It seems, then, that modern Democrats are on board with the constitutional reasoning employed by their pro-slavery, secessionist counterparts more than a century and a half ago.

CATCHWORD OF A PARTY

Responding to Taney and Democrats who embraced the *Dred Scott* decision—among them Stephen Douglas, his famous rival in Illinois—Abraham Lincoln issued one of the most startling challenges in American political history. Addressing Taney's claim that the founders did not regard blacks as included in the Declaration of Independence, Lincoln said, "I believe the entire records of the world, from the date of the Declaration of Independence up to within three years ago, may be searched in vain for one single affirmation, from one single man, that the Negro was not included in the Declaration of Independence."

Naming South Carolina Democratic senator John C. Calhoun, Lincoln concedes right away that in the recent past there were prominent Democrats who, finding the Declaration's insistence that all men are created equal "constantly in the way of their schemes to bring about the ascendancy and perpetuation of slavery, denied the truth of it." Still, he says, even they did not "pretend to believe it and then assert it did not include the Negro."

But now, for the first time, Lincoln says, the Democratic Party has produced men like Taney and Douglas who claim that the founders shared an understanding about the Declaration that no living person in their time actually believed. Even more, Lincoln said, their lies about the founders have "become the catchword of the entire party."[11]

Lincoln's claim is just as much a surprise to the modern reader as it must have been to his contemporaries, because modern Democrats, no less than Taney and Douglas, claim the founders were pro-slavery men who had no genuine intent to include blacks in the Declaration of Independence. Yet Lincoln accused Taney of doing "obvious violence to the plain unmistakable language" of the founding documents.[12] So how can Lincoln make such a claim about the founding era? What was he getting at?

Lincoln deepens the mystery by repeatedly insisting that as far as slavery is concerned, the entire objective and platform of the Republican Party is merely to restore to America the principled statesmanship of the founders. Lincoln refuses to put any moral distance between him and the founders, between himself, say, and slave-owner and Virginia planter Thomas Jefferson.

This is fascinating and relevant because there are many today who insist that Abraham Lincoln was a liberal and a progressive, that he took on the radical task of correcting the founding and remaking of America. Garry Wills, in *Lincoln at Gettysburg*, credits Lincoln with a "giant swindle" and "open sleight-of-hand" in altering the meaning of the Constitution to include people the founders had no wish to include.[13]

Yet Lincoln would undoubtedly decline this praise from a left-wing scholar seeking to appropriate him to the progressive cause. Lincoln viewed himself as a conservative. In a speech in Columbus, Ohio, Lincoln said, "The chief and real purpose of the Republican Party is eminently conservative. It proposes nothing save and except to restore this government to its original tone in regard to this element of slavery, and there to maintain it, looking for no further change . . . than that which the original framers of the Government themselves expected and looked forward to."

Again, in an 1854 speech on the Kansas-Nebraska Act, Lincoln said of slavery, "Let us return it to the position our fathers gave it, and there let it rest in peace." He added in his Cooper Union speech, "This is all Republicans ask—all Republicans desire—in relation to slavery . . . For this Republicans contend, and with this, so far as I know or believe, they will be content."

In Lincoln's time, some Democrats tried to portray themselves as conservative and Lincoln as the radical. At Cooper Union, he challenged them. "You say you are conservative—eminently conservative—while we are revolutionary, destructive, or something of the sort. What is conservatism? Is it not adherence to the old and tried, against the new and untried? We stick to, contend for, the identical old policy on the point in controversy which was adopted by our fathers who framed the government . . . but you are unanimous in rejecting and denouncing the old policy of the fathers."[14]

These assertions by Lincoln should be sufficient to refute the progressive propaganda about the Great Emancipator being one of them. But it still raises the question of what Lincoln meant when he insisted that the founders were antislavery men. Lincoln took up this question directly in his Cooper Union address, the speech that, according to historian Harold Holzer, won Lincoln the presidency by convincing the influential Republicans of the Northeast that he was their man.

Let us consider some key items of evidence that Lincoln adduces to show how the framers of the Constitution actually thought and acted with regard to slavery.[15] At the Congress of Confederation in 1784, Lincoln noted, four future signers of the Constitution were asked to vote to prohibit slavery in the immense Northwest Territory that would come to include the states of Ohio, Indiana, Illinois, Michigan and Wisconsin. Of these, three of the framers voted to ban slavery.

Three years later, a similar Northwest prohibition came up for consideration and two more future framers voted for a ban. Then in 1789, at the first official gathering of Congress, presided by George Washington, all sixteen framers present—Lincoln methodically names each of them—voted unanimously to enforce the slavery ban of the 1787 Northwest Ordinance.

Again in 1804, Lincoln records, two framers were called upon to adjudicate similar restrictions in the newly acquired Louisiana Territory. Again, they voted for federal restrictions, including a ban on future importation of slaves from abroad. And in 1820, when Congress considered the Missouri Compromise, Lincoln points out that two surviving framers cast votes, one to ban slavery extension, one to allow it.

In the manner of a lawyer—which Lincoln was—summing up his case, Lincoln unveils his statistical tally, which he reminds his audience does not include any double counting. He has twenty-three of the thirty-nine framers—"a clear majority," he points out—voting on the question of slavery expansion, and of these he counts twenty-one, a near unanimity, placing themselves on the side of banning or restricting it.

Finally, in a kind of addendum, Lincoln considers the sixteen framers who left no voting record on the subject, including Benjamin Franklin, Alexander Hamilton and Gouverneur Morris. With the exception of one, John Rutledge, Lincoln notes that all the others were confirmed antislavery men. So taking into account how they would likely have voted had the question been before them, Lincoln records his final tally of thirty-six to three, a decisive endorsement by the framers of the Republican position on slavery restriction.

Whatever one thinks of Lincoln's algebra, he would seem to have decisively refuted Taney's contention that the founders were unanimous in considering blacks to be so far inferior to whites that they were fit objects only for slavery. Moreover, Lincoln's challenge to the Democrats to name a single person—not just a single founder but any single individual—of the founding era who claimed blacks were not included as men in the Declaration of Independence was never met by a Democrat of his time and has not been met to this day. Clearly there is something very wrong with the conventional wisdom, both about Lincoln and about the founding era.

JEFFERSON AGONISTES

One of the striking aspects of Lincoln's demonstration of the founders' attitudes toward slavery is the role of the Southerners in the group. The South had a dominant role in the founding and several of the early presidents—Washington, Jefferson, Madison, Monroe—were Southerners. Yet all these men, Virginia slave-owners every one of them, railed against slavery. Their expressed attitude toward it and toward blacks was radically different, as Lincoln noted, from that of the Democrats of his own day.

Even so, the nagging question remains: why did the founders nevertheless elect to permit slavery when presumably they could have banned it outright? If the equality clause of the Declaration articulated, as Lincoln insisted, "abstract truth, applicable to all men and all times," how can its enforcement be denied or even delayed? To answer this question, let's begin with the man Lincoln turned to, Thomas Jefferson, whom Lincoln termed "the most distinguished politician of our history," and examine his views on slavery and white supremacy.[16]

In doing so we should realize we are considering the hard case, because Jefferson was clearly the most racist of the leading founders. He owned more than 200 slaves and did not free them. He seems to have had his way with a female slave on his plantation, Sally Hemings, and produced children by her. Today's progressives take a dim view of Jefferson, with some calling for his ouster from America's canon of revered forefathers.[17]

By contrast with Jefferson, Washington made provision to free his slaves upon his death and said of slavery, "There is not a man living who wishes more sincerely than I do, to see a plan adopted for the abolition of it." Madison owned slaves but devised numerous emancipation schemes, terming slavery "the most oppressive dominion ever exercised by man over man." Another slave-owner, Hamilton, was nevertheless one of the founders of the New York Society for Promoting the Manumission of Slaves. John Jay, America's first chief justice, was elected president of that society. Neither Adams nor Franklin owned slaves. Adams sought "the eventual total extirpation of slavery," and Franklin, who termed slavery "an atrocious debasement of human nature," was elected president of the Pennsylvania Abolition Society.[18]

What, then, made Jefferson different from these men? Probably the single greatest difference was that Jefferson was a man of the Enlightenment and in tune with the latest ideas in science and anthropology. Jefferson was probably the only one among the founders who avidly read ethnological travel accounts of Europeans who penetrated the heart of Africa.

In *Notes on the State of Virginia*, Jefferson writes that when it comes to intellectual ability, "I advance it therefore as a suspicion only that the blacks, whether originally a distinct race, or made distinct by time and circumstances, are inferior to the whites." Jefferson recognizes, of course, that the condition of blacks in America is largely determined by their enslavement. Still, he says, in ancient societies, slaves, upon becoming free, rose to become eminent figures in philosophy, literature and mathematics. Yet he does not observe this to be true among

America's free blacks, not one of whom, in Jefferson's experience, has "uttered a thought above the level of plain narration."[19]

Jefferson never went beyond this "suspicion," and the suspicion itself was challenged when the black naturalist and mathematician Benjamin Banneker sent Jefferson his writings. Jefferson responded, "Nobody wishes more than I do to see such proofs as you exhibit, that Nature has given to our black brethren talents equal to those of the other colors of men, and that the appearance of a want of them is owing merely to the degraded condition of their existence, both in Africa and America."[20]

Jefferson's writings about blacks and Native Americans are suffused with anthropological speculation that, in one notable case, seems deeply offensive. Jefferson speaks of black women in Africa having sex with chimpanzees, making reference to "the preference of the Oranootan for the black women over those of his own species."[21] Here Jefferson seems to echo the most vicious strains of bigotry that degrade blacks to the level of animals.

Where did Jefferson get this? Historian Winthrop Jordan writes, "There was in Africa a beast which was likened to men. It was a strange and eventually tragic happenstance of nature that Africa was the habitat of the animal which in appearance most resembles man. The animal called 'orang-outang' by contemporaries (actually the chimpanzee) was native to those parts of western Africa where the early slave trade was heavily concentrated . . . The startlingly human appearance and movements of the . . . orang-outang aroused some curious speculations." Jordan proceeds to cite travel accounts that speculated about "the sexual association of apes with Negroes."[22]

Despite Jefferson's indulgence in some of the most ridiculous conjectures of Enlightenment naturalism, he flatly refuses to use the supposed primitivism and intellectual inadequacies of blacks to justify their enslavement. "Whatever be their degree of talent," he writes of blacks in a letter to Henri Gregoire, "it is no measure of their rights." Jefferson goes on to argue that just "because Sir Isaac Newton was superior to others in understanding, he was not therefore lord of the person or property of others."[23]

Jefferson was, again on account of his Enlightenment sympathies, one of the least religious of the founders. Even so, he thundered against slavery in biblical cadences and with the fury of a biblical prophet. "And can the liberties of a nation be thought secure when we have removed their only firm basis, a conviction in the minds of the people that these liberties are the gift of God? That they are not to be violated but with his wrath? Indeed I tremble for my country when I reflect that God is just: that his justice cannot sleep forever." And if the slaves should ever rise up against the masters, Jefferson confesses that "the Almighty has no attribute which can take side with us in such a contest."[24]

No abolitionist was ever so eloquent. And then, in making the case against British rule in a draft of the Declaration of Independence that Congress amended, Jefferson blames the Crown for introducing and sustaining slavery in America. Jefferson alleges that with regard to blacks, King George "has waged cruel war against human nature itself, violating its most sacred rights of life and liberty in the persons of a distant people, who never offended him, captivating and carrying them into slavery in another hemisphere." Jefferson holds the king responsible for "this execrable commerce" since the Crown was "determined to keep open a market where men should be bought and sold."[25]

CONSENT OF THE GOVERNED

At first this foisting of the blame for slavery on the British seems incredible, yet we forget that by the 1770s slavery had already existed in America for 150 years, the first slaves having arrived around 1619 in Virginia. Historian David Brion Davis reminds us that "almost two-thirds of the history of North American slavery occurred before the American Revolution."[26] The founders are often portrayed as instituting slavery in America, whereas in reality they were contending with an institution long established before they contemplated what to do with it.

A few years before the Declaration, Jefferson in *A Summary View of the Rights of British America* makes this astounding statement against the Crown: "The abolition of domestic slavery is the great object of desire in those colonies where it was unhappily introduced in their infant state."[27] Abraham Lincoln regarded this statement as of the highest importance. Here is Jefferson basically asserting that most Americans—Southerners no less than Northerners—wish to have slavery ended even while the British Crown insists upon sustaining it against their will. Note that Jefferson does not speak merely of "emancipation"; rather, he uses the term "abolition." What, one wonders, would Taney have made of this?

In 1779, Jefferson proposed a law that would provide for gradual emancipation of slaves in Virginia, a law that he knew would apply also to him. In 1784, he proposed a law in Congress that would ban slavery from the entire Western territory of the United States; the proposal failed by a single vote. And in 1807 President Jefferson publicly supported the abolition of the slave trade, urging Congress to close it down, which it did.

Why then did Jefferson—and other founders who in general had even stronger antislavery credentials than he did—not act once and for all to end this nefarious institution? Jefferson's answer cannot be better given than in the quotation at the beginning of this chapter: "We have the wolf by the ear, and we can neither hold him nor safely let him go. Justice is in one scale, and self-preservation in the other."

Jefferson elaborates on why he considers the emancipation of blacks and their integration into American society not just problematic, but impossible. "Deep rooted prejudices entertained by the whites; ten thousand recollections, by the blacks, of the injuries they have sustained; new provocations; the real distinctions which nature has made; and many other circumstances, will divide us into parties, and produce convulsions, which will probably never end but in the extermination of the one or the other race."[28]

That this is not an affirmation of white supremacy can be seen in Jefferson's fear that either the whites will exterminate the blacks, or the blacks will exterminate the whites. Jefferson must have considered blacks as a group pretty formidable if he thought they might become the oppressive class.

Even so, Jefferson's tone here is a bit hysterical; to a progressive, I'm sure he sounds like a modern-day Trumpster, inveighing against illegal immigrants. "They will overrun us. They will wipe us out." We can agree with the progressive that such fears may be overblown—we can rejoice in hindsight that Jefferson's ghoulish vision has not come true—but they cannot be dismissed, even if they are irrational. "A universal feeling," Abraham Lincoln said in precisely this context, "whether well or ill-founded, cannot be safely disregarded."[29]

The reason for this has to do with why people join together in a social compact in the first place. According to John Locke and the theorists of classical liberalism, they do so primarily for security, or what Jefferson calls "self-preservation." And this security is not merely an actual condition; it is also a perception. In other words, people must not just be secure, they must also feel secure. Their security is in part in the minds of the people themselves, which is why liberal society is based on "the consent of the governed."

The "consent of the governed" is that other, often overlooked, phrase in the Declaration. Yet it is no less fundamental, of no less importance, than "all men are created equal." The two would seem to be the twin foundational principles of democracy, yet as the founders and Lincoln all recognized, they are not always compatible. Sometimes they can even become rivals.

What if a majority of Americans believe that to free a million or several million slaves and release them into the general population would endanger the safety and welfare of that population? The progressive answer is: Well, that's just ridiculous! Too bad for them! Let them learn to deal with it! But in a democratic society, the deference of rulers to people's opinions and even to their fears is no mere technicality.

The case for democracy, no less than the case against slavery, relies on the consent of the governed. Consider Alexander Hamilton's definition of freedom: "The only distinction between freedom and slavery is this: in the former state, a man is governed by the laws to which he has given his consent; . . . in the latter, he is governed by the will of another."[30] This applies no less to democracy than to slavery. The freedom principle in both cases is the same.

If it is wrong to govern a man without his consent—the essential definition of slavery—it is equally wrong to govern a people without their consent. To outlaw slavery without popular consent would be to destroy democracy, and thus to outlaw the very basis for outlawing slavery. Lincoln understood this, as did the American founders.

All statesmen must deal with the gap between principle and practice. But the founders also had to deal with the tension between two principles that had become rivals, "created equal" and "consent of the governed." It is this tension that produced the founders' plantation dilemma, or what political scientist Harry Jaffa calls the "crisis of the house divided." Let's see how the founders attempted to solve it.

LESSER EVIL

It is tempting when considering the problems of the past to ascribe to the people involved a freedom they did not have. It is tempting to ask them to choose things that were not on the table to choose. This may be termed the utopian temptation, which in this case has become a progressive strategy deployed against the founders. The key to the strategy is to blame the founders for not securing ideals of perfection that they affirmed in principle but were not in a position to secure in practice.

Let's put ourselves in the place of the founders, gathered in that small dusty room in Philadelphia, and ask: what were the actual choices available to them with regard to slavery? The question before them was not slavery but union, the challenge of forming a durable union. This was a hugely controversial issue, with powerful opponents—the so-called Antifederalists—contending against the new constitutional union being proposed in Philadelphia.

So the choice before the founders was not, should we have a union based on slavery or one based on antislavery? Rather, the choice was to have a union that permitted slavery to continue, at least for a time, or to have no union at all. Slavery was less prevalent in the North but nevertheless legal in all of the thirteen states represented in Philadelphia, and it was obvious to all that many states—and certainly the Southern states—would never join a union that forbade slavery at the outset.

Let's suppose the founders chose to outlaw slavery and form a union only made up of states that agreed to join on that basis. In that case, at best, America would be a northern confederacy made up of a handful of northern states. The southern states might quite likely have formed their own confederacy—similar to the one they attempted to form in 1861—entirely free of pressure from the other one. So, not one America but two.

Let's assume that as western territories were formed, they could join either the northern or the southern confederacy and become states, and that in general the northern ones joined the northern union and the southern ones the southern union. Now we still have two Americas, each one significantly larger than before. If things had happened this way—the most reasonable conjecture in this exercise of counterfactual history—there would be virtually no leverage on the part of the north over the south: the south would have created a slave empire that would most likely have lasted much beyond 1865, and the predicament of blacks today would be far worse than it is.

Given the choices before them, the founders, who were mostly antislavery men, made what they considered to be the best antislavery choice. They founded a union on antislavery principles, anchored in the Declaration. Their hope and expectation was that the people of this union would recognize, as Lincoln repeatedly stressed, that if they wanted freedom for themselves, they could not tyrannize over others. Consequently, the founders believed, in their *novus ordo seclorum* or new order for the ages, slavery would be placed, as Lincoln put it, in a "course of ultimate extinction."

According to Michelle Alexander, in her influential book *The New Jim Crow*, "Under the terms of our country's founding document, slaves were defined as three fifths of a man, not a real, whole human being."[31] We can't fault Alexander alone; we've heard this before, and Alexander is simply echoing progressive orthodoxy. Yet the implication of her statement—that the three-fifths clause represents the founders' dehumanization of blacks—is completely wrong.

The three-fifths clause of the Constitution emerged as a consequence of the founders' balancing act to secure a union. The issue between the Northern and Southern states involved political representation. The South, of course, wanted more representation—which meant more power—and thus Southern states wanted blacks to count as full persons. Northern states wanted blacks to count as zero, to reduce the power of the slave-owning faction. The three-fifths clause was the compromise that enabled the North and South to come to terms on this issue.

While historians debate its impact, this was a compromise that seems to have favored the South. Historian David Brion Davis points out that the Democratic Party's national domination, beginning with Andrew Jackson in the late 1820s and continuing through 1860, was made possible largely by the added voting power supplied to Southern states by the three-fifths clause.[32] It should be obvious from this context that the clause had nothing to do with the intrinsic worth of black people and that progressive efforts to invoke it to prove the white supremacy of the founders is both unfair and ridiculous.

The bottom line is that the founders chose the lesser of two evils. It was a difficult choice, yet both Lincoln and the abolitionist leader Frederick Douglass, himself a runaway slave, considered it the right choice. Douglass noted that by keeping the slave-owning South within the union, the founders enabled Northern political pressure to work against slavery. "I am, therefore, for drawing the bond of Union more closely, and bringing the slave States more completely under the power of the free States."[33]

Lincoln compared slavery to a cancerous growth on the body and argued that "just as an afflicted man hides away a wen or cancer, which he dares not cut out at once, lest he bleed to death; with the promise, nevertheless, that the cutting may begin at the end of a given time," in the same manner the founders treated slavery as an evil they must tolerate with a view to its future removal.[34]

Lincoln's argument was that lesser evils are always preferable to greater ones, and it is the task of the statesman to achieve as much good as is practical under the circumstances. If the framers had sought to guarantee all the rights of all men, they would most likely have ended up securing no rights for anyone. The statesman must not merely know what is good but also how much good is achievable, and to achieve it without foolishly striving for more.

"Much as I hate slavery," Lincoln said in Peoria in 1854, "I would consent to the extension of it rather than see the Union dissolved, just as I would consent to any great evil to avoid a greater one."[35] For Lincoln, the union is the mechanism—the only mechanism—for permanently ending slavery, which is why saving the union becomes his paramount goal. Lincoln implies that it is in the slaves' interest too to sustain the union, even if the cost involves continuing or prolonging their servitude.

Of the Declaration's assertion of equality, Lincoln said of the founders, "They did not mean to assert the obvious untruth, that all were then enjoying that equality, nor yet, that they were about to confer it immediately upon them. In fact, they had no power to confer such a boon. They meant simply to declare the *right,* so that the *enforcement* of it might follow as fast as circumstances should permit."[36]

In other words, the founders declared the timeless rights that apply to all men at all times, while also creating a political union in their time that would eventually elect an antislavery government in Lincoln's time, one that could finally make good on the rights that could not be secured for blacks until then. This is how the founders, not in their lifetime but two generations later, finally reconciled human equality with democratic consent.

LAYING THE FOUNDATION

In the end, we may ask: was it worth it? The founders may be exonerated of the charge of being white supremacists or being pro-slavery. But did their project succeed, not just in the end, but also in their own time? Here we must recall that up through the American founding, slavery was a universal institution. "If slavery be wrong," one of the founders, Charles Pinckney, said, "It is justified by the example of all the world."

While progressives term slavery America's "peculiar institution," political scientist Orlando Patterson responds, "There is nothing notably peculiar about the institution of slavery. It has existed from before the dawn of human history . . . in the most primitive of human societies and in the most civilized. There is no region on earth that has not at some time harbored the institution. Probably there is no group of people whose ancestors were not at one time slaves or slaveholders."[37]

American Indians had slaves on the American continent before the white man arrived here. The British, as we have seen, supervised slavery in the American colonies for a century and a half prior to American independence. Before 1776, slavery was legal in every part of America. In Northern states like New York and New Jersey, slaves didn't work on plantations but built roads, cleared land, cut timber and herded cattle; they also worked in skilled trades like carpentry, stonemasonry and blacksmithing, and also as domestic labor.

Yet after the Revolution, there was a big change. By 1804 every state north of Maryland had abolished slavery, either immediately or gradually. Thus by the end of the founding era, more than a hundred thousand slaves had been freed—around one-sixth of the total number in the country at the time—and slavery was gone, or on its way out, in seven of the thirteen original states. Southern and border states prohibited further slave importations from abroad. Congress was committed to outlawing the slave trade in 1808, which it did. Slavery was no longer a national but a sectional institution, and one under moral and political siege.

How did this happen? The simple answer—the only answer—is what historian David Brion Davis terms "the effects of Revolutionary ideology." Historian Gordon Wood, the preeminent scholar of the founding, concurs. It is no coincidence, he points out, that Americans in Philadelphia in 1775 started the first antislavery society existing anywhere. It was the Revolution that made American slavery "peculiar" in that it was out of place in a nation dedicated to the proposition that all men are created equal. In this sense, as Wood writes, "The Revolution in effect set in motion ideological and social forces that doomed the institution of slavery in the North and led inexorably to the Civil War."[38]

The founders are not to blame for killing America or giving America a "false start." Far from introducing slavery or white supremacy, they laid the moral and political foundation for a new country that became a model for freedom in the world. Based on the principles they enunciated, this country would, in the measure of time, overthrow slavery and establish equality of rights under the law. Lincoln recognized this.

The progressive attack on the founding is a decoy, an attempt to shift the blame for other, far greater sins perpetrated by other, far greater sinners. We—especially those of us who are nonwhite—owe the founders a debt of gratitude, and if we ever "take a knee" for the flag or the national anthem, it should be to say a prayer and thank God for the United States of America.

3

PARTY OF ENSLAVEMENT

The Psychology of the Democratic Master Class

Socialism proposes to do away with free competition; to afford protection and support at all times to the laboring class . . . these purposes, slavery fully and perfectly attains.

—GEORGE FITZHUGH, *Sociology for the South*[1]

The early nineteenth century saw the emergence of a new, expanded slave plantation, with a new ideology to sustain and promote it. For the first time in world history, slave-owners had an elaborate philosophy—actually two elaborate philosophies—to protect slavery from moral and political attack. This ideology was formulated by the leading thinkers of a new political party, the Democratic Party, which became, from the 1820s to 1860, the party of the plantation. This chapter explores the mind of this Democratic master class, because it has shaped Democratic thinking and strategy right down to the present.

The Democratic Party's deep involvement in administering the slave plantation and vigorously defending slavery is a historical truth that progressives and Democrats have desperately sought to camouflage. This is the significance of the left-wing rampage through the South, in the wake of the infamous Charlottesville rally, which resulted in the pulling down of Confederate monuments. The Charlottesville rally itself was called to block the proposed removal of Confederate general Robert E. Lee's monument from Emancipation Park.

In the heated aftermath of Charlottesville, Black Lives Matter and Antifa groups forced the dismantling of dozens of other monuments, with still others under consideration for relocation or removal. In Austin, Texas, the statues of Lee and another Confederate general, Albert Sidney Johnston, were taken down. Maryland authorities removed a statue of native son Roger Taney from in front of the State House.[2] On social media, I watched a video of angry protesters yanking down a statue to an unnamed Confederate soldier, shouting obscenities at him and kicking him.

Seeing the sheer venom of the protesters, I thought to myself, "Oh wow. They're acting like this lifeless statue can actually hear them and feel pain." I tried to imagine this soldier, most likely a dirt-poor farm worker who didn't own any slaves. One of these soldiers was asked after the war what his reason was for fighting in the war and he replied, "Because the Yankees are down here." In Chicago, strangest of all, someone even tried to burn a bust of Abraham Lincoln, the president who won the war and freed the slaves.[3]

This campaign is far from over. Some Democratic activists demand that all Confederate monuments go, including, for example, the ones that stand alongside the monuments to Union generals and soldiers at Gettysburg National Monument. So far the Gettysburg authorities have said no, which is why leftists are keeping up the pressure with articles in Politico like "Why There Are No Nazi Statues in Germany." The author, Joshua Zeitz, remarks, "In Germany, you won't see neo-Nazis converging on a monument to Reinhard Heydrich or Adolf Hitler, because no such statues exist."[4] In this view, the Confederacy is Nazi Germany, and America needs its own thorough denazification.

What can we make of this? At first glance, we see Democratic activists pulling down the statues of other Democrats. With the exception of Lincoln, every other statue defaced or removed seems to be one of a Democrat. The naive may be forgiven for thinking, just for a minute, that Democrats may finally be acknowledging and taking responsibility for their history. This the Democratic Party has never done before. Is it possible—could it be—that Democrats are now actually apologizing for their past history of oppression and demanding that their own party's pro-slavery leaders no longer be publicly honored?

Wishful thinking. No, that is not what's going on at all. In all the acres of media reporting on the Confederate leaders, scarcely anyone has pointed out that they were all Democrats. In fact, the whole point of the campaign to topple Confederate statues is to disguise it. It is an effort not at historical exposition but at historical concealment. The point of blaming the Confederacy is to blame slavery entirely on the South, and the point of blaming the South is to blame the party that is now politically dominant in the South, namely, the Republican Party. Thus the left targets Confederate statues in order to promote its big lie that racism and white supremacy are the province of the right.

We can see this clearly by observing one statue that has not been pulled down, the monument in Chicago to Stephen Douglas. Douglas was far more of a white supremacist than Robert E. Lee. True, Lee inherited slaves on his wife's side, but he was also opposed to slavery, as he admitted in a letter to his wife in 1856: "There are few, I believe, in this enlightened age, who will not acknowledge that slavery as an institution is a moral and political evil."[5] In this respect, Lee sounds exactly like his political idol and fellow Virginian, Thomas Jefferson.

Douglas lived in Illinois—a free state—and did not own slaves. But unlike Lee, he never expressed any opposition to slavery as an institution. On the contrary, he was, together with South Carolina Democrat John C. Calhoun, the most effective political defender of slave society. Douglas did far more to uphold slavery than Lee, who as a military man was not even involved in the antebellum debate, opposed secession when it was proposed, and joined the Confederacy, refusing Lincoln's offer of command of the Union army, only when his home state of Virginia seceded against his will.

Moreover, Douglas derided blacks in the classic language of white supremacy; nothing from Lee corresponds to this. Here's Douglas, in one of his debates with Lincoln: "Now, I do not believe that the Almighty ever intended the Negro to be the equal of the white man . . . He belongs to an inferior race, and must always occupy an inferior position." And again, "This government of ours is founded on the white basis. It was made by the white man, for the benefit of the white man, to be administered by white men."

In another speech—cited by Lincoln—Douglas said that in any contest between a Negro and a white man he was for the white man, although in any contest between a Negro and a crocodile he was for the Negro. Here, as Lincoln pointed out, Douglas' reference to the crocodile was to reduce blacks, from the white man's perspective, to the level of beasts. "As the Negro ought to treat the crocodile as a beast, so the white man ought to treat the Negro as a beast."[6]

One might expect, then, that Black Lives Matter and Antifa activists would by now have vandalized or toppled Douglas' monument. But it remains untouched. In fact, there is no controversy about it at all. The reason is obvious. Douglas was a Northern Democrat, and to target Douglas' statue would be to remove the focus from the Confederacy, which was of course Southern. Thus toppling Douglas' monument would expose the involvement of the Northern Democrats—in short, the national Democratic Party—as the political champions of slavery. So Douglas must be allowed to stand, serene and unchallenged, so as not to disrupt the progressive lie about where the political responsibility for slavery truly lies.

KING COTTON

On August 2, 1862, after Lincoln had informed his cabinet about the Emancipation Proclamation, the president met with a committee of five free blacks. He told them he looked forward to the end of slavery, but ended with this grim assessment: "Even when you cease to be slaves, you are yet far removed from being placed on an equality with the white race. On this broad continent not a single man of your race is made the equal of a single man of ours. I cannot alter it if I would. It is a fact."[7]

Lincoln was referring to something that involved slavery but went beyond slavery, what he termed the debauching of the public mind regarding blacks and white supremacy. Basically Lincoln understood that a great change had come over America between the founding period and his own, a change not merely in the nature of the slave plantation but also in the prevalence of the plantation philosophy being peddled by the Democratic Party both in the North and in the South. This change goes almost unnoticed today in progressive historiography—because it does not fit the progressive narrative—so let's draw it out.

By 1828—the year Andrew Jackson was elected, the official date for the formation of the Democratic Party—the plantation was vastly bigger and more powerful than it had been in Washington and Jefferson's day. In 1776, the slave population in all thirteen states was around 650,000, but by 1828 it had grown to around two million, doubling again to four million by 1860. In sum, the plantation had grown sixfold since the founding era, and from the 1820s to 1860 it was the cornerstone of the economy of the South.

The founders had hoped slavery would gradually die out, but they did not anticipate Eli Whitney's invention of the cotton gin in 1793. Whitney's simple device for separating short-staple cotton from its seeds revolutionized the plantation. Southern cotton production grew from 6,000 bales in 1792 to 178,000 in 1810, and up from there. From the diversified agricultural economy of Jefferson's day, the South became largely a single-crop economy. And as the nation expanded the cotton kingdom grew, too, the number of slave states expanding from eight to fifteen.

Since "King Cotton" was the basic raw material of the Industrial Revolution, it made the planters rich. By the 1830s, cotton accounted for more than half of all U.S. exports. Cotton planters were the wealthiest people in America, and there were more millionaires in the South, living off the big plantations, than there were in any other region of the country. The significance of this is that the plantation economy generated a powerful political lobby, and a new political party was ready at hand to take up the cause of the slave-owners.

Most Americans don't realize that around the time of the Revolution, there were powerful antislavery currents in the South no less than in the North. Historians Eugene Genovese and Elizabeth Fox-Genovese inform us that "antislavery expressions . . . reverberated in the South during and after the American Revolution." Winthrop Jordan notes that in Virginia—which had 40 percent of the slaves in the entire nation at the time—denunciations of slavery, though not universal, were "acceptable and widespread."[8]

Speaking in July 1773 at the Virginia Constitutional Convention, George Mason described slavery as "that slow Poison, which is daily contaminating the Minds and Morals of our People." Two years later,

Patrick Henry urged his fellow Southerners to look for a time "when an opportunity will be offered to abolish this lamentable evil."[9] This was the tone. And Southern states joined Northern states in excluding slavery from the Northwest Territory and in abolishing the African slave trade.

The tone persisted through the early nineteenth century. "Until the 1820s," John Blassingame writes in *The Slave Community,* "many planters, convinced of the immorality of bondage, joined with clergymen in seeking its abolition." During this period, the South had more than a hundred antislavery organizations, and manumissions of slaves were fairly common, especially in Maryland, Delaware and Virginia. Yet historian Stanley Elkins points out that by the 1830s "the hostility to slavery that had been common in Jeffersonian times . . . all but disappeared."[10]

How did this happen? According to Blassingame, planters launched a massive campaign to uphold slavery in the wake of the abolitionist and antislavery pressures generated by the Revolution. The goal was to unify the slave community in defense of the plantation. Mob attacks were organized against antislavery ministers. "By the 1840s," Blassingame writes, "the propagandists had largely succeeded in silencing the churches."[11] Then they began browbeating the clergy into becoming advocates of slavery.

Around the same time, planters organized a campaign throughout the South—largely successful—to block literature from antislavery societies from being delivered through the mail. In response to political pressure, every Southern state except Maryland and Kentucky passed laws prohibiting teaching slaves to read and write. Many Southern legislatures adopted measures banning manumissions, some forced free blacks to leave the state, and a few even invited free blacks to enslave themselves. By the 1850s some slavery apologists like William Yancey and Robert Barnwell Rhett were calling for the reopening of the African slave trade.

This was a new and different South, and to the incredible good fortune of the planter aristocracy, there was a political party, the Democratic Party, to represent their interests and press their claims, both at the local and the national level. Working with and through this party, the planter class found itself equipped with a full-blown moral, legal and political philosophy of the plantation, one that historians say no previous class of slave-owners ever developed.[12]

Two features of the Democratic apologia for the plantation stand out to distinguish this mode of thinking from anything that came before. First, slavery was defended not as a necessary evil but rather as a "positive good." Typical of this rhetoric is Democratic congressman James Henry Hammond's 1936 speech in Congress: "Sir, I do firmly believe, that domestic slavery, regulated as ours is, produces the highest toned, the purest, best organization of society that has ever existed on the face of the earth."[13]

Hammond and others insisted that slavery was not only good for the master, but also for the slave. Slaves were happier under slavery that they would have been as free laborers. The Democratic propagandist George Fitzhugh—who remarkably enough regarded himself a socialist—declared slavery so good for the slaves that he thought it might be worth trying not just on blacks but also on whites and all laborers worldwide. The sheer audacity of these claims is worth noting. No previous slave community dared say such things. Evil as the Nazis were, they didn't have the chutzpah to claim that what they did to the Jews was somehow good for the Jews.

Second, leading Democrats rejected the principles of the founding, including the Declaration of Independence. According to Democratic senator John C. Calhoun, founding documents like the Declaration provided "an utterly false view of the subordinate relation of the black to the white race," and his fellow Southerners like Jefferson should be blamed for "admitting so great an error" into the South, which was now suffering its "poisonous fruits." Needless to say, Calhoun's defense of slavery was constructed on the premise of white supremacy.

Calhoun acknowledged that the mood in the South fostered by the Democratic Party in the nineteenth century was quite different from what it had been in the founding era. "Many in the South once believed that it was a moral and political evil; that folly and delusion are gone; we see it now in its true light, and regard it as the most safe and stable basis for free institutions in the world."[14]

The Democrats were the majority party in the Jacksonian era. Yet it took more than Southern Democrats to defend the plantation; the

Northern Democrats too did their part. Through their leader Stephen Douglas, they concocted a second, entirely independent pro-slavery philosophy, one equally imbued with racism and one that identified the cause of slavery with the cause of democracy itself. This was Douglas' doctrine of "popular sovereignty."

Working in concert, the Northern and Southern Democrats didn't merely secure slavery and fight for its expansion into the territories. The pro-slavery ideologies of the Democratic Party made slavery seem, morally and politically, beyond reproach. Thus in the wake of mounting political criticism of the plantation, these ideologies produced a political intransigence in the planter class that led to—indeed caused—the Civil War.

Sectional differences, intense though they may be, do not inevitably lead to war. As historian David Potter points out, "Sectionalism has been chronic in American history. At times, the divisions between East and West have seemed even deeper and more serious than those between North and South."[15] The Democrats enabled the planter class to refuse political accommodation, and thus the North-South difference took the form of lethal political strife. In this respect, it may be said that the Democratic Party unleashed the malignant forces that started the Civil War.

LIFESTYLES OF THE DEMOCRATIC PLANTERS

"There's a cotton nigger for you! Genuine! Look at his toes! Look at his fingers! There's a pair of legs for you! . . . He's just as good for ten bales as I am for a julep at eleven o'clock." This is from the travel journal of Frederick Law Olmsted, witnessing a slave auction in New Orleans. On another occasion, Olmsted saw a small white girl stop a slave on the road, wag her finger and order him to return to his plantation. To Olmsted's astonishment, the grown man promptly obeyed.[16]

This was slavery. I want to probe further the pro-slavery ideologies of the Democratic Party in the nineteenth century, but first I wish to give some account of how slavery was actually experienced, not so much by the slaves—I cover that throughout this book—but mainly by the Democratic master class. What were they actually doing throughout this period?

Turns out, not much, because they had slaves to do it for them. Booker T. Washington, born a slave in Franklin County, Virginia, reports that during his childhood servitude, "My old master had many boys and girls, but not one, so far as I know, ever mastered a single trade or special line of productive industry. The girls were not taught to cook, sew, or take care of the house. All of this was left to the slaves."[17]

The slaves, of course, worked not because they wanted to but because they had to. Slavery was, at its core, a system of labor extortion that took on a racist cast because the slaves were all black. (The slave-owners were not: some American Indians owned slaves, and between 1830 and 1860 there were approximately 3,500 black slave-owners who owned upward of 10,000 black slaves.) Yet the vast majority of planters were, of course, white, and inevitably this master class drew a sharp caste line between their own white community and that of the slaves.

These slave-owners never forgot what slavery was in its essence. "For what purpose does the master hold the servant?" asked Democratic planter John Tompkins in the North Carolina *Farmer's Journal* in 1853. "Is it not that by his labor, he, the master, may accumulate wealth?"[18] While historians would later debate whether slavery retarded the economic welfare of the South, it is indisputable that it advanced the economic welfare of the planters. As one of my college professors wryly said, it strains credibility to think that the planter class would have taken on slavery as a nonprofit venture.

With the wealth of slavery, the Democratic master class developed a lifestyle based on leisure. In the words of historian Gordon Wood, "They came closest in America to fitting the classical ideal of the free and independent gentleman."[19] Self-consciously imitating the English gentry, the upper tier of Democratic planters built country homes, traced family genealogies and held sumptuous banquets. Their day was designed for people with time on their hands. A good part of it was taken up with gambling and sports: croquet, cards, cockfighting and hunting. One magazine suggested that the most enjoyable way to hunt deer was to camp alongside a stream for a week.

At the same time, there was a dark underside to the culture of the Democratic slave-owning class, vividly exposed in Kenneth Greenberg's *Honor and Slavery*. As Greenberg shows, the slave-owners developed a code of honor and respect based on values they took to be the inverse of slave values. Slaves were considered persons without honor and unworthy of respect. Not only did they lie and steal; the master class expected them to lie and steal.

Consequently, the Democratic master class developed a code in which the slightest implication that they were dishonest or dishonorable provoked a prickly, sometimes murderous response. Greenberg gives a telling example. In the North, he says, professional entertainers like P. T. Barnum made fortunes putting on shows in which jokesters made fools of people, pulled out chairs while unsuspecting people plumped down on the floor and so on. North of slavery, these antics were perceived as hilarious by the jokester and the audience—everyone, that is, except the butt of the joke.

But when a young gentleman, Marion Sims, tried that at a South Carolina college, sending his classmate Boykin Witherspoon crashing to the ground, "no one thought this was funny." A deadly silence filled the room of onlookers. Sims, Greenberg notes, apologized in the most profuse terms, "in the humblest manner." Why? Because a failure to do so could easily have resulted in serious injury or an invitation to a duel. "Everyone understood that this kind of joke in South Carolina did not end in laughter and a round of drinks. It was likely to end in death."

Duels, Greenberg writes, were the "central ritual of antebellum plantation life." They far outlasted the practice of dueling in the North, and the culture of dueling was sustained by slights to honor or respect. But not any slights; typically they were slights to honesty or status. Slaves were considered ineligible for duels because they had no honor to lose; only the master class could be "dissed," and only by another member of the master class.

Greenberg cites the example of a planter who was challenged to a duel because he told a fellow planter that he smelled bad. "When the man of honor is told that he smells," Greenberg writes, "he does not draw a bath—he draws his pistol." Today we would find it crazy that two people could fight to the death over this. Even in the nineteenth century, Americans far removed from the plantation were baffled by such behavior. Not only does the resolution seem disproportionate to the slight, but in addition, how could a duel possibly settle the factual question of whether the guy smelled bad or not?

But for the Democratic planter class, duels had nothing to do with establishing who was right over a disputed issue. The issue was not whether the fellow smelled bad or not. Rather, the issue was the questioning of a man's honor and reputation, which was to him as important as life itself. As Greenberg puts it, "The man of honor does not care if he stinks, but he does care that someone has accused him of stinking."

A further objective of duels, in addition to upholding reputation, was for the participants "to demonstrate they did not fear death." This display of fearlessness at the possibility of dying was, Greenberg says, even more important than prevailing in the duel. Moreover, planters loved to gamble and the duel was the ultimate form of gambling. "The duel was the type of gamble in which a man could achieve the highest honor because he assumed the greatest risk."

Incomprehensible though this code of behavior may be to most of us, I believe the only place that it would be comprehensible today is in our inner cities. There too is a prickly culture of honor and respect. There too slights to status and respect are not taken lightly and provoke fights and duels. Two antebellum planters might duel over who had a legitimate claim to a downed pigeon; two gang members now might duel over a pair of sneakers. Now too in places like Oakland, Baltimore and Chicago stand men ready to risk death in order to humiliate and shame an opponent who has insulted them.

And on the plantation as in the inner city today, duels were public rituals—Greenberg calls them "theatrical displays for public consumption"—aimed at saving face and shaming others. One dueler stood triumphantly over his slain opponent and announced, "This is not the profile of a man; it is the profile of a dog." Duels required the presence of witnesses, and large numbers of people participated in duels as principals, seconds, adjudicators, physicians, timekeepers or general audience.[20]

ENFORCED SUBORDINATION

Another common practice of the slave-owners that would be recognizable in our inner cities was informal polygamy. As overlords of their plantations, male planters took advantage of their position with young female slaves. "I hate slavery," fumed Mary Boykin Chesnut. "Under slavery, we live surrounded by prostitutes . . . God forgive us, but ours is a monstrous system, a wrong and an iniquity! Like the patriarchs of old, our men live all in one house with their wives and their concubines; and the mulattoes one sees in every family partly resemble the white children. Any lady is ready to tell you who is the father of all the mulatto children in everybody's household but her own."[21]

One such "patriarch" was James Henry Hammond, Democratic senator from South Carolina, who was quite candid with his son Harry about his extracurricular activities. As Hammond wrote young Harry in 1856, "In the last will I made I left to you . . . Sally Johnson, the mother of Louisa & all the children of both. Sally says Henderson is my child. It is possible, but I do not believe it. Yet act on her's rather than my opinion. Louisa's first child *may* be mine. I think not. Her second I believe is mine . . . Do not let Louisa or any of my children or possible children be the Slaves of Strangers. Slavery in the family will be their happiest earthly condition."[22]

Hammond drapes his sexual predation in the language of philanthropy. He speaks, some might say, as a true Democrat. And I agree—I see in Hammond a forerunner to Bill Clinton. Hammond displays the same sanctimony, the same quivering upper lip, even as his behavior reveals a ruthless selfishness. While Hammond is partial to slave women that he has bedded, and to slave children who might have resulted from those liaisons, he does not for a minute consider freeing any of them. Rather, he wants them to continue as slaves, although slaves "in the family." Democrats in those days liked to affectionately refer to their slave households as "our family, black and white."

A favorite discussion theme within the Democratic master class was the laziness and worthlessness of the slaves. It was a running joke among overseers that "it takes two white men to make a black man work" and that "it takes two to help one to do nothing." Even clear-eyed Mary Boykin Chesnut frets, "A hired man would be a good deal cheaper than a man whose father and mother, wife and twelve children have to be fed, clothed, housed, and nursed, their taxes paid, and their doctor's bills, all for his half-done, slovenly, lazy work."[23] Yet in reality it was the slaves who did most of the work and the planter class that was lazy and slovenly.

The slaves were property and therefore—it is true—they had little incentive to work. After all, they did not receive the fruits of their labor.

With a straight face, the Democratic master class investigated the supposed maladies that led to slaves feigning illness and shirking work responsibilities. A Louisiana doctor active in the Democratic Party, Samuel Cartwright, diagnosed slaves as suffering from Dyaesthesia Aethiopica, a supposedly tropical ailment that caused malingering, irresponsibility and "rascality" in slaves. Cartwright also identified Drapetomania as "the disease causing Negroes to run away."[24]

Recognizing they would have to make the slaves work, masters introduced the whip as the main management solution of plantation society. The whip was sometimes used sparingly, but it was used nevertheless by severe and kind masters alike. And the whip left enduring scars, emotional no less than physical. During his slave days, Frederick Douglass was whipped so badly by the slave-breaker Edward Covey that he says his mind broke down, "the dark night of slavery closed in upon me, and behold a man transformed into a brute!"[25]

Andrew Jackson, the founder of the Democratic Party, is sometimes compared to Thomas Jefferson. Both were admittedly Southern slave-owners who owned around 200 slaves. Yet Jackson was in his early career a slave-trader, a profession that was universally loathed by Jefferson and the whole founding generation and looked down upon even in Jackson's own day. Yet Jackson's era was not Jefferson's, and Jackson truly represents the Democratic Party of his time in that he shows none of the qualms about slavery that are so characteristic of Jefferson.

When one of his slaves ran away, Jackson purchased an ad in a local Tennessee paper offering a $50 reward for his capture "and ten dollars extra for every hundred lashes a person will give to the amount of three hundred."[26] Three hundred lashes may be considered something close to a death sentence! It is this barbarism in Jackson—unthinkable for Jefferson—that defines his era and, weirdly enough, coexists with Democratic rhapsodies about how slavery is wonderful not only for masters but also for slaves.

No system of tyranny can be sustained, however, entirely through force. The Democratic master class recognized that it needed carrots as well as sticks, and beyond that, it needed a whole social system that would bind the slaves physically and emotionally to the plantation. So the master class created a slave system based on total dependency.

The slaves, as Olmsted puts it, were encouraged to develop "a habit of perfect dependence," so that even without the whip they could see no way out.

This enforced subordination, according to the progressive black sociologist W. E. B. Du Bois, was the true meaning of slavery. "But there was . . . a real meaning to slavery different from that we may apply to the laborer today," Du Bois wrote. "It was in part psychological, the enforced personal feeling of inferiority, the calling of another Master; the standing with hat in hand. It was the helplessness. It was the de-fenselessness of family life. It was the submergence below the arbitrary will of any sort of individual."[27]

For most of us now, such observations are telling because they give us a window into the past. Du Bois understood the psychology of the plantation. But for many Americans—especially poor blacks, Latinos and Native Americans—what Du Bois writes will seem all too familiar. The past has not disappeared from the present. As we will see, there is a continuity between the Democrats of the mid-nineteenth century and the Democrats now, and a system of enforced dependency is the precise way in which Democrats today maintain their ethnic plantations.

SLAVES WITHOUT MASTERS

The positive-good school of slavery that emerged in the Democratic South is associated with such names as John C. Calhoun, James Henry Hammond, Henry Hughes, George Frederick Holmes, Thomas R. Dew and Edmund Ruffin. Calhoun and Hammond led the charge in the Senate. All these men, needless to say, were Democrats. But its most notorious and charismatic spokesman was George Fitzhugh, author of *Sociology for the South* and *Cannibals All!* and a regular writer for pro-slavery publications such as the Richmond *Enquirer* and *De Bow's Review*.

Fitzhugh was hardly a typical member of that school, or even a typical Southerner. Unlike many who celebrated rural agrarianism, Fitzhugh wanted the South to become a manufacturing powerhouse like the North. Virtually alone among pro-slavery apologists, he kept up a lively correspondence with abolitionists. He seems to have con-vinced the labor reformer George Henry Evans, once a committed abo-litionist, to switch allegiances and back the cause of the Confederacy.

For all his uniqueness and eccentricity, Fitzhugh was also widely influential; we hear his arguments echoed by other pro-slavery writers. Lincoln, too, was familiar with Fitzhugh and found his arguments repulsive, but also interesting. The reason, as scholars like Eugene Genovese have recognized, is that Fitzhugh "spelled out the logical outcome of the slaveholders' philosophy and laid bare its essence."[28]

Fitzhugh was also a self-professed leftist and socialist, and progressive scholars, while seeking to keep their distance from him today, cannot resist praising this aspect of his thought. Writing as a Marxist, Genovese confessed his delight in Fitzhugh's attacks on free-market capitalism. Many passages of Fitzhugh's work, writes Junius Rodriguez in *Slavery in the United States,* seem "lifted directly" from Marx, and others "foreshadow twentieth-century leftist thought."[29]

Here, then, is Fitzhugh in a nutshell.[30] He begins by noting that in every labor system there are basically two kinds of labor: free labor and slave labor. Fitzhugh concedes that at the first glance, free labor seems preferable to slave labor because the farm or factory laborer can leave his employer and go work for someone else or not work at all. By contrast, slaves cannot quit, cannot work for themselves and cannot refuse to work.

But Fitzhugh is unimpressed by this distinction, which he regards as meaningless in practice. He goes on to make an outrageous point. Free labor is actually enslaved labor, and slave labor is actually free. Free labor, Fitzhugh says, is dog-eat-dog. "The maxim, every man for himself," he writes, "embraces the whole moral code of a free society." The harsh competition of capitalism, Fitzhugh says, benefits the few and the strong while crushing the many and the weak. As a consequence of freedom, "the rich are continually growing richer and the poor poorer."

Drawing on a term frequently used by Engels and subsequently used in Marxist theory, Fitzhugh terms laborers in a free market "wage slaves." Of course he is referring here to white slaves. They are slaves because they are no less dependent on their masters than legal slaves. They too must work in order to eat and to live. And yet they have no protection, no provision, no security in the manner that legal slaves do.

In a free market, Fitzhugh notes, the interest of masters is opposed to that of the "wage slaves." When the slaves lose, the masters gain. The masters are always contriving to pay their workers less—playing them off against each other—even though the workers are the ones who produce all the products. Free society is a "war of the rich with the poor, and the poor with one another." In such society, Fitzhugh memorably observes, "virtue loses all her loveliness, because of her selfish aims."

Fitzhugh takes note of Northern travelers who unfavorably contrast the prosperity of the North with the backwardness of the South. Free labor, they argue, is more efficient and profitable than slave labor. Fitzhugh agrees, but turns the argument against them, contending that precisely to the degree that capitalism is profitable, that is the measure of capitalist exploitation of the working class.

Capitalists earn more, he says, by paying their workers less. They pay the worker only for time spent actually working, even though workers and their families also require support when the worker is disabled, or old, or sick. Capitalist entrepreneurs, Fitzhugh says, are basically slave masters "without the obligations of a master." That's how they generate so much efficiency and profits.

The beauty of slavery, according to Fitzhugh, is that it establishes an organic relationship between master and slave, not a relationship of contract but something more like a family. To those who say that slaves receive no compensation, Fitzhugh thunders that the considerable cost of maintaining a slave is the compensation. Moreover, the slave is provided for from cradle to grave. He is compensated, and his family is compensated, with food, shelter and care even when he is injured or sick or too old to work.

In a manner that echoes Marx's famous doctrine, "From each according to his ability, to each according to his need," Fitzhugh contends that a farm or plantation is a sort of commune "in which the master furnishes the capital and skill, and the slaves the labor, and divide the profits, not according to each one's in-put, but according to each one's wants and necessities."

The problem with the socialist theory coming into vogue in Europe and the northeastern states, Fitzhugh writes, is that it is "an ever receding and illusory Utopia." Socialists, he says, are attempting the impossible task of changing human nature. Slavery, he declares, is an actually existing form of socialism that happens to be its only workable form because it is based on human nature as it is. Slavery achieves "the ends all Communists and Socialists desire."

Fitzhugh concedes that there are masters who mistreat or abuse slaves, but even here, he writes, such abuse is qualified by the master's recognition that the slaves are expensive. "Labor in slave society is property," he writes, "and men will take care of their property. When slaves are worth near a thousand dollars a head, they will be carefully and well provided for." So paradoxically the slave's status as chattel provides him a sort of protection.

By contrast, Fitzhugh triumphantly notes, free laborers are not property, and this makes them disposable to their employers. If a capitalist entrepreneur has a dangerous job that may cost a worker his health or his life, Fitzhugh says, he won't risk having a slave do it; rather, he would be sure to get an immigrant laborer who, if he falls and kills himself, does so at his own risk. Free laborers, Fitzhugh says, are basically "slaves without masters," the worst possible situation for them to be in.

Unlike other pro-slavery writers who wrote paeans to slavery but could not answer the objection, "If slavery is so great, why not try it on white people?," Fitzhugh argues that a national or even worldwide slave system would benefit all workers, white as well as black. In this respect he was consistent, and he did not flinch when some of his fellow Democrats balked as he pursued the rationale of the pro-slavery philosophy to its logical conclusion. Ultimately, Fitzhugh says, the world will either adopt the slave system or the free-labor system, and his own preference was clear.

Yet in America, in his own day, Fitzhugh made the case to whites that they could escape being slaves because there were blacks to fill the task at hand. This racial hierarchy he attributed to the Democratic Party, of which he was a proud member. With blacks as the enslaved class, he says, white citizens "like those of Rome and Athens, are a privileged class." Here, from the mouth of a Democratic pro-slavery propagandist, are the roots of our contemporary term "white privilege." Fitzhugh also hints at what whites get out of white supremacy. They get the privilege of belonging to a superior caste, whether or not they own slaves.

Even so, like his Democratic successors today, Fitzhugh would have hotly rejected the idea that he was anti-black. Negro slaves, he says, are "the happiest and in some sense the freest people in the world." While the supposedly free white laborer of the North is constantly agonizing over how to support himself and his family, Fitzhugh says the black slave does his work and beyond that has not a care in the world because he and his family are fully provided for in any possible situation.

Slavery, Fitzhugh argues, is especially well-suited for blacks because "the Negro . . . is but a grown up child . . . His liberty is a curse to himself, and a greater curse to the society around him . . . The master occupies toward him the place of parent or guardian." So convinced is Fitzhugh about the benefits of blacks in captivity that in a pamphlet, *What Shall Be Done with the Free Negroes?*, he recommends that they should recognize what's good for them and voluntarily enslave themselves. "Let them select their masters."

Fitzhugh insists that the slave community is a kind of extended family in which "the interests of the various members of the family circle . . . concur and harmonize." His rhetoric on this point seems akin to, and reminiscent of, Democratic governor Mario Cuomo's 1984 Democratic Convention speech in which he likened the whole nation to a single family working toward a common purpose, one that takes care of all its members.

It seems almost eerie to hear Fitzhugh speak the modern language of compassion and social justice. For him, slavery is the ultimate expression of both. Without slavery, Fitzhugh warns, blacks would be "an intolerable burden" to themselves and society. As slaves, they are provided for in a manner that may seem meager but is in fact better than they could provide for themselves. For Fitzhugh, the slave plantation is a sort of welfare state, offering at least a basic provision of food, healthcare and security for all of its inhabitants.

Fitzhugh's sharp break with the American founders can be seen in his ridicule of Thomas Jefferson. In this he is not alone. Calhoun, Hammond and Jefferson Davis all attack the equality clause of the Declaration of Independence, proclaiming it not self-evidently true but self-evidently false. Here, again, we see what Lincoln means when he says that the Democrats introduced a new spirit of receptivity to tyranny that was not present at the founding.

In response to the Declaration of Independence, Fitzhugh quips that blacks "have a natural and inalienable right to be slaves." Seeking to refute Jefferson's famous remark that "the mass of mankind has not been born with saddles on their back, nor a favored few booted and spurred, ready to ride them legitimately, by the grace of God," Fitzhugh responds that some people are meant to be ridden, "and the riding does them good. They need the reins, the bit and the spur."

Fitzhugh pungently attacks not merely Adam Smith's free-market philosophy—"a system of unmitigated selfishness . . . rotten to the core"—but also John Locke's theory of the social contract, which posits that humans have natural rights and societies are formed with limited power to enforce only those rights that are delegated to the state.

Nonsense, says Fitzhugh. "Man is born a member of society . . . He has no rights whatever, as opposed to the interests of society . . . Whatever rights he has are subordinate to the good of the whole." Here, as we will see, Fitzhugh proves a forerunner to the fascist glorification of the state, an ideology that would strongly influence Franklin D. Roosevelt and the Democratic Party in the twentieth century.

As you may have begun to suspect by this point, George Fitzhugh was a statist and a supporter of a strong and powerful government, which in his time admittedly involved state power, not federal power. In this Fitzhugh was not alone. Most of the members of the Democrats' positive-good school were statists. Henry Hughes, for example, condemned abolitionist agitation as "a rebellion against the state."

Once again, however, Fitzhugh spells out the position with the greatest clarity. While some people say "the world is too little governed," Fitzhugh insists that "the masses require protection and control." He adds, "More of government is needed . . . Government is the life of a nation, and . . . it is absurd to define on paper . . . what they shall do and not do." For him, government power is unlimited and its exercise is controlled only by the exigencies of a given situation.

Fitzhugh places his hope for realizing his vision, at least in the United States, in the Democratic Party. A political commitment to the common interests of master and slave on the plantation is "the true and honorable distinction of the Democratic Party." Thrilled that the Democrats are dominant in the South, he predicts that "soon the Democratic Party will be in a majority again at the North." The outlook and mores of the Democratic plantation, he feels, would surely become universal. "Give the North a little more time, and she will eagerly adopt them."

Here of course Fitzhugh proved to be wrong. Despite resolute attempts by the Northern Democrats to "sell" the plantation, the Northern states did not adopt the plantation way of seeing things. Rather, they adopted the way of a new and, from Fitzhugh's perspective, most dangerous party, the Republicans, under a man Fitzhugh found surpassingly strange, Abraham Lincoln. Yet Lincoln agreed with Fitzhugh that the house would not stay permanently divided; either his way or Fitzhugh's way—the free system or the slave system—would eventually prevail.

Fitzhugh's run was of course ended by the Civil War. His home in Port Royal, Virginia was leveled by Union troops, and he fled to Richmond. After the war he was employed, strangely enough, by the Freedman's Bureau. Refusing to retract his theories, Fitzhugh, as a judge of the Freedman's court, lectured emancipated blacks about how they were better off under slavery. In 1857, he even told a group of snickering abolitionists, "Is our house tumbling about our heads? No! No! Our edifice is one that never did fall, and never will fall."[31]

In a sense, he was right. Certainly the plantation that Fitzhugh knew and loved—populated with what he took to be happy, contented slaves—was no more. But Fitzhugh's paternalistic philosophy of the plantation as a kind of infant welfare state did not completely die with it.

Fitzhugh's arguments—we cannot expect people to compete in the market, self-reliance is a chimera, people are happiest when they are looked after in the Big House—have a startling contemporary relevance. In fact, we see recognizable elements of his thinking among our own progressive Democrats, confirming my point that the pro-slavery Democrats of the South, for all their distance in time, are not so distant in ideology from the Democrats of today.

LINCOLN'S REFUTATION

Before I get to Lincoln's refutation of these pro-slavery schools of thought, it's important to emphasize that Lincoln was not merely refuting Southerners; he was refuting Democrats. Lincoln was not a hater of the South. "I have no prejudice against the Southern people," he said in his first debate with Stephen Douglas at Ottawa in 1858. "They are just what we would be in their situation. If slavery did not now exist among them, they would not introduce it. If it did now exist among us, we should not instantly give it up." If Southerners were reluctant to abolish slavery at one stroke, Lincoln said, "I surely will not blame them for not doing what I should not know how to do myself."[32]

Yet Lincoln showed no comparable gentleness in taking on the Democratic apologias for slavery, whether coming from the North or the South. "Whenever I hear anyone arguing for slavery, I feel a strong impulse to see it tried on him personally." That's what Lincoln told the 140th Indiana Regiment toward the end of the Civil War. It echoed what Lincoln had said earlier. "Slavery is good for some people!" he wrote in an undated fragment around 1858, mimicking the Democratic positive-good argument. Then he commented on it. "As a good thing, slavery is strikingly peculiar, in this, that it is the only good thing which no man ever seeks the good of, for himself." Here Lincoln's charge of hypocrisy is evident. And he deepened the charge with what followed. "Nonsense! Wolves devouring lambs, not because it is good for their own greedy maws, but because it is good for the lambs!"[33]

Here, with deadly accuracy, Lincoln struck at the Democratic pose of taking advantage of the slave while pretending to be his best friend. Yet while Lincoln was sarcastically dismissive of the Southern Democrats, he took a more serious—though ultimately not less indignant—stance against the Northern Democrats led by Stephen Douglas. Douglas was a follower of Andrew Jackson. A fiery, diminutive man, Douglas was called the Little Giant because of his formidable intellect and debating prowess. Lincoln regarded him as his supreme antagonist.

On slavery, Douglas took what we may call the pro-choice position. Like Taney, he insisted he was not in his personal views pro-slavery. But neither, he acknowledged, was he antislavery. Rather, his was a stance of public indifference. "It is none of my business which way the slavery clause is decided. I care not whether it is voted down or voted up." This was something for each particular state or community to decide for itself. The issue, for him, was not one of principle. The issue was one of free choice.

Douglas noted that we live in a big country. Naturally, people will have differing views on a subject as contentious as slavery. In some places slavery seems to make sense, in others it doesn't. "In Illinois," Douglas said, "We tried slavery, kept it up for twelve years, and finding that it was not profitable, we abolished it for that reason, and became a Free State." Illinois' approach illustrated Douglas' national model: let's agree to disagree. "Diversity," he said, "is the great safeguard of our liberties."[34]

Why impose a uniform position—whether it be pro-slavery or antislavery—on the whole country? This was a recipe for confrontation and strife. To prevent that, Douglas took a stance that he regarded as disinterested and statesmanlike. Essentially his stance was not to take a position, but to step aside and let each community or territory or state make its own decision and live with it. What, Douglas asked, could be a more democratic remedy than that?

Douglas called his stance "popular sovereignty." In a famous article in *Harper's*, Douglas affirmed "the right of every distinct political community . . . to make their own local laws, form their own domestic institutions, and manage their own internal affairs in their own way." Applying popular sovereignty to Kansas, he said, "If the people of Kansas want a slaveholding State, let them have it, and if they want a free State, they have a right to it."[35] And this approach, Douglas insisted, was congruent with the intentions of the founders.

Douglas may have been indifferent regarding slavery, but he was not indifferent regarding blacks. In one of his debates with Lincoln Douglas said, "I do not question Mr. Lincoln's conscientious belief that the Negro was made his equal, and hence is his brother, but for my own part I do not regard the Negro as my equal, and positively deny that he is my brother or any kin to me whatever."[36] As I mentioned earlier in this chapter, Douglas was a white supremacist. So were virtually all Democrats in the antebellum era.

From Douglas' abstemious rhetoric it might seem that his position on slavery was quite modest, seeking for it a limited reach and legitimacy. But in fact Douglas envisioned a massive slave empire south of the Mason-Dixon line, one that stretched from the Atlantic to the Pacific and incorporated Mexico, Central America and the islands of the

Caribbean. "Expansion was the keynote of Douglas's foreign policy," Harry Jaffa writes, "popular sovereignty of his domestic policy."[37]

Let us now zoom in on Douglas' reasoning about slavery. If we pay attention to it, we can see how close Douglas' position is to the progressive Democratic stance today on abortion. Obviously Douglas referred to a choice made by communities, not individuals. But that is the sole difference. Otherwise, the reasoning is the same. Who is to say when life begins? Let's agree to disagree. The right to choose is paramount.

This pro-logic was directly challenged by Lincoln. First, Lincoln showed the radicalism behind Douglas' supposedly modest stance. He pointed out that not only did Douglas seek to create a transcontinental slave empire, but "he has no desire there shall ever be an end of it."[38] Douglas emphatically rejected the founders' wish that slavery be placed on a path to ultimate extinction. If Douglas had his way, states and communities in America now would be deciding for themselves whether or not to enslave blacks.

Lincoln also exposed the inner contradiction in Douglas' position, and in doing this also supplies us today with the most powerful refutation of so-called pro-choice logic. Lincoln argued that for individuals no less than communities, choice is in general the correct approach. No one would dream, Lincoln said, of interfering with "the cranberry laws of Indiana or the oyster laws of Virginia." But slavery laws, Lincoln emphasized, are not in the same category. In other words, choice is not an absolute principle. Choice, Lincoln suggested in response to Douglas, can never be unequivocally affirmed without regard to the content of the choice.

Lincoln's argument applies equally to slavery and abortion. Let us consider what is being chosen. In these cases, we are talking about enslaving other people—forcibly taking away their lives and liberties. Or, in the abortion case, killing them in the womb. In both instances, choice is invoked in order to cancel out the choices of others. In both cases, self-government is a pretext for the denial of self-government. In both cases, persons who have the same rights as everyone else are being sacrificed to the convenience and welfare of others.

The problem with Douglas, as Lincoln put it, is that he has "no very vivid impression that the Negro is a human." Lincoln took Douglas to be arguing that "inasmuch as you do not object to my taking my hog to Nebraska, therefore I must not object to you taking your slave. Now, I admit this is perfectly logical, if there is no difference between hogs and Negroes." Lincoln summarized Douglas' position this way: "If one man choose to enslave another, no third man shall have the right to object."[39]

In the end, Lincoln regarded the position of Douglas and the Northern Democrats to be no less pro-slavery than that of the Southern Democrats. It would do as much "to nationalize slavery as the doctrine of Jeff Davis himself." In some ways Douglas' view was more dangerous than that of Davis, Fitzhugh or Calhoun, because Douglas' professed neutrality could seduce well-meaning people into believing that popular sovereignty was the solution for slavery.

Yet Lincoln saw that popular sovereignty was merely a cover for the protection and even extension of slavery. In a manner that echoes contemporary pro-lifers who contend that pro-choice really means pro-abortion, Lincoln contends that pro-choice really means pro-slavery. Of Douglas' popular sovereignty he said, "This declared indifference, but as I must think, covert real zeal for the spread of slavery, I cannot but hate." In the end, he warned, it will "blow out the moral lights around us."[40]

Here, in the muck and meanness of slavery, lie the roots of the Democratic Party. The plantation was its original stomping ground. The Democrats fought tenaciously for the plantation, and when they were defeated they fought just as tenaciously for the revival of the plantation. But the first step for the party, taken even before the Civil War, was to figure out how to apply the plantation model to the North, where immigrants by the millions and ultimately tens of millions were pouring into this country. The party of enslavement had big plans for them.

4

URBAN PLANTATION

Martin Van Buren and the Creation of the Northern Political Machine

Everybody is talkin' these days about
Tammany men growin' rich on graft, but
nobody thinks of drawin' the distinction
between honest graft and dishonest graft.

—GEORGE WASHINGTON PLUNKITT,
Plunkitt of Tammany Hall[1]

To hear the Democrats tell it, their love for the Mexican people has simply grown, and grown, and grown. This is now reflected in the unabashed loyalty that leading Democrats—and the Democratic Party platform—show toward illegal aliens. In the past, Democrats at least paid lip service to the necessity for immigration laws to be enforced, and for all people to obey the law.

No more. The Democratic platform of 2016 didn't even use the term "illegal" or any variation of it. It described America's immigration system as a problem, but not illegal immigration. "A decade or two ago," remarked Jason Furman, chairman of Obama's Council of Economic Advisers, "Democrats were divided on immigration. Now everyone agrees and is passionate and thinks very little about any potential down-sides."[2] The Democrats as a party are on the side of the illegals.

Under the Obama administration, illegals became a sort of privileged lawbreaking class. Initially, Obama did not hesitate to deport illegals, essentially carrying out the law and continuing the policies of the preceding Bush administration. Then Obama changed course and publicly announced that through an exercise of "prosecutorial discretion," immigration laws would only be enforced against certain types of illegals—namely violent criminals—while ordinary, run-of-the-mill illegals would be left alone.

Now, under Trump, Democrats in blue states are fighting hard to protect illegals from being sent back to their home countries. We all know about the sanctuary cities that now dot blue states across the country. Mayors of these cities have made it clear that they have no intention of cooperating in the enforcement of immigration laws. On the contrary, they will give sanctuary to lawbreakers who seek to evade those laws.

Progressives in California and New York go even further. California Democrats recently passed a law forbidding law enforcement from asking anyone's immigrant status or holding them for Immigration and Customs Enforcement (ICE) agents—unless they have been convicted of a crime. California also passed a law making it a crime for landlords to report illegals to the federal government. And recently the mayor of Oakland, Libby Schaaf, generated controversy for tipping off illegal immigrant groups that they were going to be raided by ICE authorities.[3]

In New York, even a criminal conviction is not enough to deny illegals the protection of the state. New York's Democratic governor Andrew Cuomo recently pardoned eighteen alien criminals—no murderers, mostly thieves and drug dealers—for the express purpose of saving them from potential deportation back to Mexico. "These actions," Cuomo said, "take a critical step toward a more just, more fair and more compassionate New York."

What idealism! What moral fervor! Ah, yes. I can envision Cuomo—himself descended from Italian immigrants—staring wistfully at the Statue of Liberty and Ellis Island as he signed those pardons.

He was probably remembering his parents and grandparents, who still spoke with Italian accents, or his original ancestors, not many generations removed, who came to this country speaking no English at all. Democrats, Cuomo believes, are the party of the new immigrants just as they were the party of the old immigrants, the Irish, the Italians, the Jews.

Trump, Cuomo alleges, "continues to target immigrants" and "threatens to tear families apart." Democrats are quick to tar immigration enforcement policies with the brush of racism and white supremacy. Part of the strategy is to disguise the fact that illegals are lawbreakers. The *New York Times* headline reads, "In Rebuke to Trump, Cuomo Pardons 18 Immigrants."[4]

But illegal aliens are not immigrants. An immigrant is someone who has emigrated legally to this country through a sanctioned immigration process. The point of conflating illegals and immigrants, however, is to pretend that in resisting illegal immigration, Trump and the Republicans are against immigrants themselves.

So the media is complicit with the Democrats in making the case that progressives are the partisans of the poor wretched masses that have poured into this country for nearly two centuries and have inevitably faced intolerance, bigotry and exclusion. Look, say the Democrats—with media outlets like the *New York Times* cheering wildly in the background—the Latinos are voting for us over the Republicans two to one, and this by itself proves that we are their friends and protectors.

Yet imagine if Latinos voted two to one for the Republican Party. Imagine if illegals, upon securing citizenship, started wearing Make America Great Again hats. How enthusiastic would Democrats be about fighting for illegal aliens and giving them a path to citizenship? It seems safe to say, not very. Progressive affinity for illegals seems contingent upon a kind of implicit bargain, one in which Democrats secure benefits for illegals and in exchange illegals agree to become Democrats.

Remove this condition and Democratic support for illegals evaporates. My wife, Debbie, a native of Venezuela, is sympathetic to the plight of the so-called DACA children of illegals who have grown up in this country. She cannot see sending them all back to their parents' nations. Many of them, she points out, don't even speak Spanish. They could not survive there.

So why not—she suggests—give them a way to live and work legally in this country? Give them all rights except one: the right to vote. This is not unfair because they are, after all, lawbreakers. (As a convicted felon, I can't vote either.) In the Rio Grande valley of South Texas, where Debbie grew up, virtually everyone is a Democrat. Yet not a single Democratic official to whom Debbie has mentioned this idea has expressed any interest in pushing forward with it. Very telling.

In 2010, speaking to a group of Hispanics, Obama emphasized Democratic fealty to Latinos as a group and invoked border security and strict immigration enforcement as proof that Republicans "aren't the kind of folks who represent our core values." Obama warned that if Hispanics stayed home on election day, Republicans would be elected and "then I think it's gonna be harder." He urged Hispanics to coalesce as a group and say to themselves, "We're gonna punish our enemies and we're gonna reward our friends."[5]

While he later denied it, recasting his argument in the anodyne language of Democrats fighting for the little guy, Obama knew he was appealing to ethnic resentment as a form of political motivation. This is a core part of Democratic political strategy in the twenty-first century. The rest is largely humbug to camouflage this fact. So progressive enthusiasm for the masses clamoring to get into this country seems rather more self-interested than progressives are generally willing to admit.

Some of them, however, do admit it. As progressive political scientist Adam Bonica told the *New York Times,* the immigration issue offers a "strategic advantage for the Democrats."[6] What he means is that the politics of ethnic mobilization work, as long as the ethnics keep their end of the bargain. Democrats are happy to bring more Latino illegals here as long as Latinos deliver the vote for Democrats. Politics is a two-way street and as long as the Latinos appreciate this, there is a place reserved for them on the Democratic urban plantation.

A NOVEL THEFT SCHEME

This chapter is about the formation of the Democrats' urban plantation, otherwise known as the urban political machine. Of course there were some Republican machines too, in cities like Philadelphia, in the second half of the nineteenth century. But the urban machine was a creation of the Northern Democrats in the Jacksonian era, and it reflected Democratic power in the cities of the North. So far to my knowledge no one has examined the relationship between the rural and the urban plantations, even though this was the basis for the unification of the Democratic Party and for its political domination from the 1820s through the Civil War.

The urban plantation was characterized by the fact that it produced nothing. In this respect, it was very different from the rural slave plantations, which produced cotton, sugar cane, rice, tobacco and so on. Rural slave plantations were designed to be productive. Urban plantations were not. They were both designed as mechanisms for stealing. In this respect, one might say that the urban plantation had the same basic purpose as its rural counterpart. Both were systems of larceny on a grand scale.

Yet the thefts in the two cases were different kinds. On the rural slave plantation, the theft was fairly straightforward. One man—let's call him A—steals from another man, B, by making him a slave. A is white and B is black, and the product stolen is B's labor. A benefits by appropriating the fruits of B's work and making them his own. In this case the larceny is effectuated by force. A purchases B and reduces him to a possession, holds him in captivity and makes him work through whips and intimidation, providing him with just enough to keep him healthy and useful to A's bottom line.

In the urban plantation, the theft is more sophisticated, although, in the end, no less profitable. It's worth noting that on the rural plantation A can become wealthy through stolen labor, but for this to happen he must have lots of Bs. A single B won't suffice, because B is a poor man and he has nothing that can be taken from him except his labor.

The thieves on the urban plantation, however, have a much bigger prey. Here they steal from a much larger group, one made up of the entire body of productive citizens. The target of the urban plantation is taxpayers of all income levels and also corporations—anyone who contributes to the public treasury. Here the thief, A, makes a deal with B, or actually many Bs. B is a poor, recently arrived immigrant, typically

Irish, German, Scandinavian, Italian or Jewish. These Bs are recruited into a theft scheme, but they have no idea how it operates. They are merely poor fellows trying to survive in a new country.

A promises B—these nameless immigrants whom we'll collectively call B—some meager favors (a job reference, a place to stay for a few days, a turkey dinner or flask of whiskey) in exchange for something that doesn't cost B anything, his vote. There is no compulsion here, except that of necessity. B is in dire straits and he agrees to the deal; he might have agreed to do it for even less.

A then uses B's votes to accumulate sufficient political power to get his hands on the public treasury. This for A is Fort Knox, and the immigrant vote has now supplied him with the key. Since no one is minding Fort Knox—the taxpayers who have paid into the system have no idea what is being done with their money—A is in a position to loot the treasury. So A uses B's vote to steal from another man—let's call him C. Then he uses the proceeds to pay for the pittances he provides to B, ensuring not merely his election but now his reelection.

Does all of this sound familiar? It should. It is, at least in rough outline, the modus operandi of the contemporary Democratic Party. Yet all of this started in the mid-nineteenth century through the model of the urban plantation, the urban political machine, which was also an ethnic machine. Yet the full scoop on the formation of the urban ethnic machine is an untold story in American politics.

We do have, of course, the progressive version of the tale, and we should note that this version has itself undergone a change in recent years. For most of the twentieth century, progressive historians portrayed urban ethnic machines like New York's Tammany Hall as hotbeds of corruption, bravely challenged by progressives and eventually dispatched by progressive icon Franklin Roosevelt in the 1930s.

Of late, however, Tammany and the machines are getting much better press. Here's a recent headline in the *New York Times*: "The Forgotten Virtues of Tammany Hall." The author, Terry Golway, concedes that Tammany became "the very face of political corruption." The bosses "stole elections," "intimidated political antagonists" and "shook down contractors and vendors."

But even so, he insists—elaborating his argument in his book *Machine Made*—Tammany illustrated how the Democrats "extended the hand of friendship" to new immigrants. In an interview with NPR, Golway credited the Democratic bosses with creating in essence "an informal welfare system when of course none existed." In this respect, Tammany foreshadowed and ultimately enabled the "reform" politics of the New Deal and the modern Democratic Party.[7]

The urban ethnic machine, historian Ted Widmer writes, "allowed democracy to grow beyond the founding documents into something tangible for millions of disenfranchised Americans." The ethnic machines were an "elaborate mechanism" to "put the theoretical ideas of the founders into everyday, working practice." In Widmer's progressive portrait, the ethnic machines gave a "voice" to new immigrants who didn't have anyone to speak for them until the Democratic Party came to their rescue.[8]

There is more, much more, in this vein. In 2016 Kevin Baker published a remarkable essay in the *New Republic* arguing that ethnic "political machines were corrupt to the core—but they were also incredibly effective. If Democrats want to survive in the modern age, they need to take a page from their past."[9] In other words, bring back the old ethnic machine!

That won't happen. The old ethnic machines were too obviously corrupt, and progressives gained a lot of political traction in railing against this corruption and portraying their man FDR as the great reformer. But what the progressives don't say is that Democrats legalized this corruption and made it part of their customary way of doing politics. Today the Democrats are once again active in the politics of ethnic mobilization, and the reason progressives are soft on the ethnic rackets of the past is that they know they are still running those rackets today. In this respect, Tammany is still with us in modified form.

But where did Tammany come from? What was the origin of the machines themselves? Here's a clue that reveals the nexus. The ethnic machine produced what historians now term "pork-barrel" politics. The pork barrel is the treasury, and pork-barrel politics refers to the familiar practice of politicians conspiring with each other and ripping off the treasury to fund largely useless projects that buy votes.

This term, however, can be directly traced to the old plantation. In Chester Collins Maxey's 1919 article in *National Municipal Review,* "A Little History of Pork," we find this revealing tidbit: "On the southern plantations in slavery days, there was a custom of periodically distributing rations of salt pork among the slaves. As the pork was usually packed in salt barrels, the method of distribution was to knock the head out of the barrel and require each slave to come to the barrel and receive his portion. Oftentimes the eagerness of the slaves would result in a rush upon the pork barrel to grab as much as possible for himself."[10]

So the rural and urban plantations were connected closely enough that the customs of the former could be drawn upon to describe the practices of the latter. Both operated on a principle that has defined the Democratic Party since its founding: the principle of dependency. While the slave plantation was based on the dependency of helpless black slaves, the urban plantation was based on the dependency of helpless white immigrants. Both became fodder for the exploitative machinations of the Democratic Party. The man who figured this out was Martin Van Buren.

THE LITTLE MAGICIAN

Van Buren has proven to be an enigma, both in his own time and in ours. Today the enigma may be partly due to the man's contemporary obscurity. If we remember what he looks like, his distinguishing feature is his absurdly large sideburns. Some will recall his unsuccessful presidency from 1836 to 1840, when he was defeated for reelection by William Henry Harrison. Van Buren played a bit role as a villain in Steven Spielberg's film *Amistad,* in which he was accurately shown as spurning the Africans' plea for freedom. His obscurity was the butt of a running joke on *Seinfeld* about a secret group that called itself the "Van Buren Boys."

In his own time, however, Van Buren was a colossus. This seems like an odd term to use for a short guy like Van Buren, barely five feet six inches tall, whom his contemporaries nicknamed Little Van. Yet there was no diminishing the importance of the dapper New Yorker who had risen from the obscure origins of a tavern-keeper's son to become the most powerful politician in the state. In the country, his influence was second only to Andrew Jackson's. And by all accounts Van Buren "made" Jackson, securing his election in 1828 and assuring his reelection in 1832.

In the process—here contemporary and modern accounts agree—Van Buren virtually singlehandedly created the urban political machine, and he also created the winning alliance that not only propelled Jackson and then Van Buren himself to the presidency but also sustained the Democratic Party as the majority party for forty years. Incredibly Van Buren did all this before he became president. His was a life in which his unsuccessful presidency was merely an appendage and footnote to an amazingly successful career.

Yet his contemporaries—friend and foe alike—also considered Van Buren to be a mystery. Biographer Ted Widmer writes of Van Buren's peers confessing that "no one knows exactly what he is up to" and then adds that he himself cannot trace a "thousand cat steps" that "brought him invisibly to his destination." Biographer Robert Remini lists several of the names his peers used to describe him: Little Magician, Red Fox of Kinderhook, the Enchanter and Master Spirit.

Remini cites the example of Davy Crockett, the fiery whimsical frontiersman who was no fan of Van Buren. Crockett dismissed Van Buren as an "artful, cunning, selfish speculating lawyer" who can "lay no claim to pre-eminent services as a statesman; nor has he ever given any evidences of superior talent." Asked to account for his success, however, Crockett could do no better than to term Van Buren a "riddle [that] must puzzle the devil."[11]

Modern scholars like Remini and Widmer, two progressive biographers of Van Buren, portray the man in glowing colors—a very different portrait from Crockett's—yet they too profess to be mystified by him. Widmer confesses that "Van Buren eludes us" today and "has been escaping pursuers since they began chasing him." While admitting that Van Buren's "creation of the Democratic Party was the achievement of a lifetime" Widmer nevertheless adds, "Even with all the hindsight that history can confer, it is unclear how exactly Van Buren wrought this great change."

Widmer attributes the mysteriousness of Van Buren in part to the fact that "he apparently destroyed those parts of his correspondence that would have revealed his innermost secrets." Moreover, in his own life Van Buren was famously evasive; he was known never to commit himself fully to a position. Acting on a bet that he could force Van Buren to take a stance, a senator once asked him if it was true that the sun rose in the East. Van Buren dryly replied, "I sleep until after sunrise."[12]

The puzzle is not over what Van Buren did; it is over how he did it. The normal way to tell the story is chronologically: first an account of how Van Buren built up his New York machine, and then a subsequent account of how he used it to create the party organization that propelled Jackson to power as the first president from the Democratic Party.

I believe, however, that we can understand Van Buren better by considering his life in reverse: first, how he created a new party under Jackson—a legacy that lasted forty years—and then how he laid the foundation for ethnic machine politics, a legacy that is with us to this day. Our story, then, breaks with narrative history and gives us Van Buren's two feats in ascending order of importance.

We begin around 1821 with Van Buren as the newly elected senator from New York and the undisputed leader of the New York Democratic machine—known as the Albany Regency. Let's pick up the progressive narrative from biographers like Remini and Widmer. I have no dispute with the basic details of this narrative, which goes like this. Van Buren recognized that any majority coalition in America would have to politically unite the North and the South. A New York–Virginia alliance, assembled during the founding era, had elected in turn Jefferson, Madison and Monroe.

In that era, however, Virginia was top dog and New York had second place. Van Buren's New York, however, had grown prodigiously in population and wealth by the second decade of the nineteenth century. So Van Buren's idea was to create a new political party based on reuniting North and South, New York and Virginia. Only this time New York would play the leading role and Virginia would be invited to go along.[13]

At first, Van Buren sought to work this plan through Secretary of State William Crawford of Georgia. Crawford was Van Buren's candidate for the presidency in 1824. But when Crawford suffered a stroke and fared poorly in the balloting, Van Buren switched his allegiance to another man of the South, Andrew Jackson. Van Buren knew Jackson—the two got to know each other when they were both in the Senate together. Jackson didn't make it to the Oval Office that year, but four years later he rode the North-South alliance that Van Buren painstakingly assembled all the way to the White House.

This is the official story. The one little thing—which turns out to be the most important thing—that the progressive narrative leaves out is: on what basis did Van Buren convince Virginia to go along with New York? How did he woo the South to join his Northern alliance? Here the progressives resort to mumbo-jumbo, invoking Van Buren's political perspicuity, his patient courting of Calhoun and other Southerners, his assiduous vote-counting abilities and his indisputable personal charm and savoir faire.

HIS MAGIC TRICK, EXPLAINED

Without discounting Van Buren's abilities, however, we have to read between the lines of these progressive narratives to figure out how Van Buren really sold the South on his grand unification plan. He did so by making several trips to the South in the period from 1822 to 1828. In 1822, Van Buren announced he was making a visit to Jefferson's Monticello in Virginia. He went to Virginia, but he didn't go to Monticello. Van Buren was actually on other business.

He seems instead to have secretly visited Thomas Ritchie, the editor of the Richmond *Enquirer*. I say "secretly" because there is no formal record of the visit, yet we know it took place because Ritchie alluded to it in his subsequent articles. Ritchie was the head of the Richmond junto, which controlled politics in Virginia, and undoubtedly one of the most powerful political figures in the state. His newspaper was a ferocious defender of the interests of the slaveholding class. Van Buren cultivated Ritchie, proposing to him a union between his Albany Regency machine in New York and the Richmond junto.

In this way Van Buren sought to create the beginnings of a powerful North-South coalition that could vanquish any political rival. Ritchie was interested but noncommittal. He was sold on Van Buren—whom he praised as a friend and a statesman—but not sold on the bargain. In particular, Ritchie was unconvinced about what benefits such a bargain would bring to the planter interests that the Richmond *Enquirer* so aggressively promoted.

Van Buren failed the first time, but he didn't give up. In 1826, as Andrew Jackson prepared to run a second time—he was thwarted in

1824 by what he termed a "corrupt bargain" between Henry Clay and John Quincy Adams that put Adams in the White House—Van Buren announced that he was making an extensive tour through the South, visiting Virginia, North Carolina, South Carolina and Georgia.

He didn't get to all those places because, as it turns out, he didn't need to. Van Buren spent the Christmas holidays of 1826 making a deal with Calhoun at the home of their mutual friend William Fitzhugh of Virginia. The details of the bargain are not known, but it is known that Calhoun was satisfied and agreed to back Van Buren's candidate, Andrew Jackson, for the presidency in 1828. Van Buren then drafted a letter to Thomas Ritchie, proposing a formal alliance between his New York Regency and the Richmond junto.[14]

Van Buren's progressive admirers focus on their man's blueprint for a new party united behind "General Jackson's personal popularity" as a war hero who had been supposedly cheated of the presidency the last time around. Van Buren also called for a new political organization that would "substitute party principle for personal preference." We can see in this 1827 letter to Ritchie the first traces of the new Democratic Party that existed in Van Buren's head before it existed in reality.

Yet Van Buren did not hesitate this time to spell out for Ritchie what this new party would deliver for the planter class: it would recruit the political power of the North to the protection of slave interests in the South. This is the bombshell only partially concealed in Van Buren's letter by his antiquated and somewhat overbearing rhetoric.

Van Buren argued that party attachment, "by producing counteracting feelings," was an antidote to Northern sectional prejudice against the South. Absent party attachments, "the clamor against the Southern Influence and African Slavery" was bound to gain momentum in the North. Van Buren proposed that his new intersectional alliance take on the role of defeating that momentum through its shared ideological commitment to the planter interests of the South.

Imagine, Van Buren said, an attack by antislavery men on Southerners who were also members of this new party. Naturally, he promised, Northerners belonging to that same party would rush to the Southerners' defense, regarding the attack as "assaults upon their political brethren and resented accordingly." The planters sought to uphold their peculiar institution, and the creation of a new party alliance along the lines proposed by Van Buren would be "eminently serviceable in effecting that object."[15]

This is incriminating stuff—very inconvenient to report in a laudatory biography—so Remini rushes to assure us that "it would be a mistake to interpret Van Buren's words as a defense of the slave system of the South."[16] Strictly speaking, this is true. Van Buren was not himself pro-slavery. His family had owned a handful of slaves, and Van Buren himself owned a slave named Tom before he ran away.

We may say of Van Buren what we might say of the younger Democrat Stephen Douglas who would rise to prominence in the 1850s: neither of them cared whether slavery was voted up or down. What Lincoln later said of Douglas—that he had "no very vivid impression that the Negro is a human"—would also apply to Van Buren. He was an unscrupulous man in the process of creating an unscrupulous party.

Van Buren's interest in the planter class of the South was merely political. He needed a national coalition and they were the ones who supplied the Southern power that Van Buren needed to fuse with the power of his New York Regency. Yes, it could be called the coalition to protect slavery, but had the Southern powers been cannibals instead, Van Buren would willingly have created the coalition to protect cannibalism.

Ritchie was sold on this deal. So, it seems, was Calhoun. No doubt Van Buren pitched his scheme to others and they shook hands on it. The planter class was "in." Van Buren was elated. He had pulled it off. By making them an offer they could not refuse, Van Buren had united the planter class of the South with his own, as we will see, equally grasping and opportunistic political establishment in the North. The political realignment that Van Buren sought was now underway.

Progressives seek to portray Van Buren's achievement differently. "His remodeling of Jefferson's party," writes Robert Remini, "constituted a major step in transferring the government from the control of the few to the many."[17] This is the usual left-wing balderdash, aimed at camouflaging a sordid deal between elites, specifically the sordid pact that Van Buren actually made with the forces of slavery and exploitation.

So this was Van Buren's achievement—yes, I speak sarcastically—in creating the Democratic Party or "The Democracy," as Van Buren and others called it. This party then carried Andrew Jackson to the presidency in 1828 and 1832. Jackson's opposition organized itself into a rival party in 1833 that began to call itself the Whigs in 1834. Now we turn to Van Buren's even greater achievement—I speak even more sarcastically—that defines the modus operandi of the Democratic Party right down to the present.

THE UPROOTED

Starting in the mid-nineteenth century and continuing through the early twentieth, America experienced one of the largest immigrations in human history. Some thirty-five million people left their homelands in Europe and moved to the United States. Six million came from the lands that became the German empire in 1870, four and a half million from Ireland, four million from Great Britain, almost five million from Italy, two million from the Scandinavian countries, three million from Greece, Macedonia and Armenia, and eight million or so more from the east: Poland, Hungary, Slovakia and the Ukraine.[18]

In an epic account of this migration, historian Oscar Handlin terms this group "the uprooted." While we think of these people as immigrants, Handlin shows that most of them in fact were refugees. They were fleeing something. In the case of the Irish—the most destitute of them all—they were fleeing a series of potato famines in the 1840s and early 1850s that had spread the stench of starvation, disease and death throughout Ireland.

So these were the people who washed up on the shores of the United States.

They had permanently cut their ties with the past. They had arrived in a new country with little or nothing. Many of these exiles didn't even speak English. They crowded into American cities, which were completely unfamiliar; many of them were rural peasants in their homelands. They had no transferable job skills. Now denizens of American ghettos, they were scared, confused and lost.

"They reached their new homes," Handlin writes, "worn out physically by lack of rest, by poor food, by the constant strain of close, cramped quarters, worn out emotionally by the succession of new situations that had crowded in upon them." Yet there was no time to recuperate. The immigrants faced "the immediate, pressing necessity of finding a livelihood and of adjusting to conditions that were still more novel, unimaginably so."[19] In their misery, Van Buren saw a political opportunity.

Van Buren knew these people well. The son of Dutch immigrants, Van Buren was a first-generation American, the first U.S. president to be so. He was also the first ethnic president, not descended from Anglo-Saxon roots. Thus Van Buren saw America, as I do, both from the outside and from the inside. And seeing the starving hordes—lost souls if there ever were such—wandering aimlessly in cities like New York, Van Buren noticed that they resembled a group that he had become quite familiar with in his travels through the South: American slaves.

Van Buren had an idea, one that could only have come from a complex, conniving brain such as his. We have to tread carefully here, because nowhere did Van Buren write his idea down. If he did, it must have been in the manuscripts that he—ever the circumspect strategist—subsequently destroyed. Yet the idea can be seen in its implementation. We know, for example, that Lincoln had the idea for the Emancipation Proclamation because of the Emancipation Proclamation he issued. So, too, with Van Buren, we can see his idea in the thing he built. The blueprint can be inferred from the building itself.

So here is Van Buren's idea, which, for all its subtle ingenuity, in its essence was quite simple: Why not re-create the Democratic model of the rural plantation in the Northern cities? Why not make the new immigrants just as dependent on the Democratic Party in the North as the slaves were dependent on the Democratic planters of the South? Then the two plantation systems would together form the political backbone of the Democratic Party. Such an idea, Van Buren knew, was not a matter of rote application. It would require some creative improvisation, which, fortunately for the Little Magician, happened to be his forte.

Obviously the immigrants and refugees were not slaves; they could not be held by force. Also the new immigrants were white. But the deeper point is that both groups—the immigrants and the slaves—were wretched, impoverished, helpless. Both had experienced the shock of displacement. Family separation was a common experience for these refugees, just as it was for the slaves. The challenges the new immigrants faced were the same. Their great need was to learn how to survive—the first challenge—and then to restore a modicum of security to their lives.

As for the immigrants, their whiteness didn't matter; they saw themselves in ethnic terms as Irish, Italians, Jews. Their distinguishing feature, Van Buren saw, was a clannish solidarity that was based on their origins. The people in each group huddled together and looked for solace and assistance from fellow countrymen. For many, their countrymen were the only people they could talk to, since they were the only ones that spoke their native language. By necessity, the immigrants sought to meet their challenges not individually but rather through the communal existence of their ethnic groups.

Van Buren saw that the slaves, in a parallel if not similar situation, had created precisely this sort of communal solidarity to survive on the plantation. From the immigrant yearning for survival and security that he well understood, and from their collective ethnic identity that he carefully observed, Van Buren realized the possibility for creating the same type of enduring dependency he had witnessed on the slave plantation but this time in Northern cities.

How to do this? Here Van Buren was in a unique position, because in New York he had already created the first political machine in American history. Leading a group called the Bucktails—so named because they wore deer tails on their hats—Van Buren in 1821 displaced New York's most powerful politician, DeWitt Clinton, and created a powerful machine called the Albany Regency. He did it, biographer Ted Widmer admits in a telling comparison, "like a nineteenth-century Vito Corleone."[20]

While politicians like DeWitt Clinton based their success on their popularity or on personal political accomplishments—Clinton was a noted abolitionist and the acclaimed champion of the Erie Canal—Van Buren's machine functioned in a different way. Basically, the machine demanded the complete allegiance of organizers and constituents from the state right down to the local level. The machine's agenda became their agenda. The machine told them how to vote and required them to campaign for its entire slate during election periods.

Its currency wasn't patriotism; it was party loyalty. Such loyalty required a certain toleration for corruption and even criminal behavior;

machine operatives had to learn to look the other way. No deviation, no backsliding, no independence of mind was permitted; as one Regency man, Silas Wright Jr., vowed, "The first man we see step to the rear, we cut down."[21] In exchange for this devotion, the machine rewarded its members with political and financial patronage.

For Van Buren, the treasury was not a fund of tax money accumulated to promote the common good; rather, it was a prize to be distributed to those who enabled politicians like Van Buren to dip their hands into the treasury. Asked to defend Van Buren's patronage policies, William Marcy, a prominent member of the Regency, famously responded, "To the victor belong the spoils."[22] For Van Buren and the Albany Regency, politics wasn't a vocation; it was a business.

Thus, long before the immigrants themselves arrived, Van Buren had already created the basic formula for organizing Democratic power in the Northern cities, which were filling up with immigrants and—over subsequent decades—the children of immigrants. The immigrants could be organized into clans based on their already-existing ethnic identification. These clans, Van Buren figured, could then be ruled by Democratic Party bosses who would demand ethnic loyalty in exchange for political patronage.

This, then, was the Frankenstein that Van Buren created. He was the inventor of the politics of ethnic mobilization. Other elements would be added later, such as the politics of ethnic resentment: hate masquerading as a campaign of resistance to hate. Yet the basic elements are already there. So Van Buren's Democratic urban machine proves to be his most enduring legacy. Although devised by Van Buren as a political complement to the slave plantation, for the purpose of consolidating Democratic power in the North as well as the South, one can see here, in embryo, the Democratic Party as it functions even today.

MAGNANIMITY, TAMMANY STYLE

One can draw a straight line from Van Buren's Albany Regency to the full-fledged Democratic machine as epitomized by Tammany Hall. The Regency and Tammany were both in New York, the former based in the city, the latter at the upstate capital in Albany. And eventually there were Tammany-style machines in virtually all the cities: Buffalo, Philadelphia, Chicago, Detroit, and San Francisco. While most of the machines were Irish at first, eventually other ethnic groups were also incorporated or started their own machines.

There were even a few Republican machines, such as George Cox's turn-of-the-century machine in Cincinnati and the statewide machine run out of Philadelphia that W. E. B. Du Bois wrote about in *The Philadelphia Negro*. But the vast majority were Democratic machines that, then as now, delivered the Democratic vote even in predominantly Republican states. Lincoln, for example, won New York State in the 1860 election but he lost New York City, which was just as much a Democratic stronghold as it is today. In American politics, we should note the continuities no less than the discontinuities.

The machines, as we know, were founts of political corruption. Tammany bosses like William "Boss" Tweed, Richard Croker and Charles F. Murray ran Democratic fiefdoms, dispensing favors and accumulating wealth culled not only from the public sector but also by coercing private-sector corporations to pay under-the-table fees to secure public contracts and project approvals. In Brooklyn, "Uncle John" McCooey ruled the roost; in Jersey City, Frank "I am the Law" Hague; in Kansas City, Tom Pendergast; in Boston, the duo of James Michael Curley and John "Honey Fitz" Fitzgerald. All of them were Democrats.

In his book *Machine Made,* progressive Terry Golway gives us a window into Boss Tweed's operation in the late 1860s. "The great raid on the public treasury was underway. Tweed and his friends raked in millions as they took their cuts from inflated bills for public works projects, including construction of a grand new courthouse . . . and the continued construction of Central Park."

Journalists knew about some of this but didn't report on it because many of them had been bought off by Tweed. Only in mid-1871 did the *New York Times* run an exposé, showing how Tweed had billed "nearly $3 million for furniture and half a million for carpets to outfit the new courthouse . . . hundreds of thousands of dollars for 'repairs' and 'alterations' paid to a firm with ties to Tweed. A carpenter named George Miller received more than $350,000 for a month's work."[23]

Tweed was eventually removed as grand boss, or "sachem," of Tammany and found guilty on corruption charges in 1873. Yet he escaped from Ludlow Street Jail, where he awaited trial, and fled to Cuba and then to Spain, where he was finally apprehended and extradited to the United States. He died in prison in 1878. Golway's account of Tweed's malpractices is vivid, yet it reveals a streak of genuine sympathy for him; Golway knows and approves of the fact that Tweed-like practices, which he calls "transactional politics," continue today under the auspices of the modern Democratic Party.[24]

The bosses frequently did not hold office themselves, but they controlled those who did. And yes, if you were unswervingly loyal to the Democratic machine, the bosses would help you in whatever way they could: fix your immigration problem or intervene with a local judge, say, to get your delinquent son a suspended sentence. Tammany sachems were known for such magnanimities as sustaining widows' lifestyles by keeping their dead husbands on the payroll.

Tammany's magnanimity toward widows illustrates how the Democratic urban machines were also employment bureaus. They got their people jobs, whether or not the workers actually did anything useful. The point was to keep them and their families on the payroll so that their loyalty to the Democratic Party would be continuing and secure. How well people like FDR, LBJ and Obama would have fit in as city bosses had they lived in the Tammany era. And it is no wonder that progressive chroniclers of Tammany are sympathetic to bosses who engaged in practices that progressives themselves advocate on behalf of the federal government today.

I am no more impressed by progressive accounts of good bosses than I am by earlier Democratic invocations of the good slave master. We should remember that the Democratic bosses always got the largest share of the heist—Boss Tweed of Tammany accumulated a vast fortune for himself before finally being convicted and sent to prison, and even Tammany underboss George Washington Plunkitt parlayed his influence to hold down four public offices at the same time and become a multimillionaire—and every machine generosity was at someone else's expense; the bosses never paid out of their own pocket. Moreover, if you crossed the bosses in any way, they would make sure you suffered for it.

ELECTION RIGGING

Just as tightly as the Democratic bosses controlled political appointments and the dispensing of patronage, they also controlled the voting process. In several cities, including New York, the bosses didn't rely on immigrants to vote correctly. Rather, they supplied the immigrants with filled-in ballots. The immigrants then showed up at the voting booth, where they were handed empty ballots. When the supervisor was not looking, they would simply substitute the filled-in ballot for the empty ballot. Thus outcomes were assured for Democratic bosses.

As the machines grew established they also grew bolder, now going beyond filled-in votes to also deliver dead people's votes in favor of Democratic machine candidates. Here immigrants would be directed to show up multiple times to vote, sometimes in the names of characters culled from novels or their dead relatives or dead people listed on tombstones in local cemeteries. Tammany carried on in this way for nearly a century, from the 1840s through the 1930s.

The bosses could be entertaining. Asked by an investigating committee whether he was "working for his own pocket," Tammany boss Richard Croker fired back, "All the time—same as you."[25] Despite this refreshing candor, I find it strange to read the progressive paeans to these Tammany thugs. Progressives seem to think that what they did was quite amusing and, although pushing the envelope in terms of legality, nevertheless healthy for democracy. I notice a high tolerance for pork-barrel schemes that are, even now, viewed as a normal way of conducting politics in a democracy. Progressives do not seem overly concerned that politicians are looting the treasury, and no one seems to be minding the store on behalf of the hapless taxpayer.

While progressives admit that the Democratic urban machines were a for-profit enterprise, thoroughly imbued with corruption and election-rigging, they insist, as Widmer says, that the bosses gave immigrants a "voice." Yet this "voice" was nothing more than the ventriloquist preferences of the bosses themselves. The ethnic exploitation of vulnerable people and the callous use of their votes to rip off the general population are somehow presented as triumphs of democratic inclusion.

I suspect that progressive sympathies for such exploitation are based on the realization that not very much has changed, and that modern-day progressives are into the same sorts of rackets. Even today, as we saw in the 2016 Hillary-Bernie contest, the Democrats are not above rigging elections—even while accusing Trump of electoral collusion. And Democratic resistance to voter identification laws seems to be less based on the honest conviction that poor people cannot produce valid IDs than on the Democrats' shared belief that, now as in the Tammany era, a vote is a vote regardless of whether it comes from an illegal, a dead guy or a fictional character.

In reality, this type of Democratic Party corruption and election-rigging was and is a thorough perversion of the democratic process. Even more, the whole basis of Tammany and the Democratic urban machine is a usurpation of the political system that the founders created. I don't mean this in the sense that the founders failed to create a party system and Van Buren did. The party system was not anticipated by the founders but by itself is not incongruent with the founders' *novus ordo seclorum.*

Nor do I mean it in the sense that the founders created a nation with a homogeneous population and Van Buren's machine was based on organizing ethnically diverse people. Yes, Book 2 of *The Federalist* declares that "Providence has been pleased to give this one connected country to one united people—a people descended from the same ancestors, speaking the same language, professing the same religion . . . very similar in their manners and customs."[26] It was not to be. Yet ethnic diversity by itself can be accommodated in the founding scheme.

As Lincoln recognized, the founders wisely framed their arguments in universalistic terms: not "all Englishmen" or "all Anglo-Saxons" are created equal, but rather "all men." In 1858 Lincoln said, "Perhaps half our people" have "come from Europe—German, Irish, French, and Scandinavian." These people did not, Lincoln admits, have anything to do with writing the Declaration of Independence, ratifying a Constitution. In this sense, they might feel excluded from the founding bargain of their new country.

Yet when they read the Declaration, Lincoln said, they see that it applies also to them. Then they recognize that "they have a right to claim it as though they were blood of the blood and flesh of the flesh of the men who wrote that Declaration, and so they are." The Declaration's teaching that all are created equal, Lincoln said, is the "electric cord in that Declaration that links the hearts of patriotic and liberty-loving men together."[27]

So ethnic diversity can be integrated within an inclusive American nationalism. The real perversion lies elsewhere. We can see it by consulting Book 10 of *The Federalist,* where Madison considers what he calls the problem of faction. Madison, like the other founders, worried about subgroups or factions motivated by particular interests conspiring against the public treasury and the public interest. Madison considered factions of this sort incompatible with the republican form of government. How, he asked, can America protect itself against them?

Madison's solution was the constitutional republic itself. Minority factions, he said, would be voted down by a majority. Moreover, in a large, extended republic like America, Madison predicted that while there may be a multiplicity of factions, organized perhaps around regional claims or occupational interests, none would be strong enough to steal the public purse or achieve its particular good over and against the public good. Madison was confident that any faction that attempted such "sinister designs" would surely be thwarted by other factions that would see through its nefarious scheme.[28]

Working at the state level rather than the federal, Van Buren showed how Madison's "republican remedy" could be defeated. Van Buren demonstrated how factions could indeed prevail, how particular goods could in fact vanquish the public good. The solution involved rigging the democratic process through ethnic stooges—suckers really—who would deliver the vote on behalf of helpless, dependent populations.

These populations would be courted through favors and then, when they did what was expected of them, rewarded through nepotism and patronage. The key was to keep these ethnic populations so dependent that they would continually retain the corrupt Democratic machine in power. The Democratic machine would then work assiduously not for any public good but rather for the particular good of the ethnic constituencies under its sway.

Van Buren went on to an undistinguished presidency marked by economic depression and what even progressive historians now concede is the disgrace of supervising the notorious displacement of the

Cherokee, an event otherwise known as the Trail of Tears. Perhaps repenting of his previous Faustian pacts with slavery, Van Buren joined
the Free Soil movement and made an abortive third run for president
in 1848. He was soundly defeated. In his later years, while no longer a
partisan for the plantation, he refused to follow the Free Soil Democrats who left the Democratic Party and joined the Republicans. Van
Buren stayed a lifelong Democrat.

The Tammany system was challenged by reformers in the late nineteenth century and finally routed by progressives in the early twentieth century. Working through a Republican ally, Fiorello La Guardia,
FDR finally crushed Tammany and in general brought down the urban
machines. As Jay Cost shows in his recent book *A Republic No More*,
FDR's motives were hardly pure. Rather, his intention was not to get
rid of the machine but to substitute a national machine for the various
local ethnic machines, not to eliminate corruption but to legalize it
and make it a "permanent feature of our government."[29] FDR replaced
several local scams with one big national scam.

Much has changed. The Democrats gave up their system of ethnic mobilization under Franklin Roosevelt in the 1930s, then took it
up once again under Lyndon Johnson in the 1960s. Today Democrats
don't bother to mobilize white ethnics anymore; they have moved on to
other groups: blacks, Latinos, feminists, homosexuals. Yet as Plunkitt
says, "The Democratic Party . . . can't die while it's got Tammany for
its backbone."[30] In a sense, Tammany remains the backbone of the
Democrats. The old Tammany regime is gone, but what Tammany
represents—the dehumanizing system of Democratic ethnic exploitation that Van Buren created—is still very much with us today.

5

THE PLANTATION IN CRISIS

How Democrats North and South Fought to Extend Slavery

What did we go to war for,
but to protect our property?

—ALEXANDER STEPHENS, Democrat and
vice president of the Confederacy[1]

One of the most powerful weapons of historical revisionism is silence. From ancient times, the wise have recognized the uses of silence. In Plato's *Republic*, Socrates convinces Glaucon that Greeks should not enslave other Greeks. Glaucon reluctantly goes along, but then blurts out that surely it is fine for Greeks to enslave barbarians. This assertion, Plato informs us, Socrates greeted only with silence. In this case, Socrates' silence is prudential. He has gone as far as he can go to convince Glaucon; to attempt to go further is to risk losing what has painstakingly been accomplished.

Then there is Lincoln's silence during the great secession winter of 1860-61. There was a four-month interregnum between Lincoln's election and his inauguration, and during this period several states seceded and, in a panic, Democrats as well as some Republicans considered various proposed measures to appease the South and prevent a civil war. The most famous was the Crittenden proposal, which would have extended the Missouri Compromise line across to the Pacific, allowing slavery permanently south of the line and prohibiting it north of it. While there was strong pressure on Lincoln to react publicly to these proposed measures, he said nothing, while working behind the scenes to defeat them. Thus Lincoln's silence, like that of Socrates, was in service of prudence. He had to wait until he was inaugurated to have the power to actually implement the mandate he had just won.

While I have just given two instances of the noble use of silence, this chapter focuses on a very ignoble use of silence to distort historical truth. Here I focus on progressive revisionism about the Civil War and Reconstruction. The purpose of this revisionism is to blame the conflict mostly on the South, and to blame the South again for the postbellum resistance to Northern Reconstruction. What is left out of this narrative is the role of the Democratic Party. This is how silence can be used not passively, to withhold information, but actively, to deceive.

For example, in both of Ta-Nehisi Coates' books and in his numerous articles for *The Atlantic,* there is no mention of the Democratic Party affiliation of the Confederates. They are typically named as Southerners, not as Democrats. This is particularly interesting because Coates is himself a Democrat and he apparently has no intention of holding his party responsible for its historical crimes, even though these are precisely the crimes for which Coates seeks reparations and restitution. Coates does not wish to explain why he continues to belong to a party that perpetrated the very offenses about which he is apparently inconsolable. So Coates disingenuously uses silence to serve his ideological purpose, which is to shift the blame to Trump and the Republican right.

But the pattern goes even deeper. Coates and the historians he relies on—figures such as Barbara Fields, Annette Gordon-Reed and Eric Foner—go beyond minimizing the Democratic affiliation of Southern apologists for slavery. They also leave out or at the very least downplay the role of the Northern Democrats in upholding slavery before and during the Civil War, and then reestablishing a form of neo-slavery in the South after the war. This use of silence here is critical, because to implicate the Northern Democrats is to undermine the progressive narrative that assigns virtually exclusive culpability to the South.

Ultimately progressives seek to cast blame not merely on the South but also on America. In this way they can smear the Republicans, whose base is in the South and who see themselves as reviving an American nationalism. So in addition to blaming the South—the current base of the GOP—progressives also cast some of the blame on Abraham Lincoln. Yes, Abraham Lincoln. Leading figures of modern-day historiography including George Fredrickson and Fred Kaplan, not to mention progressive outlets like the Huffington Post, fault Lincoln with being a bit of a racist, not quite as enlightened as progressives themselves.[2]

A sample work in this genre is Lerone Bennett's *Forced Into Glory: Abraham Lincoln's White Dream,* which presses the case for Lincoln being a racist by raising all the familiar issues.[3] Didn't Lincoln say that if he could save the union without freeing a single slave, he would do it? Didn't Lincoln emphasize in his debates with Douglas that he did not support social equality or intermarriage between the races? Didn't Lincoln specifically come out against giving blacks voting rights or letting them serve on juries? And didn't Lincoln's celebrated Emancipation Proclamation free the slaves only in the Confederacy—where Lincoln had no power to free them—while not freeing any of the half million slaves in Union states like Maryland, Delaware, Kentucky and Missouri?

Lincoln's words and actions seem the incriminating hallmarks of a racist, if not a full-blown white supremacist. And this progressive indictment of Lincoln may be responsible for the vandals who defaced the Lincoln statue as part of their campaign to take down or destroy racist monuments. They might well have been the acolytes of Coates, or of Reconstruction historian Eric Foner, who emphasizes that not only is Lincoln guilty, "the whole nation is guilty, even though the main effort is in the South."[4]

Foner is one of the most subtle, cunning revisionists of the left. Here, from his magnum opus *Reconstruction,* are a few telling sentences. "Conservatives, however, were not the only delegates to raise questions of social equality." In Foner's bizarre nomenclature, Southern Democrats who oppose equality are "conservatives." By contrast, "On the party's left stood the radical Republicans." Incredibly, the most zealous Republicans are now positioned on the left. And then, "Long into the twentieth century, the South remained a one-party region under the control of a reactionary ruling elite." Somehow the Democratic racist ruling class of the South is classified as a group of right-wing reactionaries, the natural predecessors in Foner's view to Trump, the GOP and modern-day conservatives.[5]

One inaccuracy on top of another. Clearly I have my work cut out for me. And my task is made even more complex by the fact that modern progressive revisionism about the Civil War and Reconstruction was preceded by a separate Democratic and progressive revisionism that developed in the late nineteenth and early twentieth centuries. Immediately following the war and Reconstruction, Democrats got to work fashioning a narrative of concealment aimed at fooling future generations about what had just happened.

The old lies and the new historical accounts parallel each other—the lying Democratic narratives of the past, sitting alongside the sanitized progressive narratives of the present—but they are not the same. The old Democratic liars pretended that the Civil War was not about slavery. Here the classic examples are Alexander Stephens and Jefferson Davis, who were respectively the vice president and president of the Confederacy. Two decades after the war, Davis insisted that "African servitude was in no wise the cause of the conflict, but only an incident." Stephens portrayed the war as "a strife between the principles of Federation on the one side, and Centralism or Consolidation on the other. Slavery, so-called, was but the question on which these antagonistic principles . . . were finally brought into actual and active collision with each other on the field of battle."[6]

Davis and Stephens appear to us as creatures of the distant past. Can we reasonably link them with the progressive Democrats who came of age a few decades later, in the early twentieth century? Yes, we can. We see a very similar understanding of the Civil War promoted in the early twentieth century by the progressive historians Charles and Mary Beard. The Beards, who agreed with Davis and Stephens that slavery had little or nothing to do with the war, famously coined the term "Second American Revolution" to characterize the shift of power, caused by the war, from the "planter aristocracy" of the South to "Northern capitalists and free farmers."[7]

The same period saw the rise of the so-called Dunning School—named after William Dunning and his colleagues at Columbia University—which portrayed Reconstruction as a vicious intrusive Republican effort to impose Negro rule on the South, happily thwarted

by independence-loving Southerner Democrats who brought the uppity blacks under heel and sent the no-good Republican carpetbaggers
packing. It comes with some surprise for us to discover that Dunning
and his colleagues saw themselves as progressives and regarded themselves as writing progressive history.

Blowing these Democratic big lies out of the water and exposing
the truth—that is my task here. First, I show that the Civil War arose
not out of a North-South debate but rather out of a bitter struggle between a Republican Party that sought to block the spread of slavery and
a Democratic Party North and South that sought to continue it. Then
I show the role of the Northern Democrats, even during the war, to
undermine the Union war effort, to force a peace treaty with the South
and to give slavery a permanent place in America's future.

When this failed, I show how the Northern Democrats attempted
to block the Thirteenth, Fourteenth and Fifteenth Amendments and
worked closely with the Southern Democrats to defeat Reconstruction,
which was a Republican project to create multicultural democracy in
America. Instead the Democrats deployed a new weapon, racial terrorism, to disperse white Republicans, subjugate blacks and reestablish
their political hegemony in the South.

THE DIFFERENCE BETWEEN THE TWO PARTIES

On December 22, 1860, in a final effort to avert the looming prospect of
civil war, Abraham Lincoln wrote a brief note to his former colleague
Alexander Stephens of Georgia, soon to become vice president of the
Confederacy. Both Lincoln and Stephens had been Whigs, and they
had worked together in opposition to the Mexican War and other issues. They respected each other.

Moreover, Stephens had in his native Georgia given an impas-
sioned speech opposing secession, arguing that despite the election of
a Republican president, slavery would be "much more secure in the
union than out of it."[8] Lincoln admired the speech so much that he had
requested an official copy of the transcript. If there was ever a chance
that two men—one a Northerner, the other a Southerner—could work
things out, this was it.

Lincoln reassured Stephens that, as his campaign statements repeatedly stressed—and as the Republican platform made absolutely

clear—the new government had no intention of interfering with slavery in the states where it already existed. "The South would be in no more danger in this respect," Lincoln wrote, "than it was in the days of Washington."

Then Lincoln added, tellingly, "I suppose, however, that this does not meet the case. You think slavery is *right* and ought to be extended; while we think it is *wrong* and ought to be restricted. That I suppose is the rub. It certainly is the only substantial difference between us."[9] And upon this difference—as Lincoln dolefully predicted—America went to war with itself in the following year.

As Stephens undoubtedly knew at the time, but which has been subsequently muddied by progressive scholarship, Lincoln was not actually distinguishing the positions of the North versus the South. The North certainly did not unanimously share the view that slavery was wrong. Only Republicans in the North held that position. Democrats in the North—Stephen Douglas notably among them—emphatically rejected that view. Northern Democrats led by Douglas contested the 1860 election against Lincoln on the basis of that disagreement.

That the slavery debate was not a North-South debate but rather a partisan debate can be verified by the startling truth I first reported in *Hillary's America* and that has gone unchallenged since. In 1860, at the time Lincoln wrote this letter, no Republican owned a slave. I don't mean merely that no Republican leader owned a slave. No Republican in the country owned a slave. All the slaves in the United States at the time—all four million of them—were owned by Democrats. Stephens himself crossed over from the Whigs to the Democratic Party in 1855, five years prior to the civil war.

In the years leading up to the war, in multiple addresses and in the Lincoln-Douglas debates, Lincoln himself stressed the main issue that separated the two parties. "The difference between the Republican and the Democratic parties," Lincoln said in a September 11, 1858, speech at Edwardsville, Illinois, "is that the former consider slavery a moral, social and political wrong, while the latter do not consider it either a moral, social or political wrong."

Keeping Douglas' popular sovereignty in mind, Lincoln added, "I will not allege that the Democratic Party consider slavery morally, socially and politically right, although their tendency to that view has, in my opinion, been constant and unmistakable . . . up to the Dred Scott decision, where, it seems to me, the idea is boldly suggested that slavery is better than freedom.

"The Republican Party," Lincoln continued, "hold that this government was instituted to secure the blessings of freedom, and that slavery is an unqualified evil to the Negro, to the white man, to the soil, and to the State . . . They will use every constitutional method to prevent the evil from becoming larger and . . . will oppose, in all its length and breadth, the modern Democratic idea, that slavery is as good as freedom, and ought to have room for expansion all over the continent.

"This is the difference," Lincoln concluded, "as I understand it, between the Republican and Democratic Parties." And Lincoln repeated his same description of the Democrats in the sixth debate with Douglas at Quincy and in the following debate at Alton.[10] Nor did Douglas contest his opponent's understanding of the core division between the parties; unlike his successor Democrats of today, Douglas had no interest in concealing his own position or in blaming the defense of slavery solely on the South.

The strategy of the Democrats, both in the 1858 Senate contest and in the 1860 presidential campaign, was to launch racist attacks against Lincoln and the Republican Party. Democrats routinely called Republicans "Black Republicans," "nigger lovers" and "wooly heads." We can find online Democratic posters contrasting the prototypical dignified Democratic white man with the menacing, stereotypical Republican Negro. In 1858, the Democratic Chicago *Times* warned that if Lincoln were elected senator, Illinois would become "the nigger state of the Northwest."[11]

In 1860, Democrats spread the false rumor that Hannibal Hamlin, himself a former Democrat who had quit the party in disgust over its pro-slavery position and was now vice presidential candidate of the Republican Party, was half black. A Democratic campaign banner in New York claimed that "free love and free niggers will certainly elect Old Abe."[12] Both in 1858 and 1860, Douglas appealed to racist sentiments among the electorate in accusing Lincoln of supporting intermarriage and social equality between the races, not to mention of favoring blacks having the right to vote and to serve on juries.

Lincoln's response to these attacks shows the manner in which he embodied the philosophical statesmanship of the founders. Indeed,

Lincoln's plight was eerily similar to that of the founders. Just as they inherited slavery, and had to figure out what to do with it, Lincoln was running at a time when racist prejudice against blacks ran strong nationwide, and he had to figure out how to handle it. There was virtually no constituency that believed blacks should be allowed to intermarry or to have social equality with whites.

Even Americans who agreed blacks should not be deprived of their natural rights—that they should not be enslaved—strongly opposed the idea that blacks should be immediately granted civil rights, which they saw as an entirely different matter. Natural rights are the prerogative of every human being—conferred, if you will, by nature or by God—while civil rights are granted by the consent of a community that has every right to withhold them if it chooses.

If Lincoln were perceived as promoting intermarriage, social equality or civil rights for blacks, his electoral defeat both in the 1858 Senate contest and in the 1860 presidential election was certain. Lincoln had the choice, as the founders did, of going down in flames or taking the strongest antislavery stance that was viable to secure the consent of the governed. This stance would involve accommodating racist sentiment—while not encouraging it—just as the founders accommodated slavery—while not encouraging it—and thus achieving a result that would help create the conditions for the ultimate defeat of both racism and slavery.

Consider the artfully conditional way in which Lincoln responded to Douglas: "Now I protest against that counterfeit logic which concludes that, because I do not want a black woman for a *slave* I must necessarily want her for a *wife*. I need not have her for either, I can just leave her alone. In some respects she certainly is not my equal, but in her natural right to eat the bread she earns with her own hands without asking leave of anyone else, she is my equal, and the equal of all others."[13]

Notice how little Lincoln concedes here to racist prejudice. He doesn't say that he rejects racial intermarriage. He merely rejects the equation that holds that a man who opposes slavery necessarily endorses racial intermarriage. Lincoln rightly points out that this is a fallacy; one can be for one without being for the other. What Lincoln does here is refuse to be drawn into a side debate about miscegenation. He keeps the focus on the actual policy issue dividing the parties, which is slavery or more precisely the extension of slavery.

Admittedly, Lincoln in his Charleston debate on September 18, 1858, said "I have no purpose to introduce political and social equality between the white and black races."[14] Lincoln also said he did not support the right of blacks to vote or to serve on juries. Later, toward the end of the Civil War, Lincoln actually did support—albeit through the democratic process, which is to say, through popular consent—the extension of those rights to blacks. Yet in 1858 Lincoln took a position that modern progressives have interpreted to suggest that he too was a white supremacist.

Why, then, would Lincoln bow to racial prejudice in this way? Let us recall Lincoln's admonition to a group of blacks on the eve of the Emancipation Proclamation that freedom would still leave blacks free in a country whose citizens rejected them as equals. If that was true in 1862, it was certainly true earlier.

So in denying his intention to give blacks the right to vote and serve on juries, Lincoln was refusing to do what he could not in any case do. For Lincoln, as for the founders, the American people were not yet ready to confer civil rights or social equality on blacks, and thus the granting of such rights must await the readiness of popular consent. Lincoln bowed to popular prejudice because even prejudice must be considered part of the "consent of the governed," and because he wanted to be in a leadership position to tame that prejudice in the future.

The progressive attack on Lincoln as a white supremacist fails. Nowhere did Lincoln ever say he considered whites to be inherently superior to blacks. The left today condemns Lincoln for taking the course he did without being able to recommend a better one. Blacks secured the right to vote and to serve on juries in large part because of what Lincoln did in assembling a Republican coalition to win the Civil War, and Lincoln's ability to do that was made possible only by his patient determination to get to first base before charging on to second.

We can draw from the reasoning above the astonishing conclusion that it was even in the interest of blacks for Lincoln to deny their right to social equality in the 1858 and 1860 campaigns because the alternative course—the one seemingly advocated by modern-day progressives—would have ensured his defeat and consigned him to political oblivion. And that would have surely resulted in a much longer delay for blacks to secure their freedom, let alone any additional rights and privileges that would be granted through amendments to the original Constitution.

THE CONFEDERACY'S NORTHERN ALLIES

The Civil War was a deliberate attempt by the Democratic Party, both in the North and the South, to kill America by carving her into two. Had secession worked, Lincoln would have been viewed as a failed president. The North and the South would have come to terms over the bifurcation long before 1865. Slavery would have continued, and on a firmer foundation than before. White supremacy would have continued to be its bedrock, and would have reigned unchallenged throughout the United States. Lincoln's dark warning about all of America becoming a plantation might have proven prophetic in his own lifetime.

The Democrats' attempt on America's life is the simple truth about the Civil War that is left out of every historical account and textbook. Progressive historians like Eric Foner and Barbara Fields don't even go near it. Even the most reliable and objective accounts of the war—such as those of James McPherson and Harry Jaffa—at most allude to it. So powerful is the influence of progressive historiography that virtually all accounts of the Civil War succumb to the North-South dichotomy that is at best a partial and oversimplified account of the truth.

Once again, the key to the whole truth is the role played by the Northern Democrats. We must begin by noting their indispensable role in any possibility of the South winning the war. In 1861, the North had twenty million people and the South nine million, four million of whom were slaves. Besides this four-to-one population advantage, the North dominated the manufacturing and munitions industries and had complete naval supremacy. These facts were known by every intelligent Southerner at the outset of the war.

How, then, did the South hope to succeed? The answer is that the Democrats of the South hoped to fight hard and long enough to debilitate public opinion on the Union side and thus strengthen the political hand of their fellow Democrats in the North. They were counting on the Northern Democrats to thwart Lincoln and the Republicans and ultimately to defeat them, so that Democrats North and South could then make a peace that permanently protected slavery.

In 1862, fresh from his success at Second Bull Run, Robert E. Lee prepared his Army of northern Virginia to invade Maryland. "The present," Lee wrote on September 8, 1862, to Confederate president Jefferson Davis, "seems to be the most propitious time since the commencement of the war for the Confederate Army to enter Maryland." Lee had successfully repelled Union attempts to penetrate the heart of Virginia. Now he wanted to capture and hold Union territory. One might think that his motives were military, but in fact they were largely political.

"It is plain to my understanding," Lee wrote to Davis, "that everything that will tend to repress the war feeling in the Federal States will inure to our benefit." Ever the cautious tactician, Lee added, "I do not know that we can do anything to promote the pacific feeling, but our course ought to be shaped as not to discourage it." Voters would go to the polls in November 1862 "to determine . . . whether they will support those who favor a prolongation of the war, or those who wish to bring it to a termination."[15]

Progressive accounts of the Civil War dwell needlessly on the South's efforts to draw England and France into the war on the Confederate side. In reality, both were far-fetched prospects and the Southerners knew it. Lee's letter does not even mention foreign intervention. Rather, Lee focuses on Northern public opinion and the forces that he knew were working diligently to steer it in the upcoming election against Lincoln and the Union armies, namely, the Northern Democrats.

Lee chose Maryland carefully. He knew that there was strong pro-Confederate sentiment in that state, and citizens of Baltimore had rioted against Lincoln in April 1861. Many secessionist members of the legislature, as well as the mayor of Baltimore—every one of them a Democrat—had been locked up for weeks that fall. Lee hoped that his incursion would embolden the pro-Confederate Democrats in Maryland to withdraw the state from the Union, dealing a crippling blow to Lincoln and the Republicans.

Thus Lee's military actions in the second year of the war were closely attentive to the effect they would have on Northern Democrats.

And Lee's assessment proved to be at least partly sound. Maryland did not secede, but the Northern Democrats did very well in the 1862 midterm election, winning several states that had gone for Lincoln just two years earlier. Undoubtedly both Lee and Jefferson Davis monitored those results. From their point of view, the Northern Democrats were going to be the ones who would help them save the plantation.

FIRE IN THE REAR

Lincoln, for his part, understood the grave threat posed by the Northern Democrats. In January 1863 he told Republican senator Charles Sumner that he feared the "fire in the rear," which is to say a faction of Northern Democrats, even more than he feared the Confederate army.[16] Here Lincoln was not thinking of his old political nemesis Stephen Douglas. Douglas, in what was surely his finest moment, vigorously opposed secession. He undertook a dangerous journey south to Tennessee, Alabama and Georgia to attempt to convince his fellow Democrats not to break from the Union. But Douglas died unexpectedly in June 1861, shortly after the war commenced.

Nor was Lincoln concerned about the Democratic Party as a whole, at least not initially. The Democratic Party in the North had split into two factions, the so-called War Democrats and the Peace Democrats. Many Northern Democrats—including hundreds of thousands of German and Irish immigrants—fought gallantly for the Union, and the battlefield heroism of the Irish Brigade, including its Regiment 69 charge at Fredericksburg into incoming cannon fire, became legendary among Tammany Irish families back home in New York and elsewhere.

Lincoln was worried about the Peace Democrats, a group that included former Ohio congressmen Clement Vallandigham and Alexander Long, former New York governor Horatio Seymour, New York City mayor Fernando Wood, and Indiana senator Daniel Voorhees. In line with Lincoln's statement about them, Republicans called the Peace Democrats "Copperheads," likening them to deadly snakes who seem harmless enough until they strike without warning.

The Peace Democrats were strengthened by early Confederate successes in the Civil War. They sought to rally public opinion against what Vallandigham called a wicked and senseless conflict. "Stop fighting," Vallandigham urged Lincoln and the Republicans. "Make an armistice . . . Withdraw your army from the seceded states."[17] Such a recipe, in Lincoln's mind, would surely spell the death of the union or at least of any union worth preserving.

Lincoln could take solace, at least in the early years of the war, from the support of the War Democrats. Yet this group was not without its problems as far as Lincoln and the Republicans were concerned. War Democrats opposed secession as unconstitutional rebellion and treason. They were, in this respect, union men. Yet for the most part, they had no intention of fighting a war over slavery. They communicated this unambiguously to Lincoln.

Lincoln needed the allegiance of the War Democrats. As historian David Herbert Donald tells us, Lincoln was fully cognizant that he had been elected in 1860 with a minority of the vote, and that only the schism in the Democratic Party that produced two separate candidates—Douglas in the North and Breckinridge in the South—had divided the Democratic vote and enabled his victory. Lincoln knew that notwithstanding its advantage in population and resources, the North needed a united front of Northern Democrats and Republicans to defeat an undivided South.[18]

This is why Lincoln, in his famous letter to Horace Greeley, wrote that "my paramount object in this struggle is to save the Union, and is not either to save or destroy slavery. If I could save the Union without freeing any slave I would do it, and if I could save it by freeing all the slaves I would do it; and if I could save it by freeing some and leaving others alone I would also do that."[19]

Lincoln framed the war as a war over union rather than a war over slavery in part to keep the allegiance of the War Democrats. Remarkably, Democrats today invoke Lincoln's words to portray him as insufficiently antislavery, even though he was politically constrained to speak that way to keep a majority of Democrats on the side of the Union.

The second reason for Lincoln's tactical decision to define the Civil War as a war over the union was to prevent the border states from seceding. The border states—Maryland, Delaware, Kentucky and Missouri—all had slaves. In fact, there were 450,000 slaves in those four states. Yet they had opted not to secede, even though powerful forces in those states continued to push them to join the Confederacy.

Lincoln did not believe he could afford to lose these states and still win the war. He once joked that he hoped that God was on his side, but without Kentucky, he wasn't sure that was even enough. Thus Lincoln believed he would best hold the border states, and thus serve the anti-slavery cause itself, by pretending that this was not a war fought over slavery. Yet of course Lincoln could have avoided the war and saved the union had he embraced the Crittenden proposal or simply adopted Douglas' doctrine of popular sovereignty. The fact that he refused to do so proves that Lincoln was willing to go to war to prevent slavery from spreading into the territories.

Once Lincoln was convinced he had secured the loyalty of the border states, he candidly acknowledged that the root cause of the Civil War was in fact slavery. "Without slavery the rebellion could never have existed," Lincoln wrote in his Annual Message to Congress in 1862, "Without slavery, it could not continue." In a later correspondence with a group of British workingmen, Lincoln said the rebellion was "an effort to overthrow the principle that all men were created equal" and that the ensuing war was a test of whether a free government "can be maintained against an effort to build one upon the exclusive foundation of human bondage."[20]

In saying this, of course, Lincoln was doing no more than agreeing with the Confederate leaders Jefferson Davis and Alexander Stephens, who insisted that they were fighting on behalf of racism and slavery. Davis, for instance, told the Confederate Congress on April 29, 1861, that the goal of the Republicans was one of "rendering the property in slaves so insecure as to be comparatively worthless," and thus it was worth going to war to save slave "property worth thousands of millions of dollars."[21]

In what has come to be known as the Cornerstone Speech, delivered on March 21, 1861, Alexander Stephens said that while the American founders considered all men created equal, "Our new government is founded upon exactly the opposite idea . . . its foundations are laid, its cornerstone rests, upon the great truth that the Negro is not equal to the white man. That slavery—subordination to the superior race, is his natural and normal condition. This, our new Government, is the first, in the history of the world, based upon this great physical and moral truth."[22] What could be clearer about the defining issue that produced the cataclysm of the American Civil War?

Ultimately Lincoln revealed his hand regarding the centrality of slavery to the war with his issuance of the Emancipation Proclamation. Yet even this, the decisive measure that Lincoln emphasized had been taken not under his normal constitutional powers—which, he had previously insisted, gave him no power over slavery in the states where it existed—but only under wartime necessity, is now derided by progressive pundits and historians. They scornfully point out that Lincoln freed slaves only where he had no power to free them and kept them in captivity in states where he could actually have freed them.

Once again, Lincoln carefully calibrated what he was doing. He sought to weaken the Southern slaves' attachment to the plantation. He sought to motivate free blacks in the North to offer their services to the Union cause. And he was determined to keep the slave-owning border states in the Union. Had Lincoln freed the slaves in the border states, most if not all of those states would have promptly defected to the Confederate side.

THE EFFECT OF THE EMANCIPATION PROCLAMATION

Yet the Emancipation Proclamation gravely weakened Lincoln's support among Northern Democrats. These Northern Democrats used the pretext of its promulgation to turn irrevocably against Lincoln. As historian Jennifer Weber writes in her book *Copperheads,* "Deeply racist Democrats who had supported the war when its only purpose was maintaining the Union jumped to the opposition when the confrontation became an effort to free the slaves."[23]

Emancipation, in other words, was the alchemy that turned War Democrats into Peace Democrats. The tone of Democratic opposition can be seen in resolutions passed by Democratic majorities in Indiana and Illinois demanding that Lincoln retract his "wicked, inhuman and unholy" Emancipation Proclamation. The Chicago *Times,* a Democratic paper, denounced emancipation as "a monstrous usurpation, a criminal wrong, and an act of national suicide."[24]

By 1864, the Peace Democrats dominated the Democratic Party. The party nominated a War Democrat, George McClellan, to challenge

Lincoln's reelection bid. But the platform was completely controlled by the Peace Democrats. The Democrats' very slogan, "The Constitution as It Is, and the Union as It Was," reflected the Peace Democrats' insistence that they wanted America to go back to the union as it was prior to the Emancipation Proclamation and the Civil War itself. In sum, they demanded a restoration of slavery.

The Democrats had a good chance to win. The war had dragged on, seemingly interminably, with even Republican stalwart Horace Greeley grieving for "our bleeding, bankrupt, almost dying country," eager nearly above all else to halt "the prospect of fresh conscriptions, of further wholesale devastations, and of new rivers of human blood." Once again, in their customary style, the Democrats launched racist attacks against Lincoln, nicknaming him "Abraham Africanus the First" and announcing his Ten Commandments, the first of which was "Thou shalt have no other God but the Negro."[25]

Lincoln dourly remarked in 1864 that "there is no proposal offered by any wing of the Democratic Party but that must result in the permanent destruction of the Union." And here he was referring to the Northern Democrats as a whole, the War Democrats no less than the Peace Democrats. By this point, historian David Herbert Donald tells us, "he gave up on winning the support of the War Democrats, most of whom quietly returned to their allegiance to the Democratic party."[26]

For Lincoln, the Northern Democrats no less than the Southern Democrats were dedicated to the dissolution of the nation as a *novus ordo seclorum,* which is to say as the founders envisioned it. It is hardly an exaggeration to say that Democrats nationwide were intent on murdering that America. The murder attempt failed. Lincoln was reelected, and the Union armies finally prevailed in the Civil War. This convinced a man from Maryland, who thought of himself as a Northern Democrat with Southern sympathies, that "our cause [is] almost lost" and "something decisive and great must be done."[27]

The man was John Wilkes Booth. Booth finally fulfilled the numerous calls for Lincoln's assassination that had been ringing in Democratic newspapers, pamphlets and public rhetoric. In the heat of the 1864 campaign, for instance, the La Crosse Wisconsin *Democrat,* edited by Copperhead Marcus Pomeroy, urged that if Lincoln were reelected, "we trust some bold hand will pierce his heart with dagger point for the public good."[28]

Today progressives portray Booth as a deranged lone wolf, but his view that America would be better off with Lincoln dead was shared by other Democrats, both in the North and in the South. Booth merely put their thoughts into action by actually killing the president. The incident that seems to have activated Booth's conspiracy was a speech by Lincoln endorsing the idea of black suffrage. "That means nigger citizenship," Booth said, taking the orthodox Democratic position on the subject. "That's the last speech he will ever make."[29]

As he jumped onto the stage in the theater where the assassination took place, Booth shouted out, "Sic semper tyrannis." Thus be the fate of tyrants. But of course it was a lie in the classic Democratic fashion. The supreme irony is that Booth's was the cause of tyranny and human bondage. So deluded was Booth that he regarded the right to enslave other humans as a form of liberty worth killing—and in the end dying—for.

Thus we see a Democrat who represented the cause of the plantation, the cause of tyranny, using the mask of anti-tyranny to justify murdering a man who perhaps more nobly embodied the striving for human freedom than any figure in history. And today the Democrats— the party that protected slavery and killed the man who ended it—have the chutzpah to blame the institution's legacy on the very party that stopped them.

A SQUID-LIKE CLOUD

Now we turn to Reconstruction, a period whose storytelling is dominated by the towering figure of Eric Foner. Foner is a capable historian who nevertheless, as a progressive leftist, does his best to hide Democratic responsibility for resisting Republican Reconstruction. He also attempts to flip the blame for slavery and racism onto the Republican right. Foner wants his readers to think that the plantation was somehow a right-wing institution that was bravely overthrown by an early generation of American progressives.

Earlier we saw how Foner disingenuously portrays the South as "conservative," even though its leaders were Democrats who advanced a pro-slavery ideology that, far from being conservative, was unique in world history and represented a radical break with the founding. Foner also counts Lincoln as a progressive even though, as we have seen, Lincoln was a self-described conservative who insisted he was merely implementing the shared principles of the founders. Foner is shameless in the way he distorts ideological labels, relying on his peers to recognize his service to the progressive cause and to uphold his distortions, as most indeed do. Even so, as we will see, Foner's squid-like cloud of ideology sometimes dissipates and a ray of truth breaks through.

Reconstruction wasn't just about extending rights to blacks. Nor was it just about settling the terms for the readmission of rebel states into the union. While he lived, Lincoln considered this an administrative rather than a constitutional problem, because as far as he was concerned secession was unconstitutional, and therefore the rebel states had never actually left the union. Reconstruction in its broadest sense was about rebuilding the nation in a manner that realized the full vision of the founders. It was about achieving Lincoln's goal of reconciling the Declaration's twin propositions, "created equal" and "consent of the governed."

The Republicans in Congress who drove Reconstruction realized that, perhaps for the first time in history, there was an elected government that supported not merely emancipation from slavery but also full equality of rights and full enfranchisement for blacks. Admittedly this majority would not have existed had Southern Democrats also been represented. By their own choice, however, they had resigned their positions in Congress and thus forfeited their right to have their votes counted.

Reconstruction represented a mortal threat to a Democratic Party whose national prospects depended upon an alliance to save the slave plantation. Some Democrats during this period wondered whether the Democrats would now go the way of the Whigs and become extinct. Perhaps the Republican Party would now, in the 1860s, become the sole party in America in the same manner that Jefferson's Democratic Republican Party had been the sole party when the Federalist Party dissolved. Democrats during the Reconstruction period vowed they would not let this happen. One way or another, they would fight Reconstruction and make a last-ditch effort to save the plantation.

The magnificent scope of Republican Reconstruction can be seen in three landmark constitutional amendments: the Thirteenth Amendment abolishing slavery; the Fourteenth Amendment extending equal rights under the law to all citizens; and the Fifteenth Amendment granting blacks the right to vote. These amendments went beyond unbinding the slave and making him a freeman; they also made him a U.S. citizen with the right to cast his ballot and to the full and equal protection of the laws.

These amendments represented the most important moment for American constitutionalism since the Constitution was first drafted and ratified. The entire civil rights movement of the 1960s would be impossible without them. The Civil Rights Act of 1964 relied heavily on the equal protection clause of the Fourteenth Amendment and the Voting Rights Act of 1965 on the Fifteenth Amendment.

Yet progressive historical accounts as well as progressive textbooks say very little about the debate over the Thirteenth, Fourteenth and Fifteenth Amendments. The reason becomes obvious when we break down the partisan vote on those amendments. One might have thought that after the Civil War, the Thirteenth Amendment would be a fait accompli. One might expect that every Democrat—at least every Northern Democrat represented in Congress—would now vote for it. In fact, only sixteen of eighty Democrats did.

Let's pause to digest that for a minute. Even in the aftermath of the Civil War, so strong was their attachment to the plantation that an overwhelming majority of Northern Democrats refused to vote to permanently end slavery. Again, we are speaking of Northern Democrats; Southern Democrats who may have been expected to vote against the amendment were not permitted to vote at all. And when the Thirteenth Amendment went to the states for ratification, only Republican states carried by Lincoln voted for it; Democratic states that went for McClellan all voted no.

On the Fourteenth and Fifteenth Amendments, the Democratic Party's performance was even more disgraceful. Not a single Democrat, either in the House or the Senate, voted for either amendment. To repeat, these were not Southern Democrats who were excluded from voting; these were Northern Democrats so averse to extending equal rights under law or voting rights to blacks that not a single one of them could bring himself to vote for either measure. So the Fourteenth and Fifteenth Amendments can be considered exclusively Republican achievements, since no Democrats contributed to making them part of the Constitution.

Now we see why progressives don't want people to know about these amendments, despite their obvious importance. They belie the progressive narrative that the Northerners were the good guys and the Southerners the bad guys. They show the Republican Party to be the only friend of blacks in the critical period following the Civil War, and they expose the Democratic Party as the true party of white supremacy, still fighting to hold onto the slave plantation.

Thus Eric Foner conveniently omits the partisan roll-call vote on each one of these amendments. He gives us all kinds of minutiae about Reconstruction but somehow leaves out how the Republicans and Democrats each voted on the crucial issues of whether blacks could no longer be slaves, vote, and enjoy equal rights under the law. Is this omission a mere oversight? Whatever his intention, Foner's narrative leaves the false impression that Reconstruction was driven by a series of political conflicts between enlightened Northern progressives and wicked Southern conservatives.

Republicans included two other significant measures as part of their Reconstruction. The first was the Civil Rights Act of 1866, significant not merely in that it was America's first civil rights law, but also in that it invalidated racially discriminatory laws in the North no less than in the South. Thus it represented a powerful Republican blow against white supremacy.

Second, Republicans sought to give freed slaves a start in life by giving them access to education and also ownership of land confiscated from the Confederacy. The Civil War itself supplied a precedent for this; toward the end of the war, Union general William Sherman issued Special Field Order No. 15, which reserved coastal land in Georgia and South Carolina for liberated slaves.

Using this model framework, Republicans through the Freedman's Bureau attempted America's first reparations law, colloquially described as "forty acres and a mule." In its most expansive reading, reparations meant, in the words of Republican senator Charles Sumner, seizing the land of the slave planters and dividing it "among patriot soldiers, poor whites, and freedmen."[30]

THE POLITICS OF TERROR

These measures were opposed by Lincoln's successor, President Andrew Johnson. By this time, it will come as no surprise for anyone to learn that Johnson was a Democrat. Lincoln put him on the ticket because he had opposed secession and was a Union man. Lincoln hoped that Johnson might attract Southern unionists to the cause and also help generate bipartisan support for the war. Yet Johnson remained a Democratic loyalist and, once he became president, connived to defeat Republican Reconstruction and restore, as much as possible, the Southern status quo ante.

Democrats at the time loved Johnson and cheered his efforts. Today's progressive Democrats take the opposite view, publicly distancing themselves from Johnson. They downplay his Democratic affiliation and claim that as a Southerner he always had secret plantation sympathies. This is actually false; as Foner himself tells us, Johnson grew up dirt poor in Tennessee and hated the planter aristocracy. Johnson's real reason for opposing Reconstruction was that he always had not-so-secret party sympathies. After the war, he spoke openly about attempting to restore the coalition of Northern and Southern Democrats that had ruled the country since the Jackson–Van Buren era in the late 1820s and early 1830s.

Johnson vetoed the Civil Rights Act of 1866, but fortunately Republicans had a strong enough majority to override his veto. Johnson was more successful in thwarting the Freedman's Bureau, the Republican mechanism for giving newly freed blacks a fresh start. Through a systematically enforced policy of lax pardons, Johnson restored plantations to their former owners, thus depriving the bureau of land that was available to issue to blacks. Thus ended "forty acres and a mule," a policy worth trying that was abolished by a Democratic president intent on restoring what he could of the plantation and of the ideology of white supremacy.

In December 1867, Johnson in his annual message to Congress asserted that African Americans possess less "capacity for government than any other race of people." He added that "no independent government of any form has ever been successful in their hands. On the contrary, wherever they have been left to their own devices, they have shown a constant tendency to relapse into barbarism." Foner admits that Johnson's diatribe is "probably the most blatantly racist pronouncement ever to appear in an official state paper of an American president."[31]

Democrats also struck at the Republicans' attempts to include blacks in the Southern economy. Republicans sought to do this by protecting the rights of blacks to make contracts and by assuring that they could also exercise their newly won right to vote. The black ballot in particular was a serious threat to the Democratic Party. Starting in 1866, blacks organized themselves into Union leagues throughout the South. They allied with Northern whites who had moved south—the group that Democrats called carpetbaggers—as well as with sympathetic Southern whites—the group that Democrats called scalawags.

In 1867–69, during the constitutional conventions, blacks and whites jointly participated in political deliberations for the first time in the nation's history. During this "golden decade," approximately two thousand blacks were elected to important political office in the South. There were two black senators, sixteen black Congressmen, and more than six hundred blacks in the state legislatures. In addition, nearly a thousand blacks held various local offices. Many of them were former slaves. Every single one of them was a Republican. In fact, blacks dominated the Republican Party in the South during the Reconstruction era.

Democrats in the South resolved not merely to crush the black Republicans but also to kill in its cradle America's embryonic experiment in multiracial democracy. This time the Democratic weapon was a deadly and murderous one, the Invisible Empire of the Ku Klux Klan, an organization led by Nathan Bedford Forrest, a former slave-trader, Confederate general and delegate to the 1868 Democratic National Convention. Democrats also founded dozens of other domestic terrorist organizations.

For nearly a decade, in the late 1860s and early 1870s, the Klan and similar groups conducted a reign of terror through the South, targeting not only blacks but also white Republicans who had gone south to help educate blacks and help integrate them into the political process.

Klansmen murdered black officials, black voters, and also carpetbaggers and scalawags. They hated blacks for being blacks, and Republicans for attempting to treat blacks as human and extend to them the same rights enjoyed by whites.

As David Chalmers writes in his book *Hooded Americanism*, the Klan's preferred techniques of political action were shooting, burning and lynching, and these gruesome acts were often conducted with large Democratic crowds in attendance, eating and drinking as they took in torture as a form of entertainment. Traveling through the South, the Republican official Carl Schurz was horrified to see, in one county after another, decomposing corpses suspended from trees or lying in ditches and on roadways.

The Republican Congress held hearings on Klan atrocities and passed laws—collectively called the Force Bill—authorizing the prosecution of these terrorist lawbreakers. As a consequence of Republican pressure, the Klan went defunct and shut its doors, although it would see a revival early in the twentieth century. During this period when the KKK ceased to exist, other terrorist groups like the Knights of the White Camelia took up the Democratic cause. Moreover, the Klan had in its short but extremely violent tenure largely accomplished its purpose: to intimidate black voters and drive Republican reformers out of the South. In a remarkable admission, Eric Foner writes that in the postbellum era, "The Klan was a military force serving the interest of the Democratic Party."[32]

Foner's admission is remarkable because it is so rare. Foner, for once, actually makes an incriminating generalization about the Democratic Party. And what a damaging admission it is. Foner makes it clear that, as a domestic terrorist group serving at the behest of a political party, the Klan resembles the Nazi Brownshirts of the 1920s and 1930s. They were the domestic terrorist arm of the Nazi Party.

There is that glimpse of ideological truth in Foner, and then he is back to his old ways. Foner concludes his book with the glum observation that Reconstruction came to a rude halt in the late 1870s, but he never gives the root cause for this. The root cause is that partly through political obstructionism, but mostly through domestic terrorism carried out by organizations like the Klan, the Democrats defeated the Republican attempt to protect blacks, enfranchise them, and give them a chance to make their own American dream. Weary Republicans—reeling from what historian Joel Williamson terms "battle fatigue"—finally retreated from the South, leaving it in the dirty hands of the Democratic Party.[33]

The Democrats lost the Civil War, but they denied the Republicans the chance to build a decent peace. This is the whole meaning of what Foner writes and yet it is the conclusion that he peremptorily resists. So do Barbara Fields, Ta-Nehisi Coates, and the whole procession of progressive scholars and pundits. I guess I shouldn't be shocked that these intellectual partisans aren't particularly eager to tell us that their own party destroyed the postbellum hopes of the African American community.

Still, for all their limitations, we should not lose sight of what the Republicans did accomplish. They saved the country and vanquished the old Democratic plantation, which lay in ruins after the Civil War. Even though progressives keep telling us about the Lost Cause—supposedly the cause of the Confederacy—the death of the Democratic plantation was the real Lost Cause. The Confederacy was merely the means to save the Democratic plantation. It was the plantation that gave rise to the Democratic Party, and it was for the plantation that Democrats fought so viciously and so bitterly.

Now that it was gone, the Democrats found themselves in a miserable position. They were like the rebel angels in Milton's *Paradise Lost,* "hurled headlong flaming from the ethereal sky" and now confused and dazed in a hell of their own making. For a time, before they gathered their wits, it was dark despair and pure pandemonium. Yet just like Lucifer and his "horrid crew," as Milton describes them, the Democrats were not about to submit.

Rather, in the manner of Belial, Beelzebub and the rest, they drew resolution from despair and shook their fists in rage at the Republicans, seeking not merely to undermine Republican projects like Reconstruction but to make a full comeback themselves. They vowed not, as progressives would have us believe, that "the South will rise again," but, rather, what the progressives like to conceal from us, that "the Democratic Party will rise again." They were determined to reinvent the plantation.

6

PROGRESSIVE PLANTATION

White Supremacy as a
Weapon of Reenslavement

It was a menace to society itself that the
Negroes should thus of a sudden be set free
and left without tutelage or restraint.

—Woodrow Wilson,
History of the American People[1]

In the critical election year of 1912, the progressive African American scholar W. E. B. Du Bois faced a choice. Should he endorse the former Republican, Theodore Roosevelt, now running on the progressive "Bull Moose" ticket, or the Democrat, Woodrow Wilson, also running on a progressive platform? In general ideological terms, both men were similar, and Du Bois, sharing the same outlook, could hardly distinguish them on that basis.

Even so, on racial grounds alone, the choice for Du Bois should have been an easy one. Du Bois knew that the Democrats, both in the North and the South, had been the party of the old plantation. They had fought to protect the plantation through the Civil War and had largely successfully blocked Republican Reconstruction. Far from repenting of their long legacy of bigotry and enslavement, the Democrats—especially in the South—were scheming for ways to restore and reinvent the plantation in the twentieth century.

Wilson was part of this scheme—a Virginia Democrat who as a young boy had watched in horror as Union armies occupied the South. This trauma had inevitably shaped his basic worldview. True, Wilson as a young man migrated north to New Jersey, where he became the president of Princeton and governor of the state. This Northern experience changed Wilson, but not in the way we might think. Instead of moving away from his old bigotries, Wilson acquired new fortification for them in the so-called scientific racism of the fin de siècle. In short, he became even more racist than he had been before.

We see this in Wilson's scholarly output, which we can assume that Du Bois—himself a historian and sociologist—knew well. In 1889 Wilson published *The State,* a survey on the origins of government and civilization. Drawing on a new scientific taxonomy devised in Europe but gaining ground in American universities—much of it deriving from an attempt to apply Darwin's theories to human populations—Wilson argued that the history of civilization is best understood in terms of the accomplishments and failures of various races.

American democracy, in Wilson's view, was not an American creation; rather, it was a racial legacy dating back to the ancient German Teutonic tribes, whom Wilson dubbed the "Aryans." Wilson credited most achievements in the area of government and social development to these Aryan people. Other races, Wilson insisted, lack the capacity for democratic self-government, which was essentially an Anglo-Saxon product.[2] Wilson, in short, was an early apostle of the nineteenth-century movement to invoke science on behalf of white supremacy.

In 1901, Wilson published an article in the *Atlantic Monthly* in which he made the case for the segregation laws that the Democratic Party was at the time enacting throughout the South. Free blacks, Wilson argued, were "unpracticed in liberty, unschooled in self-control; never sobered by the discipline of self-support, never established in any habit of prudence . . . insolent and aggressive; sick of work, covetous of pleasure." Obviously they needed segregation, Wilson concluded because otherwise they would be "a danger to themselves as well as to those whom they had once served."[3]

Wilson's magnum opus was his five-volume *History of the American People,* the tone of which can be captured in a telling section. Returning to his theme of the unschooled Negro, Wilson wrote that as a result of his indolence and viciousness, "The tasks of ordinary labor stood untouched; the idler grew insolent, dangerous; nights went anxiously by, for fear of riot and incendiary fire . . . until at last there had sprung into existence a great Ku Klux Klan, an Invisible Empire of the South, bound together in loose organization, to protect the southern country from some of the ugliest hazards of a time of revolution."[4]

Running against Wilson was the Rough Rider nicknamed TR, who would seem from his record to be the far better candidate for Du Bois to support. Roosevelt was not uncontaminated by the Darwinian racialism that was all the rage in progressive intellectual precincts. He too spoke of the survival of the stronger races and the ultimate extinction of the lesser ones. Yet TR was a New Yorker, a Union man and a Republican. He embraced Lincoln and Reconstruction. He condemned lynching and the Klan. Unlike Wilson—and at considerable political risk to himself—he sought to build bridges to the black community and integrate blacks into the postbellum South.

In 1901, Roosevelt, as the newly elected president, invited the most prominent black leader in America, Booker T. Washington, to dinner at the White House. TR's natural decency can be seen in his description of the offhand way the invitation came about. "It seemed to me natural to ask him to dinner to talk over his work, and the very fact that I felt a moment's qualm on inviting him because of his color made me ashamed of myself and made me hasten to send out the invitation."[5]

Born a slave, Washington had risen to prominence as a black educator and statesman, founder of the Tuskegee Institute in Alabama. Washington, like TR, was a Republican who subscribed to the Republican ideology of free people, free labor and free markets. TR knew Washington's deep ties to African American farmers, teachers, small businessmen and clergy, and he sought to create a working relationship with them. A few years later, in 1905, Roosevelt visited Washington's Tuskegee Institute in Alabama.

The significance of these actions—especially the 1901 dinner at the White House—can hardly be grasped today. America just had a two-term black president, Barack Obama, and it is commonplace now to have blacks at state functions and at the White House. Blacks and other minorities, from Ben Carson to Nikki Haley, are a visible presence in the Trump administration. The atmosphere could not have been more different a century ago, in the early 1900s. Roosevelt's dinner invitation provoked the tempestuous ire of Democratic racists throughout the South.

"The action of President Roosevelt in entertaining that nigger," fumed Democratic senator Benjamin Tillman of South Carolina, "will necessitate our killing a thousand niggers in the South before they will learn their place." Mississippi's James Vardaman, a former congressman who would be elected to the Senate as a Democrat that year, said following the dinner that the White House was now "so saturated with the odor of the nigger that the rats have taken refuge in the stables."[6]

What, you might ask, was the big deal? The big deal was that once blacks were freed from slavery, the issue became whether they should enjoy equality of rights with whites. The most potent symbol of this was "social equality," which included the right to socialize on equal terms with whites, to sit down to dinner with them, even to marry their sons and daughters. This was the explosive significance of the Roosevelt-Washington rendezvous at the White House. It was the original, real-life *Guess Who's Coming to Dinner?*

WILL THE REAL UNCLE TOM PLEASE STAND UP?

Yet it was precisely that 1901 meeting that fortified Du Bois' hatred of Roosevelt. Du Bois, you see, was the second-most-famous black leader in America. He was undoubtedly the country's leading African American intellectual and was the first black to get a Ph.D. in philosophy from Harvard.

Even so, Du Bois was a prickly and pretentious figure. Since most people pronounced his name Du-Bwah, he insisted that they should say it as Du-Boys. He wore three-piece suits, and adorned his outfits with a hat and a cane. When challenged in academic quarters, he was known to convey a European sophistication and superiority by drawing out his monocle. He sought to inherit from Frederick Douglass the position of the leading representative of the African American community.

In dismay he watched as this title seemed to pass seamlessly from Douglass to Washington, one Republican to another. To Du Bois' horror, Timothy Thomas Fortune, editor of the *New York Age* and the most influential black journalist of the era, explicitly likened Washington to Douglass and even published an article raising the question of whether

Washington was the "Negro Moses." Du Bois found it hard to believe that American elites, in the North no less than the South, kowtowed to the homespun former slave whom Du Bois considered barely an educator, let alone his equal.

In his best-known book, *The Souls of Black Folk*, Du Bois launched an intemperate attack on Washington, accusing him of being a sellout and an Uncle Tom. To my knowledge, this is the first time that the Uncle Tom accusation appears in American politics. Du Bois alleged that while he and others were fighting for blacks to have civil rights and full access to American opportunities—including higher education—Washington sought to accommodate Southern segregation and to teach blacks nothing better than vocational skills in preparation for manual occupations.

This critique of Washington, launched by a leading progressive, has now become standard fare in progressive academia and media. Typical is the left-wing historian Louis Harlan's unremittingly hostile two-volume biography of Washington. Harlan portrays his subject as a racial and ideological sellout, while he views Du Bois as a heroic resister on behalf of full legal and social equality. Today Republican intellectuals like Thomas Sowell and Republican cabinet officials like Ben Carson are scornfully dismissed as Uncle Toms in the Booker T. Washington mode. Progressive intellectuals like Ta-Nehisi Coates and Cornel West like to think of themselves in the Du Bois role of glorious resisters.

Yet a closer look reveals that Washington was the resister and Du Bois was the sellout. After all, it was Du Bois who, largely on grounds of personal arrogance and resentment, backed Woodrow Wilson over TR. As we will see in this chapter, Wilson was almost single-handedly responsible for the national revival of the Ku Klux Klan, an organization that had been defunct since the 1870s. Wilson also segregated the federal government and promoted vicious schemes of forced sterilization of racial minorities. These schemes were eventually taken up by the Nazis in a macabre succession of policies that moved from mass sterilization to mass murder to the Holocaust.

Thus I agree with Jonah Goldberg's assessment that Wilson was "the most racist president of the twentieth century."[7] And this is whom Du Bois actually supported. Washington, by contrast, did nothing so egregious to harm and set back his fellow African Americans. Why, then, is Du Bois portrayed as a hero and Washington spurned as an Uncle Tom by progressives?

To fully appreciate the absurdity, we need to probe more deeply the meaning of the term "Uncle Tom." In Harriet Beecher Stowe's novel *Uncle Tom's Cabin,* the slave character Tom is the noble long-suffering protagonist. He is not a sellout or a traitor to blacks. That use of the term came decades later, as blacks and others looked back at slavery and sought to distinguish those who resisted the institution and those who sustained it. Somehow poor Tom's name became a symbol of shameful collaboration.

In this context, it's helpful to consider how Malcolm X in the 1960s used the term "Uncle Tom." He used it to designate the House Slave as compared with the Field Slave. As Malcolm X saw it, the Field Slave was the true resister of slavery. He was the "bad nigger." By contrast, the House Slave made his peace with slavery. In the Malcolm X narrative, when the Big House on the plantation was burning, the Field Slave rejoiced while the House Slave rushed to the owner and said, "Massa, our house is burning." Our house! The House Slave identified with the master, and accommodated himself to the oppression of slavery.

Now Malcolm X did not suggest the House Slave liked slavery, merely that he accommodated himself to it. On this basis Malcolm X dubbed him an Uncle Tom. But concealed in Malcolm X's distinction was the fact that the Field Slave also accommodated himself to slavery. He might have tried to run away or organize a slave revolt—in reality, there were hardly any slave revolts and no successful ones—but the Field Slave, no less than the House Slave, was powerless to actually stop slavery. So both in the end accommodated an institution they were in no position to do anything about, and the House Slave was therefore no more of an Uncle Tom than the Field Slave.

In the same manner, Booker T. Washington accommodated segregation in the South because he had no power to end it. He emphasized black self-help because this was the only practical way for blacks to advance in the entirely inhospitable Democratic environment of the Deep South. Even so, it may be asked whether he adopted available measures to fight for legal equality. The answer—generally suppressed in progressive accounts of him—is that yes, he did.

In a recent biography, historian Robert Norrell highlights facts that have been downplayed or omitted in progressive accounts. He shows that Washington spoke out regularly against lynching and lobbied Congress for legislation to outlaw it; condemned railway segregation in speeches and articles and lobbied the rail companies to stop it; funded lawsuits to block Democratic campaigns to deprive blacks of their voting rights; condemned the unfairness of the sharecropping system that robbed black farmers of their earnings; and supported a black defendant, Alonzo Bailey, in a landmark 1911 Supreme Court case, *Bailey v. Alabama,* striking down the discriminatory and oppressive practice of peonage.[8]

Taken as a whole, Washington did more in practical terms than Du Bois to combat segregation in particular, and white supremacy in general. Note that while Du Bois railed against segregation throughout the early part of the twentieth century, he accomplished nothing in terms of curtailing it. Washington's "accommodation" is reminiscent of how the founders and even Lincoln accommodated slavery. These men did what they could within their power to restrict what was beyond their power to instantly eliminate. No one can be reasonably criticized for that.

AN APPRECIATION FOR HITLER

While we can understand Du Bois' attack on Washington as the bitter recriminations of a lesser man, this still doesn't fully explain Du Bois' bizarre endorsement of Wilson. Du Bois insisted in 1912 that Wilson "will treat black men and their interests with far-sighted fairness . . . he will not seek further means of Jim Crow insult, he will not dismiss black men wholesale from office, and he will remember that the Negro in the United States has a right to be heard and considered."[9]

These absurd predictions sound like those of a man insisting that a scorpion that has already shown its sting is not going to sting anyone. Why, then, would an intelligent man like Du Bois say such nonsense? In other words, notwithstanding his personal desire to settle scores with Washington and Roosevelt, why didn't Du Bois go with the higher cause of stopping Wilson and his party's known racism? We can answer this question by looking at Du Bois' subsequent career. In the years following Wilson's two terms—in which Du Bois' predictions proved to be the very opposite of the truth—Du Bois moved on from Wilson and proceeded to become enamored with both Stalin and Hitler.

In 1936–37, Du Bois made a trip to Europe that included visits to Russia and Germany. He praised Stalin for making "a brave start at scientific planning" by "investing the ownership of all land and materials in the public and then using natural wealth and resources for the ultimate good of the mass of inhabitants." Du Bois refused to criticize Stalin's purge trials and actually defended his forced relocation of small landowning peasants, apparently regarding such repressive measures as necessary to establish a state-run egalitarian paradise.

What attracted Du Bois to Stalin was his socialism, which Du Bois came to understand as the most uncompromising form of progressivism. On Stalin's death, Du Bois proclaimed him a "great man" who pursued "real socialism." And this is also what Du Bois appreciated about Hitler. Traveling through Nazi Germany, Du Bois praised Hitler's dictatorship as "absolutely necessary to put the state in order" and praised Hitler's social programs such as "national health, living wage, new public housing projects and new public works of all kinds." Du Bois found the Nazi state to be a "content and prosperous whole." While Du Bois deplored Hitler's racism toward blacks, he attributed Hitler's vilification of Jews to "reasoned prejudice or an economic fear."[10]

Du Bois' blind appreciation for Hitler mirrors his blind appreciation for Stalin, and indeed the two dictators—notwithstanding their subsequent clash on the battlefield—were close ideological cousins. They were, in fact, both national socialists. While Marx and Lenin both viewed communism as international socialism, Stalin had emphasized "socialism in one country," socialism for Mother Russia—in short, national socialism. Hitler too was a national socialist who headed the German National Socialist Workers' Party.

Historian Stanley Payne, in *A History of Fascism,* remarks on the parallel between Stalinist socialism and German national socialism. Much earlier the Russian socialist Trotsky recognized the similarity, contending that Stalinism and fascism were "symmetrical phenomena."[11] Both Hitler and Stalin were champions of the all-powerful state, and they sought a remaking of society and even of human nature in subordination to the centralized state.

Du Bois' naked admiration for tyrants like Stalin and Hitler proved an embarrassment to his allies at the National Organization for the Advancement of Colored People (NAACP), whose magazine, *The Crisis,* Du Bois edited for many years. The NAACP fired Du Bois, who eventually left America in disgust and became a citizen of Ghana, where he eventually died a bitter and broken man. This progressive icon came to hate America because in his view America did not take the strong measures that Stalin and Hitler did to bring strongman socialism and centralized state power to their countries.

This, then, is the tragedy of America's leading African American progressive. He backed Wilson against TR, identified with the Democratic Party at a time when most blacks were Republicans and then later became a devotee of Stalin and Hitler, all because he embraced the progressive vision of the centralized state. In 1912, Du Bois saw Wilson as a more reliable champion of centralized state power than TR. Ultimately that—and Du Bois' personal grudge—counted more for Du Bois than even Wilson's blatant, documented commitment to white supremacy.

Du Bois' betrayal of the black cause was not just about Wilson; it was also about the two political parties. Even though Republicans were the party of emancipation and civil rights, they were also the party of individualism and self-reliance. Du Bois didn't believe in self-reliance; he believed in reliance upon the centralized state. And he detected a subtle but unmistakable movement in the Democratic Party from the party of state's rights to the party of centralized state power.

Du Bois realized that the Democrats under Wilson were creating a new plantation, to be run by a new elite progressive class that would replace the old planter class. Du Bois was not entirely against such an arrangement; indeed, he had argued that the black community should be led by a "talented tenth" of its smartest men. One might reasonably suspect that Du Bois envisioned himself at the helm of this group. Yet this was not Wilson's idea at all—his progressive plantation had no room for blacks at the top—and consequently Du Bois grew disenchanted with Wilson.

Du Bois' disenchantment with Wilson is today shared by most progressives. Wilson's racist progressivism is an embarrassment to their current political strategy. But progressives still revere Du Bois. So they ignore Du Bois' role in putting Wilson in the White House, pretending that it never happened. But in fact Du Bois didn't just give Wilson his personal endorsement, he also drew other influential blacks, including Boston activist William Monroe Trotter, to the Democratic Party, helping Wilson and the Democrats win a very close election.

This is part of a bigger story that tells us as much about progressives as it does about Du Bois. They continue to lionize Du Bois because they too are aficionados of centralized state power. They too, as Du Bois did, envision a role for black progressives as overseers on their new plantation. They too, as we will see, were complicit in the great schemes of twentieth-century tyranny, not merely Stalinism but also Nazism. Thus for the Democrats and the progressives who led them, the tyranny of the old slave plantation was replaced by the tyranny of the state.

The state, in fact, became the new plantation, run not by an elite class of Democratic planters but by a single Democratic Big Boss—initially Wilson and later Franklin Roosevelt, Harry Truman, Lyndon Johnson, Bill Clinton and Barack Obama—operating from a Big House that we know as the White House. Wilson began this reinvention of the Democratic plantation from a rural network specializing in black exploitation to a national network of ethnic exploitation involving multiple minority groups. But Wilson could only take the new progressive plantation so far; it took FDR to actually build it and other Democratic presidents to give it its current shape and form.

In this and the following two chapters, we see how the progressive Democrats creatively reinvented the plantation. They did this by deploying new weapons, white supremacy and ethnic mobilization, that had existed under slavery but were developed by progressives into a comprehensive system of exploitation. At the same time, we should be cognizant that a subsequent generation of progressives has rewritten history to pin the blame for ethnic mobilization and white supremacy onto their adversaries, the very party that fought against Democrats' vicious and bigoted schemes from the outset.

WHY WILSON ADMIRED LINCOLN

Here we move from the progressive intellectual, Du Bois, to the progressive president, Wilson. Wilson, FDR and LBJ are acknowledged to be the three leading progressives of the twentieth century. Consequently, they are all celebrated in the historiography of the left. In a recent article, "The Do Gooder," the *New Republic* ranks Wilson "among America's greatest presidents."[12] Wilson is praised by progressive biographers for his supposed dedication to global self-determination and for his progressive reforms, including the introduction of the income tax, the Federal Reserve and greater federal regulation of industry.

But Wilson's blatant record of racism is too much for today's progressives to ignore. (I find it comical how Democrats today are in the awkward position of having to repudiate the embarrassing bigotry of virtually all their early presidents, from Jackson through Wilson.) In fact, it is crucial for their narrative to distance themselves from the deep racism not only in the Democratic Party's history but also in early progressive history. So progressive activists assail Wilson—always careful to identify him as a Southerner rather than a Democrat—and demand that the Woodrow Wilson School at Princeton change its name, while of course keeping its progressive intellectual thrust.

But if Wilson was a progressive racist, shouldn't Princeton get rid of the progressivism and not just Wilson's contaminated name? No one on the left is pressing for this, because virtually no one on the left admits that progressivism has anything to do with racism. Wilson's biographers like Arthur Link and John Milton Cooper insist his racism was a regrettable leftover from his Southern roots. So Wilson did these wonderful progressive things, but occasionally—we hear—his Southern background reasserted itself and he did some bad stuff like show the Ku Klux Klan propaganda movie in the White House and segregate the federal government and so forth.

Yes, even the progressive critique of Wilson is part of the big lie to blame the South for the bigotry of progressivism and of the Democratic Party. Wilson regarded himself as having transcended Southern provincialism. Having absconded for Princeton at a young age, he believed he embodied the most enlightened progressivism of the early twentieth century, a progressivism far more associated with the North than the South.

That Wilson was in no way representative of Democratic thinking in the South can be seen in a single fact: his almost over-the-top admiration for Abraham Lincoln. This is a surprise: America's first progressive Democratic president modeled himself upon America's first Republican president! Our initial bafflement and incomprehension, however, gives way to understanding when we see what it was that Wilson admired about Lincoln.

Wilson did not admire Lincoln for his Republican dedication to the principles of the American founding. On the contrary, Wilson was the first American president to denounce the founders. Wilson ridiculed the founding system of separation of powers and checks and balances. Wilson did not share the founders' belief that an all-powerful centralized state poses a grave threat to the rights and freedom both of individuals and of states. Wilson rejected the founding scheme of distributing power between the federal government and the states, and also among various branches of the federal government, to minimize abuses of power.

What Wilson admired most about Lincoln was his willingness to greatly increase the power of the federal government at the expense of the states. Lincoln had simply refused to let the states secede, a marvelous display of federal control over renegade subdivisions that wanted to go their own way. Wilson also admired Lincoln's willingness to undercut the constitutional system of checks and balances when the situation warranted: Lincoln, for instance, suspended habeas corpus even though the Constitution clearly gives that power to Congress.

Lincoln also earned Wilson's praise for his readiness to revoke civil liberties, as when he had Ohio Copperhead Clement Vallandigham arrested for incendiary speeches opposing the war. Yes, Vallandigham was a Democrat and Wilson sympathized with him in that regard. But in the broader sense, Wilson admired how Lincoln handled the Vallandigham case because he saw in Lincoln a man who represented unlimited state power concentrated in the executive branch, a Republican model for Wilson's own Democratic administration.

How would Lincoln, had he lived to see them, have responded to Wilson's commendations? I believe he would have been deeply offended by them. Let's begin with Lincoln's use of federal power to prevent states from withdrawing from the union. Lincoln's point was that the sole reason for seceding was the Southern Democrats' refusal to accept the result of a free election. What was the point of having elections if the losers could then invalidate them by escaping the governance of an electoral majority?

Lincoln viewed the concentration of federal power that occurred during his administration as a military strategy necessary to put down an armed rebellion and win a civil war. He perceived the measures he took—on habeas corpus, on suspending civil liberty, even the Emancipation Proclamation—as acts taken under duress. He considered none of these measures the normal conduct of government, and with the exception of the Emancipation Proclamation, he intended none to outlast the war.

Consider Lincoln's argument for suspending habeas corpus. Yes, this power was given to Congress by the Constitution, but the very existence of an armed assault on the government prevented Congress from being able to meet and act promptly. Therefore, Lincoln insisted his executive branch had the temporary authority to act on behalf of Congress, and this action was legitimate provided Congress, upon considering it, approved the measure, which it did.

Lincoln did not himself call for the arrest of Vallandigham, although he approved the move when one of his generals, Ambrose Burnside, ordered it. Lincoln's reasoning was that Vallandigham had gone beyond criticizing war policy to actively encouraging antidraft riots and exhorting soldiers to leave the front, and this posed a danger to war recruitment and military rules.

"Must I shoot a simple soldier boy who deserts," Lincoln asked, "while I must not touch a hair of a wily agitator who induces him to desert?"[13] Yet Lincoln was fully aware of how Democrats used the Vallandigham case to portray him as a tyrant. He did not wish to give fodder to such accusations. So shortly after Vallandigham's arrest, Lincoln ordered him released and turned over to the Confederacy.

Lincoln's commitment to the founders' scheme can probably be seen most vividly in his insistence that the 1864 election go ahead, even though it took place in the desperate and decisive stage of the war. Lincoln could have argued for postponing the election until the war was over, but such a thought seems not even to have entered his mind. Moreover, for several months while the conflict dragged on, Lincoln himself believed it possible, even probable, that he would lose the election. For a time, it was not even clear he would be the Republican nominee.

Ultimately the victories of the Union armies led by Grant and Sherman revived Lincoln's popular support and ensured his reelection. Even so, his willingness to risk defeat—to risk what in his mind represented the continuation of the plantation, this time in the North as well as in the South—confirms his determination to respect the founding formula of government by popular consent even under conditions of extreme duress.

In sum, Lincoln was an American nationalist while Wilson was a statist. What Lincoln considered to be extraordinary powers, used by government only in the event of a national emergency, Wilson saw as powers to be used in the ordinary course of government. Essentially Wilson turned what was provisional and most problematic about Lincoln—and recognized as such by Lincoln himself—into a new progressive creed alien to the spirit of Lincoln and also to the spirit of the American founding.

Why, we may ask, was Wilson himself and the whole progressive Democratic movement that grew around him so enamored of the power of centralized government? The usual progressive answer is that progressives came to realize that they were the smartest people and that society runs most efficiently with the smartest people at the helm. This is the theme of progressive manifestos like Herbert Croly's *Progressive Democracy* and E. A. Ross' *Social Control,* in which Croly and Ross argue that societies don't run themselves; someone has to control them, and it may as well be highly educated and highly specialized social scientists like themselves.

"The state is an organization that puts the wise minority in the saddle," Ross writes. "The state aims more steadily at a rational safeguarding of the collective welfare than any organ society has yet employed." While in theory the state is supposed to be democratically chosen by the society, Ross argues that "as a matter of fact, the state, when it becomes paternal and develops on the administrative side, is able in a measure to guide the society it professes to obey." It becomes, in a sense, "an independent center of social power."[14]

Here we see how progressive intellectuals sought, with a certain measure of rat-like cunning, to subvert the democratic process. Their goal was the administrative state that, while being installed by the people, would govern for rather than by people. The true rulers would be the progressives themselves, guided by the mind of the progressive intellectual. And this progressive longing is with us today. It explains why so many in academia and the professional sectors count themselves as progressives. They aspire to join the ruling class that administers the centralized state.

Many conservatives and Republicans don't seem to get this. The conservative response—influenced by writers like Friedrich Hayek and Milton Friedman—is to make the case for why centralized societies don't work. Conservatives argue in the Hayekian mode that societies are organisms that are far too complex for even the most intelligent and dedicated administrators to run from central command. This response, however, misses the thrust of what is so appealing to progressives about the centralized state, and why progressives don't really care whether the centralized state makes the best or most efficient decisions compared to alternative ways of organizing society.

Look at the problem this way. Imagine going to a plantation owner and giving him the macroeconomic argument that he shouldn't use a forced-labor system because slavery is a very inefficient way of organizing society. After all, slaves, being unpaid, have little motivation to work, and blah, blah, blah. Some Republicans and abolitionists did at the time make this sort of case to planters. Not surprisingly, they made very few converts.

What would a plantation man say to someone who talked like this? Most likely he would respond with a scornful laugh. If pressed, he would say he doesn't give a damn about the profit to society; what motivates his enterprise is its profit to him. Sure, the slaves are reluctant to work, but that problem has had a workable solution ever since the invention of the whip. From the planter's point of view, unpaid labor is obviously the best form of labor because it costs close to nothing and the planter keeps the vast share of the profit.

Back to Woodrow Wilson and the early generation of progressive Democrats. What motivated their enthusiasm for the national government—for the centralized state—was their realization that it was the centralized state that had defeated the old plantation. Consequently, they reasoned that the only way to reestablish the plantation and make it invulnerable was to create a new type of plantation run by the centralized state itself. This way they could become the new plantation bosses, with power incomparably greater than that exercised by any slave-owner.

One national plantation with one big boss and lots of overseers, organized on an ethnic basis like the old plantation, just as effective as a system of exploitation but adapted to new circumstances and therefore structured somewhat differently—this became Wilson's model and indeed the model of the Democratic Party in the twentieth century, right up to the present.

Wilson represented a great shift in the Democratic Party from being the party of state's rights to the party of the strong centralized state. The reason for the shift is obvious. State's rights was the most effective way to protect the old slave plantation. But in the early twentieth century Roosevelt and the progressives had no slave plantation to protect. They needed a way to revive the plantation, to create a new type of plantation that they could run from a central location. Thus the Democratic Party switched its allegiance to a strong centralized state because that was the best way to reinvent the plantation. Notice that for the Democratic Party this represented a change of tactics, but not a change of purpose.

Wilson and his progressive cohorts created the embryo for this new type of plantation. Here we focus on its genesis, constructed on the cornerstone of white supremacy. Although white supremacy is the very charge progressive Democrats today make against Republicans, I will show that in its most virulent form it is an invention of progressivism and the Democratic Party. I will also identify the three distinguishing features of the new Democratic engine of exploitation: racial terrorism, segregation and forced eugenic sterilization. Some of this surrounding apparatus is now gone, but the progressive plantation itself is in full operation today.

INVENTING WHITE SUPREMACY

How do you reconstruct a plantation? How do you go about rebuilding not a single plantation but an entire plantation system that has been wiped out by the Civil War? This was the challenge confronting Wilson and his generation of progressive Democrats. At first, they had to accept what they had lost. They had lost the slaves, who were now free. This represented a financial loss of $4 billion, a number I arrive at by multiplying the number of slaves (four million) by the average cost of a slave ($1,000).

We can convert $4 billion into today's money and get a much larger number. But let's think about what the loss of the slaves actually represented to the planter class. Historian David Brion Davis points out that in 1860 the total value of the slaves was around 80 percent of the nation's gross national product.[15] That means that, in today's terms, the total loss to the slave-owners was not $4 billion but something closer to $13 trillion. No wonder the Democratic planters went to war, as Jefferson Davis himself said, to protect their very valuable property.

The loss of slavery wasn't merely a financial disaster; it changed the rules of an entire culture that had previously been based on status, leisure and idleness. A Maryland Unionist described the new situation facing former Democratic slave-owner Tench Tilghman and his family: "The younger ladies on Wednesday and Thursday milked the cows, while their father the General held the umbrella over them to keep off the rain . . . The General has to harness his own carriage horses and probably black his own boots."[16]

Fanny Andrews, the daughter of a Georgia Democratic planter, complained that "it seems humiliating to be compelled to bargain and haggle with our own servants about wages."[17] One gets the idea that the true source of her outrage wasn't the bargaining but rather that the slave-owner class, which previously got this labor for free, now had to pay for it. Such was the angst of the postbellum Democratic leisure class. And yet there was nothing they could do to get their old way of life back.

Sure, the Democrats in the South had some consolations. They had replaced slavery with sharecropping. Under the sharecropping system blacks still worked in the rice, tobacco, cane and cotton fields. Now they were wage laborers and in theory entitled to a share of the crop, typically one-third if the planter provided the implements and seed, one-half if the sharcroppers provided their own.[18]

Moreover, since sharecroppers lived on the plantation, owners found ways to impose charges on them for tools and living expenses that typically left them with little to call their own. Owners also controlled the freedom and, to some extent, the lives of their workers, who were also their tenants. So dependent were sharecroppers on their employers that some scholars have not hesitated to term sharecropping a form of "neo-slavery."

Still, sharecroppers were contract laborers. They were not actually slaves. However subjugated they were, they could round up their family and leave the plantation. So if sharecropping was to be part of the new Democratic plantation system, Democrats in the South would have to find ways to force sharecroppers to stay, no matter how onerous the conditions they faced. The great instrument for keeping the slaves on the old plantation—namely, the whip—was no longer available to the postbellum planter class.

Increasingly, Wilson and his fellow Democrats noticed the competitive threat posed by free blacks in the South. Partly this threat was economic—slaves who had developed practical skills were now in a position to compete with white laborers for employment. Part of it was cultural—free blacks could in theory intermingle socially with whites and even intermarry with them, while this had been unthinkable for slaves. Moreover, blacks posed a serious political threat to Democratic hegemony because, overjoyed at being freed by the Republicans, they were now overwhelmingly Republican in their loyalties.

The Democrats no longer had slavery to sustain the plantation, but they did have something else—they did have racism. Racism, after all, predated the slave plantation. It continued through the slave period. And it outlasted slavery, becoming in many respects stronger after emancipation than it had been before. Moreover, slavery had been confined to the South, at least in the nineteenth century, while racism seemed to be a potent force in the North no less than in the South.

These statements require clarification. Racism—specifically the belief in inherent black inferiority—dates back to the first European encounters with Africans in the early modern period. I have written about this in my book *The End of Racism*. Basically, Europeans could not account for the primitivism of black Africa entirely in environmental terms, and therefore blamed a good portion of it on inherent—and ultimately biological—inferiority. This perception of blacks as uncivilized and perhaps incapable of civilization—this original racism—was imported to America when Europeans settled this continent.

Slavery fortified racism and fostered an early version of white supremacy. It did so for the reason given by historian C. R. Boxer: "One race cannot systematically enslave members of another for centuries without acquiring a conscious or unconscious feeling of racial superiority."[19] The point is that unlike slavery in many other parts of the world, where slaves and slave-owners belonged to the same race, American slavery was racial slavery. Not all the slave-owners were white—there were also a few thousand black slave-owners in the South between the 1820s and 1860—but all the slaves on the Democratic plantations of the South were black.

Boxer's point is that when the slave-owners are white and the slaves are black, the whites will inevitably presume themselves suited to rule and the blacks suited to be ruled. The presumed logic goes like this: "We are on top and they are on the bottom; therefore, we must deserve to be on top and they must deserve to be on the bottom. We are naturally superior to them."

Here, then, is the original basis of entrenched white supremacy. But it took time for this self-consciousness to develop. That's why we see very few virulent denunciations of blacks, even in the South, during the founding period. Those emerged in the early nineteenth century as the plantation expanded and a political party arose in the 1820s that reflected the will and interest of the planter class. That's why I say that white supremacy is a creation of the Democratic master class.

This psychological rationalization for slavery then became corroborated by the wretched condition of the slaves. Even though this wretchedness was imposed by the Democratic slave-owner, who prevented his slaves from being educated and civilized, the planter would point to the wretchedness of black slaves as proof of their racial inferiority.

Yet racism was also tempered by slavery not only because the plantation system necessitated close and constant interactions between the slaves and the master class but also because slavery as an institution prevented open economic competition between whites and blacks. Both blacks and whites worked for the benefit of the white master class, and this pleased the masters just fine—as long as the slaves went along with the arrangement, there was no reason for the masters to direct racial hostility to the slaves. After slavery, however, the free blacks became a problem not merely in the economic sense but also in the political and cultural sense.

Wilson and the progressive Democrats observed what modern scholars have subsequently corroborated: there was more potent racism in America in the late nineteenth and early twentieth centuries than any time before or since. "Anti-black racism," historian George Fredrickson writes, "peaked in the period between the end of Reconstruction and the First World War."[20]

And in this sea of racism, Democrats thrived. They didn't have slavery, but they did have this. Moreover, slavery was an institution that could be abolished. The slaves could become free. But race, thankfully, for the Democrats, was unalterable. Blacks could not stop being black, or as Democratic pro-slavery apologist Thomas Roderick Dew once put it, "The Ethiopian cannot change his skin, nor the leopard his spots."[21]

The Democrats realized they could unify the white South by fomenting a shared hatred of blacks. Racism could not offer, as slavery did, the chance to extract free labor from blacks. But it did offer every white person, no matter how poor or ignorant, the chance to belong to an aristocracy of color, placing them above every black person, no matter how successful or educated.

Thus the Democratic formula became one of white supremacy and black suppression. The Democrats would fight to expand the franchise for whites while curtailing it for blacks. They would indulge white hatred by directing it against blacks, especially educated blacks whose very presence embarrassed racist theories of white supremacy. By cultivating racism, by nourishing it and by using it, the Democrats realized they could build an enduring foundation for a new type of plantation to replace the one that had been lost.

Consider the instrument that sustained the old plantation: the whip. The whip was the tool of force employed by the old Democratic planter class to get the slaves to the plantation, to keep them there, and to make them work. Wilson and his progressive Democrats realized that they needed something similar, a new whip if you will, a new instrument of force that would take these disorderly emancipated slaves and beat them back down, then keep them down, and ideally reduce the threat they posed by reducing their actual number in society.

At this point, in early 1915, who should walk through Wilson's door in the Oval Office but his old college friend Thomas Dixon, author of *The Clansman: An Historical Romance of the Ku Klux Klan.*

THOMAS DIXON'S PROGRESSIVE RACISM

Wilson and Dixon were buddies; they had attended Johns Hopkins University together. Today progressives call Dixon a "right-winger" on the basis of his Southern roots and racism, but by now we can recognize this as part of the big lie. The South was a Democratic stronghold and racism was virtually the official doctrine of the Democratic Party. Dixon had served in the North Carolina General Assembly as a Democrat. Moreover, Dixon was a self-described progressive associated with the social gospel movement. His slogan was, "Politics is religion in action."

In his early career, he had been an avowed socialist. A champion of the homeless, he was also an animal rights activist known for his opposition to hunting. He railed against capital punishment. Dixon's book *The Root of Evil* contains such a passionate denunciation against capitalism that his progressive biographer Anthony Slide remarks it "almost compensates for the worst excesses of racism to be found elsewhere in Dixon's writings."[22] That's how Wilson knew him, and their friendship was ideological no less than personal.

Legislator, lawyer, preacher, actor and author, Dixon also claimed be an expert on Reconstruction who had mastered, in his own words, four thousand volumes of American historical records. In 1902 he published the bestseller *The Leopard's Spots: A Romance of the White Man's Burden,* and followed it up with *The Clansman,* a lurid account of a Northern Republican who colludes with vicious, lustful blacks to persecute the South and violate its lovely maidens.

The villain of *The Clansman* is a character named Austin Stoneman, explicitly modeled on the Pennsylvania Republican abolitionist Wendell Phillips. The victims are ordinary, put-upon Southern Democrats who are just trying to get on with their lives when they are set upon by this predatory alliance of Republicans and Negroes. And the heroes of the book are the Night Riders of the Ku Klux Klan, who swoop down gallantly and overthrow the bad Republicans and Negroes, reestablishing a reign of virtue in the South.

Here is a sample passage by Dixon: "At night the hoof-beat of squadrons of pale horsemen and the crack of their revolvers struck terror into the heart of every Negro, carpet-bagger and scalawag." No wonder Dixon dedicated his book to the memory of "A Scotch-Irish leader of the South, My Uncle, Colonel Leroy McAtee, Grand Titan of the Ku Klux Klan."[23]

The Clansman was another publishing success, and Dixon even wrote a stage play based on it. But now, he told Wilson, the acclaimed Hollywood producer D. W. Griffith had turned the story into a powerful movie, *Birth of a Nation*. Dixon was right about this. The film is even today acknowledged to be a technical masterpiece, using the latest cinematic techniques to convert Dixon's literary melodrama into arresting scenes that build inexorably toward an explosive climax. Dixon wanted Wilson to screen the movie in the White House and invite his cabinet and other influential figures.

Progressive historical accounts of this meeting typically depict Wilson as the gullible fellow who went along with Dixon and Griffith's nefarious scheme. But Wilson was obviously too intelligent not to recognize the publicity that a screening would provide the new movie. It would be the first-ever film shown at the White House. I believe Wilson knew exactly what he was doing. Dixon promised that the film would "transform every man in my audience into a good Democrat," and this was exactly what Wilson had in mind.[24]

What Wilson may not have realized—I suspect he did realize it, but he may not have—is that the White House screening of *Birth of a Nation* would help to inspire a Klan rejuvenation. If Wilson didn't know it immediately, he surely knew it soon. That's because when the film opened in theaters, the nearby streets in several cities were filled with whites on horseback wearing full Ku Klux Klan regalia. More than three million people saw it in its first year. Many of them undoubtedly constituted the original membership of a revived Ku Klux Klan.[25]

Wilson's comment on seeing the film, according to Griffith, was simply, "It is like writing history with lightning" and that the events portrayed in the film were "all true." Wilson's progressive biographers attempt to distance Wilson from this quotation, since it does not appear in official records, yet there is no reason to believe Griffith made it up. Moreover, *Birth of a Nation* itself is laced with on-screen quotations taken directly from Wilson's writings and leave little doubt that his views were congruent with those expressed in the film.

The Klan revival that Wilson inspired was a national phenomenon that went far beyond the reach of the original Ku Klux Klan. It is not widely known—in part because progressive textbooks don't mention it—that the original Ku Klux Klan was a largely regional phenomenon, concentrated in nine Southern states. But Wilson helped inspire a second Ku Klux Klan that stretched from Maine to the Midwest to California. The new Klan had more members outside the South than within it. This was a Klan no less murderously terrorist than its earlier predecessor, but one that now stretched "from sea to shining sea."[26]

Once more, the Ku Klux Klan became the domestic terrorist arm of the Democratic Party, just as it had been in the nineteenth century. Again, whether Wilson foresaw this or not, this was what actually happened. And the Klan became just what Wilson and his progressive Democrats were searching for, an institutional whip used to beat blacks down and keep them from competing with whites for jobs, socializing with whites or—most important of all—voting Republican.

In her book *White Rage,* Carol Anderson describes the typical Klan murder. "One of the most macabre formats was a spectacle lynching which advertised the killing of a black person and provided special promotional trains to bring the audience, including women and children, to the slaughter. These gruesome events were standard family entertainment; severed body parts became souvenirs and decorations hung proudly in homes."[27]

As Anderson recognizes, the new Klan was different from its predecessor in some respects. The old Klansmen wore stilts under their robes to appear nine feet tall; the new Klan was distinguished by the white sheets and pointed hats. The old Klan didn't burn crosses; the new Klan got that idea from a climactic scene in Griffith's movie. The old Klan targeted blacks and white Republicans; the new Klan targeted blacks and also Catholics and Jews.

But murder for entertainment and political gain was a common feature of the old Klan and the new. And the one little detail Anderson leaves out is that these were murders typically organized in league with the local Democratic Party, with Democratic crowds in attendance, and conducted in large part to send a message to black Republican voters.

The Klan reached its zenith in the mid-1920s, when membership in the organization stood between three and five million. During this period the Klan controlled Democratic primaries in many states. At the 1924 Democratic National Convention, informally known as the Klanbake, Klansmen defeated a motion even to condemn KKK violence. After this, enrollment in the Klan declined, but not before it largely achieved its goal of suppressing blacks and in particular the black vote, thus keeping the Southern vote solidly white and solidly Democratic throughout the first half of the twentieth century.

And what happened to Thomas Dixon? Progressive accounts typically leave their discussions of him around 1915, the date *Birth of a Nation* was released. Dixon, however, went on to a prominent career as a writer and Democratic Party activist. He was a zealous campaigner for FDR in 1932, gave numerous speeches championing FDR's National Recovery Act—the signature program of the New Deal—and was rewarded by the FDR administration with an appointment as clerk of the United States Court, Eastern District of North Carolina. Although Dixon later soured on the New Deal, he retained his judicial position from 1938 to 1946, the year of his death.[28]

MAN IN A CAGE

Now that Wilson and the progressive Democrats had found a way to beat blacks down through racial intimidation and murder, they needed a way to keep them down. If racial terrorism suppressed the black vote, something was needed to insulate white Democrats from economic competition with blacks. Here the Democratic solution was state-sponsored segregation, imposed throughout the South between the 1890s and 1910. Segregation laws required blacks and whites to attend separate schools and use separate sections in buses, trains, theaters and churches, and even to drink out of separate water fountains in public places.

While state-sponsored segregation was a Southern phenomenon—giving some support to the progressive campaign to blame racial evils on the South—it should also be noted that every Southern segregation law was passed by a Democratic legislature, signed by a Democratic governor and enforced by Democratic officials. There are no exceptions to this rule. So segregation was the work of the Democratic Party in that region.

Wilson's contribution was to take segregation to the federal government. It is not widely recognized that prior to Wilson the federal government was not officially segregated. African Americans have successive Republican administrations going back to the Civil War to thank for that. Progressive scholars don't want Republicans to get the credit, so they downplay or leave this fact out of their textbooks. It remains a fact, nonetheless. Wilson, however, expanded racial segregation from its local Southern precincts to the nation's capital. From the Treasury Department to the post office, whites and blacks were required to eat separately and use separate bathrooms.

Somewhat comically, Du Bois in 1913 wrote an open letter to Wilson in which he complained about segregation. Du Bois wrote of "one colored clerk who could not actually be segregated on account of the nature of his work has consequently had a cage built around him to separate him from his white companions of many years."[29] Wilson did not respond, but Du Bois must have realized what his endorsement of Wilson and the Democrats had produced: blacks were now being put into cages!

Around the same time, a group of activists associated with Du Bois—most of them backers of Wilson in 1912—met with the president. Monroe Trotter, editor of the Boston *Guardian*, bitterly challenged Wilson on segregation. Wilson informed him that "segregation is not a humiliation but a benefit, and ought to be so regarded by you gentlemen." One may call this the positive-good argument for Democratic segregation. And with this ended Trotter and Du Bois' hopes of having a central role in administering Wilson's emerging Democratic plantation.

If racial terrorism and segregation are the first two elements of Wilson's progressive plantation, the third and final one involves what may be termed "race conservation." Race conservation has two elements: racially restrictive immigration laws and eugenic sterilization of the supposedly "unfit," mostly poor whites and racial minorities. Wilson supported both and saw them as closely connected. Immigration restrictions would keep the racial inferiors from getting into the country, and forced eugenic sterilization would prevent those who were already here from reproducing.

The Immigration Act of 1924 was actually signed after Wilson left office, but he and other progressives—most of them Democrats, but also some Republicans—had pushed for such measures for more than two decades. It may seem odd to find Republicans in this connection making common cause with Democrats, but we see that today also. The progressive Republicans were basically half Democrats, just like their counterparts now. Thus we would not be wrong to dub these early Republican progressives the original RINOs (Republicans in Name Only).

The racist rhetoric of progressive RINOs like Madison Grant and Lothrop Stoddard shows that progressivism of all stripes—even Republican progressivism—was imbued with racism. Stoddard and Grant were both close associates of Planned Parenthood founder Margaret Sanger; Stoddard served on the board of her Birth Control League. Grant was a well-known conservationist—a cofounder of the environmentalist movement—and his racism grew out of that: he believed that just as America conserved its natural resources, it should conserve its valuable racial stock by restricting both immigration and racial intermarriage.[30]

To some degree, the zeal of the progressives is not surprising. The early twentieth century unleashed a second wave of mass immigration, this time not from Ireland and Germany but largely from southern and eastern European countries. And with the arrival of these new people, the progressive doctrines of racism and white supremacy took a new and to some degree unexpected turn. Incredibly, the same racist progressives who had previously proclaimed blacks to be inferior now declared that these southern and eastern European whites were also inferior and their numbers should be minimized.

White supremacy now became Nordic supremacy, and progressives distinguished between the superior Nordics and inferior Alpine and Mediterranean types. In order to demonstrate how America was being infested by immigrants, a Carnegie Institution report offered, as its main illustration "The Parallel Case of the House Rat," which traced rodent infestation from Europe to the ability of rats to make their way to America "in sailing ships."[31]

No doubt fearing economic competition from new workers willing to do the same job for less, unions were at the forefront of the movement to exclude immigrants. The socialist leader Eugene Debs accused "the Dago" of underbidding union workers by living even more "like a savage or a wild beast" than the hated Chinese immigrant.[32] For progressives in those days, blacks were niggers, Mexicans were wetbacks, Asians were chinks, Italians were wops and dagos, and all those people deserved to be kept out of America or prevented from reproducing.

Wilson was fully on board. In his last volume of the *History of the American People,* published in 1902, Wilson warns that America is faced with the threat of being flooded by "men from the lowest class from the south of Italy and men of the meaner sort out of Hungary and Poland." These undesirables, Wilson argues, are part of a great wave of undesirables from southern and eastern European countries that are "disburdening themselves of the more sordid and hapless elements of their population."[33]

Wilson left little doubt he thought the wave should be stopped, and in 1924 it was. The Immigration Act of that year was explicitly cast in racial terms. It essentially banned immigration to America from South Asia, the Middle East and the Far East. It severely restricted the immigration of Catholics and Jews from southern and eastern Europe by imposing national origin quotas equivalent to 2 percent of each nationality's population in the United States in 1890. For fifty years, from 1924 through 1965, progressives essentially shut the door on immigration on the basis of white supremacy.

Wilson was also a pioneer in the area of progressive eugenic sterilization. In 1911, as governor of New Jersey, he signed into law one of America's first forced-sterilization laws. The law created a "Board of Examiners of Feebleminded, Epileptics and Other Defectives" charged with determining whether prisoners and those residing in poorhouses and other charitable institutions should be coercively sterilized. Through progressive prodding, eventually some twenty-seven states enacted similar forced-sterilization laws, and some 65,000 Americans were prevented, against their will, from reproducing.

THE PROGRESSIVE ROOTS OF NAZISM

I cannot conclude this chapter without pointing out that three of the schemes of the progressive plantation—race-based immigration restriction, racial segregation and forced sterilization—provided models for the Nazi Party in the early 1930s. Hitler himself praised progressive immigration restrictions in America, noting that "by simply excluding certain races from naturalization" they displayed "in slow beginnings" Hitler's own move toward the Nazi idea of a racially supremacist state.

Hitler also praised antimiscegenation laws championed by American progressives. "The Germanic inhabitant of the American continent," he wrote in *Mein Kampf*, "who has remained racially pure and unmixed, rose to be master of the continent; he will remain the master as long as he does not fall victim to the defilement of the blood."[34]

James Whitman shows in *Hitler's American Model* that the Nazis explicitly modeled their Nuremberg Laws—laws that segregated Jews into ghettos, prevented them from intermarrying with other Germans and excluded them from citizenship—on the Jim Crow laws of the Democratic South. Whitman's documentation is thorough. He even has the records of the Nuremberg meetings, showing how the Nazis basically took the Democratic laws, crossed out the word "black," wrote in the word "Jew" and had their work largely done for them. In the crushing words of Roland Freisler, state secretary of the Nazi Ministry of Justice, surveying the Democratic segregation and state-sponsored discrimination laws, "This jurisprudence would suit us perfectly."[35]

Here was the actual scene. A senior group of Nazis is gathered around a table, with a stenographer present, to record what one of them termed a historic occasion: they were in the process of founding the world's first racist state. Then one of the Nazis, Heinrich Krieger, who studied in the United States, sheepishly raised his hand and informed his colleagues that they could not do this because the Democratic Party in the United States had beaten them to it.

The Nazis were incredulous. But Krieger was right. The Nazis wanted to segregate Jews into ghettos, and the Southern Democrats had already done this. The Nazis wanted to prevent intermarriage between Jews and other Germans; this mirrored what miscegenation laws passed mostly by Democrats did in many American states. Finally, the Nazis wanted state-sponsored discrimination that would permit confiscation of Jewish property; precisely this type of state-sponsored discrimination was the norm throughout the Democratic South.

So the Nazis reviewed the Democratic laws of the Jim Crow South and framed their Nuremberg Laws specifically on them. In doing so the Nazis knew full well they were adapting the policies of the Democrats. Yet tellingly there is no textbook in the United States to my knowledge that describes this Nazi-Democratic connection. Never once has CNN or NPR or the History Channel documented the role of the Democratic Party in shaping Nazi racism.

Whitman, a progressive legal scholar, is also reluctant to assign blame where it is due. He talks about "American white supremacy," "American racism," "American law" and "American influence on the Nuremberg Laws."[36] Surely he knows that the Democratic laws were bitterly contested under the nation's two-party system. Yes, there were antimiscegenation laws in a couple of Republican states, but America in general didn't do this; the Democrats did. Yet as the very title of Whitman's book suggests, he resorts to the familiar tactic of blaming America—not the Democratic Party—for inspiring Nazi policies.

Much in the same vein, the German historian Stefan Kuhl, whom I interviewed in Munich, shows in *The Nazi Connection* that Hitler's forced-sterilization policies of 1933 were lifted almost verbatim from blueprints supplied earlier in the century by American progressive eugenicists. Under the Nazis, forced sterilization gave way to compulsory euthanasia for the sick and disabled, and later those same killing facilities were expanded into the gas chambers that were used for Hitler's "final solution."

Did American progressives know that they had shaped Hitler's policies? Kuhl shows they certainly did. In fact they "understood Nazi policies as the direct realization of their scientific goals and political demands." In 1934 Leon Whitney, secretary of the American Eugenics Society, confessed that American progressive eugenicists "have long been working earnestly toward something very like what Hitler has now made compulsory."

Kuhl reports that Clarence Campbell, another close associate of Planned Parenthood founder Margaret Sanger, attended the 1935 International Population Congress in Berlin, where he raised a toast "to that great leader, Adolf Hitler!" Sanger herself gave speeches in the mid-1930s praising the Nazi sterilization laws and recommending that America move faster in this direction to keep up with what Hitler had done.[37]

A progressive himself, Kuhl knows how damning it is to trace Nazi sterilization and mass murder to the inspiration of American progressives. Thus, to spread the blame around, he insists that the responsibility for these atrocities falls equally on the left and on the right. Kuhl declares it ironic that a progressive Democrat like Woodrow Wilson and an avowed socialist like Margaret Sanger inspired the "right-wing" Nazis. But there is no irony involved because, as I'll show in the next chapter, the Nazis were themselves left-wing socialists with an ideological agenda closely parallel to that of their American progressive counterparts.

In the end, Wilson's progressive plantation—the centralized state—remained an incomplete project. The conditions weren't right, and Wilson himself was too much of a pointy-headed intellectual to get it done. The distinctive racist elements of Wilson's plantation—racial terrorism, federal segregation and eugenic sterilization—would eventually become a progressive embarrassment. Yet they would be retained, in modified and more palatable form, in the Democratic plantation scheme as it evolved in the 1930s and beyond.

It would require more propitious circumstances—ideally a major crisis of some sort—to make that plantation scheme a reality. It would take another Democrat with the same tyrannical impulse as Wilson, but less educated and more cunning, to get the job done. Such a man would have to be a creative improviser of the Van Buren type, but even more unscrupulous, a mafia boss unhampered by conscience. Only such a man could achieve the practical realization of the progressive plantation. In New York, there was such a man.

7

THE STATE AS BIG HOUSE

What FDR Learned from
Fascism and Nazism

If Fascism ever comes to America,
it will be in the name of Liberalism.

—RONALD REAGAN,
60 Minutes interview, 1975[1]

In 1935, Sinclair Lewis published a novel, *It Can't Happen Here,* which envisioned the coming to power of a fascist regime in the United States. Little did Lewis, progressive leftist and former socialist, know that even while he was writing the book, the administration of President Franklin Delano Roosevelt was consciously importing fascist ideas to America.

Lewis of course knew that American fascism would not be identical with Italian or German fascism. It would not feature swastikas or "Deutschland Uber Alles"; it would be built on homegrown symbols and take on a uniquely American character. Even so, Lewis completely missed what was happening in front of him because he could not see the fascist elements on his own ideological side.

This chapter is about FDR and the fascist plantation. In it I will show that during the 1920s and 1930s, the Italian fascists under Mussolini and the German fascists under Hitler developed a new type of plantation governed by the all-powerful, centralized state. FDR then imported that fascist model to America, modifying it into a shape that was distinctively American. FDR created what we may call democratic fascism, fascism that could win popular support and sustain the president in office for four terms. In the process FDR permanently transformed the Democratic Party and remade the Democratic plantation.

FDR's fascist plantation is not merely recognizable in its key elements; it also supplies the basic operational template for today's Democratic Party. I recognize that for many people the very notion of a fascist plantation will come as a surprise. Fascism is a European ideology; what does it have to do with the plantation system of American slavery?

An even bigger surprise is the notion that an American president—indeed the leading progressive figure of his time—was actually influenced by fascism, let alone that he emulated the fascist leaders that he is famous for fighting and defeating in World War II. Some progressive Democrats won't just take issue—they will take umbrage—at my attempt to link FDR with the fascist and Nazi horrors of the twentieth century.

Hitler, however, was quite familiar with the slave plantation. The progressive historian Ira Katznelson writes, "Hitler denigrated blacks, admired American racism, and regretted the South's defeat in 1865." Hitler also hated Lincoln and blamed him for how "the beginnings of a great new social order based on the principle of slavery and inequality were destroyed by the war."[2]

Many scholars have noted the similarities between Nazi concentration camps and slave camps of the Democratic South. I grant that it seems wrongheaded, even obscene, to compare death camps where millions died to Democratic slave plantations. The former existed for the purpose of extermination; the latter for forced labor. The two are not morally equivalent.

I agree, and I am not making such a comparison. The perception that I am rests on a failure to distinguish between Nazi concentration camps and Nazi death camps. From Dachau to Mauthausen to Ravensbruck, there were hundreds of concentration camps throughout Germany and in German-occupied territories. By contrast, there were just a few death camps—Auschwitz, Belzec, Chelmno, Treblinka, Majdanek and Sobibor—and none of them were located in Germany.

The typical concentration camp was not a death camp. It had no gas chambers. "The vast majority of Jews killed in the Holocaust," Timothy Snyder writes, "never saw a concentration camp." Nazi concentration camps included Jews, but the majority of the captives were Russians and eastern Europeans. These were labor camps, just like the Democratic slave camps. They put between eight and twelve million people to work to serve the Nazi state, especially the Nazi armaments industry. Studies by German scholars of this topic bear titles like *Hitler's Slaves* and *Slave Labor in Nazi Concentration Camps*.[3]

In his study of concentration camps, Wolfgang Sofsky notes that slave camps and Nazi concentration camps were both forced-labor systems in which the captives received no compensation for their labor and masters had virtually unlimited power over them, not merely their work conditions but their lives. The prisoners, in both cases, were reduced to complete and vulnerable dependency. Masters in both cases could compel their captives to "work without a break, beat them, torment them, or hound them to death."

Remarkably, the captives in forced-labor systems all display similar characteristics. Sofsky describes the work routine for Nazi captives: "For the prisoner, putting on the brakes was the supreme dictate. Work tempo was reduced to a minimum as soon as the guards or Kapo were out of sight. When the superior returned, prisoners did their utmost to appear as if they were working at a brisk pace." Replace the term "kapo" with "planter" or "overseer" and Sofsky could be describing a Democratic slave plantation in Virginia or South Carolina.

What protected the slave, to a certain degree, Sofsky argues, was his or her status as property. "The slave has a value and a going market price. The master does not acquire slaves in order to kill them but to put them to work for the master's benefit . . . As barbaric as the owners often were in dealing with their slaves, the death of a slave was a loss." By contrast, the Nazi prisoners "were not the personal property of masters but the inmates of an institution. They belonged to no one." Thus if they were killed, no one cared.

Sofsky also notes that both the slave camps and the Nazi camps were systems based on racial classification. Slavery of course drew a sharp racial line between the typically white slave-owner and the black slave. In the Nazi camps, there was a variety of inferior groups, each of which wore a distinguishing badge. Criminals wore a green badge, nonconformists or "asocials" a black badge, political dissidents a red triangle, foreigners a red triangle with their nationality marked on it, gypsies brown triangles, and Jews the Star of David.[4]

The close connection between Democratic plantations and Nazi labor camps was noted in the early 1970s by progressive historian Stanley Elkins, who pointed out that both the slave plantation and the concentration camp were closed systems, cut off from the larger society. Consequently, he argued, they generated similar types of dysfunctional personalities.

Essentially Elkins argues that the captives internalized their systems of oppression. Jewish kapos served the Nazi machine just as black overseers served the Democratic planters. Even those who did not become part of the regime of oppression found their moral personality disfigured. As a survival mechanism, concentration camp victims developed submissive stereotypical patterns of behavior that were also regularly observed on the slave plantation—the so-called Sambo syndrome.[5]

Moreover, where did Hitler get his idea for reducing Russians, Poles and eastern Europeans to slavery? According to progressive historian Timothy Snyder, he got it from the Jacksonian Democrats of the nineteenth century. Hitler's initial plan had been for Germany to undertake colonial expeditions similar to those of the French and the British. Hitler realized, however, that most of the valuable real estate in Asia, Africa and South America had already been taken. German colonial opportunities in the early twentieth century were very limited.

Then Hitler remembered what Andrew Jackson and his successors did to the American Indians. Jackson's Indian Removal Act had driven tens of thousands of Indians—the Chickasaw, the Choctaw, the Creek and the Seminole—out of their ancestral homes, forcing them to relocate farther west. When the Cherokee resisted, they were forcibly removed, leading to the infamous Trail of Tears. In Hitler's own summary, Americans had "gunned down the millions of Redskins to a few hundred thousand, and now keep the modest remnant under observation in a cage."[6]

This gave Hitler a new idea. Why bother to conquer in Asia and Africa when he could conquer the natives in Europe itself? Hitler's plan was to emulate the Jacksonian Democrats in driving the Russians, the Poles and the eastern Europeans from their homes. They would be forced to relocate elsewhere. The ones who resisted would be killed. The ones who stayed would be enslaved and sent to German labor camps.

Hitler's scheme was called Generalplan Ost. Snyder reports that the Nazis sought to "deport, kill, assimilate, or enslave" some thirty to forty-five million people. They planned to create, on their land, small German farming communities. Snyder writes, "Colonization would make of Germany a continental empire fit to rival the United States, another hardy frontier state based on exterminatory colonialism and slave labor . . . As Hitler imagined the future, Germany would deal with the Slavs much as the North Americans had dealt with the Indians. The Volga River in Russia, he once proclaimed, will be Germany's Mississippi."[7]

Hitler, interestingly enough, was also a fan of the Ku Klux Klan. "He seemed to think it was a political movement similar to his own," reports Ernst Hanfstaengl, a friend of Hitler's who also served as his head of the Foreign Press Bureau.[8] Hitler appears to have recognized, as Woodrow Wilson did before him, that if the centralized state were to serve as a new type of Big House, administering a new type of state-run plantation, then it too would require an organization to serve as a kind of whip, to keep the subjugated people in line.

Hitler was undoubtedly aware of the close parallels between the Klan and the Nazi Brownshirts, because many Germans and American observers noted them at the time. At their peak, both groups had three to four million members. Both were paramilitary organizations that practiced racial terrorism. Both targeted racial minorities, in one case blacks, in the other, Jews. And both were extensions of a political party, the Klan of the Democratic Party, the Brownshirts of the Nazi Party.

Thus the concept of a fascist plantation is hardly far-fetched.

FDR AND THE KKK

FDR's relationship to fascism, however, requires a little introduction. FDR was obviously not a racial nationalist like Hitler, but he did maintain a fairly close relationship with racially nationalist groups in America. Since we are discussing the Klan, it may be useful to begin with FDR's close connection with Woodrow Wilson, the progressive Democrat largely responsible for the nationwide revival of the Klan. FDR, of course, served as navy secretary in the Wilson administration. Not once during his tenure did he criticize Wilson's KKK affinities and racist policies or indicate the slightest discomfort with them.

Yet progressives who distance themselves from Wilson—or at least from the racist side of Wilson—never distance themselves from FDR. FDR remains the great progressive hero, routinely invoked by Democrats today as their inspiration and ideal. FDR's progressive biographers such as Arthur Schlesinger Jr., William Leuchtenburg and Robert Dallek speak of him in hagiographical terms, leaving little doubt they consider him one of America's greatest—if not the greatest—president. Except for a brief, throat-clearing reference to FDR's internment of Japanese Americans, seemingly explained by the exigencies of war, little or nothing is said about FDR's racist ties or the racist policies of the FDR administration.

Yet although his ties were obviously less direct than Wilson's, FDR had a much closer association with the Ku Klux Klan than any of his biographers are willing to admit. His successor, Harry Truman, was briefly a member of the Klan. Progressives who credit Truman with desegregating the armed forces rarely mention this. If they do, they insist that Truman wasn't a racist; he was merely anti-Catholic. This is the same Truman who wrote his future wife Bess, "I think one man is just as good as another so long as he's honest and decent and not a nigger or a Chinaman."

Truman added, "Uncle Will says that the Lord made a white man from dust, a nigger from mud, then He threw up what was left and it came down a Chinaman. He does hate Chinese and Japs. So do I . . . I am strongly of the opinion that Negroes ought to be in Africa, yellow men in Asia, and white men in Europe and America." As late as 1963, Truman in a newspaper interview asked a reporter, "Would you want your daughter to marry a Negro?"[9]

One of FDR's closest political allies and most enthusiastic supporters in the Senate was Mississippi Democrat Theodore Bilbo, the state's leading progressive. Bilbo campaigned for FDR in 1932, and FDR returned the favor, helping Bilbo to win a Senate seat in 1934. In 1940, when Bilbo won reelection, FDR proclaimed him "a real friend of liberal government," and Bilbo routinely characterized himself as "100 percent for Roosevelt and the New Deal."

A longtime member of the Ku Klux Klan, Bilbo championed its agenda of segregation and resistance to racial intermarriage, which he termed "mongrelization." He tried, albeit unsuccessfully, to segregate the national parks and publicly defended lynching as a necessary punishment for "Negro rapists." Bilbo served twelve years in the Senate, from 1935 to 1947. During that time, FDR worked closely with him, not merely on New Deal initiatives but also to resist racial integration in the armed forces and to suppress antilynching legislation.[10]

In the House of Representatives, FDR relied on a whole constellation of racist Democrats to push through his agenda, notably Texas Democrat Sam Rayburn, who would become Speaker of the House. Rayburn campaigned for FDR and against Hoover on the grounds that Hoover sought "to abolish segregation and promote a deal with Negroes." What he liked about FDR presumably was that he was for segregation and against finding common ground with blacks.

Rayburn was an avid segregationist who explained to an audience at First Baptist Church in Bonham, Texas, in 1928 why he could never be a Republican. "I will never vote for the electors of a Party which sent the carpetbagger and the scalawag to the prostrate South with saber and sword to crush the white civilization to the earth."[11] This same Rayburn was a critical progressive ally not only of FDR but also his Democratic successors Truman and later Lyndon Johnson.

FDR also nominated longtime Klan member Hugo Black, an Alabama Democrat, to the Supreme Court. Black had altered his resume to camouflage his Klan association. Yet Black's Klan ties were well known. His law partner Crampton Harris, the cyclops of the Birmingham Klan, had initiated Black into the organization. Black became an active member, marching in parades and addressing Klan rallies throughout Alabama.

When Black ran for Senate as a Democrat in 1926, he had the Klan's endorsement, and his election was celebrated by the Klan in a ceremony attended by Imperial Wizard Hiram Evans, who presented Black with a gold-engraved lifetime passport to the Invisible Empire of the Klan. When all of this was exposed in the *Pittsburgh Post* following Black's confirmation to the Court, Black protested that he had merely joined the Klan to advance his career. "The Klan," he said, "was in effect the underground Democratic Party in Alabama."[12]

This statement is both true and telling. Many years later, Bill Clinton would say something very similar about another Democratic Klansman, Harry Byrd, who went on to become Senate majority leader and mentor to Bill and Hillary Clinton. Bill Clinton undertook to explain why Americans should not be too hard on Byrd for his "fleeting association" with the Klan. Byrd's association was hardly fleeting, but we'll let that pass. "What does that mean?" Clinton thundered. "I'll tell you what it means. He was a country boy from the hills and hollows of West Virginia. He was trying to get elected."[13] In other words, you simply had to be in the Klan in those days to advance in the Democratic Party.

Ever the consummate political dissembler, FDR pretended he had no idea that Black had been in the Klan. But even FDR's progressive biographer Robert Dallek, a sycophantic admirer if there ever was one, admits that "in choosing Black, there seems little question that Roosevelt was aware of his Klan membership and that his election to the Senate had partly required Klan support."[14]

Many years later, Black himself put the matter to rest in a 1968 memo. "President Roosevelt told me," he said, "there was no reason for my worrying about having been a member of the Ku Klux Klan. He said that some of his best friends and supporters were strong members of that organization. He never in any way, by word or attitude, indicated any doubt about my having been in the Klan nor did he indicate any criticism of me for having been a member of that organization."[15]

A FASCIST SUPERHERO

Notice that the Klan connections of these leading progressive Democrats are much more recent than those of, say, Confederate general Nathan Bedford Forrest, a founder of the nineteenth-century Klan. Yet Forrest's statues are torn down by progressives while FDR's are left standing. In fact, there is no indication on the part of left-wing monument destroyers that they are even ambivalent about FDR's racist legacy.

The same applies to Harry Truman, Hugo Black, Sam Rayburn and Robert Byrd. No one to date has called for the renaming of the Rayburn House Office Building in Washington, D.C. A good deal of

West Virginia is named after Robert Byrd: highways, schools, medical centers and so on. They are all given a pass by progressive activists. Apparently it's just fine to have served or worked with the Ku Klux Klan as long as you are a progressive Democrat.

In fairness, many of the Black Lives Matter and Antifa thugs who pull down monuments probably have no idea about FDR's connection to Black, or Black's deep ties to the Klan. Here we are back to the big lies of omission, the systematic progressive erasure of important events and associations to hide the complicity of big-name progressives in the worst crimes of American history. As we will see in this chapter, few people have benefited more from this left-wing cover-up than FDR.

FDR's reputation remains that of the indefatigable hero of the Depression and World War II, famously associated with the phrase "The only thing we have to fear is fear itself." I have never understood the appeal of this idiotic phrase. Imagine going to a hospital to be treated for a serious, life-threatening illness and being informed by the person in charge that "the only thing you have to fear is fear itself."

Au contraire, dummy. The only thing I have to fear is the sickness that's killing me. The fear is a natural, reasonable response to that. Fear during the Depression was fear of bankruptcy, of joblessness and starvation and total ruin. It was rational fear. The only way to remove the fear was to remove the underlying cause of the fear.

This FDR did not do; the Depression continued through all his four terms in office. In the decade of the 1930s, industrial production and national income fell by almost one-third. Historians now agree that it only ended with World War II and the manufacturing boom of the late 1940s and 1950s. Even so, just four years after he first used the phrase, FDR in his 1936 renomination speech recalled, "In those days, we feared fear. That was why we fought fear. And today, my friends, we have conquered fear."[16]

This is capital stuff, reminiscent of Peter Sellers in the movie *Being There*. Sellers plays Chance, a gardener who utters pedestrian banalities and absurdities, mostly drawing on an analogy to gardening. Yet these enigmatic pronouncements are hailed by the elite as profundities. So too with FDR, who is routinely celebrated by progressives for profundities that are not profound and for doing things that he manifestly did not do.

As I mentioned earlier, FDR deserves no credit for ending the Great Depression. I will acknowledge his role in leading the American fight against the fascists and Nazis during World War II. The soldiers and those aiding the war effort turned the tide against the enemy. The Red Army too played a critical role in defeating the Axis powers. Even so, FDR's wartime leadership undoubtedly accelerated Germany's final defeat.

Yet it must also be admitted that these later developments of the 1940s have helped progressives to conceal FDR's much friendlier and indeed more intimate relationship to fascism and Nazism in the previous decade. In truth, FDR admired Mussolini and embraced fascist principles that had been implemented both in Italy by Mussolini and in Germany by Hitler. For their part, in the early 1930s, the Italian and German fascists praised Mussolini and the New Deal. FDR and the fascists were part of a mutual admiration society.

Showing these connections is telling enough. But in order to go further, we need to make a searching examination of the true meaning of fascism. We need to understand how FDR's New Deal drew on the formulas of Italian fascism, how FDR like Hitler appealed to envy and hatred of successful entrepreneurs in order to mobilize political action against them, how fascist concepts like *Gleichschaltung*—which basically means political correctness—were embraced by progressives and how fascist economic policy is at the core of the progressive Democratic plantation even today.

True, Wilson envisioned the progressive plantation long before FDR. But FDR deserves credit—or, more precisely, blame—for the fascist plantation. Wilson cannot be held responsible for it because he preceded Mussolini and Hitler; consequently, there is no way he could have had these fascist dictators as models. FDR did learn from both of them, and moreover, like Mussolini and Hitler, he had the economic catastrophe of the Great Depression to justify moving his country in a direction that the people would never ordinarily want to go.

One way to see how FDR embraced Nazi policies is to consider the distinctive fascist approach to economic policy followed by Mussolini as well as Hitler. The fascists were socialists but not in the Marxist way. Their national socialism did not involve nationalization of industry or worker control of various industries. Rather, it involved government control of the major sectors of the private economy. Fascism is state-directed capitalism.

This became FDR's approach, and subsequent generations of progressive Democrats have made it their own. As we will see, the New Deal's signature initiative, the National Recovery Act, was explicitly modeled on fascism and administered by an FDR man who was a devotee of Mussolini. FDR's closest advisers like Rexford Tugwell openly praised fascism, which they recognized as leftist and which they considered more progressive than the New Deal.

Fascism's influence on the New Deal was recognized by contemporaries such as Herbert Hoover, who warned, "If we continue down this New Deal Road, ours can become some sort of Fascist government."[17] Reagan too, in the quotation that opens this chapter, knew from his youth the close nexus between fascism and American progressivism. Imagine what Hoover and Reagan would have said had they lived to see how much these fascist roots have blossomed among Democrats in our own time.

Case in point: Obamacare. Already I can envision the progressive eruption. "So what precisely is fascist about Obamacare?" Look at the way that Obama greatly increased government control not only over healthcare—every hospital, every doctor, every health insurance company—but also over the financial sector—every bank, every investment house—and increasingly over the energy, automobile and education sectors as well. Obama didn't nationalize these industries in the typical socialist mode, nor did he give workers control over the means of production, as Marx advocated.

Rather, he extended government control over these major sectors of the economy, giving him the power in 2009 to fire Rick Wagoner, the CEO of General Motors, or to direct health insurance companies on whom to cover and on what terms. Obama blithely went down this road—it never occurred to him to go down any other road—and whether he knew it or not, he used the fascist model of state-directed capitalism that has come down to him and to the Democratic Party from FDR.

FDR got some other big things from the Nazis—the politics of class hatred and enforced cultural conformity—and I'll get to them. But I also want to highlight that there is one big thing FDR did not share with Hitler and Mussolini. They were dictators, and he was not. Admittedly FDR had dictatorial instincts. Some leading progressives like Walter Lippmann in complete seriousness urged FDR to assume dictatorial powers. To his credit, FDR declined, but at times he moved in a dictatorial direction, as when he tried to stack the Supreme Court and thus subvert the institution of an independent judiciary.

But in general FDR remained the elected leader of a constitutional democracy. This meant that, unlike Mussolini and Hitler, FDR had to build a political coalition to get himself reelected. He had to build Democratic constituencies for his fascist agenda, which meant he had to invent a peculiarly American brand of fascism. He did this by abandoning the old Van Buren strategy of mobilizing urban plantations, each run by a big-city boss, and replacing this decentralized Tammany model with a new model of a single national plantation with the White House as the Big House and the president as Massa.

This FDR model has proven both politically successful and extremely attractive to progressive seekers of power. Here, after all, is a chance to be Massa, not of a single plantation, as in the days of old, but of an American plantation. Who said that exploitation can't be fun? LBJ, Bill Clinton and Obama all adopted FDR's model in enthusiastic succession. And how each of them has enjoyed being Massa, including Obama, the first African American inhabitant of the Democratic Big House.

FDR saw himself as a kind of fascist superhero, not in the Hitler mode but in the Mussolini mode. But even before the end of World War II, even prior to U.S. troops entering the concentration camps, FDR knew how Americans had come to view fascism and Nazism and that he had to bury his past associations with both. Fascism had become politically radioactive. So FDR himself began the project that progressives have continued ever since, one of burying and entombing their own idolization of the fascist project.

At the same time, progressives began to redefine fascism and Nazism in such a way that they could project these evils onto the right, so that future generations would be bamboozled into thinking that the Republicans, not the Democrats, the conservatives, not the progressives, were in bed with Mussolini and Hitler in the critical decades leading up to global war and Holocaust. The big lie about race thus expands to incorporate a big lie about fascism and Nazism.

HOW THE NAZIS VIEWED FDR

Very few people today, either on the left or on the right, seem to know precisely what fascism means. We can see this from the examples I cited earlier of how the progressive left routinely portrays Trump as a fascist and Republicans who support him as a kind of neo-Nazi party. Trump is said to be a fascist because he is an authoritarian, an ultra-nationalist and a racist who derides Mexicans and Muslims and seeks to keep them out of this country. Doesn't Trump say he wants to "make America great again" in precisely the same tone that Hitler promised to make Germany great again?

Actually, no. As I showed in *The Big Lie,* fascists aren't merely authoritarians. We've seen dictators around the world for more than a century, from Idi Amin to Ferdinand Marcos to Pol Pot; obviously these rulers were not all fascists. Moreover, Trump is not an authoritarian. If he were, would he permit himself to be flayed across all platforms in every form of media, from the daily news to the commentators to the late-night comedians? Mussolini and Hitler would have dispatched their goons and shut those people down overnight.

Trump's alleged racism arises out of his views on immigration. I mentioned earlier how Trump's distinguishing line is not a racial one; rather, it is between legal and illegal immigrants. Admittedly, Trump has said he wants to change immigration laws to restrict immigrants who come merely through "chain migration" via the so-called family unification provision. Trump wants to admit more productive immigrants, but he includes in this definition capable Indian engineers and software guys.

In any other country Trump's proposal would be unremarkable. Most countries that take immigrants do so on the basis of national self-interest. If Canada and Australia need more doctors and nurses, they open their doors to more doctors and nurses. They understand that, even under the liberal theory of the social contract, there is no "right to immigrate"; immigration is a pact between those who want to move to another country and the people of that country who want to have them. Whatever you think of Trump's view on immigration, it is not racist.

Trump's nationalism is nothing more than traditional American patriotism, surrounded by the familiar symbols of the flag, the anthem and soldiers' graves. It should be emphasized that nationalism is not a distinguishing feature of fascism or Nazism. To take a few examples, Gandhi was a nationalist, as was Mandela. Other anticolonial leaders were, to a man, nationalists. Winston Churchill was a nationalist, as was de Gaulle. The American founders were nationalists, and so was Lincoln. It makes no sense to call all these people fascist.

Moreover, Mussolini and Hitler were not nationalists in the traditional or Trumpian sense. Mussolini once reviled the Italian flag as a "rag" to be "planted on a dung hill." Traditional patriotism, Mussolini wrote, was a scheme for the capitalist class—the bourgeoisie—to win the loyalty of the people and protect its class privileges.[18] Mussolini resolved to "remake" Italy much as Obama in 2008 resolved to remake America. Mussolini's allegiance was never to the nation in general but only to a fascist conception of the nation.

Hitler too emphasized he was not a patriot, because patriotism, as he understood it, involved affirming the ideas, institutions and rituals of an existing society. Like Mussolini, Hitler sought to overthrow that society and replace it with something entirely new. His loyalty was neither to traditional Wilhelmine Germany nor to Weimar Germany, both of which he viewed as decadent. Hitler's dedication was only to his own futuristic ideal of what he termed the *Volkish* or fascist state.

Perhaps the strongest evidence for Trump's fascism and neo-Nazism is that self-styled fascists or neo-Nazis today have been seen shouting Trump slogans and wearing Trump hats. I examine this phenomenon in a later chapter. But here I want to focus not on neo-Nazis but on real Nazis. A neo-Nazi, after all, is a Nazi wannabe. Hitler admirers circa 2018 are not the same as the people who actually served Hitler and administered the fascist state with all its attendant horrors. Whom did those people—including the fascist leaders Hitler and Mussolini themselves—support on this side of the Atlantic?

Mussolini, it turns out, was an admirer of Franklin Roosevelt. Historian Stanley Payne writes in *A Short History of Fascism* that initially Mussolini thought better of FDR than of Hitler. Mussolini condescended toward Hitler at their first meetings and only changed his view after Hitler's successful conquests. But he was positively disposed to FDR from the outset "and the Duce and Roosevelt established personal contact even before Roosevelt was inaugurated."[19]

Shortly after FDR unveiled the early programs of the New Deal, Mussolini reviewed his book *Looking Forward* in an Italian magazine. Mussolini concluded that FDR's policies and outlook were "reminiscent of the ways and means by which Fascism awakened the Italian people." Adopting a ponderous tone, Mussolini wrote, "The question is often asked in America and in Europe just how much Fascism the American president's program contains."

Mussolini's answer: a lot. Fascism, Mussolini said, "is the principle that the state no longer leaves the economy to its own devices." Terming the New Deal "boldly interventionist," Mussolini identified as its main goal replacing America's free-market economy with an economy controlled and regulated by the centralized state. FDR, Mussolini concluded, was moving his country in the direction of national socialism, and "without question the mood accompanying this sea change resembles that of Fascism."[20]

Around the same time, the official Nazi newspaper *Volkischer Beobachter* provided its views of America's new president. "We too as German National Socialists are looking toward America." FDR, the Nazi publication said, was replacing "the uninhibited frenzy of market speculation" of the 1920s with the "adoption of National Socialist strains of thought in his economic and social policies." Of his policies the paper concluded, "We fear only the possibility that they might fail."

On another occasion, the *Volkischer Beobachter* examined FDR's leadership style, which it found comparable to Hitler's own dictatorial style or *Fuhrerprinzip*. Returning to FDR's New Deal policies, the Nazi paper noted that "if not always in the same words," FDR too "demands that collective good be put before individual self-interest. Many passages in his book could have been written by a National Socialist. In any case, one can assume he feels considerable affinity with the National Socialist Philosophy."[21]

I get these quotations from historian John Patrick Diggins' *Mussolini and Fascism*, published in 1972 and virtually unknown today, and also from the German historian Wolfgang Schivelbusch's equally obscure study *Three New Deals.* Not a single prominent FDR biography or progressive history of the period gives us the scoop on fascist and Nazi enthusiasm for FDR. Even Ira Katznelson's admirable recent study *Fear Itself*—the most honest progressive treatment of the links between the New Deal and fascism—artfully leaves out the most incriminating quotations.

So the whole subject of fascism and Nazism is surrounded today by a thick vapor of vagueness and obfuscation. Young progressives go around screaming about fascism and Nazism even though they have no idea what fascists and Nazis actually believed. We cannot fault them; they cannot find this information in their standard textbooks or in the general media. This darkness—this mirror of concealment—is a product of design, necessary to advance the progressive lie that fascism and Nazism are phenomena of the right. Let us therefore turn on the light and look behind the mirror.

FASCISM AT ITS CORE

What is fascism? In his April 29, 1938, message to Congress, FDR warned that "unhappy events abroad" had taught Americans a simple truth. "The liberty of a democracy is not safe if the people tolerate the growth of private power to a point where it becomes stronger than their democratic state itself. That, in its essence, is fascism—ownership of government by an individual, by a group, or by any other controlling private power."[22]

We see here how FDR himself is one of the earliest inventors of the progressive big lie about fascism. Fascism is not about the growth of private power; it is about the unchecked growth of government power. Fascism is not about the private sector taking over the government; it is about the government taking over the private sector. FDR redefines fascism to make it look like he is saving American democracy from a fascist takeover by big business. He inverts the meaning of fascism to portray his Republican opponents as fascists while presenting himself as, well, the antifascist.

FDR's lies live on in the present. In May 2017 the *New York Times* published an op-ed by Henry Scott Wallace—grandson of FDR's second vice president, Henry Wallace—defining fascism as "a merger of state and corporate power." Wallace portrayed his grandfather as a champion of the people against the rise of fascist tendencies in America, drawing a straight line from the fascist Republicans of the 1930s to Trump and the GOP today.[23]

Nowhere does Wallace point out that his grandfather was a socialist and that Hitler was the head of the National Socialist German Workers' Party. In line with contemporary progressives, Wallace is desperate to get the socialism out of national socialism. Leftists regularly tell me on social media, "Hitler wasn't a socialist. The Nazis just said that to get elected. They didn't enact any socialist policies. Don't you know Hitler persecuted the socialists and fought against the Soviet Union in World War II?"

Yes, I know. I also know that fascism in its essence is the centralization of power in the national state. "Everything in the state, nothing outside the state, and nothing against the state." That was the fascist slogan, drafted by Giovanni Gentile, the leading philosopher of fascism, and echoed by Mussolini, who created the first fascist regime in the world. Gentile adds, "The authority of the state is not subject to negotiation. It is entirely unconditioned. Morality and religion must be subordinated to the laws of the state."[24]

"For fascism," the fascist theoretician Alfredo Rocco wrote, "society is the end, individuals the means, and its whole life consists in using individuals as instruments for its social ends."[25] As this quotation suggests, the fascists of the 1920s and 1930s described the state as a living organism, with each individual being a cell within the organism. Obviously the cell had no value or identity or rights outside the organism; its value was solely what it contributed to the larger whole.

The second distinguishing feature of fascism was its forward-looking or progressive element. Progressives routinely portray fascism as "reactionary" in order to make it seem right-wing. But even the progressive historian Roger Griffin rejects this as a mischaracterization. "Fascism is anti-conservative," he writes. It had a "revolutionary, forward-looking thrust . . . It thus represents an alternative modernism rather than a rejection of it."[26]

One of the groups that strongly supported and eventually merged with the fascists was the Italian Futurists. In Germany too, self-described progressives and futurists embraced the revolutionary promise of fascism. Historians like A. James Gregor point out that fascists and communists recruited from the same sorts of people, malcontents who hated their society and sought to create another one from the ground up. Fascists, like communists, sought to create a new man and a new society freed from the shackles of traditional mores, religion and morality.

Now ask yourself: does this sound right-wing or left-wing? You don't have to guess. In 2012, at the Democratic National Convention, Obama unveiled the slogan, "The government is the one thing we all belong to." This fascist apotheosis to the centralized state is a sentiment that Gentile and Mussolini would surely have applauded. It couldn't be more different from the American founders' view, which is that we don't belong to the government; the government belongs to us.

Mussolini was a Marxist—together with Antonio Gramsci, the most famous Marxist in Italy. Mussolini was "the strongman of the revolutionary Left" who, in the words of historian Zeev Sternhell, "never said a single word against socialism as a system of thought."[27] Together with a group of revolutionary socialists known as the Syndicalists, he created the first fascist party in the early 1900s and the first fascist state in 1922. Around the same time, fascist movements were started in England, in France, in Germany and elsewhere in Europe.

All the founders and leaders of early fascism—there are no exceptions—were men of the left. The leading French fascists were Jean Allemane, the "grand old man" of French socialism; Marcel Déat, founder of the Parti Socialiste de France; and Jacques Doriot, a French communist. The Belgian fascists were rallied by the socialist theoretician Henri de Man. In England, Oswald Mosley broke with the Labour Party, which he considered insufficiently leftist, and founded the British Union of Fascists. In Italy, Mussolini's fascists were all revolutionary socialists, and one of his regime's closest advisers was Nicola Bombacci, a founder of the Italian Communist Party.

Hitler too was a man of the left. The leading Nazis were all committed socialists, as we can see from the Nazi twenty-five-point platform, released in the 1920s. The Nazis called for nationalization of large corporations and trusts, government control of banking and credit, the seizure of land without compensation for public use, the splitting of large landholdings into smaller units, confiscation of war profits, prosecution of bankers and other lenders for usury, abolition of incomes unearned by work, profit sharing for workers in large companies, a broader pension system paying higher benefits, and universal free healthcare and education.

Doesn't exactly sound like Trump's agenda, does it? It's not, and yet much of it is creepily familiar. Sure, some of the language is dated. Try crossing out the word "usury" and replacing it with its modern equivalent: "interest." Also cross out the word "Jew" and substitute "Wall Street greed." Now the Nazi platform of 1920 reads like a progressive platform jointly drafted by Elizabeth Warren and Bernie Sanders. If read aloud at a left-wing gathering on campus, I am sure it would provoke thunderous applause.

Mussolini and Hitler were national socialists not just in theory but also in practice. They established state control over all the major industries in their countries. Germany also created massive new state entities, such as the Hermann Göring Reichswerke, a state-run conglomerate charged with increasing industrial output in preparation for war. Hitler went much further than Mussolini, largely because he had more power. Mussolini's regime included nonfascist elements, and he had to compromise with them.

Unhampered by such constraints, Hitler enforced what the Nazis termed *Gleichschaltung*, the subordination of all the institutions of the culture to the ideological priorities of Nazism. Mussolini's regime had its own version of this—as Gentile put it, "For fascism, the state and the individual are one"[28]—but it was enforced in the Italian, which is to say lackadaisical, way. The Nazis, with German punctiliousness, implemented *Gleichschaltung* by forcing the media, the universities and the film industry into full conformity. They called it "working toward the fuhrer." Even private citizens were supposed to work toward the fuhrer at all times.

This was the true meaning of draping the swastika on your balcony, or giving the "Heil Hitler" salute. It signaled your willingness to be a servant or even a slave of the Nazi state. Thus *Gleichschaltung* in its own way corresponded to the Democratic master's dream on every slave plantation to have his slaves in full conformity with his dictates, one may say at all times "working toward the master."

Does all of this sound alarmingly familiar? It should. Today on the American left, *Gleichschaltung* has a different name: political correctness. Political correctness reflects the left's desire to impose voluntary ideological compulsion throughout the culture. No one is exempt, not even the poor Christian baker who simply wants to live by his conscience. He too must be browbeaten into submission and forced to serve the gay wedding couple whose lifestyle he finds objectionable and immoral. He too must in his own way give the Heil Hitler salute to contemporary leftist orthodoxy.

While Hitler's national socialism paralleled Mussolini's fascism in many respects, it differed in one big one. Hitler despised the Jews and Mussolini did not. (In fact, some prominent founders of Italian fascism such as Angiolo Olivetti were Jewish.) Hitler was much more of a rabid racist than Mussolini. Yet even this racism, the German historian Gotz Aly shows in two important recent books, served the cause of the left and thus bears comparison with Democratic racism on this side of the Atlantic.

Aly's work stands out in the vast corpus of German scholarship on the Nazi regime because he asks questions others don't. Aly's first question is: why did Hitler hate the Jews? It is not sufficient to answer that Hitler was a racist. Aly wants to know why he selected the Jews as his political targets. Aly's answer: Nazi anti-Semitism was rooted in envy. Hitler hated the Jews not because they were failures but because they were successful.

Hitler's own rhetoric concedes this. He fulminates against Jews for being unscrupulous selfish capitalists engaged in exploitation of the ordinary German citizen. Distinguishing between productive capitalism and finance capitalism, Hitler accuses Jews of engaging largely in finance capitalism, in other words of being greedy swindlers who make obscene profits for producing nothing. FDR, as we will see, also embraced this politics of envy and bequeathed it down to progressive Democrats of our own day.

Aly then poses a second question: why did the German people remain loyal to Hitler even through a protracted war that reduced their nation to rubble? They had barely voted Hitler into office in 1933; did they believe in him so much that they would stick with him to the bitter end? To answer these questions, Aly writes, "It is necessary to focus on the socialist aspect of National Socialism." Aly concludes that German allegiance to Hitler was not out of pure conviction. They weren't just suckers for Goebbels' propaganda.

Rather, Aly shows in a recent book, *Hitler's Beneficiaries,* that Hitler robbed from the Jews and other nations in order to fund Nazi socialist and redistributionist schemes. Once the Nazis had ousted the Jews from high positions in Germany, those positions went to other Germans. The Nazis confiscated Jewish property and art treasures. At the same time, Hitler pillaged other European countries of their wealth, and these resources were used by the state treasury to fund an expansion of the *Volksstaat,* or welfare state.

Aly reports that by using all this stolen money, "the Nazi leadership gave Germans their first taste of what it might be like to own an automobile. It introduced the previously almost unknown idea of vacations." Moreover, "It insured farmers against the vagaries of the weather and the world market." Nazis pioneered "the beginnings of environmental conservation." The national socialists expanded the state pension system and passed rent-control laws, tenants' rights laws and laws restricting the rights of creditors. Thanks to Nazi largesse with the booty of war, many German workers also had their first taste of French silks, Belgian lace and Dutch cheese.

No wonder, Aly concludes, that the Germans stuck with their man. They were Hitler's "satisfied thieves." Other socialists merely made extravagant promises, but the Nazi welfare state delivered the goods. Hierarchical though Nazism may have been in its organizational structure, it was also in this respect egalitarian.[29] One may say that any government that robs Peter to pay Paul can usually rely on Paul's support. Once again, there would be a valuable lesson for FDR in this Nazi principle of building popular loyalty by using the government for the purpose of confiscation and wealth redistribution.

THAT ADMIRABLE ITALIAN GENTLEMAN

Now let's see how FDR viewed fascism and how he created a uniquely American brand of it, in the process permanently transforming the progressive plantation. In 1933, FDR responded to a journalist who asked him his view of Mussolini. "I don't mind telling you that I am keeping in fairly close touch with that admirable Italian gentleman."

That same year FDR again gave his view of Mussolini to Breckinridge Long, U.S. ambassador to Rome. "There seems to be no question that he is really interested in what we are doing and I am much interested and deeply impressed by what he has accomplished and by his evidenced honest purpose of restoring Italy."[30]

FDR's enthusiasm for Mussolini and Italian fascism was echoed by other progressives of his time. The left-wing historian Charles Beard wrote of Mussolini's regime, "An amazing experiment is being made here . . . It would be a mistake to allow feelings aroused by contemplating the harsh deeds and extravagant assertions that have accompanied the Fascist process . . . to obscure the potentialities and lessons of the adventure."

Herbert Croly, editor of the *New Republic,* insisted that fascism offered the potential for the spiritual reconstruction of society. Progressives in popular culture picked up the fascist tune. "You're the top, you're Mussolini," crooned Cole Porter in an early thirties hit song whose Mussolini reference was tactfully removed a few years later when the Italian fascists invaded Ethiopia.[31]

Mussolini dispatched members of his so-called brain trust to fascist Rome to study fascist policies. He sent a second administrative team to examine the fascist organizational structure for the government. FDR adviser Rexford Tugwell, upon returning from Rome, wrote of fascism, "It's the cleanest, neatest, most efficiently operating piece of social machinery I've ever seen. It makes me envious."[32]

FDR regarded his National Recovery Act (NRA) as the most important of his New Deal programs. It was directly modeled on Italian fascism. The NRA empowered the federal government to establish coalitions of labor and management in every industry to set production targets, wages, prices and even maximum and minimum working hours. These agreements would be reviewed by a government-run Industrial Advisory Board answerable to FDR himself. According to Tugwell, the NRA was designed to "eliminate the anarchy of the competitive system."[33]

FDR's man to run the NRA, General Hugh Johnson, was an avowed admirer of fascism who loved to associate himself with what he termed the "shining name" of Mussolini. Johnson carried with him, and routinely quoted from, a fascist propaganda pamphlet, *The Structure of the*

Corporate State, written by one of Mussolini's aides. Under Johnson, the NRA issued its own brochure, *Capitalism and Labor Under Fascism.* It acknowledged that "the fascist principles are very similar to those which have been evolving in America."[34]

We have seen how FDR was ideologically shaped by fascism; now let us explore how, like the Nazis, he made political use of racism. FDR wasn't a racist, at least not of the extreme form that Hitler was, but he was not above making a Faustian pact with his party's worst bigots in order to get his agenda passed. The conventional progressive wisdom is that FDR won political support for the New Deal by assembling an amazing coalition of big-city bosses, poor white Southerners, farmers, laborers, Catholics, Jews, other ethnics and blacks.

But as progressive historian Ira Katznelson points out, these groups were not equally important for FDR.[35] Consider blacks. Most blacks in the South did not vote, courtesy of voter suppression by the Democratic Party. True, a great migration had begun in which blacks were moving from the rural South to northern cities. But FDR already had the cities. So he didn't care about the black vote there.

What FDR needed was the votes of the racist Democrats from the South who sat on powerful committees that had the power to accelerate or block his New Deal programs. These racists were also progressives who were generally behind FDR's programs, especially New Deal initiatives, like the Tennessee Valley Project, that benefited their region. Yet recognizing how indispensable they were to FDR, the Democratic racists made three demands.

First, they demanded that most New Deal programs, like Social Security, be designed in a way to exclude blacks. FDR agreed. Consequently, most New Deal programs excluded farm labor and domestic workers, recognizing that these were the two areas in which most blacks were employed. In Katznelson's words, blacks were "excluded from the legislation that created modern unions, from laws that set minimum wages and regulated the hours of work, and from Social Security."[36] These exclusions continued through the Truman administration and were only ended by Republicans in the 1950s.

Second, the Democratic racists demanded that FDR protect segregation. FDR was on board. He refused to desegregate the armed forces, even though he had the power to do so. As Katznelson puts it, in World War II, "The United States in effect had two armies—one white, one black. Not entirely separate, they were utterly unequal."[37] Desegregation would have to wait until the Truman era. FDR and progressive Democrats also prevented congressional Republicans from attaching antidiscrimination provisions to social programs. Again, it took Republicans in the Eisenhower era to finally remove these racist restrictions.

Third—and most damning—the Democratic racists insisted that FDR block antilynching legislation. FDR was up for it. Despite a surge in lynching that provoked Congressional Republicans, and even some Democrats, to get behind antilynching legislation, that legislation had no chance to pass without FDR's support. He withheld it, and the laws failed. Later Truman followed in FDR's footsteps by refusing to make lynching a federal offense.

We might expect this from a former Klansman like Truman, but why FDR? FDR seems to have agreed with his fellow Democrat, James Byrnes of South Carolina, who warned that laws against lynching would "arouse ill-feeling between the sections" and "destroy the Democratic Party."[38] FDR in other words was less concerned about black lives than he was about getting programs through and maintaining the Democratic Party's balance of support between the northern cities and the solid South.

We should not unilaterally fault FDR here; the northern Democrats were (as we have seen throughout this book) complicit in the underlying racism. When an antilynching bill came to the Senate floor in 1937, it was a progressive northern Democrat, William Borah of Idaho, who denounced it as ill-timed, ill-advised, and unconstitutional. Seeing their cause was hopeless, proponents of the bill retreated, and FDR made no objection.

Katznelson gives a second example of what happened when southern Democrats launched a procedural amendment to kill an antilynching bill. Northern Democrats, who might be expected to align with Republicans, did not. "What is striking about this," Katznelson writes, "is not the overwhelming support of southern Democrats or the comparable degree of opposition by Republicans. It is, rather, the critical support for adjournment provided by non-Southern Democrats, almost half of whom voted to support the South's procedural move."[39]

Equally striking for me is that a progressive like Katznelson has blown the cover of FDR and the northern Democrats. Katznelson doesn't just expose how the Democratic Party, North and South, accommodated racism; he even links Democratic racism to Nazi racism. And notice how he admits in passing that Republicans could be expected to oppose Democratic racism. Republicans, in other words, were the party of civil rights not just in the 1860s but right through the 1930s and 1940s. Katznelson's work is remarkable because he is virtually the only honest historian who has lifted the lid on FDR, revealing aspects of the man that have been concealed by two generations of biographers.

Yet in the end, even Katznelson disappoints. Basically Katznelson argues that even though FDR made a Faustian pact with the worst racists in his party—which is to say, in the country—it was all worth it. Despite FDR's "dirty hands"—a term that Katznelson defines as "taking wrong action in a right cause"—he got the New Deal passed. In the end, Katznelson contends, echoing progressive conventional wisdom on this subject, the same New Deal coalition evolved in a manner that made civil rights legislation possible.[40] So: two cheers for FDR!

Had the New Deal ended the Depression, one could make an argument that it constituted harsh medicine that required all sorts of shortcuts and ugly compromises. But it didn't, and, as we will see, its long-term effects have been mostly negative. Katznelson's second point about the evolution of the Democratic Party will have to wait for the next chapter, but again we will discover that the truth is quite different from progressive conventional wisdom.

SHIFTING THE BLAME

Finally, let's see how FDR reconstructed the Democratic coalition by taking a page, actually two pages, from the early record of the Nazis. First, FDR identified and demonized an internal enemy: rich Republicans. Starting with his inaugural address in 1933 and continuing with his 1936 Democratic Party Nomination Address, FDR castigated wealthy Republicans and conservatives in the same type of language that Hitler used against the Jews.

Calling Republican businessmen "money changers" and "economic royalists," FDR accused them of "creating a new despotism," an "economic tyranny." The New Deal in FDR's view had challenged these "privileged princes" who sought to oppress "political freedom" by imposing "economic slavery" on the American people. "They are unanimous in their hate for me," FDR thundered, "and I welcome their hatred." Only by exposing and routing these greedy swindlers, FDR concluded, could he and his valiant New Dealers create "the largest progressive democracy in the world."[41]

I am tempted to say that FDR invented the language of class warfare that was then taken up by subsequent generations of Democrats and has now become a staple of progressive politics. In his election campaign of 1948, Truman railed against "princes of privilege" and "bloodsuckers with offices in Wall Street."[42] And today we have the same language from Pelosi, Schumer, Hillary and Obama.

But in truth FDR didn't invent that language; Hitler did. Sure, we find the same language in Marx and in socialist rhetoric, but let's remember that Hitler too was a socialist. He was the first political leader to actually use such language. FDR was the second. Thus the class warfare rhetoric of today's progressive Democrats doesn't just go back to FDR; it goes back to the Nazis.

FDR recognized, as Hitler did, that envy is a very powerful human force. Its power derives not merely from its sheer wickedness—we detest others for the mere fact that they are more successful than we are—but also from its secrecy. We rarely confess envy to another, "Hey, my neighbor is doing better than I am and I can't take it." We are reluctant to admit it even to ourselves. Thus envy is the worst of the deadly sins, even more potent for operating covertly.

No politician can openly appeal to envy. Both Hitler and FDR knew they couldn't publicly say, "We cannot stand those Jews and Republicans and entrepreneurs who are smarter and more hardworking than we are. Let's go get them." Consequently, envy has to be mobilized behind the banner of social justice. "Those guys have been stealing from us. It is right and proper that we seize their possessions and distribute them among ourselves." This is the strategy that Hitler and then FDR seized upon.

So the point of creating an internal enemy, whether Jews or Republican businessmen, is to justify stealing from that group. But notice how FDR, like Hitler, laid the political groundwork for the theft by accusing his intended victims of being thieves. Hitler had accused the Jews of manipulating the German economy and leeching off the productive labor of the German people. FDR claimed that rich businessmen were tyrannizing the American people and ripping them off. How exactly? Hitler didn't say, and FDR didn't either.

Presumably FDR meant that businesses were not hiring enough people or paying them enough. This was Hitler's usury argument: "The Jews are exploiting you because they are charging too much for their money." But even if this were true, it hardly constituted tyranny. If you don't like what the moneylender is charging, don't borrow from him. In a market system, businesses are not required to hire people any more than people can be forced to work for such businesses. Salaries are settled through a bargaining process involving the mutual consent of the employer and employee.

Yet having identified the group from which he intended to extract money—wealthy Republican businessmen—FDR proceeded to build the Democratic coalition to do it. Here, we see, his technique was very different from that of Hitler and Mussolini. They didn't need to build wining electoral coalitions. FDR did. So how did he do it? Here the progressive narrative focuses on how FDR replaced the Democratic urban machine system of local big bosses with a single big boss, himself, administering the federal government.

I have no quarrel with this narrative. It shows, for example, how FDR worked with the bosses when he needed their support and got rid of them when it was politically safe to do so. In New York, for example, FDR as a state senator opposed the Tammany machine. The machine, in retaliation, supported FDR's rival Al Smith for the Democratic nomination in 1932. But when FDR secured the nomination, he made peace with the Tammany sachems because he needed them to campaign for him in the general election.

The very next year, however, FDR turned against Tammany once again. He shrewdly allied with the newly elected progressive Republican mayor of New York, Fiorello La Guardia, and even distributed federal patronage through him, bypassing and thus rendering impotent the Tammany machine. That's how La Guardia got one of New York's two major airports named after him. "FDR could have saved the Tammany machine," Jay Cost writes, but instead "he took the kill shot."[43]

In the end, Tammany was doomed not merely because of FDR's political wiles but also because the federal government, not the local city treasury, became the source of largesse and Democratic patronage. By the 1940s, the Tammany system had collapsed, replaced with a new patronage operation from Washington, D.C. Yet FDR still needed a mechanism to rally the political support necessary to sustain this patronage system—in other words, to keep Democrats in power.

TAMMANY ON THE POTOMAC

He found that support in the unions. Here the progressive account gets romantic and dewy-eyed. Even Katznelson indulges in rhapsodic descriptions of how FDR empowered unions, giving them the power to negotiate with management, to get a better deal for workers. Since union membership was voluntary—workers had to vote to start a union—how could anyone deny that this was an arrangement that combined freedom of choice with a more just outcome for workers?

I deny it. My basis for doing so is that this was not the arrangement that really matters. Once again we have to look behind the mask of progressive concealment. The truly significant deal was not the one between unions representing workers and management; rather, it was the one between unions on the one hand and the Democratic Party on the other. Let's try to see the arrangement from FDR's point of view.

Here's the deal that FDR and the Democrats offered the unions: We will pass laws that not only enable unions to exist but also force workers who don't want to join unions to join them as long as a majority of workers approves the union.

We will also enable unions to collect dues, again from the willing and the unwilling. We will thwart the ability of employers to fire union workers who strike, and force them to hire those workers back after the strike.

Even more, we will use the government to force management to give in to union demands, in effect putting the full power of the state behind the unions. What private corporation can resist Uncle Sam? The good news, from the government's point of view, is that we don't have to raid the treasury to fund union demands. Rather, we intervene to make the auto industry or the energy industry or the construction industry pay. The government is simply the "heavy" that beats the private sector into submission.

And there's more. We don't want the unions to focus narrowly on worker benefits, as they historically have. Now we want them to join with other Democratic groups in pressing for greater welfare benefits, the whole New Deal package. This means that union workers benefit not merely through higher wages and unemployment benefits but also through more lavish Social Security payments to more lucrative welfare programs.

Unions, in short, were given the opportunity to facilitate not merely the rip-off of the employer but also the rip-off of the taxpayer.

It was a good deal for unions. Since nothing in the world is free, however, the Democrats wanted something in exchange for all this federal protection, or to be blunt, for running this extortion racket. They wanted the unions to pressure their members to vote for Democratic candidates—saving politicians the trouble of having to persuade them individually—and to use a significant portion of union dues to fund the campaign war chest of the Democratic Party. This would ensure Democrats could stay in power so the racket could continue indefinitely.

Ironically it was a Tammany man, New York senator Robert Wagner, and not FDR, who first spotted the potential for a union racket. Wagner sponsored the National Labor Relations Act of 1935, which created a pro-union federal board for the purpose of actively intervening in labor disputes. FDR was not actively involved. But Wagner and the unions themselves saw the basis for an alliance that would deliver benefits for the unions and voters and funds for the Democratic Party.

The following year, 1936, FDR showed workers what the federal government could do for the unions. The United Auto Workers announced a major strike against General Motors, and in response GM shut down its huge plant in Flint, Michigan. UAW men then occupied GM facilities, refusing to leave or permit any work to be done there. They also shot at strikebreakers and policemen who sought to remove them from GM property.

GM turned to the government for support, but neither Democratic governor Frank Murphy nor FDR backed the eviction of strikers. Instead, FDR's labor secretary Frances Perkins urged GM president Alfred Sloan to come to Washington, D.C., and negotiate with UAW head

John Lewis under federal auspices. Sloan declined, saying he could not in good conscience enter into negotiations while GM property was being unlawfully occupied.

While the public in general supported Sloan, FDR attacked GM management for its recalcitrance, and finally Sloan, having no federal or state support to recover his property, succumbed to the UAW and agreed to its demands. Soon the entire auto industry got the message that unless they gave in, they were subject to the combined force of the unions in cahoots with the federal government.[44]

Not every union embraced FDR at first. The oldest and most powerful union, the American Federation of Labor (AFL), remained aloof. But a breakaway group, the newly formed Congress of Industrial Organizations (CIO), climbed aboard FDR's bandwagon and endorsed his reelection in 1936. So did the United Mine Workers and the Amalgamated Clothing Workers. And once FDR himself got behind the union movement and showed how he could deliver for them, the AFL was soon also on the Democratic team.[45]

In sum, the unions went for FDR's deal, and through this union racket, FDR remade the Democratic plantation. And although unions, having provided the political backbone of the Democratic Party for two generations, are now much weaker than they used to be, the racket still continues. In the aftermath of the 2008 crash, for instance, Obama used the power of the government to bludgeon General Motors into making its shareholders and bondholders take a hit, but not its union workers, who were shielded by federal protection.

The Nazi state didn't need to negotiate with unions. Essentially it displaced the unions and incorporated worker protections into its own state-run socialist schemes. FDR, however, had to ensure his reelection in 1936, 1940 and 1944. He also wanted to create an enduring national Democratic plantation system that would outlast him. And so he did. While the fascist plantations in Europe all collapsed by 1945, FDR's incorporation of fascist ideology and fascist strong-arm tactics into a new Democratic plantation system is still with us today.

8

CIVIL RIGHTS AND WRONGS

LBJ, Nixon and the Myth
of the Southern Strategy

Let's face it. Our ass is in a crack. We're
gonna have to let this nigger bill pass.

—Lyndon Johnson
to Senator John Stennis, 1957[1]

An interesting phenomenon in politics is the flip-flop. What would cause a politician who takes a stand on an issue to reverse himself or herself and take precisely the opposite stand on the same issue? Even more interesting is the about-face, or *volte face*. The *volte face* goes beyond the flip-flop because it represents a total and usually lasting shift of course, as when Reagan abandoned the Democratic Party and became a Republican.

More interesting even than the *volte face* is when a whole group or party makes this shift. Perhaps the most dramatic example in our lifetime is when the Soviet Communist Party in 1991 abolished itself. It's one thing for an individual to undergo a wrenching conversion, but what would cause a whole party to reverse itself in that way? Could it be a transformation of collective conscience, or a new perception of group interests, or what?

Our exploration of the subject is deepened by a new possibility introduced by Winston Churchill, who in one of his essays takes up the subject of consistency in politics. Accused on more than one

occasion of reversing himself and taking inconsistent positions on issues, Churchill defends himself by invoking the apparent *volte face,* the
change of tactics that is not a change of goals or values.

Churchill writes, "A Statesman in contact with the moving current of events and anxious to keep the ship on an even keel and steer a
steady course may lean all his weight now on one side and now on the
other. His arguments in each case when contrasted can be shown to
be not only very different in character, but contradictory in spirit and
opposite in direction: yet his object will throughout have remained the
same . . . We cannot call this inconsistency. In fact it can be claimed to
be the truest consistency. The only way a man can remain consistent
amid changing circumstances is to change with them while preserving
the same dominating purpose."[2]

Keeping this in mind, let's examine a series of critical transformations or switches in American politics over the past few decades.
Why did blacks, who were once uniformly Republican, become, as
they are now, almost uniformly Democratic? Why did the South, once
the "solid South" of the Democratic Party, become the base of the Republican Party? How did the GOP lose what used to be its base in the
Northeast and become the party of the South, the Midwest and the
West, not counting the West Coast? How did Democrats go from their
longstanding approach of demonizing blacks to championing black interests and, at least in terms of political rhetoric, demonizing whites?
Why did a racist and segregationist like Lyndon Johnson spearhead the
enactment of the Civil Rights Act of 1964, the landmark legislation of
the civil rights movement?

No understanding of current politics is possible without answering these questions. And progressives have put forward their answer,
which is now conventional wisdom, commonly invoked as if it were
too obvious to require any proof. Even some Republicans believe it, as
evidenced by RNC chairman Ken Mehlman going before the NAACP
in 2005 and apologizing for the racist history of the Republican Party.
In 2010, the first black chairman of the RNC, Michael Steele, conceded
the GOP's supposed Southern Strategy had "alienated many minority
voters by focusing on the white male vote in the South."[3]

You know you've got a powerful ideological indictment when even
its targets are willing to make a confession. And what is this indict-

ment? Its essence can be expressed in a few key propositions. The parties switched platforms, at least on the race issue. This big switch was brought about in the late 1960s by the GOP, which under the leadership of Richard Nixon employed an infamous Southern Strategy based on an appeal to racism and white supremacy.

The racist wing of the Democratic Party—the so-called Dixiecrats—responded by switching allegiances and becoming Republicans. Meanwhile the Democrats under LBJ pushed through the signature civil rights laws: the Civil Rights Act of 1964, the Voting Rights Act of 1965 and the Fair Housing Bill of 1968. So the Democrats, once the party of racism, became the party of civil rights, and the GOP, once the party of Lincoln and emancipation, became the new home of bigotry and white supremacy.

There is no limit to the number of articles chanting this progressive tune. "The Southern Strategy was the original sin that made Donald Trump possible," Jeet Heer writes in the *New Republic*. Heer contends that while the GOP has relied for decades on "coded appeals to racism," or what Heer terms "winking racism," Trump with his overt racism is the party's "true heir, the beneficiary of the policies the party has pursued for more than half a century."[4]

"Reagan, Trump and the Devil Down South" is the title of a recent article in the left-wing *The Guardian* that faults the GOP with making a "deal with the devil." Yes, it's the Southern Strategy all over again. "Goldwater discovered it; Nixon refined it; and Reagan perfected it into the darkest of the modern political dark arts." While these Republicans preferred "dog whistle" appeals to racism, "Trump blows it out," and "that's why the base loves him; he feels their rage."[5]

And from *The Atlantic* we get the headline, "How Trump Remixed the Republican 'Southern Strategy.'" Here the author Robert Jones blames the Southern Strategy on "the speeches of Richard Nixon . . . who polished George Wallace's overtly racist appeals for mainstream use in the Republican campaign playbook." Jones too says Trump has upped the ante. "In a demonstration of just how successful the old strategy was—he's discarded the dog whistle in favor of a bull horn."[6]

And again—just to highlight the omnipresence of this stuff—we have Salon informing us that "the idea that today's Democratic Party is the party of militant white supremacy is profoundly wrong." Why? You see, there was a Southern Strategy and a big switch. "White southern Democrats were explicit about their racism, and it's no mystery that they left the party." These people then "joined a Republican Party waiting with open arms."[7]

There is a considerable body of progressive scholarly literature behind this rhetoric. This includes Earl and Merle Black's *The Rise of Southern Republicans* and Dan Carter's *From George Wallace to Newt Gingrich: Race in the Conservative Counterrevolution*. These are the progressive spinmeisters of the narrative of the Southern Strategy and the big switch. Most recently, historian Kevin Kruse's study *White Flight: Atlanta and the Making of Modern Conservatism* invokes the Southern Strategy and the big switch to make the case that white supremacy is now a core doctrine of the Republican right.[8]

What dividends this explanation provides for progressive Democrats! Basically it erases most of their history and gives them a Get Out of Jail Free card. Democrats have never publicly admitted their role over nearly two centuries of being the party of slavery, segregation, Jim Crow, racial terrorism, the Ku Klux Klan and also fascism and Nazism. Yet when pushed up against the wall with the mountain of evidence provided in this book, how can they deny it?

They cannot deny it. Therefore, their ultimate fallback—their only fallback—is to insist that they changed. The bad guys became the good guys. The biggest payoff for them is the corollary to this. Supposedly the Republicans also changed, in the opposite direction. The good guys became the bad guys. So now the Democratic left not only gets to accuse Trump, conservatives and Republicans of being the party of racism, they also get to take their own history of white supremacy—with all its horrid images of slavery, lynching and concentration camps—and foist it on the political Right.

But is it true? Or—as you are entitled to suspect by now—is the whole doctrine of the LBJ moral transformation and the Southern Strategy and the big switch yet another case of progressive deception? More than that, is it an elaborate cover-up for yet another Democratic scheme of exploitation, which is to say, yet another modification of the progressive plantation?

We've covered the role of two of the most prominent progressives, the pedantic bigot Woodrow Wilson and the quasi-fascist dissembler

FDR; here I give you the untold story of the third one, LBJ, who happens to be the most cynical conniver of them all. And the real question about LBJ is not how and when he made his conversion—he didn't—but rather why an old-time segregationist bigot would become convinced that it was in his and his party's interest to promote a landmark Civil Rights Act. The plot thickens.

HOW DOES A RACIST CHANGE HIS SPOTS?

We begin with LBJ because he was the man in the White House who drove the Civil Rights Act and the Voting Rights Act. He was a man of the South who lived through the transformation of the two parties. Moreover, he himself embodied the big switch. He was a progressive racist who appears to have become a progressive antiracist. He was a Democratic bad guy who became a Democratic good guy. My wife Debbie graduated from the university LBJ went to, Texas State University in San Marcos, and LBJ is regarded there as a sort of demigod. On the campus I walked across LBJ Street to the LBJ Student Center and along the way passed a statue of LBJ in the quad.

Antifa and Black Lives Matter activists wouldn't dream of yanking down LBJ statues. That's because the progressive narrative on LBJ is even more positive than it is on FDR, at least as far as race is concerned. LBJ was the "flawed giant," in the title of a biography by historian Robert Dallek. Marshall Frady in the *New York Review of Books* affectionately calls him "the big guy" and revels in his "brawling, uncontainable aliveness," his "galumphing conviviality."[9]

The story that Dallek and other progressives tell about LBJ goes like this. He used to be a sort of a racist, given his dirt-poor, Texas hill country background. LBJ's story, however, is a triumphant account of how a redneck white country boy underwent a moral transformation. To paraphrase Obama, the arc of his life bent toward justice. When he got the power, he used it for good.

According to the left-wing journalist Bill Moyers, LBJ once told him that as a consequence of supporting civil rights laws, "we just delivered the South to the Republican Party for a long time to come."[10] This seems so altruistic on the part of a famously cynical man as to almost inspire wonder. And as progressives tell it, the political transformation of the Democratic Party was no less altruistic and wondrous.

That's because in miniature the progressive narrative about LBJ mirrors the progressive narrative of the Democratic Party. As the narrative goes, civil rights was no less of a political risk for a party previously wedded to white supremacy than it was for LBJ. Yet the Democrats were up to the challenge and came out better for it. For LBJ as for the Democrats, an unfortunate start led to a happy ending.

This account of LBJ is unbelievable and fantastic, by which I mean it cannot be believed and is the product of fantasy. Biographer Robert Caro found in LBJ "a hunger for power in its most naked form, for power not to improve the lives of others, but to manipulate and dominate them, to bend them to his will." Is it really plausible that this sort of man, whom historian Doris Kearns Goodwin termed "the greatest political bargainer of them all," a man who once said he thought about the subject of politics for eighteen hours a day, would bargain away his party's interests and get nothing in return "for a long time to come"?[11]

If such strange behavior was indeed the result of a wrenching transformation, there is no plausible evidence for it, not from Dallek, not from Goodwin, not even from biographer Robert Caro, who seems to have followed LBJ's life virtually day by day for decades and wrote a four-volume biography of him. LBJ told no one of his great conversion; he never wrote about it or made a speech about it, so if it happened he kept it entirely to himself.

Here is a man who, according to a memo filed by FBI agent William Branigan, seems to have been in the Ku Klux Klan. This memo was only revealed in recent months, with the release of the JFK Files. Progressive media—even progressive historians—have largely ignored it, trying to pretend it does not exist. Branigan cites a source with direct knowledge, even though he does not name his source. As one blogger notes, no one with even a cursory knowledge of LBJ's background can regard his involvement with the KKK to be a shock or a surprise.[12]

So how does a Klansman change his spots and become a moral idealist without telling anyone? Moreover, it seems difficult to credit moral idealism to a manifestly dishonest man. Here my exhibit is LBJ's 1965 address at Howard University, which progressives celebrate because in it LBJ makes a bold defense of affirmative action. "You do not take a man who, for years, has been hobbled by chains, liberate him, bring him to the starting line of a race saying 'You are free to compete with all the others' and still believe you have been fair . . . We seek not just freedom of opportunity; not just legal equity but human ability; not just equality as a right and a theory, but equality as a right and result."[13]

Impressive stuff, as far as it goes. But how far does it really go? The merits of LBJ's argument have been debated ever since by the left and the right. But what typically goes unnoticed is LBJ's telling silence on why blacks were for so long hobbled by chains and who it was that hobbled them. Let's recall that here we have a longtime Southern segregationist giving an account of the sins of segregation in the third person as if he were a mere observer, not a participant.

Even so, Dallek's only comment about LBJ's Howard address is that, in retrospect, it seems "excessively hopeful," as if LBJ's only problem was an excess of moral idealism.[14] The progressive historian Ira Katznelson, one of the few to notice LBJ's sly omission of his own role in the events he was describing, nevertheless downplays its significance by noting of LBJ, "His personal record and sense of pride were at odds with the quality of his history." In short, he lied.

Katznelson adds that LBJ "missed the chance to come to terms with the most dismal, even exploitative, aspects of the New Deal." This, he frets, must have been "particularly agonizing" for him.[15] I don't know whether to regard this as naïve or sneaky on Katznelson's part. Surely Katznelson is smart enough to know LBJ had not the slightest intention of fessing up that he was a member of the racist group that hobbled blacks. If he had, his audience would have immediately recognized that the very dude who poisoned the waters was now hypocritically pretending to show up as the water commissioner.

Finally, by every account, LBJ was a nasty, bullying, crude, selfish, mean-spirited and personally and sexually abusive individual. These are not qualities that we associate with a moral exemplar undergoing a crisis of conscience. There was the time he gave dictation to a female secretary while urinating in a corner washbasin. In the account of a Senate aide, on another occasion, while sitting next to a woman in his car with his wife Lady Bird on his other side, "Johnson made a point of placing one of his hands under the woman's skirt and was having a big time, right there in front of Lady Bird."[16]

There is much, much more in this vein in Caro's biography. I don't need to go into LBJ's serial infidelities, even in the Oval Office, his chronic boasting about the women he had conquered, the name that he gave to his penis, his boasting about its size and so on. Suffice to say that Johnson would not survive five minutes of scrutiny by the #MeToo movement. LBJ, like JFK and Bill Clinton, reflects the priapic aggression of the prototypical plantation boss.

Yet even more than the other two, he liked to lord over people, not just women but everyone. As Caro shows on page after page, LBJ derived pleasure from degrading and humiliating others. He was known to converse with aides in his office bathroom while emptying his bowels, which Marshall Frady interprets as a sign of his "Rabelasian earthiness" but which less charitably reveals an ugly demonstration of his power over subordinates.

LBJ was a pervert in every sense of the word; if I can pursue the excremental theme, he was into this shit. As LBJ himself put it, he wanted the type of person working for him "who will kiss my ass in Macy's window and stand up and say, 'Boy, wasn't that sweet!' "[17] Surely many Democratic plantation bosses of the nineteenth century could have said pretty much the same thing.

These traits do not describe the "old" LBJ, prior to some moral transformation. This is who LBJ was the whole time. And the same is true of LBJ's racism. We can see this in LBJ's use of the term "nigger" or "uppity nigger." LBJ didn't just use these terms in the early days, when, under the tutelage of his segregationist mentor Richard Russell, he upheld segregation and the poll tax and fought to undermine antilynching laws. No, LBJ showed a special fondness for them when he was Senate leader, vice president and president—in other words, the very time he was supposedly undergoing his moral transformation.

In the mid-sixties, LBJ nominated African American lawyer Thurgood Marshall to the Supreme Court. When an aide suggested to LBJ that there were other qualified black jurists he could have chosen, suggesting as an alternative possibility Judge A. Leon Higginbotham, LBJ responded, "The only two people who ever heard of Judge Higginbotham are you and his momma. When I appoint a nigger to the court, I want everyone to know he's a nigger."[18]

This was in 1965, one year after LBJ helped secure the passage of the Civil Rights Act. The man he called a nigger was the nation's most prominent African American attorney, who had argued the landmark 1954 *Brown v. Board of Education* case. Yet progressive historian Robert Dallek, who recounts this episode, interprets it in a way to minimize LBJ's culpability. "Johnson's pejorative language was partly his way of intimidating a new staff member or of showing how tough and demanding he was."[19]

Yet for LBJ this kind of talk was a consistent pattern. The same year, LBJ told his aide Joseph Califano that the black riots in the Watts area of Los Angeles showed how blacks could not control themselves. Pretty soon, Johnson warned, "Negroes will end up pissing in the aisles of the Senate and making fools of themselves, the way . . . they had after the Civil War and during Reconstruction."[20] The very fact that LBJ continued to embrace this view of Reconstruction—once promoted by the progressive racists of the Dunning School and popularized by Thomas Dixon in *The Clansman* and *Birth of a Nation*—suggests that contrary to progressive rumor, LBJ's racism was never rehabilitated.

Biographer Robert Caro describes an incident involving Robert Parker, LBJ's chauffeur. Parker recalled an occasion when Senator Johnson asked him whether he would prefer to be called "boy," "nigger" or "chief." Parker asked to be called by his name. Johnson erupted, "Let me tell you one thing, nigger. As long as you're black, and you're going to be black till the day you die, no one's gonna call you by your goddamn name. So no matter what you are called, nigger, you just let it roll off your back like water and you'll make it. Just pretend you're a goddamn piece of furniture."[21]

Historian Doris Kearns Goodwin, in the otherwise positive biography *Lyndon Johnson and the American Dream,* cites LBJ telling Senator Richard Russell during the debate over the Civil Rights Act of 1957, "These Negroes, they're getting pretty uppity these days and that's a problem for us since they've got something they never had before, the political pull to back up their uppityness. Now we've got to do something about this, we're got to give them a little something, just enough to quiet them down, not enough to make a difference."[22]

This admission is telling not merely because of its use of the insulting reference to the "uppityness" of blacks but also because it shows that LBJ's support for civil rights legislation wasn't the result of some moral awakening on LBJ's part; rather, it was part of a strategy. This notion is confirmed by what LBJ allegedly told two governors regarding the Civil Rights Act of 1964: "I'll have them niggers voting Democratic for two hundred years."[23]

Some progressives—notably the "fact-checking" site Snopes—have questioned this quotation, which appears in Ronald Kessler's *Inside the White House* but not in any other source.[24] Kessler attributes it to Air Force One steward Robert MacMillan, who claims to have heard LBJ say this. And as we can see the quotation is consistent with several others whose veracity is undoubted. My conclusion is that LBJ remained the vile bigoted Democrat he always was, and the notion that he underwent some sort of enlightened conversion is pure humbug.

LBJ'S SHREWD CALCULATION

It is time to reinterpret LBJ's "conversion," and to do this, we must try to imagine the political landscape that LBJ saw before him, a landscape very different from the one that FDR encountered a generation earlier. Two big things were changing and fast. First, white racism was declining precipitously all over the country, but especially in the South. Second, blacks were getting up and moving out of the rural South, and many of them were voting for the first time. Both these things were a big problem for the Democratic Party.

Let's take them in sequence. As innumerable surveys confirm, white racism—at least white racism of the old sort, which is to say old-fashioned hatred of blacks, holding them to be inferior beings and sanctioning violence and degrading treatment of them—plummeted through the late 1940s, 1950s and 1960s.[25] So sweeping is the change that many survey questions routinely asked prior to World War II—Are blacks entitled to the same legal rights as whites? Would you consider voting for a black candidate for political office?—are no longer even asked because white support for these things is now nearly universal. Harry Truman saw the change happening even in the late 1940s, and this—not some moral evolution to a higher state of being—was the sea change in American public opinion that pressured him to desegregate the military. LBJ also knew this because he could see it, even in the Texas backcountry.

Now it is tempting to believe that racism declined in America be-cause of the moral suasion of the civil rights movement, but to believe this is to put the cart before the horse, as most progressive accounts predictably do. The reason they do this is so that they can credit LBJ and progressive activism with the civil rights laws, and then credit those laws not only with creating legal equality but also with combat-ing racism. In reality, however, the steep decline in racism preceded the civil rights movement. The civil rights movement didn't cause it; it caused the civil rights movement.

Think about why Martin Luther King Jr. encountered so little in-tellectual resistance to his challenges to segregation. Fifty years earlier, he would have. This is not to deny that local officials, like Birmingham sheriff Bull Connor, unleashed dogs and hoses on civil rights protest-ers. King himself served time as a political prisoner in the Birming-ham jail, an experience that strikes a chord with me. But by this time the intellectual fight had been won. The local segregationist establish-ment, not King, was on the defensive. That's because popular opinion in America had shifted dramatically between the time FDR died in 1945 and the 1960s.

So what caused the shift? The obvious answer is: Adolf Hitler. In the end, the horrific crimes of Hitler overthrew the doctrine of white supremacy. Once American troops entered the concentration camps, once people saw those ghostly emaciated figures emerge out of the camps, they could no longer subscribe to theories of Nordic superior-ity they might once have held. Those doctrines were now permanently discredited.

The progressive historian George Fredrickson points out in *Racism: A Short History* that the very word "racism" came into common use only in the 1930s "when a new word was required to describe the theories on which the Nazis based their persecution of the Jews."[26] This shows how closely linked racism and Nazism were in the popular mind and helps confirm that it was the Nazis who, against their intentions of course, finally put white supremacy into the grave.

We can imagine that LBJ watched with horror the decline of rac-ism in America, not simply because he was a nasty bigot himself—and bigotry loves company—but also because white supremacy had been the central political doctrine of the Democratic Party for at least a century. Once the Republicans ended slavery the Democrats turned swiftly to white supremacy, which became the glue, both in the North and the South, that held the party together.

With racism dwindling fast, LBJ knew his party would lose voters whose allegiance to the Democrats had been based on the party's support for racist policies. This was a serious problem. From the Democrats' point of view, it meant that if racism could not be revived—and there was no way after Nazism to revive it—then the party would need new voters, and lots of them, in order to compensate for the loss of white racist voters who were regrettably losing their prejudices.

Where to look? There was only one place: black voters. And blacks in the 1950s and 1960s were voting in greater numbers than ever before. For the first half of the twentieth century, the Democrats had through racial intimidation and other means largely suppressed the black vote in the South, where the vast majority of blacks lived. But starting around World War I, a great migration occurred in which blacks over the next several decades literally got up and moved.

As Isabel Wilkerson writes in *The Warmth of Other Suns,* some six million blacks—nearly half of the entire black population of the rural South—left the farms, plantations and cotton fields of that region and moved to cities like New York, Detroit, Chicago, Los Angeles, Philadelphia. Some moved to smaller cities like Milwaukee and Oakland. The great migration was, as Wilkerson puts it, "an unrecognized immigration within this country."[27]

Here in the cities, blacks could vote and did vote, so for the first time in American politics, the black vote became significant, particularly so by the late 1940s and 1950s. The black vote was especially important in swing states like Illinois, New York and Pennsylvania. Fully aware of this, Republicans offered the most sweeping and forceful endorsement of civil rights for blacks to appear in any party platform since the nineteenth century. The party of Lincoln was making a bid for these new black voters.

Again, this was a major problem for LBJ and the Democrats. LBJ knew that in order to make up for the racist vote, the Democrats must win not just some black votes, not just a majority of black votes, but virtually all the black votes. The Democrats needed blacks to be just as uniformly loyal to the Democratic Party as white racists had previously been. LBJ had to figure a way for blacks to vote for Democratic candidates automatically, habitually, regardless of the qualities or qualifications of the Democrat on the ticket.

PLANTATION CONFESSIONS

But how to achieve this? After all, Democrats had been segregating, degrading and abusing blacks for a long time. LBJ knew this as well as anyone because he had been one of the abusers. How then to convince blacks, who were now voting, to vote en masse for a party that had enslaved them, segregated them, terrorized them and was still the party of bigotry in the 1960s?

LBJ realized that the Democrats could no longer whip the blacks into submission, as in the past. The Democrats needed a new relationship with blacks and on different terms than before. However reluctant LBJ may have been to admit it—we see that reluctance in his statements to fellow Democratic bigots in the Senate—he was also a realist. If he wanted virtually unanimous black support for the Democrats, he knew he couldn't just beat it out of them; he would have to woo them for the first time in the party's history. He would have to make it worthwhile for them to stay on the Democratic plantation.

But how? This is a difficult topic to talk about, and I am about to go into controversial territory. (You're thinking, "Controversial territory? Where else have we been throughout this book?" What I mean is that I'm now entering territory that is controversial even by my standard.) I have to tread carefully. I don't know a better way, however, than to illustrate the state of mind of a sizable segment of African Americans in the aftermath of slavery—a state of mind that became critical to LBJ as he attempted to solve his political conundrum.

I turn to Eugene Genovese's study of slavery, *Roll, Jordan, Roll,* widely considered to be the best work on the subject. Genovese relays the testimonies of several slaves who were interviewed after they became free. We might expect them to vividly describe the travails of enslavement, and they did. But they also confessed to something else. I quote verbatim from these accounts.

Here's Andrew Goodman, interviewed at the age of ninety-seven: "I was born in slavery and I think them days was better for the niggers than the days we see now. One thing was, I never was cold and hungry when my old master lived, and I has been plenty hungry and cold a lot of times since he is gone. But sometimes I think Marse Goodman was the bestest man God made in a long time. The slaves cried when told we were free 'cause they don't know where to go, and they's always 'pend on old Marse to look after them."

Here's Henri Necaise of Mississippi: "To tell de truth, de fact of de business is, my marster took care of me better'n I can take care of myself now. When us was slaves Marster tell us what to do. He say, 'Henri, do dis, do dat.' And us done it. Den us didn't have to think where de next meal comin' from, or de next pair of shoes or pants. De grub and clothes give us was better'n I ever gets now."

Here's Ezra Adams: "De slaves on our plantation didn't stop workin' for old marster even when dey was told dat dey was free. Us didn't want no more freedom than us was gittin' on our planation already. Us knowed too well dat us was well took care of, wid plenty of vittles to eat and tight log and board houses to live in. De slaves, where I lived, knowed after de war dat they had abundance of dat something called freedom, what they could not eat, wear and sleep in. Yes, sir, they soon found out dat freedom ain't nothin' 'less you got somethin' to live on and a place to call home. Dis livin' on liberty is lak young folks livin' on love after they gits married. It just don't work."[28]

As an immigrant who came to America with $500 in my pocket and no family here, no connections, nothing to fall back on, I know at least a little what it's like to be flung into freedom. I am hardly comparing my experience to that of former slaves, but in India I did see the people known as Dalits, or "untouchables." Those people have historically been treated worse than slaves; they are so reviled that traditional Hindus would not allow their shadow to cross over them. The untouchables too fell into a kind of collective stupor in which they could hardly imagine a route of escape from their degraded lot.

Based on that experience, I have nothing but sympathy for these poor slaves who had been turned into complete dependents during slavery and were then hurled into freedom in a society where, to put it mildly, they were not welcome. Thus I am not criticizing their longing for the security of the old plantation; I am merely recognizing it as a natural and powerful response to their dire situation.

LBJ would have recognized it just as I do. The difference is that I get it from books, reinforced by my own, admittedly quite different, experience. But LBJ grew up in the Texas hill country. He was a redneck from the rural backwoods. He knew people like Andrew Goodman, Henri Necaise and Ezra Adams. He understood their insecurity; he understood their fear, in part because he was helping to create it. And now, years and even decades later, LBJ saw a way to exploit that insecurity and fear to offer blacks a new arrangement. This arrangement became the essence of LBJ's Great Society.

"I'm gonna put $500 million in this budget for poverty," LBJ told black leader Roy Wilkins, "and a good deal of it ought to go to your people."[29] Both LBJ and Wilkins understood that these types of "handouts" weren't free. They were offered as part of a bargain between LBJ and the Democrats on the one side, and the black community on the other.

Here's the bargain that LBJ offered African Americans: We Democrats are going to create a new plantation for you, this time in the towns and cities. On these new plantations, unlike on the old ones, you don't have to work. In fact, we would prefer if you didn't work. We are going to support you through an array of so-called poverty programs and race-based programs. Essentially we will provide you with lifetime support, just as in the days of slavery. Your job is simply to keep voting us in power so that we can continue to be your caretakers and providers.

Here's the part LBJ did not say: We are offering you a living, but it's going to be a pretty meager living. Basically you get public housing, food stamps, retirement checks every month and medical care for the poor. If you have children we will subsidize them, provided they are illegitimate. More than this we cannot offer you, because we have to make sure that you stay on the plantation. This means that we need you to remain dependent on us so that you keep voting for us. Your dependency is our insurance policy to make sure that this is an exchange, not a giveaway.

In sum, LBJ modified the progressive plantation so that blacks, for the first time, would be treated as constituents, much as the Irish were in the Tammany days. No longer would Democrats directly rip off the blacks by stealing their labor. Now blacks would become partners with

Democrats in a scheme to extract resources from other Americans. Through a variety of taxes, regulations and mandates, those other Americans would be the ones paying for the Democratic plantation.

What made the scheme irresistible, from the Democrats' point of view, was that through the state the Democrats could force even Republicans to pay for their new urban plantation. In fact, the very sufferings that Democrats had historically imposed on blacks would now supply the moral capital for demanding that "America" make blacks whole. Future arguments for reparations and affirmative action would emphasize not what the Democrats did but what "America" did. Now the American taxpayer would be on the hook for correcting the wrongs perpetrated by the Democrats.

LBJ knew, of course, that not all blacks lived in inner cities. Less than half of African Americans today do, and that was also the case in the mid-sixties. It was never LBJ's intention for all blacks to actually inhabit the urban plantation. Rather, he wanted about half to live there, dependent on the government, and the other half to work for the government, serving the urban plantation. These blacks could now be considered overseers of the Democratic plantation.

LBJ knew that if the government employed blacks on a large scale, it would draw blacks out of fields like teaching, preaching and small business. Teachers, pastors and entrepreneurs would become administrators, service providers and social workers. In sum, they would lose their skills for succeeding in the private sector and learn only how to administer the agencies of government. They too would become captives of a sort, fatally dependent on the Democratic plantation. They too would have no way to leave.

From the perspective of LBJ's deal, African Americans could now look to the federal government as a new type of Big House. LBJ himself would be Massa, although he could be considered a good master as long as blacks lived up to their end of the deal. And LBJ probably genuinely believed it was a good deal for blacks. After all, who else gets a living from cradle to grave without having to work! Even so, shrewd artificer that he was, LBJ must have known that he was making blacks complicit in their own captivity, a captivity no less real for being voluntary. Few would actually have a chance to escape from the Democrats' urban plantation. Some would even learn to love the plantation.

Blacks took the deal for the following reasons. First, having come out of the haunting experience of slavery and sharecropping, many of them were terrified of what African American writer Shelby Steele terms the "shock of freedom." To them a meager security seemed preferable to the risk of not being able to survive. Second, some blacks had come to believe—as some do now—that because of past oppression, America owed them a living.

Republicans of course know there is some truth to this, which is why during Reconstruction Republicans attempted to give blacks a fair start but were thwarted in these efforts by racist Democrats. Today's Democrats, however, are all too eager to affirm that blacks require the lifetime support of the U.S. government, because this then provides the pathway to political dependency on the Democratic Party.

One consequence of LBJ's deal was that race, which black leaders from Frederick Douglass to Booker T. Washington to Martin Luther King Jr. had been trying to eradicate from public life, took on a new significance. Blacks wanted to be known as black, and black even became "beautiful." No one was surprised when progressive pundit Cornel West published a book called *Race Matters.* As Shelby Steele wryly noted, race never mattered to such people when there was no profit in it for them.[30]

Also as a consequence of LBJ's deal, Democrats became the new champions of blacks voting. From LBJ on, Democrats wouldn't merely advocate that blacks vote; they would in many cases supply the buses to take them to the polls. In her book on the great migration, Isabel Wilkerson writes, without irony, "Suddenly the very party and the very apparatus that was ready to kill them if they tried to vote in the South was searching them out and all but carrying them to the polls."[31] If LBJ were around to read this, I'm sure he would have found it hilarious.

That's why LBJ "converted" from a racist Democrat who sought to keep blacks down on the old sharecropping plantation to a racist Democrat who sought to create a new type of plantation where blacks would willingly vote for their Democratic providers. That's why LBJ pushed the Civil Rights Act and the Voting Rights Act and the Great Society. That's why progressives lionize LBJ even though they know what a vile scumbag he was. He's their guy; he was the creator of their urban plantation in its most modern and most recognizable form. And that's why blacks have become, as a group, the lifetime servile dependents of the Democratic Party.

PARTY OF CIVIL RIGHTS

Despite the ingenuity of LBJ's plantation deal, the Democrats still had a major problem, and LBJ himself had no idea how to solve it. That problem was that blacks have long memories. Even blacks living in the 1960s had parents who endured the slights and humiliations of segregation, grandparents who were sharecroppers, great-grandparents who were slaves on the Democratic plantation. Progressive Democrats realized there was no way to con blacks into forgetting about all this stuff.

What they needed was a way to convince blacks that while Democrats may have been their enemies in the past, Democrats were their friends now. Hence progressives needed to sanitize LBJ sufficiently to give him full credit for the Civil Rights and Voting Rights acts. And this project of persuasion would work even better if somehow they could persuade blacks that Republicans, who were blacks' liberators in the past, were their enemies now. In this way black fear—including the nightmarish memories of the past—could be channeled into political hatred directed at the Republicans.

This is the significance of the Southern Strategy and big switch arguments. The left needed to make the case to African Americans that the parties switched platforms and switched sides: somehow the cops became robbers and the robbers became cops. Consequently, we must never lose sight of how these arguments are weapons to cover up the tracks of the bad guys and to project the blame onto the good guys, making it seem like they are the bad guys. It's naïve to consider these arguments apart from their political utility.

Still, in the two sections that follow I am going to do exactly this. I am going to examine propositions apart from their manipulative use and merely ask of each one: is this true? Let's start by asking: which party actually passed the landmark civil rights laws of the 1960s, the Civil Rights Act, the Voting Rights Act and the Fair Housing bill? Progressives give full credit to LBJ, as if he single-handedly got the legislation through Congress.

Yet LBJ knew that the main opposition to these laws didn't come from the Republican Party; it came from the Democratic Party, from the group of racist segregationists loosely called the Dixiecrats. These Dixiecrats, led by former Klansman Robert Byrd and LBJ's own mentor Richard Russell, mounted filibusters to block the legislation. The filibuster against the Civil Rights Act continued for eighty-three days. Byrd himself spoke for over fourteen hours.

LBJ's only way to get the laws passed was to turn to Senate Republican leader Everett Dirksen. Dirksen knew that the Civil Rights Act of 1964 was merely a restatement of the Fourteenth Amendment that Republicans had passed—and Democrats had turned into a practical nullity—a century earlier. Even the whole color-blind doctrine articulated by Martin Luther King Jr. was hardly original; Frederick Douglass said the same—and said it better—many decades earlier.

In the mid-nineteenth century, Douglass insisted there was no self-esteem to be found in skin color: "Let the sun be proud of its achievement." He added, "It is evident that white and black 'must fall or flourish together.' In the light of this great truth, laws ought to be enacted, and institutions established—all distinctions, founded on complexion ought to be repealed . . . and every right, privilege, and immunity, now enjoyed by the white man, ought to be as freely granted to the man of color."[32]

Dirksen got behind the legislation. And proportionately more Republicans than Democrats voted for the Civil Rights Act, the Voting Rights Act and the Fair Housing bill. In the House, the Democratic vote for the Civil Rights Act was close: 152 for and 96 against. The Republican vote was 138 for and 34 against. In the Senate, the Democrats voted 46 for and 21 against; the GOP voted 27 for and 6 against. So 80 percent of Republicans in the House and 82 percent in the Senate voted yes; only 61 percent of House Democrats and 69 percent of Senate Democrats did. Had Congress been made up entirely of Democrats, none of these laws would have secured the votes to defeat the filibuster and thus none of them would have passed.

If one expects progressive pundits to give Republicans credit where credit is due, one would be sorely mistaken. In various ways, progressives have been misleading the public on this topic for decades. While running for president in 2000, Al Gore said his father Al Gore Sr. lost his Senate seat because he championed equal opportunity, even though Gore Sr. voted against the Civil Rights Act of 1964, losing his seat in 1970 because of his positions on the Vietnam War and school prayer. More recently in 2013, MSNBC host Chris Hayes identified segregationist George Wallace—who in 1963 coined the phrase "segregation now, segregation tomorrow, segregation forever"—as a Republican. MSNBC was forced to issue a correction.[33]

A subtler attempt at progressive revisionism comes from Harry Enten, writing in *The Guardian*. Conceding greater Republican than Democratic support for civil rights, Enten writes that nevertheless "geography was far more predictive of voting coalitions on the Civil Rights [Act] than party affiliation." Enten proceeds to control for regional affiliation, and based on this revised mathematics, he concludes that Democrats are no less the party of civil rights than Republicans.[34] Here we see the familiar progressive tactic of saving the Democrats by blaming the South.

The question that Enten avoids, however, is: which is the party that cultivated and nourished racism in the South in order to establish a one-party monopoly in that region? As we have seen, the answer is: the Democrats. Moreover, northern Democrats allied with southern Democrats in making the party the official vehicle of white supremacy from the 1860s through the 1960s. Enten insists "it just so happened southerners made up a larger percentage of the Democratic than Republican caucus," but this is a flat-out lie; it didn't "just so happen"; it was the result of calculated, long-standing Democratic strategy beginning when Republicans shut down the old slave plantation.

DID THE PARTIES SWITCH PLATFORMS?

Now let's turn to a second question: did the two parties switch platforms? We can test this claim by examining the core philosophy of Abraham Lincoln, the first Republican president, and then seeing whether it is still the core philosophy of the Republican Party today.

On multiple occasions, Lincoln defined slavery in this way: "You work; I'll eat." In his Chicago speech of July 10, 1858, Lincoln put it slightly differently: "You toil and I will enjoy the fruits of it." In its essence, Lincoln said, slavery gave men the right to "wring their bread from the sweat of other men's faces." As historian Allen Guelzo pointed out in a recent interview I did with him, for Lincoln the most appalling feature of slavery was that it was a form of theft, theft of a man's labor.

Lincoln went on to argue that for centuries monarchs and aristocrats had stolen the labor of working people through a variety of mechanisms, from confiscatory taxation to outright confiscation. Lincoln insisted that notwithstanding its lofty rationalizations, the Democratic slave plantation was based on this ancient principle of thievery. "No matter in what shape it comes, whether from the mouth of a king . . . or from one race of men as an apology for enslaving another race, it is the same tyrannical principle."

Lincoln contrasted slavery with the Republican principle, which is that the man that makes the corn has the right to put the corn into his own mouth. In Lincoln's words, "As each man has one mouth to be fed, and one pair of hands to furnish food, it was probably intended that that particular pair of hands should feed that particular mouth." The social philosophy underlying this is that "every man can make himself" and "the man who labored for another last year, this year labors for himself, and next year he will hire others to labor for him."

Lincoln calls this the free-labor system, by which he means the free-market system. It operates on self-improvement, as Lincoln's own story illustrates. "I am not ashamed to confess that twenty five years ago I was a hired laborer, mauling rails at work on a flat-boat." The free-labor system, in Lincoln's words, "gives hope to all and energy and progress and improvement of condition to all."

Naturally, Lincoln says, people want to keep what they earn. "Even the ant who has toiled and dragged a crumb to his nest," he says, "will furiously defend the fruit of his labor against whatever robber assails him." And while the temptation to envious confiscation is inevitable, Lincoln told a delegation of workingmen during the Civil War, "Let not him who is houseless pull down the house of another; but let him labor diligently and build one for himself."

Failure to succeed, Lincoln said, is "not the fault of the system, but because of either a dependent nature which prefers it, or improvidence, folly or singular misfortune." As political scientist Harry Jaffa interprets Lincoln's words, "The brain surgeon and the street sweeper may have very unequal rewards for their work. Yet each has the same right to put into his mouth the bread that his own hand has earned. The brain surgeon has no more right to take the street sweeper's wages than the street sweeper to take the brain surgeon's."

Why not? Because for Lincoln such schemes of confiscation are a restoration of the slavery principle where "*some* have labored, and *others* have, without labor, enjoyed a large proportion of the fruits." Lincoln added, "This is wrong and should not continue. To secure to each laborer the whole product of his labor, or as nearly as possible, is a most worthy object of good government."[35]

Lincoln's philosophy can be seen in its practical implementation when his own stepbrother, age thirty-seven, wrote him to ask for a small loan to settle a debt. Lincoln responded, "Your request for eighty dollars, I do not think best, to comply with now." Lincoln reminded him this was not the first time he was being importuned for money; they had been down that road before. The problem, as he put it, is that the man was "an idler . . . You do not very much dislike to work; but you do not work much, merely because it does not seem to you that you could get much for it."

Here's what Lincoln proposed: "You shall go to work, tooth and nails, for somebody who will give you money for it." Lincoln added an incentive. "If you hire yourself at ten dollars a month, from me you will get ten more, making twenty dollars a month . . . Now if you will do this, you will soon be out of debt, and what is better, you will have a habit that will keep you from getting in debt again."[36]

It should be obvious from this that Lincoln's basic ideology—that people have a right to the fruits of their labor, and that government, if it gets involved at all, should merely provide idlers and indigents with the means to become self-supporting—is even today the basic ideology of Republicans. And it is equally clear that the confiscatory principle "You work, I eat" is even today the basic ideology of Democrats. The entire welfare state, from the New Deal through the Great Society to contemporary Democratic schemes, is rooted in the same plantation philosophy of legally sanctioned theft that Lincoln identified more than a century and a half ago.

WHY BLACKS BECAME DEMOCRATS

Now we turn to our third question: why did blacks become Democrats? They were once at home in the Republican Party. As Frederick Douglass put it, "The Republican Party is the deck; all else is the sea."[37] How different things are now. After the Civil War nine out of ten blacks voted Republican; now nine out of ten blacks vote Democratic. So something happened to cause blacks to switch their allegiance. But what?

For progressives, the huge backing of blacks for the Democratic Party proves that the Democratic Party is the party of racial enlightenment and black interests. It follows by the same reasoning that the GOP must be the party opposed to blacks. As Jamelle Bouie put it in the Daily Beast, "If the GOP is so supportive of African-Americans, then why have black voters abandoned the party in droves?"[38]

Here I give a surprising answer to that question. The data show that blacks did not switch from Republican to Democratic in the 1960s. They did not do it because of civil rights. Rather, a majority of blacks became Democrats in the 1930s. This was at a time when the Democratic Party was manifestly the party of segregation and the Ku Klux Klan. FDR, who got less than one-third of the black vote in 1932, got 75 percent of the black vote in 1936.

Why would blacks leave the party of emancipation and resistance to segregation and lynching and join the party of bigotry and white supremacy? The depressing answer is that blacks did it in exchange for the pittance that they got from FDR's New Deal. We have seen earlier how FDR designed the New Deal to exclude African Americans and preserve Jim Crow. How delighted and amused FDR must have been to see blacks coming over to his camp even as his administration worked closely with racist Democrats to screw them over.

It should be noted, in mitigation of this horrible decision on the part of African Americans—and it was a horrible decision—that conditions for blacks during the Great Depression were almost inconceivably bad. Historian Ira Katznelson points out that median black family income was around $500 a year, which means most blacks lived at subsistence level without electricity, hot water, refrigeration, adequate plumbing or gas for cooking. "Under these circumstances," Katznelson writes, New Deal benefits "limited though they were" and "however discriminatory" still offered some relief and solace to a "desperate population."[39]

So FDR bought off the African American vote at a bargain-basement price in the 1930s. Yet this secured the Democrats a decisive, but not unanimous, black vote. Democrats had around 75 percent of the black vote, and they remained in that range from the 1930s through the 1960s. Then LBJ consciously directed a large portion of his Great Society benefits to blacks and bought off another big chunk of the black vote for the Democratic Party. Since LBJ, blacks have voted for Democrats in the 90 percent range.

As we will see in the next chapter, the political decision to become part of the Democratic plantation has proven to be disastrous for blacks, although not necessarily for the black overseer class that administers the Democratic plantation. However this may be, the timing and motivation of the black switch is a decisive refutation of the progressive lie that blacks wisely left the Republican Party because they recognized it as the party of white supremacy and joined the Democratic Party because they knew it had become the party of civil rights. That wasn't the perception; neither was it the reality.

REEXAMINING THE SOUTHERN STRATEGY

Now we turn to Nixon's Southern Strategy and the reasons for the other switch: the switch of the South from being the political base of the Democratic Party to now being that of the GOP. Here the progressive narrative is that Nixon was convinced by his malevolent advisers—notably Kevin Phillips, author of the bible of the Southern Strategy—to make a racist appeal to the Deep South, winning over Dixiecrats and segregationists to the GOP and firmly establishing the Republican Party as the party of white supremacy, a mantle that has now been inherited by Trump.

The first problem with this Southern Strategy tale is that progressives have never been able to provide a single example of an explicitly racist pitch by Richard Nixon at any time in his long career. One might expect that a racist appeal to Deep South racists would actually have to be made, and to be understood as such. Yet quite evidently none was.

This is not to deny that privately Nixon harbored all kinds of prejudices, not only against blacks but also against Jews, the Irish, the Italians, Ivy Leaguers and others. The private Nixon, as shown by the Watergate tapes, was a veritable cauldron of resentments. He even called the ancient Greeks "fags." Yet even in private the worst that

Nixon says about blacks is that it may take them 500, not 50, years to fully integrate in America.[40] In public, however, Nixon was quite the Machiavellian, and his public statements—including his campaign appeals—are free of these private resentments.

The two biggest issues in the 1968 campaign were the war in Vietnam and, closely related, the antiwar movement in the United States. Nixon campaigned on a strong anti-communist, law-and-order platform. While embracing the welfare state—Nixon was no conservative on domestic issues—he also railed against what he termed the "excesses of bleeding heart liberalism." Some progressives contend that while not explicitly racist, Nixon's campaign themes reflected a covert or hidden racism. Nixon was supposedly sending "coded" messages to Deep South racists, speaking as if through a political "dog whistle."

Now I have to say I consider this "dog whistle" argument to be somewhat strange. Is it really plausible that Deep South bigots, like dogs, have some kind of a heightened awareness of racial messages—messages that are somehow indecipherable to the rest of the country? Not really. Even so, let's consider the possibility. I concede of course that most public policy issues, from taxes to crime to welfare, are entangled with race. A tax cut, for instance, will have a disproportionate impact on some groups as compared to other groups.

Precisely for this reason, however, it's incumbent on progressives to have some basis of distinguishing "dog whistle" tactics from ordinary political appeals. Yet never have I seen anyone make this distinction. Progressive rhetoric almost inevitably assumes that Nixon is speaking in racial code. How can this be established, however, without looking at Nixon's intention or, absent knowledge of his intention, the particular context in which Nixon said what he did? Context, in other words, is critical here.

Consider Nixon's famous law-and-order platform, which is routinely treated as a racist dog whistle. Now a call for law and order is not inherently racist, and this theme from Nixon resonated not merely in the South but throughout the country. It should be noted that Nixon's law-and-order argument was directed not merely at black rioters but also at mostly white violent antiwar protesters. Nixon condemned the Black Panthers but also the Weather Underground, led by a man whom I've subsequently debated, Bill Ayers, and his wife, Bernardine Dohrn.

In 2016, my wife Debbie and I had lunch with them in Chicago. Last time we checked, both of them were white.

What of Nixon's supporters? Were they the stereotypical segregationist bigots we have encountered throughout this book? The left-wing historian Kevin Kruse thinks so. Kruse portrays as racist the phenomenon of "white flight," which refers to middle-class whites moving out of the crime-ridden inner cities to the suburbs. Kruse terms this the politics of "suburban secession," a deliberate invocation of the Confederacy itself, as if whites were "seceding" from the cities and establishing their own white nations in the suburbs.[41]

Yet Kruse conveniently omits the equivalent phenomenon of "black flight," which refers to middle-class blacks doing the same thing as soon as they acquire the means to move to safer neighborhoods. Witness today the prosperous black suburbs of Washington, D.C., heavily populated with both whites and blacks who got out of the city. Does it make any sense to call all these people bigots? No. Wouldn't Kruse himself do the same thing for the safety of his family? Of course he would.

Kruse's portrait of Nixon's base of white middle-class Republicans as a reincarnation of the Old South racists is contradicted by Norman Mailer, who reported on the Republican Convention in Miami Beach in 1968. He found "a parade of wives and children and men who owned hardware stores or were druggists, or first teller in the bank, proprietor of a haberdashery or principal of a small-town high school, local lawyer, retired doctor, a widow on a tidy income, her minister and fellow-delegate, minor executives from minor corporations, men who owned their farms."[42]

As Mailer recognized, this was not a rally of Ku Klux Klansmen of the type that attended, say, the Democratic Convention of 1924. In fact, this was not a Southern-dominated group at all. Most of the attendees were from the Northeast, the Midwest and the West. This was Nixon's "silent majority," the ordinary Americans whom Nixon said worked hard and played by the rules and didn't complain or set fire to anything and, precisely for this reason, had been ignored and even reviled by the Democratic Party.

Nixon had an excellent record on civil rights. Unlike Barry Goldwater, who opposed the Civil Rights Act of 1964, Nixon supported it.

He also supported the Voting Rights Act the following year. When Nixon was elected in 1968, nearly 70 percent of African American children attended all-black schools. When he left, in 1974, that figure was down to 8 percent.

Tom Wicker, progressive columnist for the *New York Times,* gave his appraisal of Nixon's desegregation efforts. "There's no doubt about it—the Nixon administration accomplished more in 1970 to desegregate Southern school systems than had been done in the 16 previous years or probably since. There's no doubt either that it was Richard Nixon personally who conceived, orchestrated and led the administration's desegregation effort . . . That effort resulted in probably the outstanding domestic achievement of his administration."[43]

The Nixon administration went even further, putting into effect the nation's first affirmative action program. Dubbed the Philadelphia Plan and carried out by Nixon's labor secretary, Arthur Fletcher, it imposed racial goals and timetables on the building trade unions, first in Philadelphia and then throughout the country. Basically Nixon moved to kick in the closed union door and to force racist Democratic unions to admit blacks. The progressive legal scholar Neal Devins admits that Nixon's Philadelphia Plan was "the genesis of affirmative action in government contracting (and arguably all federal affirmative action programs)."[44]

Let's pause to consider: would a man who is seeking to build an electoral base of white supremacists in the Deep South promote the first program that actually discriminates in favor of blacks? Once again, progressives here go into their familiar hemming-and-hawing mode. Historian Howard Gillette is typical in that he insists Nixon only did this as a "wedge issue," to break up the New Deal coalition that included both African Americans and racist white unions.[45]

But even if Nixon's objectives were purely strategic, one would have expected him to break up this coalition by courting the white unions. Instead he courts black workers. He could hardly have expected that forcing white unions to hire blacks would have endeared him to the supposed racist constituency that had just elected him. Nixon's resolute backing of affirmative action alone makes nonsense of the progressive view that his electoral base was made up of Deep South bigots.

LEARNING FROM GOLDWATER'S MISTAKE

Moreover, Nixon lost the Deep South. Goldwater won five Deep South states in 1964, the only states he carried other than his native Arizona. Not that Goldwater was a racist—he was a founding member of the Arizona NAACP and had pushed to integrate the Arizona National Guard and the Phoenix public schools. He had supported the Civil Rights Act of 1957, which established a Civil Rights Division in the Justice Department, as well as another civil rights bill in 1960.

Goldwater objected to the Civil Rights Act of 1964 on libertarian grounds; he did not believe the federal government was constitutionally authorized to regulate discrimination in the private sector. Sadly, Goldwater's principled stand was misunderstood by many African Americans, who saw Goldwater as a racist and his party, the GOP, as the party of racism.

These sensitivities on the part of blacks were, of course, understandable. Unfortunately for the GOP, they cost the party dearly. Previously Martin Luther King Jr. had maintained his independence from both parties; now he joined the Democratic camp. And Goldwater paid not only with a disastrous election loss but also with the loss of his reputation: the characterization of Goldwater as a racist, although false, has endured as a staple among today's progressives.

Even so, Nixon learned from Goldwater's mistake. This point is made with unmistakable clarity in Kevin Phillips' *The Emerging Republican Majority,* published in 1969. A recent article in the Huffington Post makes the standard progressive claim that Phillips "helped construct" Nixon's Southern Strategy. Historian Dan Carter calls him its "nuts and bolts architect." Yet Phillips admits that Nixon could not have read the book prior to the 1968 campaign since it didn't come out until the following year. What Phillips set forth was not a recipe for Nixon's success but an ex post facto explanation for how Nixon had succeeded.[46]

According to Phillips, Nixon understood that he could never win a majority by appealing to the Deep South. He had just seen Goldwater win that region and lose the rest of the country in considerable part because of his position on the Civil Rights Act. We should remember that in 1968 the Republican base was in the Northeast, the Midwest and some parts of the West. Nixon was not foolish enough to endanger this entire base while seeking merely to bag a handful of Deep South states.

What Nixon did, according to Phillips, was appeal to the Sun Belt, "a new conservative entity stretching from Florida across Texas to California."[47] The Sun Belt reflected a modernizing economy grounded in defense, manufacturing, technology and services and was—and still is—the fastest-growing part of the country. Phillips argued that whoever won the Sun Belt would win the presidency. Notice that the Sun Belt encompasses much of the South but stretches from coast to coast and includes non-Southern states like Arizona and Nixon's home state of California.

In the South itself, Nixon targeted the urban population of the Outer or Peripheral South. Nixon was not after the Deep South states of Mississippi, Georgia, South Carolina or Alabama; he barely campaigned in those states. Rather, he was after the Peripheral South states of Florida, Texas, Arkansas, North Carolina, Tennessee and Virginia, the latter four of which Phillips calls "the four most reluctant Confederate states."[48] And within these states, Nixon's campaign focused on cities: Tampa, Houston, Dallas, Little Rock, Norfolk, Raleigh, Nashville.

Nixon recognized that these voters represented the urban and suburban face of a changing South. Many were transplants from the North who came to the South in search of jobs and opportunity. Nixon appealed to these Peripheral South voters not on the basis of race but rather on the basis of Republican policies of entrepreneurial capitalism and economic success. In other words, he went after the Peripheral South's non-racist, upwardly mobile voters, leaving the Deep South racists to the Democratic Party. And sure enough, in 1968 Nixon won Virginia, Tennessee and Florida in the Peripheral South and the entire Deep South went to the racist Dixiecrat George Wallace.

What happened to all those racist Dixiecrats who, according to the progressive narrative, all picked up their tents and moved from the Democratic Party to the Republican Party? Actually, they exist only in the progressive imagination. Of all the Dixiecrats who broke away from the Democratic Party in 1948, of all the bigots and segregationists who voted against the Civil Rights Act of 1964, I count one—just one—who switched from Democrat to Republican.

That solitary figure was Strom Thurmond. The constellation of racist Dixiecrats includes Senators William Murray, Thomas P. Gore, Spessard Holland, Sam Ervin, Russell Long, Robert Byrd, Richard Russell, Olin Johnston, Lister Hill, John C. Stennis, John Sparkman, John McClellan, James Eastland, Herman Talmadge, Herbert Walters, Harry F. Byrd Sr., Harry F. Byrd Jr., George Smathers, Everett Jordan, Allen Ellender, A. Willis Robertson, Al Gore Sr., William Fulbright, Herbert Walters, W. Kerr Scott and Marion Price Daniel.

The list of Dixiecrat governors includes William H. Murray, Frank Dixon, Fielding Wright and Benjamin Laney. I don't have space to include the list of Dixiecrat congressmen and other officials. Suffice to say it is a long list. And from this entire list numbering over 200 we count only a single defection. Thus the progressive conventional wisdom that the racist Dixiecrats became Republicans is exposed as a big lie.

The Dixiecrats remained in the Democratic Party for years, in some cases decades. Not once did the Democrats repudiate them or attempt to push them out. Segregationists like Richard Russell and William Fulbright were lionized in their party throughout their lifetimes, as of course was Robert Byrd, who died as late as 2010 and was eulogized by leading Democrats and the progressive media.

HOW THE SOUTH BECAME REPUBLICAN

We still have one final mystery to clear up. If it wasn't because of white supremacy, how did the South—not just the Outer or Peripheral South, but also the Deep South—finally end up in the Republican camp? This question is taken up in political scientists Byron Shafer and Richard Johnston's important study, *The End of Southern Exceptionalism*.[49] This work, relatively unknown and with an admittedly strange title, provides a decisive refutation of the whole progressive theory of the Southern Strategy and the big switch.

The key questions that Shafer and Johnston ask are: when did the South move into the GOP camp, and which voters actually moved from Democratic to Republican? Shafer and Johnston show, first, that the South began its political shift in the Eisenhower era. Eisenhower, who won five Peripheral South states in 1956, was the first Republican to break the lock that the FDR Democrats had established in the South.

Obviously this early shift preceded the civil rights movement and cannot be attributed to it.

Shafer and Johnston, like Kevin Phillips, contend that after the postwar economic boom of the late 1940s and 1950s, the increasingly industrial "New South" was very receptive to the free-market philosophy of the Republican Party. Thus Shafer and Johnston introduce class as a rival explanation to race for why the South became Republican. In the 1960s, however, they cannot ignore the race factor. Shafer and Johnston ingeniously find a way to test the two explanations—race and class—against each other in order to figure out which one is more important.

Shafer and Johnston do this by dividing the South into two camps, the first made up of the wealthier, more industrial, more racially integrated South—this is the New South—and the second made up of the rural, agricultural, racially homogeneous South—this is the Old South that provided the historical base of the Democratic Party. Shafer and Johnston sensibly posit that if white Southerners are becoming Republican because of hostility to blacks, one would expect the Old South to move over first.

But in fact Shafer and Johnston find, through a detailed examination of the demographic data, that this is not the case. The wealthier, more industrial, more integrated New South moves first into the Republican Party. This happens in the 1950s and 1960s. By contrast, the rural, agricultural, racially homogenous Old South resists this movement. In other words, during the civil rights period the least racist white Southerners became Republicans and the most racist white Southerners stayed recalcitrantly in the Democratic Party.

Eventually, the Old South also transitioned into the GOP camp. But this was not until the late 1970s and through the 1980s, in response to the Reaganite appeal to free-market capitalism, patriotism, protection of the unborn, school prayer and family values. These economic and social issues were far more central to Reagan's message than race, and they struck a chord beyond—no less than within—the South. In 1980 Reagan lost just six states; in 1984 he lost only Mondale's home state of Minnesota. Obviously Reagan didn't need a specific Southern Strategy; he had an American strategy that proved wildly successful.

Reagan's success, however, was made possible by the sharp leftward move by the Democratic Party, starting with the nomination of George McGovern in 1972 and continuing though the 1970s. This swing to the left, especially on social and cultural issues like school prayer, pornography, recreational drugs and abortion, receives virtually no mention by progressive scholars because it disrupts their thesis that the trend in the South to the GOP was motivated primarily by race.

As far as congressional House and Senate seats are concerned, the South didn't become solidly Republican until 1994. Again, this was due to the Newt Gingrich agenda, which closely mirrored the Reagan agenda. Leftist historian Kevin Kruse spells out the Gingrich agenda— reducing taxes, ending the "marriage penalty" and more generally reducing the size of government—and then darkly implies that "this sort of appeal" also had a hidden racial component.[50] But everyone who voted for the Contract for America knows that this was not the case. Small-government conservatism is not racism.

Finally, we can figure out the meaning of the title of Shafer and Johnston's book. We are at "the end of Southern exceptionalism" because the South is no longer the racist preserve of the Democratic Party. The South has now become like the rest of the country. Southerners are Republican for the same reason that other Americans are Republican. And black Southerners vote Democratic for the same reason that blacks everywhere else vote Democratic. For whites no less than blacks, economic issues are predominant, foreign policy and social issues count too, and race has relatively little to do with it.

We can sum up this section by drawing two lines in the South, the line of racism and the line of Republican affiliation. When we draw these lines we see that they run in opposite directions. Survey data show that racism declined dramatically throughout the second half of the twentieth century, and precisely during this period the South moved steadily into the GOP camp. Thus as the South became *less* racist, it became *more* Republican. The progressive narrative is in ruins.

Still, don't expect the Democrats to quit. They have, after all, their new progressive plantation to protect. It may not have the aristocratic élan of the old nineteenth-century slave plantation, but it's the best FDR, LBJ and their cohorts could do to re-create the plantation system in the twentieth century. And as we will discover, this Democratic plantation is the true home of racist exploitation today. This fact, however, must be covered up if Democrats want to continue to win the votes of blacks and other minorities.

Consequently, we can expect the progressives to continue to chant about the Southern Strategy and the big switch, even when the evidence has collapsed all around them. They need this rationalization almost as much as they need the plantation itself to stay in power. In fact, their main goal now is to sustain the plantation and to expand it, and to that subject we turn in the next chapter.

9

MULTICULTURAL PLANTATIONS

Expanding the Culture of Dependency

> Nowhere in the ancient or modern
> world . . . is there the idea that people will
> become self-sufficient if they are given
> a lifetime income that is slightly better
> than subsistence with no requirement
> either to work or educate themselves.
>
> —SHELBY STEELE, *A Dream Deferred*[1]

In this chapter we examine the multicultural plantation, one whose foundation was established by LBJ but was built mostly by Bill Clinton and, even more, by Barack Obama. The multicultural plantation was made possible by the Immigration Act of 1965, which opened America's door to more than twenty-five million nonwhite immigrants mostly from Asia and Latin and South America. Democrats have seized on this demographic change, the third great wave of immigration in America's history, to create an expanded plantation system that incorporates blacks, Native Americans, Asian Americans and Hispanics. This plantation—fortified by an accompanying ideology of multiculturalism and identity politics—is the new venue for the most crippling racism that exists today.

Let's recapitulate our story about racism so far. Throughout this book we have been examining the exploitation schemes put into place by racism and white supremacy. These schemes have been quite varied, even as racism and white supremacy have remained the same. Thus the slave plantation from the 1820s through 1860 generated its own type of racism to justify the ownership of human beings by other human beings. In a country built on the proposition that "all men are created equal," it was difficult to have slavery without introducing the rationalization that the slaves were an inferior type of human or perhaps even subhuman, so that it would be acceptable to treat them like brutes or merchandise.

The slave plantation was also a self-contained ecosystem, transmitted through generations, with its own rules and codes. Work was mandatory—it was the point of the system—but masters knew slaves had no incentive to work, because they did not receive the fruits of their labor. Hence even masters who were ordinarily kind people knew they needed the whip to make the slaves work against their will.

Stealing in general was regarded indulgently by slave-owners because they recognized they owned not just the stolen property but also the thief who stole it. In no slave state were slave marriages legal, and there were special laws governing mulatto children who turned up. If a plantation owner impregnated a female slave, the law held that the offspring of that union remained a slave. Slave status, in other words, was transmitted through the mother. This was the way of the old slave plantation.

This rule was quite different from the one that operated under the second phase of racism and white supremacy, which was the progressive plantation phase, from the post-Reconstruction 1880s through the 1950s and 1960s. Here black identity was established by the one-drop rule, in which any discernible black heritage—theoretically a single drop of black blood—consigned one to inferior legal and social status. One progressive writer termed it "the mark of the Ethiopian."

This phase was defined by racial segregation and racial terrorism. This too was an intergenerational system with its own norms, defined by such features as separate schools and separate water fountains, the exclusion of blacks from public life with the possible exception of sports and entertainment, and the use of various forms of intimidation—lynching being only the most gruesome—to punish suspected black criminals and to suppress the black vote. This was the way of the progressive plantation.

But where are racism and white supremacy today? Since those earlier schemes of racist exploitation have ended—we don't have slavery of the antebellum type anymore, legal segregation has been abolished and no longer do roving hordes of costumed Klansmen ride roughshod over black communities—some might hold that racism and white supremacy have largely disappeared. I entertained this possibility in my 1995 book *The End of Racism*, in which I argued that while one could find episodic instances of racism, racism as a system of organized exploitation no longer controlled the lives of blacks or anyone else in America.[2]

That book stirred up a hornet's nest of progressive criticism. I remember a debate I had with Jesse Jackson at Stanford University in which I challenged him to show me evidence of racism now that was strong enough to prevent his children or my daughter from pursuing their dreams. Jackson confessed he couldn't, but he insisted that was not because racism had diminished. Rather, he said, it had gone underground and now operated covertly rather than overtly to thwart the aspirations of blacks and other minorities. The less we actually observe this racism, Jackson declared, the more insidious and powerful it is. You can imagine my frustration in attempting to refute this charge of invisible racism.

Yet in the past few decades the progressive left has become obsessively focused on invisible racism. The textbooks are full of concepts such as "subtle racism," "unintentional racism," "neoracism" and "cryptoracism." On one campus, a left-wing psychologist elaborated for me the distinctions between what he termed the three phrases of racism, the "oral phase," the "anal phase" and the "phallic-oedipal phase."

Progressive pundits insist that racism doesn't have to manifest itself through individual acts of racial discrimination; rather, there is "symbolic racism," involving the use of coded symbols like the flag to provoke racial animosity, and "institutional racism," operating through seemingly race-neutral practices such as university admissions policies, corporate hiring, bank lending and government contracts. Since those selection processes—merit-based though they might appear—disproportionately benefit whites over blacks, they are manifestations, we hear, of "white privilege" and "white supremacy."

This search for invisible racism strikes me as looking for racism in all the wrong places. Why pursue hidden racism when there is obvious racism staring us in the face? We can clarify this idea by asking a different question: is there a system of subjugation today that reveals the most blatant manifestation of racism and white supremacy and also represents the third phase of the plantation? This question generates a series of others. If so, how does it operate? Why don't the people who run the system want to fix it? Why don't the inhabitants get up and leave? Is such a system limited to blacks or does it also involve other minorities: Native Americans, Asian Americans and Latinos?

Clearly such a system exists and it is no less an intergenerational ecosystem of racial exploitation than were slavery and segregation, only its reach is much wider. Indeed, all the progressive gobbledygook about covert racism, institutional racism and white privilege seems designed to draw attention away from it. But here, in plain sight, is a racism for the twenty-first century, a whole ecology of human exploitation that is not just protected but cherished by progressive Democrats. It is time to visit the urban plantation.

STREETWISE

I've seen the urban plantation myself, up close, in cities like Detroit and Chicago, which I visited most recently in connection with my films. But for my guide I'd like to use progressives who grew up on the plantation or specialize in studying it. I'll begin with writer Ta-Nehisi Coates, who was raised on the rough streets of Baltimore. "To be black in the Baltimore of my youth," he writes, "was to be naked before the elements of the world, before all the guns, fists, knives, crack, rape and disease . . . Everyone had lost a child, somehow, to the streets, to jail, to drugs, to guns."

The underlying emotion of the urban plantation, for its inhabitants, is fear.

> The only people I knew were black, and all of them were powerfully, adamantly, dangerously afraid . . . It was always right in front of me. The fear was there in the extravagant boys of my neighborhood, in their large rings and medallions, their big puffy coats and

full-length fur-collared leathers, which was their armor against the world. They would stand on the corner of Gwynn Oak and Liberty, or Cold Spring and Park Heights, or outside Mondawmin Mall with their hands dipped in Russell sweats.

I think back on those boys now and all I see is fear . . . I learned that "Shorty, can I see your bike" was never a sincere question, and "Yo, you was messing with my cousin" was neither an earnest accusation nor a misunderstanding of the facts. These were the summonses that you answered with your left foot forward, your right foot back, your hands guarding your face . . . Or they were answered by breaking out, ducking through alleys, cutting through backyards, then bounding through the door . . . into your bedroom, pulling the tool out of your lambskin or from under your mattress or out of your Adidas shoebox, then . . . returning to that same block, on that same day . . . hollering out, "Yeah, nigger, what's up now?"

Coates understands that for young men on the urban plantation, it's all about power expressed through the ability "to crack knees, ribs and arms." He also knows how abnormal this environment is, and that there's another one in which "there were little white boys with complete collections of football cards, and their only want was a popular girlfriend and their only worry was poison oak. That other world was suburban and endless, organized around pot roasts, blueberry pies, fireworks, ice cream sundaes, immaculate bathrooms, and small toy trucks."[3]

Impressed as I am by Coates' raw, vivid descriptions, I notice he never asks the question: How exactly did my world get so screwed up? How can my Hobbesian world, where life is nasty, brutish and short, be converted into a happier, more peaceful one? Here Coates is maddeningly unhelpful, giving us nothing more than dark hints that the urban plantation is a creation of public policy. Yes, it is, but whose public policy? Coates does not say.

Nor is Coates impressed by attempted solutions. In another, more recent book, he lashes out at neighborhood gentrification, which refers to the project to transform poverty-stricken, crime-ridden neighborhoods by attracting new businesses, coffee shops and a young, upwardly mobile residential population. "Gentrification is but a more pleasing name for white supremacy," Coates writes. He views it as "the interest on enslavement, the interest on Jim Crow, the interest on redlining, compounding across the years, and these new urbanites living off that interest are, all of them, exulting in a crime."[4]

A much more comprehensive account of the urban plantation comes from the work of urban anthropologist Elijah Anderson, whose research focuses on the largely black neighborhoods of Philadelphia. While Anderson is a Philadelphia native, he approaches his topic in the manner of an anthropologist visiting a distant land, in other words, with clinical detachment. This makes his observations especially illuminating.

Anderson begins by describing how these same urban communities were once governed by an "old head," typically a "man of stable means who believed in hard work, family life and the church." His acknowledged role "was to teach, support, encourage and in effect socialize young men to meet their responsibilities." Young people "had confidence in the old head's ability to impart useful wisdom and practical advice." Even for those who didn't have dads to look after them, "the old head acted as surrogate father."

But today, Anderson writes, "the old head is losing his prestige and authority," displaced by drug-dealing gangs who have convinced "street smart young boys . . . that the old head's lessons about life and the work ethic are no longer relevant." Anderson's point here is the urban plantation isn't simply a continuation of earlier black communities that formed under sharecropping and segregation; rather, it is a new creation of the past few decades, with a new culture and new role models.

The gangs have created a new "code of the street," which is the title of one of Anderson's books. "At the heart of the code," Anderson writes, "is the issue of respect." Yet this respect is obtained by "taking the possessions of others." Anderson explains: "Possessing the trophy can symbolize the ability to violate somebody—to 'get in his face,' to dis him—and thus to enhance one's own worth by stealing someone else's." Even trivial conflicts, such as a dispute over a pair of sneakers or a perceived insult to one's manhood or one's girlfriend, can result in modern-day duels that leave people gravely injured or killed.

Even holdups at gunpoint, Anderson points out, are power transactions involving respect. "The holdup man wants first to relieve the victim of his property. The victim does not want to give it up. Yet the streetwise victim fully cooperates and may even help the perpetrator rob him. He says, 'All right. There it is. Please don't hurt me.' In saying this, he is effectively submitting to the power of the holdup man. Such deferential behavior is itself often a large part of what the stickup man wants. He wants the person 'with something' to recognize him, to acknowledge his power and what he can do to the victim."

Anderson contends that "central to the issue of manhood is the widespread belief that one of the most effective ways of gaining respect is to manifest nerve. True nerve expresses a lack of fear of death . . . Conveying the attitude of being able to take somebody else's life if the situation demands it gives one a real sense of power on the streets." The code of the street can turn an otherwise polite and deferential person into a potential murderer.

When a street kid is murdered, Anderson says, it is customary for friends and relatives to "vent anger at the newspaper for not running a long enough story" or to "vent at the police, calling them incompetent, racist or worse." At the funeral, "they speak of the deceased . . . They wonder aloud why this happened, but in fact they know why. They know the boy was a drug dealer. They know he violated in some way the code of the street." Yet among all the testimonials about the boy's life nothing is said about these matters.

According to Anderson, the code of the street is also built in opposition to the normal code of getting ahead in society, for example, through hard work or education. Instead, Anderson writes, gangs help to create an "oppositional culture" in which it is considered cool not to go to school, not to hold a steady job, but rather to make money through theft, extortion, selling drugs and manipulating the system of federal handouts. To play the system is, in Anderson's words, and in the title of another of his books, to be "streetwise."

Perhaps the most interesting section of Anderson's urban anthropology focuses on how streetwise males take pride in seducing women with extravagant but dishonest promises of commitment and marriage, getting them pregnant and then abandoning them contemptuously and repeating the process with other women. "The girls have a dream," Anderson writes, "the boys a desire."

In Anderson's account, "The man derides family values and . . . feels hardly any obligation to his string of women and the children he has fathered. In fact, he considers it a measure of success if he can get away without being held legally accountable for his out-of-wedlock children. To his hustling mentality, generosity is a weakness . . . Self-aggrandizement consumes his whole being and is expressed in his penchant for a glamorous lifestyle, fine clothes and fancy cars."

The sexual conquest begins with the "rap," which constitutes the "verbal element of the game . . . Among peer-group members, raps are assessed, evaluated and divided into weak and strong. The assessment of the young man's rap is, in effect, the evaluation of his whole game." The winnings of the game are described as "hit and run" or "booty." Moreover, "The young man not only must 'get some,' he must also prove he is getting it."

At first, Anderson writes, the impregnated women feel crushed because they realize they have been betrayed. Yet they soon discover that, in the culture of the urban plantation, having a baby becomes "a rite of passage to adulthood." Suddenly these young women discover they have something they can call their own, and "the teenage mother derives status from her baby." They become part of what Anderson calls the "baby club"; many similarly placed women welcome the newcomer into their fold.

Welfare is not the reason for getting pregnant, Anderson insists. But it affords "a limited but steady income" that becomes the means for teenage women to escape the often painful circumstances of their own homes and to establish their own single-parent household. Sometimes this brings the deadbeat back, seeking the woman's attention, not because he now cares for her but because he has his eye on her welfare check. Some men maintain a virtual harem of impregnated women whom they inveigle for money. And even when the actual father stays out of the picture, Anderson reports, the welfare check can still serve as a mechanism to "attract other men who need money."

Sometimes the father of the child is willing to provide as best he can. This happens rarely because "to own up to a pregnancy is to go against the peer-group street ethic of hit and run." But in these cases too, Anderson says, welfare often provides an incentive for young women to deny the paternity of the child's father, because "a check from the welfare office is often more dependable than the irregular support payments of a sporadically employed youth." Because of the relative security that births to unwed mothers bring in this way, Anderson argues that illegitimacy has lost its earlier stigma and become "socially acceptable."[5]

WORST PLACES ON THE PLANET

Reviewing these accounts of the urban plantation, I have to say that it is one of the worst places on the planet. Obviously there are more impoverished places in the Third World, such as in the favelas of Brazil or the slums of Mumbai. Crime and corruption are rife. But if you take a poor slum kid from Asia or South America and transplant him to a place with jobs and opportunity, mostly likely he or she would flourish.

The school I attended in India, St. Stanislaus in the outskirts of Mumbai, had day-schoolers like me who commuted from home but also a boarding population mostly of orphans who lived on campus and were under the care of the missionary priests who ran the school. The priests served as a kind of surrogate family for these boarding school students. Lacking every decent amenity that we day-schoolers took for granted, many of the boarders went on to careers as doctors, engineers and corporate executives.

How was this possible? As I discovered, middle-class kids had lots of games and distractions but these poor kids studied four to five hours a day. They put in an hour before school started and another three or more after school let out. This more than compensated for the family advantage that I had, coming from a home with literate and relatively cultured parents. I had to work hard to compete with these students on tests and examinations.

My experience illustrates the point that kids around the world lack money and they lack education, but the vast majority want to succeed and they want to learn. Give them education and they will eagerly seize it. Offer them employment and they will work hard and save money in order to rise up. What this means is that even the poorest communities typically sustain a culture of work and family—sometimes a surrogate family—that is necessary to survive under dire conditions and that helps produce upward mobility, perhaps even success, under more favorable circumstances.

Not so with the urban plantation. Here there is a dearth of jobs, but what type of business would want to move into areas that are so dysfunctional and dangerous? Moreover, one does not get the sense that even if there were jobs they would attract the young men that Coates and Anderson describe with their gold chains and pimp walks and confrontational mannerisms. Can we envision these guys showing up for work at Ford or Procter & Gamble, maintaining a disciplined routine, taking instructions from authority, conducting product inventory, working the assembly line, or interacting with customers?

Pastor Eugene Rivers worked for decades in the inner cities of the Northeast. His answer to this question is a resounding no. Almost twenty years ago Rivers published an article in the *Boston Review* in which he made the startling observation that "unlike many of our ancestors, who came out of slavery and entered this century with strong backs, discipline, a thirst for literacy, deep religious faith, and hope in the face of monumental adversity, we have produced . . . a 'new jack' generation, ill-equipped to secure gainful employment even as productive slaves."

Rivers' point is that the slaves had real skills, as carpenters, plumbers, weavers, masons, mechanics, cooks and so on. However reluctant they may have been to work without pay, they did work, and consequently they developed the habits of work. Once slavery ended, such people knew how to do things and they had the work ethic to hold down a job. But this does not seem to be true of the new generation on the urban plantation. These young people are so nihilistic, so lacking in skills and motivation, that in Rivers' searing words they "would be ineligible to qualify for *slavery*."[6]

This is one critical respect in which the urban plantation differs from the slave plantation. The slaves all worked while many modern urban plantation dwellers don't, nor do they aspire to do so in the normal, productive economy. To the extent they do have jobs, those jobs are criminal assignments, and unsurprisingly many young men have been convicted of a variety of offenses, from burglary to assault to drug crimes, and have served time.

So pervasive is this problem that, according to the Sentencing Commission, nearly one in three young African American men is at any given time in prison, on probation or on parole.[7] Conviction and incarceration make their lives even more difficult, as I found out myself after my felony conviction on the campaign finance issue. It was harder for me to get health insurance and life insurance, even though my offense was a white-collar one, posing no dangers to my health or life chances. For these young men, a felony conviction makes businesses reluctant to hire them even when they are released from captivity, so the prospect of lawful work becomes even more unlikely.

So let's draw out the analogy between the old slave plantation and the new urban plantation. In both cases we have a group that doesn't work, refuses to work, is sexually dissolute and obsessed with luxurious display, status and respect, and gets into duels—sometimes lethal duels—over petty objects like a pair of sneakers or insults. Just to be clear, I am not making a predictable comparison between the inhabitants of the urban plantation and the slaves. Rather, I am making one between the inhabitants of the urban plantation and the slave-owners.

The Democratic planter class, after all, was made up of people who did nothing, whiling away their time in duels, sexual chicanery, card games, cockfights and luxurious displays. And they could get by with doing nothing because they relied on the slaves to do all the work. While their ideology proclaimed the slaves to be dependent on them, they were in fact dependent on the slaves. On the urban plantation, too, inhabitants do little or no productive work. And most of them can manage without employment because in one way or another they are dependent on the federal government.

Another similarity between the old Democratic plantation and the new is that in both of them the family structure is in complete disarray. On the Democratic slave plantation, the slave-master was typically married, but this did not stop him from carrying on with the female slaves. As for the slaves, they might cohabit, but they could not legally marry, and their offspring were the property not of the parents but of the master. On the Democratic urban plantation, marriage, though legal, is virtually unheard of, and illegitimacy rates of 75 to 90 percent are common.

It is tempting to attribute the breakdown of the black family today to the legacy of slavery, and many progressive scholars and pundits do exactly this. The classic work here is E. Franklin Frazier's *The Negro Family in the United States,* published in 1939. Frazier argued that the matriarchal family structure under slavery persisted into the twentieth century. Others, including diplomat Daniel Patrick Moynihan, who worked for Nixon but went on to become a Democratic senator from New York, built on Frazier's analysis to blame slavery for the modern black family in which children typically grow up without a father.[8]

Let's think about why the matriarchal model of black family life was adaptive during slavery. Slavery as an institution depreciated the role of the man as provider and protector. During slavery, fathers did not feed, clothe or put a roof over the heads of their children. The plantation owner did this. Nor could fathers protect their spouses and daughters from being humiliated or violated by the man in the Big House. Slave mothers, by contrast, not only gave life to their children but also looked after them. Consequently, the father as father became a dispensable figure, and the black family in enslavement became a matriarchal household.

Still, the black family outlasted slavery. Recent work by scholars, notably the progressive historian Herbert Gutman, show that despite the enormous strains that slavery placed on the black family, blacks worked hard to reunite and rebuild their families after slavery, and they did so not on a matriarchal model but rather on that of the traditional "nuclear" family, which was the prevailing norm for African Americans through the first two-thirds of the twentieth century.

Gutman's work is confirmed by the data. In 1900, W. E. B. Du Bois estimated the illegitimacy rate for blacks to be around 25 percent. Du Bois attributed this mostly to slavery. The rate stayed roughly constant from 1900 through the early 1960s, when it soared to over 50 percent. Then it soared even more through subsequent decades so that today the illegitimacy rate for blacks is a staggering 75 percent.

This is probably the single factor most responsible for retarding the development of young people on the urban plantation. As anthropologist Bronislaw Malinowski put it in *Sex, Culture and Myth*, it is a "universal sociological law" that "no child should be brought into the world without a man—and one man at that—assuming the role of sociological father, that is, guardian and protector, the male link between the child and the rest of the community."[9]

Malinowski's statement was not controversial at the time. Many other anthropologists, including Margaret Mead, made the same point.[10] Today, however, anyone who says that children should not be raised without fathers is routinely attacked by progressive and left-wing activists. These activists have become intellectual apologists for the expanded Democratic plantation. They have no problem with high illegitimacy rates for blacks and other minorities and resist those who treat this problem as a problem.

The dramatic increase in black illegitimacy from 25 to 75 percent occurred during and after LBJ's Great Society. We cannot blame it on slavery. We must attribute it to things that happened during this period, notably the emergence of an urban plantation culture that produced widespread illegitimacy and a federal government willing and ready to subsidize (and thus encourage) it. In other words, we can't fault the Democrats of the Jacksonian era; we must fault the Democrats from LBJ's time to our own. These Democrats have been not merely the enablers but also the cheerleaders of family breakdown on the modern plantation.

LEARNED HELPLESSNESS

We are now in a position to answer some of the questions raised at the outset of this chapter. Why don't inhabitants of the urban planation get up and leave? The answer is that the culture of the plantation breeds a kind of "learned helplessness." The term was coined by psychologist Martin Seligman, who accidentally discovered the phenomenon while doing research on dogs. Seligman and a colleague saw that dogs subjected to electric shock turned passive and made no effort to escape even though they could easily avoid subsequent shocks by jumping over a small barrier.

Seligman subsequently applied the concept of learned helplessness to individuals. Children who do poorly on math tests begin to feel helpless about their chances for learning math. Women who are habitually shy never want to venture out into social situations because they are resigned to perpetual shyness. Torture victims develop a passivity that makes them inured to being tortured.

Learned helplessness refers to the way that once the mind is conditioned in a certain way, it can become immobilized in that state. In this sense, learned helplessness is an enslavement of the mind. Today it has become a basic principle of behavior analysis and behavior therapy. While Seligman used the concept for individual analysis, however, we can also apply it to groups. Groups can learn to be helpless just as individuals can.[11]

Learned helplessness seems to be the reason why people who live miserable lives on the urban plantation nevertheless don't get up and leave. They have become used to the plantation; even if they feel an impulse to leave they cannot, as there is nowhere for them to go. They lack the skills and sometimes even the motivation to survive outside the plantation. They are too dependent on the drug culture, the crime culture and the culture of government subsidy and support. So while they are free in theory to exit, their minds remain captive, no less to the Democratic Party than to the urban plantation.

What about the people who run the urban plantation? I am referring here to the whole class of overseers: the politicians, the intellectuals, the public defenders and class-action lawyers, the social workers and administrators who together operate and uphold the plantation. Why don't they fix, improve and rehabilitate it to make it more livable? The short answer is that they have no reason to do this. The urban plantation is run entirely by Democrats. Most of these inner cities are one-party states. There is not a Republican in sight. Every position from the mayor on down is held by Democrats. So these are Democratic plantations in the same way that the old rural plantations were Democratic plantations. Many things change over time, but some don't.

The urban plantation as currently constructed by the Democrats works just fine for the Democratic Party. It creates a dependent class that the Democrats can service, maintaining inhabitants in a position of meager provision so that they are content enough to vote to keep the subsidies coming, but not so well provided for that they might entertain the thought of leaving or making it on their own, in which case they would cease to be a reliable political constituency for progressive Democrats.

Additionally, the meager circumstances and cultural pathologies of the urban plantation create a resentment among inhabitants. The Democrats steer this resentment toward the Republicans, and the white man and the larger society, always forgetting to mention that it is they—the Democrats—who actually run these places. Instead Democrats use the racial resentment generated by the way they run the urban plantation to bludgeon society and condemn America for failing its most vulnerable citizens. The whole idea is to extract an increasing fund of capital for the urban plantation that, however, never actually fixes anything but keeps the inhabitants in a state of lasting, intergenerational dependency.

The Democrats have recruited a whole class of people, black and white, to organize, administer and defend the urban plantation. This is the new overseer class, typified by longtime Democratic congressman Charles Rangel of New York. In 2010, an eight-member panel of the House Ethics Committee found that this African American representative had brought "discredit to the House" by violating federal laws or ethics rules. He had obtained donations from people with business before his committee to fund a center named after him; failed to pay taxes on a Caribbean home; used a rent-subsidized apartment for campaign purposes; and not properly disclosed more than $600,000 in assets and income.[12]

Although the New York Times described the House Ethics Committee findings as a "staggering fall" for the senior House Democrat, Rangel was comfortably reelected in 2012, and he remained in the House until 2017. How is this possible? It is possible because like the Tammany bosses of old, today's overseers retain their power based on the patronage that they dispense to their dependents. Without the overseers, the inhabitants of the plantation cannot survive. Consequently, overseers have a virtually foolproof system for staying in power, no matter what shenanigans they pull in office.

But you don't have to be unethical to be an overseer on the urban plantation. John Lewis, a legitimate civil rights hero, is a leading overseer. He and Rangel may be opposites in moral character, but in their collaboration to sustain the Democratic plantation, they are in it together. So are Michelle Alexander, author of The New Jim Crow, and Ta-Nehisi Coates. These writers derive their moral status from being spokespersons for black suffering. Harsh though it may be to say it, they have a stake in that suffering. Their careers would not be the same without it.

Today there are two kinds of people who can be found on the urban plantation: the people who live there, and the people who control them. We can spot these people here and there in books like *Streetwise* and *Code of the Street*. But in reality they are everywhere. We are talking about hordes of social workers involved in urban planning, education, health, welfare, academic research, housing, alcohol and drug rehabilitation and innumerable other programs. In some areas this group seems to rival in size the population it is supposedly taking care of.

Here we see how the plantation, which does not create employment for its inhabitants, nevertheless does provide stable employment to a whole class of academics, social workers and bureaucrats. The employment is stable because the plantation is permanent; there are no plans for it to ever be dismantled. The "war against poverty" is a perpetual fight in which poverty always wins because the game is rigged and the combatants are not fighting to win, only to hold the line.

Not surprisingly, overseers of the urban plantation like Coates also become its tenacious defenders. They aggressively fend off criticism of the plantation and roundly abuse those who try to find ways to help people to leave the plantation.

No wonder Coates suppresses the role of the Democratic Party in creating and sustaining the plantation. Over the past few decades, we have seen how ferociously Coates and his fellow overseers respond to proposals to transform the urban plantation or to help people escape from it.

They don't want to end social policies that subsidize illegitimacy; yet they have no plans of their own to restore and stabilize the black family. They oppose law-and-order schemes to reduce black-on-black crime in dangerous neighborhoods. Meanwhile, they rail against white and even black policemen who may develop stereotypical biases by working in these rough neighborhoods but who remain, nevertheless, the best protectors of black life on the urban plantation.

The grand pooh-bahs of the overseer class despise the fight against drugs and insist that drug dealers be released from prison. Drug incarceration, they insist, is the "new Jim Crow." They hate gentrification or schemes for "enterprise zones" in the inner city. They detest parental choice and educational reforms that attempt to give young people the job skills to enable them to move out and go where the jobs are. In sum, they protect the interests of the overseer class. They don't want to dismantle the plantation and they don't want "runaways."

It is time now to revisit the concept of the Uncle Tom, which I introduced earlier with Du Bois and Booker T. Washington. I do so because this is the accusation that plantation overseers routinely and almost inevitably apply to black conservatives who promote schemes of self-help and self-reliance. These conservatives are accused of being collaborators with racists and traitors to the black community. Since I know these people I can tell you that Thomas Sowell, Shelby Steele, Walter Williams, Clarence Thomas and many others are depressingly familiar with these baseless accusations. The latest target of overseer attack appears to be the rap artist Kanye West, who is not a conservative but who has declared himself to be a freethinker and has shown his independence by appearing in public wearing a MAGA hat signed by Trump himself.

What makes the Uncle Tom charges especially ironic, of course, is that they are advanced by members of the overseer class who are, just like Du Bois, the real collaborators with a racist plantation scheme. The new overseers sustain the urban plantation just as the old overseers sustained the old rural plantation. Yet this relationship of power and dependency between overseers and inhabitants is camouflaged by the rhetoric of racial solidarity that Democratic overseers routinely employ. Their favorite term is "we," much as the old master class liked to refer to "my family black and white."

In reality, however, the interests of the overseer class and the inhabitants of the urban plantation are very different. The inhabitants want to move up and make it, and this can only be achieved by transforming the inner cities or by moving out of them, just as whites and so many others have. But this is the last thing that the overseers want. It is the mission of this group to ensure that the inhabitants of the plantation stay in perpetual dependency. Thus they can justly be considered betrayers of the people whose welfare they are charged with. So the real Uncle Toms are accusing people who are not Uncle Toms of being Uncle Toms.

OVERSEERS WITHOUT A PLANTATION

Something interesting happened when President Trump advanced a proposal to extend the so-called Dream Act (DACA), enabling the children of illegals to stay in the United States. Trump agreed to keep 1.8 million DACA "dreamers" on the condition that Democrats also support increased border security and funding for a wall to restrict the entry of illegal aliens. Trump insisted that he would not accept a DACA solution that did not involve more comprehensive immigration reform. One might expect that Trump's position would be resisted by Latino progressives like Univision host Jorge Ramos, and it was. But interestingly enough, it was also resisted by African American and Asian American activists.

At a gathering of more than one thousand African Americans at Atlanta's Ebenezer Baptist Church, organized to celebrate the legacy of Martin Luther King Jr., pastor and activist Raphael Warnock condemned Trump as "a willfully ignorant, racist, xenophobic, narcissistic con man." Taking up the DACA cause, Warnock thundered, "Some of us came on immigrant ships, others of us came on slave ships, but we're all in the same boat."[13] Interestingly Warnock made no reference to those who have come here unlawfully; in line with progressive talking points, he slyly conflated legals and illegals, putting both into the umbrella category of "immigrants."

Around the same time, Asian American activists showed up at a pro-DACA rally outside a federal building in Los Angeles, where Democratic representative Judy Chu declared that Trump's willingness to rescind DACA was "a cruel and devastating blow to the nearly 800,000 young Americans currently enrolled in the program. This indefensible action is an open attack on America's immigrant communities and undermines our core values as a nation."

Chu's rhetoric was echoed by representatives of an alphabet soup of Asian American civil rights organizations: the National Council of Asian Pacific Americans, the Southeast Asia Resource Action Center and the Asian American Legal Defense and Education Fund. I happened to see this rally on TV. Yet when the cameras panned to the audience, there were hardly any Asian Americans, just a few Asian tourists, who looked like they were from Japan, taking pictures and laughing.[14]

What's going on here? DACA is an overwhelmingly Hispanic or Latino issue. So what explains the involvement among black and Asian American activists? And they aren't just involved; their tone on the

DACA issue is one of hysteria. Clearly something bigger is going on here. We're seeing the expansion of the Democratic urban plantation beyond blacks to include other groups. None of these other groups has a full-scale urban plantation; one of them does not even inhabit a plantation.

Asian Americans don't have a plantation; in fact, as a group, they illustrate the difficulties and limits of the Democratic project to expand the plantation. There are sizable Asian American communities in Los Angeles and one or two other cities. But by and large the Asian Americans who move into the inner city move out as soon as they can, typically within a single generation. For the Democrats, this is very problematic. How do the Asians do it? They do it by succeeding academically, professionally and entrepreneurially.

Asian Americans are vastly overrepresented at the nation's top colleges and universities. Not surprisingly, Asian Americans are, despite their relatively small population, more likely than other groups to become doctors, engineers, software programmers. Asian Americans form more businesses on average than other groups, including whites. Asian American median household income is around $78,000 as compared with the white median household income of around $62,000. This success has earned Asian Americans the title of "model minority." Democrats, however, aren't into model minorities; they like dependent minorities.

Asian Americans have a history of being victimized by the Democratic Party. The Democratic unions excluded the Chinese and Japanese, and progressive Democrats lobbied for immigration restrictions that kept Asians out of the country. In World War II, FDR interned Japanese Americans under suspicion of disloyalty, although he did not even consider locking up Italian and German Americans. Today the affirmative action policies that progressives implement throughout academia discriminate both in academic admissions and job hiring against more qualified Asian Americans and in favor of less qualified African Americans and Hispanics.

Even so, the absence of an Asian American plantation and the seemingly obvious compatibility of Asian Americans with the Republican Party have not stopped Democrats from recruiting Asian American overseers. How does this process work? It works in two steps. The first is that progressives use their influence in academia and popular culture to cajole Asian Americans into their camp. Asian Americans are eager to assimilate to the culture in which they find themselves—a culture they identify with status and success—and in the university they encounter the regnant progressive culture and so assimilate to that.

The progressive appeal to the Asian American elite is through identity politics. Progressives welcome them not for their individual achievements but for their "diversity." Notwithstanding the absurdity of lumping, say, a Pakistani and a Chinese, with no cuisine, religion or culture in common, under the umbrella category of "Asian," the left manages to convince some of these people to think of themselves in that way and even to become professional Asians—that is, purported spokespeople for the Asian American community.

This offer comes with financial support. Basically the Asian American groups are not sustained through membership; there are hardly any members. Rather, they are funded by progressive philanthropic foundations like the Ford Foundation and the Carnegie Foundation. These groups create shadow ethnic organizations that then have offices and letterhead and issue statements purporting to speak for Asian Americans even though they actually speak only for themselves—or more precisely they become parrots for the progressive party line.

The presence of shadow organizations is important for what the Democrats are now trying to create, not a single African American plantation but multicultural plantations involving every ethnic minority group. In the case of Asian Americans, if Democrats can't get full-blown plantations, they want at least the simulacra of them. But the left wants every minority group to be part of the picture. In the twenty-first-century scenario, the Democrats want black urban plantations, Hispanic plantations, Asian American plantations and Native American plantations.

REZ LIFE

We see here how the Democrats are moving toward realizing Lincoln's fear. Lincoln feared the triumph of a Democratic national plantation system controlling and subjugating more and more groups of people. For Lincoln the nightmare scenario was the expansion of black plantations to some form of white plantations. The Democrats, however, have gone for a tricolor plantation featuring (to put the matter in crude stereotypes) black, brown and yellow people. To each minority ethnic group its own plantation, with a single group—the progressive Democrats—lording it over all of them.

Native American plantations don't bear that name; they are called, of course, reservations. These reservations are rural, not urban. Most native Indians don't live on reservations; just one in five—some 400,000 out of a population of 2 million—do. Yet reservations continue to define Native American identity. There are around 310 reservations in the United States. Most are on virtually uninhabitable land, the result of the forced relocation of the principal tribes in six Southern states in the nineteenth century by the Jacksonian Democrats. Yet upon closer examination, the native Indian reservations bear a striking resemblance to the Democrats' urban plantation.

I visited South Dakota's Pine Ridge reservation a few years ago while filming the movie *America*. I interviewed Sioux tribal leader Charmaine White Face, and even though we disagreed strongly about Columbus—a genocidal maniac, in her view—we had a good rapport. She took me for a drive through the vast reservation, and I was struck by the ramshackle dwellings, the filth, the cars on the lawn, the wild dogs running around and the disconsolate native people sitting around in clusters, apparently doing nothing. Struck by the absence of office buildings or businesses of any sort, I asked White Face, "Where do most people around here work?" She replied, "Our unemployment rate is 80 percent. Most people around here do not work."

Pine Ridge reservation, White Face told me, is one of the largest reservations in the country, and the poorest. Like other reservations, it is run by the Bureau of Indian Affairs (BIA), an agency of the federal government. While in theory the native Indians are separate nations, in reality they are, as the Supreme Court once termed them, "dependent nations"—dependent on the government through the BIA. Government control is virtually absolute, White Face said, and the quality of services, from housing to education to the reduction of toxic pollution, is uniformly terrible. "If you want to know what government-run healthcare looks like," White Face warned, "come see the mess that we have here."

David Treuer, a member of the Ojibwe tribe, lives on Red Lake reservation in Minnesota. In his book *Rez Life,* he describes the texture of life there.

> There aren't really any farms on Red Lake Reservation, and there are only a few backwoods businesses advertising welding, small-engine repair or logging. There are only four convenience stores I know of . . . Other than these, there is no place to buy gas or food. There were no hotels until 2010, when Red Lake opened a casino . . . Until the new casino was built the biggest building on the rez, except for the hospital, was the BIA Jail.
>
> There are no hair salons, Starbucks, Einstein Brothers Bagels, cell phone stores, Radio Shacks, Jiffy Lubes, McDonald's, Arby's, Rent-A-Centers, car dealerships, Gaps or Old Navy stores. There aren't even any real billboards. What signs do exist are often small, hand painted on plywood, as often as not propped against a tree rather than planted on the ground . . . All of this—this nothing—on a reservation the same size as Rhode Island.

Since nontribal members are not as a rule allowed to live on the reservation, Treuer turns his attention to a strange sight on the highway leading up to the reservation, which he calls the Compound. The Compound, he writes, houses what he terms the "foreign" workers—government officials, welfare bureaucrats, research teams, medical personnel, teachers and administrators—a veritable army of overseers who help oversee the reservation but don't belong to it.

Many native Indians are hostile to these "foreigners," whom they associate with "the white man." Many of their complaints seem to be legitimate, given the atrociously low levels of education and opportunity. Some native Indians, young and old, demonstrate their resistance to the white man by refusing to learn his language. Remarkably, they speak no English. I wonder what school conducted in English must be like for students who speak no English. The students who endure this must experience it as surreal.

But interestingly the overseers of the reservation do nothing to fix these problems or even to combat the racial resentment. Indeed, they encourage it. Treuer doesn't know the reason, but a pretty good guess is that they know it will keep the Indians clustered together on the reservation, under their supervision. Otherwise they may get the crazy idea to leave and make it in the white man's world.

Native American life at Red Lake, Treuer informs us, is bad as measured on a whole train of indices, in line with the situation facing native Indians on most reservations. The only affluent tribes are the ones that operate successful casinos, such as the Seminole in Florida. Red Lake has a casino, but since the reservation is in the middle of nowhere, attendance is relatively sparse. Average household income in America: over $50,000. Average household income at Red Lake: $21,000. The unemployment rate is in the range of 50 percent, and teen unemployment approaches 100 percent.

Treuer movingly describes the cultural pathologies of life at Red Lake, again quite similar to those at other reservations. Family life is chaotic, as suggested by the remarks of a native Indian policeman, Steve Hagenah. "As you know," Hagenah tells Treuer, "families are all broken up . . . Sometimes when I've got to interview someone, a witness or whatever, I go to three or four, sometimes five places before I find who I'm looking for. Kids are floating all over the place and their own families don't know where they are . . . These kids are like motor pool cars. No one takes care of them until they're broken. And then it's too late."

In confirmation of an old stereotype, there are serious problems of drugs and alcohol. Suicide rates are high. A major cause of death is traffic accidents, which apparently occur much more frequently here than anywhere else. Violence is epidemic, occurring at ten times the rate it does in the rest of the country. Treuer notes that in one town called Bena, population 140, one in six residents has done more than ten years in prison.

Sound familiar? I don't know if Treuer or Whiteface has ever been to Baltimore, Chicago or Oakland, but if they visited those places I think they would see how the federal government has wreaked the same havoc on them as it has on Pine Ridge and other Indian reservations. On the urban plantation, as on the reservation, no one seems to do much, but there is one thing that they do reliably. Red Lake Indians, according to Treuer, are conscientious voters. "More than

90 percent of Red Lakers go to the polls. Of these, 90 percent vote Democratic."[15]

THE MULTICULTURAL PLANTATION

The Democrats' new plantation, just like the old Democratic slave plantation, must expand in order to survive. Let us see why this is so. Blacks are 12 percent of the population, so with 90 percent of blacks voting Democratic, the Democrats have locked in 10 percent of the vote. American Indians are less than 1 percent of the population, and the Democrats get most of them. Asian Americans are just under 5 percent and the Democrats get around 60 percent of them. Still, this is less than 15 percent of the total population.

But there is another group, Hispanics, or Latinos, who are even more numerous than blacks, 13 percent of the population. These terms "Hispanic" and "Latino" are not racial. This group includes light-skinned and dark-skinned people who typically have a mixture, in varying proportions, of white, black and Asian heritage. "Hispanic" is linguistic, referring to people from the Spanish-speaking countries south of the border. "Latino" is a wider term, encompassing people of Central or South American descent, including, for example, Brazilians who typically don't speak Spanish. Since both terms are in popular use, however, I use them interchangeably.

Hispanics are the nation's largest minority and, being a young population, also the fast-growing. Some demographers estimate they will make up 25 percent of the population by 2040. If the Democrats could get 90 percent of Hispanics, this would add at least 10 percent to their current vote, raising them to a guaranteed base of 25 percent of the national total with the promise of an even greater harvest in the future.

Now it's just a matter of getting to 51 percent, or more accurately, to the electoral vote total needed to win elections. To their locked-in ethnic base the Democrats expect to add in other reliable Democratic voters—professors, journalists, artists—as well as other identity groups—feminists, a group mainly composed of single women and unmarried mothers, and homosexual and transsexual activists—and there is the Democrats' electoral majority. At least, this is the strategy of the Democrats today.

So now we turn to the Hispanic plantation, otherwise known as the barrio. Right away we confront a puzzle. We might expect that Democrats would be energetically courting Latino citizens, making the case for how wonderful the barrio is, for how much they are doing for the barrio and so on. But we hear none of this. Instead we hear about DACA "dreamers" and illegal immigration.

Dreamers, according to a series of recent tweets by Democratic senator Charles Schumer of New York, are America's best citizens. In 2018 Democrats briefly shut down the government in angry resistance to Trump's refusal to go along with their DACA "fix." This political allegiance to illegals is bizarre in that, with the possible exception of some cases of voter fraud (where illegals show up and cast a ballot), in general illegals can't vote. What, then, explains the priority of this issue with progressive Democrats?

Leading Democrats say that they sympathize with illegals as much as they sympathize with blacks and other minorities. I suspect this is true, and I interpret it to mean that they sympathize with all these groups to the extent that they prove to be politically useful to them. Progressives also declare that America needs illegals; without them—as Hillary Clinton suggested a few years ago—who will do the menial jobs like cleaning hotel rooms and picking fruit that illegals routinely do?

Leave aside the racist condescension of this statement, which closely mirrors the views of pro-slavery Democrats like James Henry Hammond, who defended slavery on the grounds of a so-called mudsill theory: in sum, there was dirty, degrading work to be done, and therefore we needed a dirty, degraded class of slaves to do it. In reality, between 1942 and 1964 America had a guest-worker program for Mexican Americans, the Bracero program, which allowed them to work legally in this country without becoming American citizens.

Nearly five million Mexican contract laborers came to the United States under this program, mainly as agricultural workers. Despite periodic complaints about farmers taking advantage of these foreign workers—there was even a television exposé, *Harvest of Shame*—on the whole the program was profitable for growers and beneficial to the workers, which is why the workers kept coming. Yet in 1964 a Democratic Congress with President Johnson's approval shut down the Bracero program.

Why? One of the strongest proponents of closing down the guest-worker program was the Mexican American activist Cesar Chavez. Chavez believed that Mexicans coming to America as guest workers and working for low wages would prevent Hispanics in this country from unionizing farm labor and pushing—with government backing—for higher wages from the growers. And in fact Chavez's farm worker movement only took off, and was able to secure 40 percent wage increases for grape pickers, once the Bracero program was terminated.[16]

As we might suspect after considering the fate of the Bracero program, the progressive focus has always been on recruiting citizens who can vote onto the Democratic plantation. With Hispanics today, the left is trying multiple initiatives. The first is to make the case that America stole the upper half of Mexico from Latinos and therefore Latinos should "take back their country" by rallying together as Democrats. This argument has limited validity in that the Mexicans who ended up on the American side of the border prospered far more than their counterparts in Mexico. Even so, this progressive pitch resonates with some young Latinos who like to think of themselves as aggrieved victims.

A second approach is bilingual education. Here the left emphasizes that it is not necessary for Hispanics to all learn English in the mode of earlier generations of immigrants, who shed their native languages and adopted the American lingua franca. The point of bilingual education is not merely for Democrats to show appreciation of the native language of Hispanics but also to maintain Hispanic group solidarity. The Democrats need Hispanics and Latinos united as a class in the Democratic camp.

Bilingual education is typically part of a more comprehensive progressive ideology, the ideology known as multiculturalism. Multiculturalism is a doctrine of culture, of the equality of all cultures. The basic idea here is that all ethnic cultures are equal and none is better or worse than any other. "Each human culture is so unique," writes Latino anthropologist Renato Rosaldo, that "no one of them is higher or lower, greater or lesser than any other."[17]

The point of this is not merely to teach ethnic pride or self-esteem. Nor is it, as usually advertised, a campaign to defeat "hate." Rather, it is to teach Hispanics—along with blacks, Native Americans and Asian Americans—to each affirm their ethnic identity and, even more, to define it in resistance to a white identity or even a unified American identity. While posing as a benign neutral doctrine of the equality of cultures, multiculturalism is an aggressive expression of the us-against-them ideology. Far from resisting hate, it is actually a form of hate—hate directed against what is derisively termed the "dominant culture."

Now on the face of it, the notion of the multicultural premise—that cultures are merely different, and no culture is superior or inferior, better or worse, than any other—is manifestly silly. To make this point, I don't need to prove that the American Constitution is superior to the Iroquois Charter or to raise the question, "Where is the Proust of the Papuans?" Rather, I can simply appeal to immigrant experience. Every thinking immigrant—including every thinking Hispanic—knows that all cultures are not equal.

How so? The reason is that immigration itself is a walking refutation of multiculturalism. As an immigrant myself, I know that we have a natural attachment to the place where we're born. When I left India I left everything I knew and loved: my birthplace, my family, my school, my friends. This is not easy, and no one makes lightly the decision to permanently leave.

And yet, immigrants do. In doing so they are casting a decisive vote. And what is the immigrant doing if not voting in the most telling way possible, which is to say, with his own feet, against his native culture and in favor of the new culture to which he is relocating? And why would anyone do this if they weren't confident that the new culture would provide not merely a different life but a better life?

Despite its absurdities, multiculturalism is indispensable to progressive Democrats because it is a necessary alternative to assimilation. Democrats saw what happened in the late nineteenth and early twentieth centuries when the Irish, the Italians and the eastern Europeans assimilated. Suddenly these immigrants, who previously saw themselves as Irishmen, Italians, Czechs, Slovaks and so on began to think of themselves generally as "Americans."

Their identity shifted, and this shift helped dissolve the whole ethnic urban machine system that Van Buren and others had so painstakingly assembled on behalf of the Democratic Party. When Irishmen and Italians became Americans, they were no longer reliable Democrats. By FDR's time, Democrats had to move from a system of ethnic allegiance to a new national system of worker allegiance through the labor unions. Even this new system proved fragile over time as unions lost much of their power.

Imagine the catastrophe that would face the Democratic Party if African Americans, Native Americans and Hispanic Americans stopped thinking of themselves as hyphenated Americans and thought of themselves simply as Americans! Democrats cannot afford for these groups to lose the collective solidarity that is the basis for the pact that the Democrats seek to make with them: "We will take care of you if you agree collectively to vote for us."

So multiculturalism is a way to defeat assimilation, at least for the black, brown and yellow people. It is a way to undo the historical process of Americanization and substitute for it a new formula in which each group affirms its own ethnic identity and agrees to deposit itself on its own ethnic plantation, which is then run by the progressive Democrats. Far from being an ideology of empowerment, multiculturalism is in fact an ideology of ethnic resentment toward whites that is, in the end, aimed at reconciling minority groups to their own enslavement and dependency on the Democratic plantation.

Yet none of this—not bilingualism, not "conquest of America" rhetoric, not multicultural mantras—has delivered Hispanics fully into the clutches of the Democratic Party. Hispanics do vote Democratic by substantial margins. Obama, for instance, won more than two-thirds of the Hispanic vote. But Hillary got a few points less than Obama, which could be the result of her personal flaws, or it could mean that Hispanic support for Democrats is now holding steady or even trending down.[18]

This is not good for a party that wants and needs a heavy Hispanic vote—something close to if not in the same range as the virtual monopoly that it has over the African American vote. To understand the Democrats' Hispanic problem better, and what the party hopes to accomplish by raising the banner of the illegals, let's turn to the story of my wife's cousin, Ellen Martinez, who grew up in a family of migrant workers.

DEPLOYING THE BIG LIE

Ellen and my wife Debbie grew up in the south Texas region of the Rio Grande Valley, close to the Mexican border. Debbie was born in Venezuela. Her dad was Venezuelan but her mom was Mexican American, actually a fifth-generation Mexican American from the valley. When her parents divorced Debbie moved to a barrio on the outskirts of Harlingen, Texas. Her cousin Ellen lived with her twelve other siblings and their parents, Raul and Maria Elena, in nearby La Grulla.

Yet Debbie has very few memories of Ellen, for the simple reason that Ellen's family was always gone. They were migrant workers. This meant that every summer, and often through the year, Ellen's parents would pack up the family and drive halfway across the country in search of manual labor. Typically they went to California or Oregon or Washington State, where both parents worked picking onions, apples, raspberries or asparagus at pay rates ranging around $4.25 to $4.50 an hour.

"We've had our lives in boxes for so long, it's natural for us," Ellen's mother Maria Elena told journalist Isabel Valle, who profiled the Martinez family for a book about migrant labor, *Fields of Toil*. Work hours are from 4 a.m. to sundown. The migrants live in temporary trailers in work camps that have been set up for them. Amenities are very limited, the smell of Mexican food fills the early morning and late evening air, and the only sounds of recreation are the Tejano songs blasting out from portable radios on the fields and in the camps.

The migrants share food and appliances; children from different families even share clothes. "You always have to think of others who have less than you do," Maria Elena says. "We may be poor but we have a lot more than other people, so we share what we do have." Since money is scarce, the Martinez family only buys what it absolutely needs. Ellen and her siblings never went to the movies, to the mall, nor did they participate in any athletic activities that cost money.

"I didn't like migrating," Ellen told Isabel Valle. "I didn't like that life. I kept telling myself I would make sure I would never marry anyone who migrated. If there is anything I liked, I guess it was the traveling. But once we got to our destination it was always work. We never went sight-seeing or anything." Only in her senior year in high school did Ellen stay back in La Grulla while her family went north to pick fruits and vegetables.

Ellen's family has done this for as long as she can remember, actually for more than four decades. Raul is an old man now, but he still can't sit still. "That's the way he is," his wife says, "he always has to be busy." In an interview for the book, she told Valle, "What really makes him happy is that he's earning some money. Right now we only have enough to buy food. We still need money for the road, and we'd like to have a little saved up for the winter, when there is no work."[19]

Raul has transmitted his work ethic and savings habit to his children, who are all self-supporting and who have now bought their parents a piece of land and a house so that they can be comfortable in their old age. As for their politics, Raul and Maria Elena are both Republicans. One of Raul's points of pride, his wife says—we don't get much from Raul because he speaks hardly any English—is that they have never taken government handouts even when they have been eligible for them. Ellen is now married to a bank executive, and she and her husband are also Republicans.

But this is not true of all of Ellen's siblings. I don't have an official count, but it seems that they are about one-half Republican, one-half Democratic. Why, then, might children raised in the same household under the same parental values go such different ways politically? Apparently it's because her siblings who are Democrats believe that the other party, the Republican Party, hates Hispanics. They think Democrats are the party of inclusion while Republicans are the party of hate. In short, they have drunk the progressive Kool-Aid.

So finally we are in a position to answer the question of why the progressive Democrats focus so much on illegals. Essentially they want to blur the distinction between legal and illegal immigrants, so that when Republicans speak out against illegal immigration, Democrats can portray them as being "against immigrants." This way Hispanics—not just illegals but also legal Hispanics whose families have been in America since the mid-nineteenth century—will learn to fear and despise Republicans in the belief that they are racist bigots who are opposed to all Hispanics.

It's another big lie, of course, but a toxic one. And as we see with Ellen's family, at least to a degree, it works. In this respect, it's a successful lie. The reason Democrats need the lie is that they have no other way to win over hardworking, self-supporting people like the Martinez family. The Martinez clan is a self-reliant bunch, while the Democrats need fearful, dependent people who don't believe they can survive without the Democratic Party to take care of them. Ellen's hope, Debbie's and mine is that this big lie, like all the others, is finally exposed so Democrats won't be able to con Hispanics into fatally succumbing to the party of the plantation.

10

HOLDOUTS

Democrats and the Problem of White People

All you heard from the Clinton campaign was African American this, African American that. The same with Hispanics and Latinos. . . . Nothing about white people. . . . I am a white male, no way was I going to vote for her.

—WTF1958, blog post response to an article posted on CNN[1]

The so-called Unite the Right rally in Charlottesville seemed almost scripted by a group of Hollywood progressives. Here was an event featuring neo-Nazis and Ku Klux Klansmen and white supremacists of every stripe. There they were, chanting for Donald Trump and sporting MAGA hats. And then—in a kind of dramatic climax to the narrative—one of them drove his car into a pedestrian, killing her. So the Charlottesville rally illustrated not only hate and its apparent source but also the consequence of that hate, a dead body lying in the street.

What better metaphor could the left have for Donald Trump's America? Here, blatant and undisguised, were the white nationalists who were said to have taken over the Republican Party and made up the core constituency that got Trump elected a few months earlier. Whatever might be said about how progressive Democrats were the bad guys in the past, or about how bogus the Southern Strategy and the big-switch narratives might be, here was visual, irrefutable proof that today's racists are in the Trump camp, and the people mobilized to fight them, Antifa, Black Lives Matter and the rest, are allied with the progressive cause. The progressive message following Charlottesville was clear: say what you will about history, we are the good guys now.

Trump was pressed by the left to make a full-throated denunciation of the Charlottesville rally. In a sense, the progressives in the media wanted to force him to repudiate his alleged supporters while acknowledging that Antifa, Black Lives Matter and the counterprotesters were right to confront them. Trump refused, going no further than to denounce violence from "all sides." Later Trump did sign a Senate resolution roundly condemning white supremacy.

Still, Trump's refusal to unilaterally rebuke the so-called Unite the Right ralliers brought tears of disappointment and outrage to CNN commentator Van Jones. "He's not defending the humanity of the people who were run over . . . He can't distinguish between Nazis with torches saying anti-Jewish, anti-Black stuff and . . . the people who went there to try and defend people from those thugs." Jones invoked his Jewish godmother to insist that "she can't count on the President of the United States to stand with her when a Nazi ran over an American citizen. Killed an American citizen with ISIS tactics in our country." Jones concluded with a sniffle, "I'm just hurt. I'm sitting here hurt, and I think a lot of people are hurt."[2]

The Charlottesville narrative built on top of images of Richard Spencer—the poster boy of white supremacy in America today—and a few dozen of his like-minded compatriots raising their arms in a "Heil Trump" Nazi-style salute in the aftermath of the election. The narrative came in the wake of news articles preceding the election showing that the Ku Klux Klan newspaper *Crusader* had, without endorsing Trump, nevertheless praised his candidacy.[3] For progressives, Charlottesville was the ultimate confirmation and the ultimate vindication. No wonder media coverage of Charlottesville was intense and lasted for weeks, rivaling if not exceeding the coverage of, say, the two parties' national political conventions.

At one point I almost laughed out loud when I saw a single white nationalist surrounded by a dozen or so cameramen and reporters. No one, not the white nationalist, not the reporters, not the onlookers, seemed to recognize the irony of the situation. This wasn't the Ku Klux Klan in the mid-1920s marching down Pennsylvania Avenue with 50,000 hooded Klansmen. This was one solitary guy. Yet he was the obsessive focus of the media because the reporters were convinced that he—this one guy—was the disturbing face of white supremacy in Trump's America.

For the progressive left, Charlottesville is part of a larger narrative that can be summed up by Univision anchor Jorge Ramos' assertion, in a CNN interview with Anderson Cooper, that Trump and the Republicans "want to Make America White Again."[4] So MAGA, in this view, is a disguised way for Trump and the Trumpsters to say they want to go back to a country where whites are supreme and blacks, Hispanics and other groups are second-class citizens, vulnerable to deportation and discrimination.

This theme is perhaps most fully fleshed out by Ta-Nehisi Coates. Coates takes issue with commentators across the political spectrum who say that Donald Trump got elected by winning the white working-class vote. "Trump defeated Clinton," Coates writes, "among white voters in every income category, winning by a margin of 57 to 34 among whites making less than $30,000 and $50,000; 61 to 33 for those making $50,000 to $100,000; 56 to 39 among those making $100,000 to $200,000; 50 to 45 among those making $200,000 to $250,000; and 48 to 43 for those making more than $250,000."

Trump won rich whites and poor whites. He won young whites, middle-aged whites, and the white elderly. He won whites with college degrees and whites without them. He won white women and white men. And in varying margins he won them in every part of the country. "Part of Trump's dominance among whites," Coates writes, "resulted from his running as a Republican, the party that has long cultivated white voters."

Notice, Coates says, that Trump did not win blue-collar Hispanics or blacks. If Trump made some sort of a working-class pitch to restore jobs to America, Coates asks why that appeal fell on deaf ears among working-class minorities. Only white workers seemed to have heard it. Consequently, Coates concludes, Trump didn't really win by assembling a working-class coalition. Rather, he won by forging an ethnic coalition, and therefore he is, in the title of Coates' essay, "The

First White President." Obviously there were white presidents before Trump, but Trump is the first to win election by harnessing the power of whiteness.[5]

THE KNOW-NOTHING ENDORSEMENT

Before I dive into this debate, I want to point out that we've actually been here before. I realize that many on the left consider Trump's presidency to be unprecedented, and even Republican "never Trumpers" seem to agree, justifying their defection from the GOP and their persistent attacks on Trump on this basis. Both groups are wrong. The issue of how to deal with a noxious bigoted group that professes to be in one's camp was faced by Reagan in the 1980s and also, in a more serious form, by the first Republican president, Abraham Lincoln.

During one of his election campaigns, a woman confronted Reagan with the news that an extremist group perceived as white supremacist, the John Birch Society, was supporting his candidacy. "What's your reaction," she demanded to know, "to your endorsement by the Birchers?" Reagan responded, "They will be buying my philosophy. I'm not buying theirs."[6] And that was how he successfully diffused the issue. Still, Reagan's response was, in my view, insufficient, because it made no effort to answer the question: if you don't agree with these white supremacists, why do *they* think you're their guy?

Now let's turn to how Abraham Lincoln handled this same issue. There was a powerful political party in the 1850s colloquially known as the Know-Nothings. The term came from the group's self-appropriation of an insult. Their critics called them ignorant buffoons who knew nothing, and in the manner of blacks who call each other nigger, the Know-Nothings ironically embraced the label. Officially, though, their party was called the "Americans."

When the Whig Party dissolved, many of its members joined the Know-Nothing party. The Know-Nothings were both a reform movement and an anti-immigrant movement. Know-Nothings supported antislavery, missionary projects at home and abroad, charitable aid for orphans and the poor, and temperance. They also despised the new immigrants, especially the Irish, for their "rum and Romanism." The Know-Nothing platform called for slavery restriction, alcohol prohibition, a halt to immigration, and a law banning immigrants from benefiting from the Homestead Act, which made cheap land available to settlers moving west.

The immigrants for their part hated the Know-Nothings. The Irish in particular associated them with the same English Protestants who had been oppressing them back in Ireland. We have already seen how the Democratic Party had been organized by the Van Burenites in the North to recruit Irish and other immigrants to the urban machines. Even though the immigrants were clearly being exploited by the Democrats, this was exploitation with their consent. So the immigrants identified with the Democrats, and the Know-Nothings identified first with the Whigs and then with their own American party.

By 1860 this American party had dissolved, but the underlying movement had not; it counted upward of a million supporters. Given the association of the Irish and other immigrants with the Democratic Party, the Know-Nothings were naturally disposed to vote for the opposing party. This made them potential Republican voters who, in a close election, could easily make the difference. Lincoln knew he needed the votes of these Know-Nothings if the Republican Party was to prevail in that critical year.

Throughout the 1850s, the Democratic stalwart Stephen Douglas had repeatedly and vociferously castigated the Know-Nothing movement, branding its followers a bunch of ignorant xenophobes. Douglas did not hesitate to do this even when the Know-Nothing movement was at its zenith in the mid-1850s. Lincoln, by contrast, made no such condemnations. He recognized that the nativist movement, despite its malevolent elements, was part of the antislavery movement, and he had no intention of dividing the forces of the antislavery movement.

During the 1860 campaign, Democrats circulated a rumor that Lincoln had made a secret stop at a Know-Nothing lodge in Quincy, Massachusetts. The issue was all over the papers, and Abram Jonas, a Jewish Republican attorney in Quincy who detested the Know-Nothings, wrote to ask Lincoln if it were true. Lincoln responded that it was not, but then he added this, "And now a word of caution. Our adversaries think they can gain a point if they could force me to openly deny the charge, by which some degree of offense would be given to the

Americans. For this reason, it must not publicly appear that I am paying any attention to the charge."[7]

In private, Lincoln made his position clear in an 1855 letter to his friend Joshua Speed: "I am not a Know-Nothing. That is certain. How could I be? How can anyone who abhors the oppression of negroes be in favor of degrading classes of white people? As a nation, we began by declaring that all men are created equal. We now practically read it, all men are created equal, except negroes. When the Know-Nothings get control, it will read, all men are created equal, except negroes, and foreigners, and Catholics. When it comes to this I should prefer emigrating to some country where they make no pretense of loving liberty—to Russia, for instance, where despotism can be taken pure, without the base alloy of hypocrisy."[8]

It should also be said that leading Republicans like Frederick Douglass rejected the Know-Nothing agenda and embraced the immigrants. Likening hatred for the Chinese to hatred for blacks, Douglass said, "I want a home here not only for the Negro, the mulatto and the Latin races; but I want the Asiatic to find a home here in the United States, and feel at home here, both for his sake and for ours." The Republican platform in 1860 contained no denunciation of immigrants, no call for restricted immigration and no support for excluding immigrants from the provisions of the Homestead Act.[9]

Even so, Lincoln's only denunciation of anti-foreign and anti-Catholic prejudice appears in a personal private letter. Lincoln never publicly repudiated the Know-Nothings. For this he was assailed by Democratic newspapers, just as Trump was assailed in the progressive media for not sufficiently repudiating the white nationalists in Charlottesville. And Lincoln got the Know-Nothing vote, just as we can reasonably surmise Trump got the white nationalist vote.

Lincoln never expressed guilt or qualms over this; from his point of view, the Know-Nothings came to him; he didn't go over to them. Moreover, in rejecting the bad elements of the Know-Nothings, such as their hatred of immigrants and determination to shut America's door to them, he did not hesitate to identify with the good things they stood for, such as social reform, temperance, and antislavery. In this episode, if we think about it, there is a valuable lesson for Trump and the Republican Party.

THE OBAMA-TRUMP VOTER

Now we turn to Coates' charge that Trump got to the White House through a successful appeal to whiteness or white supremacy. Progressives like Coates interpret Trump's campaign slogan "Make America Great Again" as a call to return America to a time and place where women were out of the workforce, blacks were segregated and discriminated against, Hispanics and Asians were barred from coming to America and gays were a silent group confined to the closet. Admittedly Trump never said any of this, but might his voters understand him to be saying—or at least implying—it?

More than eighteen months into Trump's presidency, scholars have crunched the numbers to figure out which voters gave him his margin of victory. This consensus holds that Trump did not win by getting out his vote, nor did Hillary lose by failing to get out her vote. Base voters of both parties showed up to vote for their candidate. American presidential elections are typically decided by the independent or "swing" voter who is captive to neither party, and Trump prevailed by winning a sufficient number of these voters in key states.[10]

In 2008 and 2012, these independent voters pulled the lever for Obama. In the 2016 Democratic primary, many of these same voters were for Bernie Sanders. So Trump won by getting Obama voters and Sanders voters. This is confirmed by the fact that Trump won blue states like Pennsylvania, Michigan and Wisconsin. Obama won all those states, even while Hillary had regarded Wisconsin as so securely in the bag that she didn't even bother to campaign there.

Consider Youngstown, Ohio, which is regarded as America's prototypical working-class town. This is union territory, so heavily Democratic that Republicans often don't field candidates in many races and think they have done well when they get one-third of the vote. Bruce Springsteen wrote a song about a father who returns to Youngstown after World War II to work in the steel mills. But "now the yard's just scrap and rubble . . . Them big boys did what Hitler couldn't do." Translation: America used to be great, but isn't anymore. The evil corporate bosses have ruined it.

Youngstown is in Mahoning County, and Mahoning—together with adjoining Trumbull County—gave Obama the margin he needed to win Ohio in 2008 and 2012. No one thought these voters would switch parties; in the words of columnist Paul Sracic, it would be "like asking a New York Yankees fan to cheer for the Boston Red Sox."[11] Yet Trump almost took Mahoning County—Hillary won it by a hair—and he did win in Trumbull County. His promise to make America great again seems to have resonated.

In Wisconsin, Trump won twenty-one working-class counties that just four years earlier had gone to Obama by comfortable margins. Howard County, Iowa—which is 150 miles northeast of Des Moines—went for Obama by a margin of 20 points in 2012; in a massive swing, Trump won it by 20 points. Maine's second congressional district, which Obama won by 8 points, went for Trump by 12. Of nearly 700 counties that twice voted for Obama, more than 200 defected to Trump.

Who are these voters? They are white voters—we can call them Bruce Springsteen voters—and we can safely dismiss the idea that they are white supremacists. White supremacists don't vote for a black presidential candidate, however well qualified. Nor was Obama well qualified; he was a community organizer who had not yet served a single term in the Senate. Clearly Obama's skin color did not prevent these swing voters from going over to his side.

The website fivethirtyeight.com examined what happened in Howard County, Iowa. Laura Hubka, navy veteran and ultrasound technician who chaired the county's Democratic Party and knocked on doors for Hillary, shared her perspective on why Democratic voters switched to Trump. "We're a blue-collar town. People who were longtime supporters didn't want to hear what we had to say anymore." As for Hillary, "she was an elitist, was what I kept hearing."

Holly Rasmussen, an Obama voter, admitted she ended up voting for Trump "just to shake up Washington, to be honest. We've been in a rut for so long. People here don't want to be multi-gazillionaires. They just want to get paid a decent wage."

Before casting her ballot, Rasmussen went to see a movie that exposed the history of the Democratic Party. Quoting fivethirtyeight.com, "The week before the election, emboldened Trump supporters took out a full-page newspaper ad and rented out the historic, city-owned Cresto Theatre and Opera House—a long-ago vaudeville haunt—for screenings of conservative filmmaker Dinesh D'Souza's documentary

Hillary's America and the Benghazi film *13 Hours.* To Democrats' dismay, the theater was packed."[12]

I may have helped, but in the end it was Trump's message that got through. A few weeks after the election, CNN's Van Jones interviewed Scott Seitz of Trumbull County, Ohio, another lifelong Democrat and Obama voter who flipped to Trump. "We put Democrats in office," he said, and they

> turned around and forgot completely about us . . . We have a ton of mills that have seemed to close up and not only did they close up, but they've been torn down and removed. They look like ghost towns . . . We truly want to make America better . . . We hope that the bleeding can actually stop in our area.
>
> . . .When we get a downturn in the economy, we need to still feed our families. And when they talk about the Second Amendment or taking our guns away, that's exactly what we think of, all the time that we have hunting together and as a family, and we go out and we harvest and we put food in the freezer.[13]

Do these sound like people who are trying to force women out of the workforce, or to reestablish segregation and state-sponsored discrimination, or to send immigrants like me home? These may be Democrats, but they are not those types of Democrats. Outraged at the defection of these voters to Trump, progressives have concocted a narrative designed to discredit them, but it is maliciously false, just another big lie.

WHAT THE HILLBILLIES FIGURED OUT

We have so far an indication of why working-class Obama voters pivoted to Trump. But we need to probe deeper, because we also have to answer Ta-Nehisi Coates' question: why didn't the white working class following the black working class and the Hispanic working class in opting for the Democratic plantation? In other words, what differentiates the white workers from their black and Latino counterparts?

Let's begin with a bit of white history. I realize this sounds strange, because we are accustomed to hearing about black history and Hispanic history. But the white working class has a history too, albeit one that is typically ignored in progressive scholarship. Progressives won't tell you, for example, that historically whites around the world have been enslaved in numbers comparable to blacks.

The Roman slaves, for example, were mostly whites, and over the centuries several million whites were captured and enslaved by the various Muslim dynasties, from the Abbasid to the Ottoman. Indeed the very term "slave" derives from the Latin word for "Slav," a reference to the large number of white slaves captured from that region of Central Europe.[14]

Nancy Isenberg's recent book *White Trash* offers a useful account of the history of white workers in America. Their ancestors, she points out, were the dregs of Europe, cast off to clean out the continent and also to do the dirty work that needed to be done in the new world. These early settlers, in Isenberg's account, included "roguish highwaymen, mean vagrants, Irish rebels, known whores and an assortment of convicts" including an English waif named Bess Armstrong, dispatched to Virginia for stealing two spoons.[15]

Although not slaves themselves, Isenberg portrays the "crackers" and "squatters" of Virginia and North Carolina as very much in the same low category. In theory, indentured servants were captives merely for a fixed period, usually between four to nine years, most typically seven. But during this period, Don Jordan and Michael Walsh write in *White Cargo,* masters had "more or less total control over their destiny."[16] And servants soon discovered that for relatively minor offenses, including attempts to run away, their terms could be extended.

In fact, planters employed these lowly whites to work in gangs alongside slaves, with the same overseer driving the whole operation, with the authority to flog the whites no less than the blacks. "The lives of white workers," historian David Brion Davis writes, "were not significantly different from the lives of most slaves."[17] Sometimes planters gave the riskiest tasks to the whites, knowing that if they were injured or killed there would be no price to pay. The whites were wage laborers after all, while the slaves cost close to a thousand dollars apiece in the early to mid-nineteenth century.

The term "white trash" made its first appearance in print in this period, in 1831. But here Isenberg goes astray because she focuses too narrowly on the poor whites of the South, flaying them for their racist condescension toward black slaves without calling out the Democratic Party that cultivated these sentiments for political gain. Isenberg implies that today's Trump voters are the descendants of those racist white Southerners.

This, however, is clearly wrong. The white working voters that delivered the election to Trump in Pennsylvania, Michigan and Wisconsin are obviously descended from ancestors who fought on the Union side in the Civil War. Even the poorest of poor whites in the South, the Appalachians, were mostly independent-minded folk who resisted the demand for secession. When the white hillbillies of Virginia refused to join the Confederacy, Lincoln carved out a new state for them, West Virginia, which remained in the union.

So much for history. Fast forward now to the second half of the twentieth century. In the postwar period, the manufacturing boom across America—especially in the Northeast and Midwest—raised the standard of living of the white working class to the point where a blue-collar plumber or electrician had the same middle-class amenities as his college-educated white counterpart. The third quarter of the twentieth century was, one might say, the golden age of the white working class.

Not that this group experienced the meteoric rise in earnings that college-educated whites saw, especially in professions like medicine, finance, business, law and later technology. But working-class whites could expect to see a gradual improvement in wages from a couple of dollars an hour in the early 1950s to $20 an hour or more in the 1970s. Adjusted for inflation, this represents a doubling of real annual income for working-class households. The annual increases may have been small, but at least the jobs were stable and the trajectory was upward.

With a comfortable and steady wage, whites built working-class communities where young people expected to follow in the path of their parents. Their lives were not defined by moving up and moving out, nor by the need for creative individual self-expression. Rather, these people found solace in staying put, devoting themselves to providing for their families, and earning respect not only through their skilled trades but also through involvement in the civic life of the community, becoming, say, volunteer firemen or Little League coaches.

Today, many of those working-class communities have been obliterated. The high-paying jobs are gone, replaced by service jobs that don't pay enough to comfortably provide for a family. Young people can no longer do what their parents did; they can stay, with much more dismal prospects, or they can leave. The disappearance of jobs doesn't merely reflect a contraction of opportunity; rather, it reflects a breakdown of community. Even the family and civic associations that contributed to a decent life for these people have frayed and corroded.

In other words, the economic catastrophe of the white working class is now accompanied by a cultural catastrophe. Some of the same cultural pathologies that were once characteristic of black America are now also part of white America. In the mid-sixties, for example, Daniel Patrick Moynihan in a famous report, *The Negro Family: A Case for National Action,* declared a national crisis over the fact that the black illegitimacy rate was approaching 25 percent. But today the white illegitimacy rate is over 25 percent.

Just as crack has ravaged the black inner city, white communities have been devastated by a drug and alcohol epidemic that seems to have affected adults and young people alike. White working-class areas have seen rising rates of depression, cirrhosis of the liver, and suicide. So serious are these problems that, according to a study by Anne Case and Angus Deaton, working-class whites who at the turn of the century had a mortality rate 30 percent lower than blacks now have a mortality rate 30 percent higher than blacks.

I make this comparison not to make a racial point; on the contrary, one can infer from these pathologies and their prevalence in white, black and Latino communities that there is nothing racial about them; rather, they are the product of dwindling prospects and the cultural dysfunction that often comes in their wake. Rather, my point is simply that the white working class now has the highest rate of premature deaths in the country. Case and Deaton chillingly term these "deaths of despair."[18]

J. D. Vance's recent book *Hillbilly Elegies* gives as good an account as can be given of what it actually feels like to grow up in these ravaged communities. Vance's own mother is addicted to drugs and moves serially from one marriage to another—five at last count—which is why he was raised by his grandparents, whom he calls, hillbilly style, Moomaw and Papaw. Moomaw and Papaw have their own problems, Papaw being known to get rip-roaring drunk and deliver some heavy blows to his wife and Moomaw, in retaliation, to set the old man on fire while he is asleep.

Yet young Vance, somehow, manages to get out of all this insanity, to get a decent education, eventually to make his way to Yale Law School and to his current job at an investment firm in San Francisco, not to mention his part-time vocation as a successful writer. How did he do it? He attributes part of his success to his crazy-ass grandparents, who for all their eccentricities loved him unconditionally, and to the Marine Corps, which taught him to stop blaming his failures on society and to start taking responsibility like a man.

When Vance traveled abroad on a Marine Corps mission, he encountered children in Third World countries who didn't have a fraction of what he did. He handed one such kid an eraser—just an eraser—and witnessed the child respond as though he had been handed the moon. This episode, and others like it, taught Vance not to see himself as a victim but rather, as he puts it, "one lucky son of a bitch." Vance learned to appreciate not his white privilege but rather his American privilege, his good fortune to be born and raised in the United States of America.[19]

LIKE VOTING FOR HIS DAD

What can we conclude from all this? First, I conclude that while the white working class is still not in as bad shape as the black and Hispanic working class, its travails are no less hard to bear because they represent a sharp reversal of fortune. These white working-class communities once prospered, but now they are in ruins. Suffering is always harder to bear when it represents a steep fall from the way things used to be. The white working class seems to be the first generation in postwar American history to experience downward mobility in this way.

At the same time, it has not escaped the notice of the white working class that the Democratic Party reserves all its attention and sympathy for black and Latino suffering, and none for white suffering. On the contrary, progressive Democrats portray poor whites as racists who refuse to recognize their ongoing white privilege. Many working-class whites are hostile to Democrats not because they are racists but because they feel discriminated against, and in my opinion they are right to feel this way.

Second, the white working class remains as ornery, rebellious and independent-minded as it always was. It hasn't given in; it hasn't thrown in the towel. The Democrats have succeeded in convincing a large portion of working-class blacks and Latinos that they are better off on the urban plantation, living off the government and delivering their votes in exchange to the party that makes that happen. And the Democrats would like nothing better than to dump the white working class there as well.

Some working-class whites have of course fallen for this con, which is why they are Democrats. But a sufficiently large number of them continue to view the Democratic plantation as a degradation and an insult. They are down, but they are not yet out. They may not have jobs, but they still have a work ethic. Their families and communities may be hurting, but they still want to pull them together. They can see what has happened to their black and Latino counterparts on the plantation; their plight is if anything considerably worse.

So, tempted though they may be with the promise of free stuff, they are not about to become leeches off the state. Their stubborn attitude can be compared to the Spartans, whose land was sometimes called Laconia. As the story goes, when Philip of Macedon contemplated an invasion, he sent a message to the Spartan ephors that said, "If I take Laconia, I will kill all the men, rape all the women, and enslave all the children, leaving no stone on top of another." To which the Spartans replied with a single word, "If." And this is the attitude of white working-class rebels. They may be surrounded by all sorts of perils, but they are not done yet.

So why Trump? When they hear Trump pledge to make America great again, what they hear is that he cares about their plight and that he will try to make their communities whole. Let's pause to consider the three forces that have combined to create this perfect storm of devastation across working-class America. These forces are: globalization, immigration, and technology. Jobs go abroad via one-sided trade agreements; immigrants come here and work for less; and technology puts machines to work doing what humans used to be required to do.

Now ask yourself: what has the Democratic Party done to address these problems? Answer: nothing. And the GOP record is not much better. Both parties, of course, are reconciled to modern technology. Both parties have in general welcomed globalization, allowing other countries to freely sell here even though they impose tariffs on American goods sold there. Finally, both parties have ignored the problem of illegal immigration, the Democrats largely because they want illegals on their plantation, the Republicans to appease their business constituency, which can get away with paying these people lower wages.

Trump, by contrast, refused to sign the Pacific trade treaty in its extant form. He vowed to reconsider the North American Free Trade Agreement (NAFTA). And to the consternation of many Republicans wedded to free-trade dogma, he imposed tariffs on steel and aluminum, 25 percent on steel, 10 percent on aluminum, exempting only Canada and Mexico, pending what Trump said was a fair rebalancing of existing trade agreements with those countries.

Trump also put the immigration issue on the map, forcing both parties to confront the impact of illegals on jobs, on crime and security and on the burden placed on scarce social services. Trump has even suggested the need to reform legal immigration, placing more emphasis on merit and on workers this country needs and less on the kind of "chain migration" that allows an immigrant like me to bring virtually limitless numbers of relatives to this country under the pretext of "family unification."

In sum, while the Democrats do nothing and the Republicans do next to nothing, Trump at least promises to try. I have never heard Trump say he knows how to restore these working-class communities, but I have never seen any other politician address the issue with Trump's forthrightness. And since his election Trump has been on it, cajoling and muscling corporations to bring their business and jobs back to the United States, and a number of them have.

Fiat Chrysler, for example, said it would shift production of heavy trucks from Mexico to a plant in Warren, Michigan. Toyota and Mazda announced the opening of a new $1.6 billion plant in Huntsville, Alabama, that will create 4,000 jobs over three years. Apple and Exxon-Mobil pledged to expand their operations in the United States. Trump's solutions have been decried by Democrats and even some Republicans as trivial and ad hoc, but however inadequate they are, he is the only one attempting a cure.

Recall the stony-faced silence with which Democrats—notably the Black Caucus—greeted Trump's announcement in his 2018 State of the Union that black unemployment rates had plummeted. Trump was right about this: the black unemployment rate dipped from 8.3 percent when Trump took office to 6.8 percent a year later.[20] One might expect this to be welcome news to a group that purports to champion black welfare. Yet upon reflection there is no puzzle here. The Black Caucus is part of the overseer class. These guys don't want people to leave the plantation.

The Trump voters certainly get it. I remember watching a working-class guy being interviewed on CNN shortly after the election. What he said was not what CNN wanted to hear. Trump, he said, reminded him of his own father, who had worked blue-collar jobs all his life, only to see that way of life essentially wiped out, not because he got lazy or stopped playing by the rules but because of decisions made by other people, by politicians and technocrats acting very much in their own self-interest.

"I don't know if Trump will change anything," the man said, breaking down and holding back tears, "and I don't really care if he does. He is the only one who spoke to my dad's broken heart. My dad is now gone, but when I voted for Trump, it was like voting for my dad."

ELEPHANT IN THE LIVING ROOM

I believe I have vindicated Trump voters of the charge that they are all a bunch of white supremacists. Still, there are white supremacists in America. There are neo-Nazis and Ku Klux Klansmen and Skin-heads—the very people who showed up in Charlottesville for the Unite the Right rally. There are Richard Spencer and his cohorts performing Hitleresque Trump salutes. If fascism and racism are, as I have shown throughout this book, phenomena of the progressive Democrats, why are these guys on the right? How to explain their support for Trump? This is the elephant in the living room.

First, it should be noted that this is a very small group. The KKK today is virtually a defunct organization. It has been defunct since the 1980s. It has, at most, a few hundred members nationwide. If the Klan were to organize a rally anywhere in the country, its members would be overwhelmed by a much larger group of counterprotesters. And no, the KKK doesn't have a real newspaper. The *Crusader*—the so-called newspaper that praised Trump—is nothing more than a crude twelve-page pamphlet that comes out four times a year.

Historian David Chalmers, whose book *Hooded Americanism* is a history of the Klan, is frequently asked by reporters to explain the KKK revival. He tells them that they *are* the Klan revival; in other words, there is no revival except in their fevered reporting. Chalmers even recounts an episode in which a KKK cross-burning was held up until the TV crews arrived.[21] The left-wing media needs the Klan to sustain their political attack on the right. So they magnify the organization, allowing the public to believe that it still poses the kind of threat that it historically posed under the aegis of the Democratic Party to blacks and other minorities.

Let's assume that the Klan has five hundred to a thousand members. What is the evidence that these guys voted for Trump? Actually, there is none. The media loves to trot out former Klansman David Duke not because he is representative of anything but because he is the only prominent name associated with the Klan that can be tied to the Republicans, notwithstanding the GOP's insistent repudiation of him on numerous occasions. It is hard to name anyone else because historically the entire leadership of the KKK—Imperial Wizards, Grand Dragons, Exalted Cyclopses, Great Kleagles and all—have all been Democrats.

Has anyone conducted a survey of neo-Nazis or Skinheads to show that they are actually Trump voters? I am not aware of any. When CNN commentator Van Jones was asked by conservative radio host Hugh Hewitt what percentage of Trump voters are white supremacists, he replied, "Probably less than one percent." Columnist Will Saletan invoked an opinion survey to show that while 3 percent of whites said they "mostly agree" with the white supremacy movement, 5 percent of Trump voters fell into this category.[22] So the data are scarce and all over the place. What we can agree on is that we are dealing with a quite marginal phenomenon.

In the aftermath of Charlottesville, there have been several media profiles of white supremacists. The intention, I am sure, is to show what clear and present dangers these individuals pose to society. Given racism's dark history, I was prepared to believe it. But reading the articles, I am struck by how pathetic and powerless these people are. Racism is only dangerous when prejudiced people have real power. It is blatantly obvious that these sorry individuals have little or no power.

Something else emerges from the profiles, peeping out from under the overwrought verbiage: many of the most prominent white supremacists have a left-wing background. The Southern Poverty Law Center looked into the past of Jason Kessler, organizer of the Charlottesville rally, and was astounded to discover that he had been an Obama supporter and active in the left-wing Occupy movement.[23]

What could be more interesting than to explain how an Obama supporter could become a white supremacist? Or how an Occupy Wall Street sympathizer transitioned into a defender of the white cause? Yet the progressive media went dead silent on this one. Only one local Charlottesville newspaper, *The Daily Progress,* bothered to dig into this, noting that Kessler's previous tweets, his neighbors and several of his friends "attest that he held strong liberal convictions just a few years ago."

In those earlier tweets, Kessler said that not only was he a former Democrat, but many of his current followers previously voted for Democrats. David Caron, a childhood friend, said Kessler became alienated when he realized that there was no place for him in a Democratic Party focused on ethnic diversity and minority issues. In Caron's words, "He was a Democrat until last year. The main thing is, he said he felt like the party didn't want him."

Laura Kleiner is a Democratic activist who dated Kessler for several months in 2013. According to the article, "She said Kessler was very dedicated to his liberal principles, and that he was a strict vegetarian, abstained from alcohol and drugs, embraced friends of different ethnicities and was an atheist."

Kleiner said that notwithstanding his Jewish heritage, Kessler showed no indication of being anti-Semitic. She also said he had a roommate for several years who was an African immigrant. Speaking of Kessler, Kleiner told the newspaper, "He broke up with me, and a lot of it was because I was not liberal enough . . . I am a very progressive Democrat, but he didn't like that I ate fish and that I'm a Christian."[24]

I mentioned Kessler's leftist background on social media and he lashed out angrily by releasing a video denouncing me. The video itself is rambling, incoherent and laced with obscenities. The most interesting thing about it is that Kessler attacks me as a rich brown-skinned guy who only stands up for big business and special interests. In other words, notwithstanding his disavowal of my portrait of him, Kessler sounds just like the left-wing racist I made him out to be. If he has undergone any kind of conversion, his video gives no indication of it.

Examining other profiles of these extremists, things only get weirder. The *New York Times* profiled Tony Hovater, portrayed as a foot soldier of various white supremacist and neo-Nazi groups. Yet despite the paper's attempt to make Hovater look menacing, his comments suggest a tone not so much of fanaticism as of irony. Hovater insists, for example, that Hitler didn't necessarily want to exterminate the Jews; that was Himmler! Hitler, he claims, "was a lot more kind of chill on those subjects."

The problem with the diversity-mongers in politics, according to Hovater, is that "at this rate I'm sure the presidential candidate they'll put up in a few cycles will be an overweight, black, crippled dyke with dyslexia." Hovater interrupted one of his tirades against democracy with the aside, "I guess it seems weird when talking about these types of things. You know, I'm coming at it in a mid-90s, Jewish, New York observational-humor way."[25] Apparently we have a Nazi Seinfeld on our hands.

And the beat goes on. *Newsweek* published a profile of Andrew Auernheimer, coeditor of the world's biggest neo-Nazi website, the Daily Stormer. Despite his notoriety in the United States, Auernheimer lives in the Ukraine. He fled there after serving jail time in America on a computer hacking conviction that was later vacated.

In its research for the article, *Newsweek* interviewed Auernheimer's mother, who disclosed that her son comes from a "large, mixed-race family" with Native American heritage and that he has Jewish lineage "on both sides of his family." So we have a mixed-race guy who hates mixed-race people and a descendant of Jews who wants, in his words, to slaughter them "like dogs"?[26]

Atlantic Monthly journalist Luke O'Brien traveled to Whitefish, Montana, to do an in-depth profile of the other coeditor of the Daily Stormer, Andrew Anglin. Anglin was apparently organizing a rally that he promised would include European nationalists, a Hamas representative and a member of the Iranian Revolutionary Guard. But no rally actually took place.

Anglin told O'Brien that he had given up on the United States and wanted to burn it to the ground. "There is rapidly approaching a time when in every White Western city, corpses will be stacked in the streets as high as men can stack them. And you are either going to be stacking or getting stacked." Yes, we are dealing with a highly disturbed individual.

But how did he get that way? O'Brien talked to Anglin's friends from the school he attended in Columbus, Ohio. They told him that Anglin was a kind of hippie who enrolled in an alternative education program. Anglin was a vegan and his girlfriend Alison was an animal rights activist. He was also an atheist who wore his reddish hair in dreadlocks. His trademark hoodie bore the sign "F*CK RACISM."

Anglin began his blogging career after high school. His early blogs are revealing. "Here his leftist leanings were on full display: He wrote posts encouraging people to send the Westboro Baptist Church death threats from untraceable accounts, and he mocked the Ku Klux Klan and other racist organizations." Reporter O'Brien is puzzled. Anglin doesn't sound like a fascist; he sounds like a member of Antifa.

In March 2007, Anglin posted about Donald Trump, attaching a video clip from a roast of former New York mayor Rudy Giuliani. Giuliani appears in the video in drag, and Trump rams his face into Giuliani's chest. It was all apparently in fun. Even so, Anglin describes them both as "fags" and writes that Giuliani is clearly involved in a "twisted homosexual transvestite affair with Donald Trump."

In 2010–11 Anglin visited Southeast Asia, where he became a rainforest activist, dated Filipina women, and railed on his podcast against Christian missionaries. "You see the way white people—and it is white people—went around the whole world and f*cked everybody. I think the white race should be bred out." This was a sentiment he routinely expressed.

While O'Brien speculates that something happened in the rain forest to make Anglin a neo-Nazi, he has no idea what that might be. Neither does Anglin, apparently.[27] So what we have is a leftist atheist environmentalist who thinks Trump is a fag and that white people screwed up the world running the world's largest neo-Nazi website. Go figure!

IDENTITY POLITICS FOR WHITES

My purpose in highlighting the leftist roots of today's white supremacists is not merely to undermine the claim that they are right-wingers. It is also to show how easily people like Kessler and Anglin have morphed from leftist political activism to white supremacy. None of them underwent any conversion or transformation. Rather, they moved, as it were, laterally, from leftist radicalism to neo-Nazi radicalism. The Nazis, let's recall, made precisely the same journey. Now, as in the past, leftism, racism and neo-Nazism go hand in hand.

I recognize that these ragtag extremists are a muddle-headed group. We should not, however, be muddle-headed about them. One of the few scholars to make a genuine attempt to study their movement is political scientist Carol Swain. Swain, who was featured in my film *Hillary's America,* is one of the leading African American scholars in the country. Swain has written two books, a detailed study of the white nationalist movement called *The New White Nationalism in America,* and another consisting of searching interviews with its most prominent members.

Swain recognizes that the "new white nationalism," as she calls it, is different from old-style racism. Most significantly, the nationalists of today vehemently deny that they are white supremacists. They insist that they are simply advocates of white identity and white power in the same mode as the advocates of black identity and black power. Incredibly, the white nationalist movement seeks to portray itself as a kind of civil rights movement, fighting for equal treatment for white people!

Jared Taylor is the editor of the white nationalist website American Renaissance. An American who spent his youth in Japan, Taylor is much more urbane and cosmopolitan than we might stereotypically expect. Pointing out that minority groups often prefer to relate to members of their own group, he says, "If a white person says, 'I like being white, and I prefer my associates to be white,' that's hate? Why?" Taylor adds, "Races are different. Some races are better at some things than others."[28]

Yet in his conversation with Swain, Taylor takes this line of thinking in a surprising direction. "I think Asians are objectively superior to whites by just about any measure that you can come up with. This doesn't mean I want America to become Asian. I think every people has the right to be itself . . . Even if Asians build societies superior to those built by white people, I think white people are perfectly legitimate in preferring the kind of societies they build."

Lisa Turner, the women's coordinator of a white nationalist group called the World Church of the Creator, also insists she is merely standing up for whites as a group, although she takes a dimmer view of Asians than Taylor. Turner tells Swain, "Asians are nothing but imitators, copycats. It's monkey see, monkey do. They have copied what white Europeans have done, and that's the only reason that Asians have any kind of civilization at all."

Despite its name, the World Church of the Creator is an atheist organization, as most white nationalist groups are. "The philosophy behind Christianity," Turner says, "is utterly poisonous. Turn the other cheek, love your enemy—these kind of ideas have put a guilt trip on the white race. The biggest enemies we have out there are the Christian churches."

Swain quotes Michael Hart, who advocates a separate nation for whites somewhere in the Pacific Northwest. "I have no desire to rule over blacks . . . or to have someone else rule over blacks on my behalf. Quite the contrary. I do not want to rule, enslave or exterminate anyone . . . All that I—and most white separatists—want is the opportunity to rule ourselves, in our own independent country."

Even David Duke is on board with this approach, as suggested by the name of the group he founded, the National Association for the Advancement of White People (NAAWP). Duke says that just as the NAACP works for black interests and La Raza Unida works for Hispanic interests, his group is "about preservation of our identity as ethnic people, our existence, our values, our culture, our traditions."[29]

One white nationalist that Swain did not interview is Matthew Heimbach, founder of the Traditionalist Youth Network. Although he has been dubbed the "Little Fuhrer" in the media, Heimbach insists that "we reject the label of any form of racial hatred . . . We have contact with comrades in Syria, comrades in the Philippines, comrades around the world and black nationalists in the United States. We believe every group of people should be able to have self-determination."[30]

I can from personal experience verify Swain's observation that this appeal to group identity and self-determination is the language of contemporary white nationalism. In the mid-1990s, as part of my research for *The End of Racism,* I attended an American Renaissance conference. There I heard Jared Taylor trace his intellectual lineage not to the Republican right but to the Democratic Party and the Confederacy. His ancestors stood up for their cause and for their race, he told me, and he intended to do the same.

At the conference, I also heard Sam Francis, then a columnist for the *Washington Times,* make an argument I had never heard anyone make in public before. "What we as whites must do," he said, "is reassert our identity and our solidarity, and we must do so in explicitly racial terms through the articulation of a racial consciousness as whites . . . The civilization that we as whites created in Europe and America could not have developed apart from the genetic endowments of the creating people, nor is there any reason to believe that the civilization can be successfully transmitted to a different people."

I quoted Francis saying this, and the *Washington Times* fired him over it. Swain mentions this episode as one of the first skirmishes between a mainstream conservative—me—and a white nationalist—Francis—who had been successfully posing as a mainstream conservative.[31] I wasn't trying to get Francis fired. I quoted his remarks because they struck me as one of the very first explicit articulations of a doctrine of white racial consciousness.

Not only is Swain right that the white nationalists are not the bigots of old, but she also correctly discerns that the point they make is not entirely wrong. It takes a courageous scholar to make this point. The progressive economist Glenn Loury is, as far as I know, the only one on the left to make it. "I really don't know how you ask white people *not* to be white in the world we are creating," Loury says. "How are there not white interests in a world where there are these other interests?"[32]

The usual progressive response to Loury is that white solidarity is dangerous because whites as a group have the power to put their prejudices into practice. Racism is prejudice plus power and whites supposedly have both. Black and Hispanic solidarity is not dangerous because minority groups may have their prejudices but they don't have the accompanying power. Moreover, the motives for minority collective associations are benign. In the progressive view, disadvantaged groups have a right to form in their desire to resist white oppression and white supremacy.

This argument, however, fails to consider the contemporary reality that minority interest groups are much more powerful than white nationalist groups. It's not even close. Which group has more clout, the NAACP or the NAAWP? Black representatives in Congress have a Black Caucus, which does not hesitate to fight for explicitly black interests; where is the White Caucus that openly promotes white interests? Moreover, black and Latino interest groups have powerful allies in Hollywood and the media.

The white nationalists have none of this. They are shunned by both political parties and they have much less power to enforce discrimination in their favor than their black and Latino counterparts. While the old-style racism is now outlawed as a consequence of civil rights legislation, affirmative action—racial preferences against whites and in favor of blacks and other minorities—is currently the law of the land.

So marginalized are the white nationalist groups today that they are the ones who feel victimized. They are the ones who are branded as hate groups. Even most whites hate them! Their ideology is so controversial that on campus it sends students fleeing in search of safe spaces. "The only occasion on which it is acceptable for whites to speak collectively as whites," Jared Taylor writes, "is to apologize."[33] Consequently, their racial solidarity, the white nationalists say, is a necessary response to being so besieged in mainstream culture.

Both Swain and Loury advocate that America move away from ethnic identity politics. Loury, in particular, calls for a "racially transcendent humanism being the American bedrock."[34] I am on board with this, and I will discuss this further in the concluding chapter, but here I should say why white nationalists should not be expected to cheerfully go along.

It is all very well to tell them that politics ideally should not be structured along the lines of race or ethnicity. Their point is: it is. And as long as the Democratic Party mobilizes groups along ethnic lines, they are going to feel justified in doing as whites what every other group does in the name of its own ethnicity. Multiculturalism has come home to roost, and white nationalists are its newest advocates.

WHO IS RICHARD SPENCER?

I had never interviewed a white supremacist before, so I didn't know what to expect when Richard Spencer showed up to talk to me, with my film team present and the cameras rolling. Spencer is often portrayed as the most dangerous man in America; a recent profile of him in the *Atlantic Monthly* likened him to Hitler with the title "His Kampf," and when he showed up to speak at the University of Florida, the governor declared a state of emergency. Normally you have to be a hurricane or an epidemic to qualify for that designation.[35]

Debbie and I had arranged security—after all, we are both immigrants from Third World countries and Spencer is not known to be a fan of our type—but from the moment we saw him we knew we had nothing to fear. Spencer came alone, unaccompanied by goons. He looked around nervously, giving me an eager-to-please smile. I saw right away he was a cordial, diffident guy. Dressed in a tweed jacket, he looked somewhat like an academic from a previous era.

"No, I'm not a Nazi," Spencer said right away. "I'm not a neo-Nazi. I'm not any of those things." Why then, I asked him, did you and your pals give the Nazi salute, the raised arm and the "Heil Trump"? At first Spencer pretended it was no big deal. "Well, you know, we have 'Hail to the Chief,' lots of things." But when I pressed him, he acknowledged it was for effect, a kind of up-yours to the politically correct class. "I was being provocative."

Spencer said he wasn't a white supremacist either, but he admitted to being a white nationalist. "I don't believe in nationalism in terms of silly or hokey flag-waving, and I definitely don't believe in nationalism in the sense of Europeans fighting one another. I believe, actually, in a greater brotherhood of European peoples." Would this, I asked, include Greeks and Italians? Spencer said yes. "We're all cousins. We're all part of a big extended family."

What's so great, I asked him, about the white race? Spencer spoke of what he termed its "Faustian spirit. The white race is expansive whether in terms of conquering, in terms of exploration of the seas or space, or scholarship and analysis of science. We possess something that's peculiar to us, and it makes us special." And was that something, I inquired, in the genes? "It is," Spencer replied. "No question. Everything is in the genes."

My real interest was to find out what Spencer really believed and where he really belonged on the political spectrum. I asked him whether he sought to conserve the principles of the American founding. He responded, "I've been critical of the American founding throughout my career." The whole concept of individual rights, he said, was "problematic."

Me: So, all men are created equal. True or false?
Spencer: False, obviously.
Me: The idea that we have a right to life, true or false?
Spencer: I don't think we have rights to really anything.

I asked Spencer about the two main prongs of Reaganite conservatism.

Me: One prong is American influence is good for the world and that American power should project American values, agree or disagree?
Spencer: If American values are wielded to destroy other cultures and bring them into one big capitalist market or something, I don't think we should be promoting American values in that sense.
Me: The second prong of Reaganism was free-market economics, promoting a global free market in which people trade with each other. Would you like to see the world be a global capitalist order?
Spencer: Absolutely not. This notion that we need to destroy our own industries, that our people are just one more competitor in a global

marketplace. Good luck, sink or swim, pal. The notion that that should be the guiding philosophy of our citizens is disgusting, actually. I totally reject that.

I asked Spencer about his advocacy of a concept called the white ethno-state.

Me: What I take you to be saying is that the white ethno-state would have a powerful state at the center of it.

Spencer: No question.

Me: But this notion of limited government . . . As you know, the founders saw the government as the enemy of our rights.

Spencer: No individual has a right outside of a collective community. You have rights, not eternally or given by God, or by nature.

Me: Who gives them to us?

Spencer: Ultimately the state gives those rights to you. The state is the source of rights, not the individual.

Me: Would it be fair to say you are not just against illegal immigration but immigration, period?

Spencer: I'm definitely against illegal immigration. That's an easy one. I'm against replacement immigration in the sense that I'm against immigration coming in from the Third World that is ultimately going to change the ethnic and cultural constitution of the United States. I wouldn't say I'm against immigration in itself. I would actually be happy to open the door to white South Africans among many who are truly suffering. I would be happy to take in those refugees.

Me: Would you be happy with an immigration policy that said, we want people from New Zealand, Australia, white guys from Europe and South Africa. We don't want people from Barbados or Bombay.

Spencer: Yes, and that was the immigration policy beginning in 1924 up until 1965. That period of time coincided with American greatness.

Me: Now this seems very different than Trump. Trump was quoted in the paper saying to Bannon, if there's an Indian guy working in Silicon Valley and his visa runs out, and we have to send him home, that's a loss. That's something we should try to prevent. You disagree?

Spencer: I do disagree with that. The H-1B Visa program has been totally detrimental to white people. I want white people to become
doctors, lawyers. I want white people to achieve their dreams.

I asked Spencer about his favorite presidents. Reagan? "I do not
think he was a great president." Lincoln: Spencer blamed him for starting "an unnecessary war" instead of negotiating a solution with the
slave-owners. Spencer wasn't too hot on Washington either. Who, then,
were his favorites? "There's something about Jackson," he said. "There's
something about Polk, who took something from Mexico and made it
ours." I pointed out to him that they were both Democrats.

Finally I asked Spencer about the movie *Birth of a Nation*.

Me: Have you seen it?

Spencer: Yes, I have.

Me: What did you think of it?

Spencer: It's an amazing film, one of the most important films ever
made.

Me: Leaving aside its technical merits, the notion that the sex-crazed
blacks are taking over the country and the Ku Klux Klan was a re-
demptive movement of white identity to clean the place up—you
agree with that?

Spencer: It was a romanticization of the first Klan in response to Republican Reconstruction. It's an idealized vision that paints in really
broad strokes.

Me: But it's your music.

Spencer: Sure. It appealed to many Americans including presidents.

As I interviewed Spencer, I kept saying to myself, obviously this
guy is not a conservative, but what is he? He's not a progressive in the
contemporary sense, either. And yet his ideas are so familiar. Only toward the end of the interview did it hit me. Spencer's views are virtually identical to those of the progressive racists of the Woodrow Wilson
era. He even dresses the part. Basically, the guy is a relic.

In a purely logical sense, Spencer should be a progressive Democrat. Progressive Democrats invented the ideology he espouses, and

even today the Democratic Party is the party of ethnic identity politics. Spencer's problem, however, is that the Democrats mobilize black, Latino and Asian identity politics against that of whites. Since whites are now the all-round bad guy, Spencer's brand of progressivism is no longer welcome at the multicultural picnic.

Thus Spencer, a man without a party, turns to Trump. Now there is very little on which Spencer and Trump actually agree. Trump is a flag-waving patriot who cherishes the American founders; Spencer isn't and doesn't. Trump is a capitalist; Spencer prefers a strong state regulating markets on behalf of white interests. Trump wants to keep illegals out so legal immigrants and other American citizens—whether white, black or brown—can thrive. Spencer wants more white immigrants, fewer—if any—black and brown ones. In sum, Trump is generally conservative in his ideology and Spencer is clearly not.

Why, then, did Spencer vote for Trump? Why does he consider himself on the right? The simple answer is that Spencer has no place else to go, so he is trying to carve out a niche for himself in the only party where he can find some measure of agreement, however small. The point here is that Trump isn't embracing Spencer, just as Lincoln didn't embrace the Know-Nothings. Rather, Spencer is going to Trump, as the Know-Nothings eventually went with Lincoln.

Look at it from Spencer's point of view. If you're a white nationalist who wants racial preferences for whites, would you rather go with the Democrats, who want racial preferences against whites, or with the Republicans, who want racial preferences for no one? Clearly the latter. If you're a white nationalist who wants to eliminate minority immigration altogether—legal and illegal—would you rather vote for the Democrats, who encourage more illegals, with a view to gaining more future voters, or for the Republicans, who support legal but not illegal immigration? Again, the answer is obvious.

We can see the same phenomenon on the Democratic side of the aisle. Consider a radical communist who wants a 100 percent tax rate and the complete abolition of private property. Would such a guy prefer the Republicans, who affirm property rights and seek to lower the tax rate, or the Democrats, who push for tax increases and more regulation of private property rights? Obviously the latter. Does it follow, then, that the Democrats are the party of communism or that they should feel morally obligated to repudiate the communist vote? Not at all; no one even asks this of them.

To sum up, white nationalism is not conservative, even if white nationalists end up in the Trump column. The left tries to portray Spencer and other white nationalists as right-wingers in the same way they claim Hitler was a right-winger; it's an attempt to conceal their own history. Nor is white nationalism the most potent form of racism in America today. The institutionalized racism of the Democratic plantation is far worse. This is the new form of progressive ethnic exploitation that whites as a group have, at least to date, bravely resisted.

11

EMANCIPATION

How American Nationalism
Can Save the Country

Go down, Moses, way down in Egypt land,
and tell old Pharaoh, let my people go.

—NEGRO SPIRITUAL

On November 19, 1863, Abraham Lincoln stood at the battlefield of Gettysburg and delivered some brief, telling remarks. Without making any specific reference to the battle of Gettysburg and without once mentioning the word "America," he said that the Civil War was a test of whether a nation dedicated to the proposition that all men are created equal "can long endure." Lincoln said it was for "us the living" to continue the "unfinished work" of the war dead, to ensure "that this nation, under God, shall have a new birth of freedom—and that the government of the people, by the people, for the people, shall not perish from the earth."[1]

For all their familiarity, these words are also strange. Clearly Lincoln was saying that in the Civil War America's very survival was at stake. But why? Wouldn't America still exist whichever side won the war? Let's say that Lincoln negotiated a settlement with the Confederacy in which the Missouri Compromise—the law that had kept the peace from 1820 to 1860—was restored in an expanded form so that slavery would be permanently allowed south of the Mason-Dixon Line, which would now be extended all the way to the Pacific.

This is not imaginary or counterfactual history. Such a solution was proposed and seriously debated. The Crittenden proposal was named after the man who devised it, Kentucky senator John Crittenden. Historians agree that it was the only way the Civil War could have been averted. Some Republicans, terrified of the prospect of war, warmed to a seemingly equitable division of territory that would have prevented it.

Had Abraham Lincoln gotten behind the Crittenden proposal, it would most likely have passed, and there would have been no Civil War. Yet Lincoln worked behind the scenes to defeat it. "Stand firm," he told his fellow Republicans. Compromise on the very core of what the Republicans campaigned for, he said, would mean "all our labor is lost, and sooner or later must be done over." Admittedly the pressure to give in seemed irresistible; that was why Republicans had to be tough. "The tug has to come, & better now than any time hereafter."

We must admit, in taking his stand against Crittenden and other compromise measures, Lincoln, notwithstanding his seeming attributions of the war to unavoidable circumstances—"And the war came"—nevertheless played a decisive role in its tragic and bloody occurrence. If Lincoln's stance here were self-serving or reckless, he could be said to have plunged the nation into an unnecessary cataclysm and, far from being America's greatest president, he would have to be considered the worst. No defender of Lincoln can agree with such an assessment.

So why did Lincoln reject the Crittenden compromise? For him, the issue was starkly simple and yet unutterably profound. He had won a free election, and now the Democratic Party was attempting to reverse the outcome of that election. He had secured an electoral mandate for halting the spread of slavery, and now the Democrats, both in the North and the South, sought to force him to bargain away his mandate. The Democratic South had not only threatened to break up the country but was in the process of breaking it up, putting Lincoln in a position of having to relinquish his Republican principles in order to discourage this process.

Lincoln said he would not and could not do it. Why not? Because, Lincoln argued, his electoral mandate was not his to give up. True, he and his fellow Republicans had campaigned on the platform of restricting the spread of slavery. Once the American people, speaking through an electoral majority, approved that mandate, Lincoln insisted that it no longer belonged to him—it now belonged to them.

"No popular government can long survive a marked precedent, that those who carry an election, can only save the government from immediate destruction by giving up the main point upon which the people gave the election." For Lincoln to bargain away his mandate would be to give up on the meaning of democracy. Only the people themselves could give up what they alone possessed. "The people themselves, and not their servants, can safely reverse their own deliberate decision."

Therefore, Lincoln said, "I will suffer death before I will consent or advise my friends to consent to any concession or compromise which looks like buying the privilege of taking possession of the government to which we have a constitutional right . . . I should regard any concession in the face of menace as the destruction of the government itself, and a consent on all hands that our system shall be brought down to a level with the existing disorganized state of affairs in Mexico."

And again, "We have just carried an election on principles fairly stated to the people. Now we are told in advance the government shall be broken up, unless we surrender to those we have beaten, before we take the offices. If we surrender, it is the end of us, and of the government. They will repeat the experiment upon us ad libitum. A year will not pass, till we shall have to take Cuba as a condition upon which they will stay in the Union."

Now Lincoln acknowledged that while majorities have a right to rule, the power of even elected majorities is strictly limited by what the Constitution authorizes. Majorities do not have unlimited power. Moreover, they are obliged to respect minority rights no less than their own. Even elected majorities have no warrant to trample on the constitutionally specified rights of minorities.

Lincoln conceded that if he had violated the constitutional rights of any individual or group—such as its right to free speech or freedom of religion or to freely assemble—then those individuals or groups would be justified in leaving the union. "Think, if you can," Lincoln said on March 4, 1861, "of a single instance in which a plainly written provision of the Constitution has been denied." Then Lincoln added, "Such is not our case."

Lincoln had violated no constitutional rights, let alone vital ones. Therefore, Lincoln said, the election and its aftermath "presents to the whole family of man the question, whether a constitutional republic, or a democracy, a government of the people, by the same people, can or cannot maintain its territorial integrity against its own domestic foes."

In his July 4, 1861, Special Message to Congress, Lincoln added, "Our popular government has often been called an experiment. Two points in it our people have already settled—the successful establishing and the successful administering of it. One still remains—its successful maintenance against a formidable internal attempt to overthrow it." Lincoln insisted, "We must settle this question now, whether in a free government the minority have the right to break up the government whenever they choose," because "if we fail, it will go far to prove the incapability of the people to govern themselves."

It was his task and the task of all patriots, Lincoln concluded, to "demonstrate to the world that those who can fairly carry an election can also suppress a rebellion; that ballots are the rightful and peaceful successors of bullets, and that when ballots have been fairly and constitutionally decided, there can be no successful appeal back to bullets; that there can be no successful appeal except to ballots themselves, at succeeding elections."

So now we can see why Lincoln went to war. He went to war to save not just the nation but a certain type of nation. For Lincoln, America would not be America once the proposition of all men are created equal—and the whole ensemble of constitutional principles that flow from it—was given up. Lincoln refused to submit to an America defined by the principles of the slave plantation, principles whose realization Lincoln regarded as tantamount to the death of the nation. Even more, in Lincoln's words, it would "practically put an end to free government upon the earth."[2]

But why did the Democratic South start the war? Even a scholar as astute as Harry Jaffa argues that the planter class made a colossal strategic mistake. These people had slavery in the South. Lincoln had pledged not to interfere with it there. Yet after the war slavery was permanently abolished throughout the country. "One might suspect," Jaffa writes, "that the Southern secessionists were financed by abolitionism as they catapulted slavery toward its destruction."[3]

I believe, however, that these Democratic planters were not so dumb. They realized what Lincoln's election signified, that the balance of power had tipped against them. Slavery was now indeed, as Lincoln promised, on its way to "ultimate extinction." The Southern Democrats went to war, but they knew that they could count on the Northern Democrats to undermine Lincoln from within Union ranks. If they waited longer, their political position was likely to deteriorate further. Yes, they might lose the war and lose it all, but they were going to lose it all in any event. Thus their best time to strike was now.

A SIMILAR SITUATION

I think the perceptive reader will know full well why I am recounting this history. Notwithstanding all the Solomonic pronouncements about how history does not repeat itself, we are in a very similar situation today with Trump. Trump, like Lincoln, came out of nowhere; both men were outsiders. Yet from the outset Lincoln showed a resolve in taking on the Democratic plantation that can provide a valuable lesson to Trump.

Lincoln was portrayed by the Democrats and their allies, just as Trump is now, as being a grave threat to their fundamental liberties. Yet we may ask about Trump the same question that Lincoln asked about himself. Has Trump actually violated any of the basic constitutional rights of his opponents? Has he deprived them of their free speech or the right to assemble or vote? No, he has not. And yet they persist in trying to drive him from office for the same reason their Democratic forbears sought to bring Lincoln to his knees, because they cannot abide the result of a free election.

We need to step back and take in the full scope of this. For all that we learn about America's two-party system, as a practical matter one party has dominated politics for a generation or more. We cannot count the founding period, because there were no parties in the modern sense then. But from the 1820s through 1860, the Democrats were the majority party. From 1865 through 1932, it was the Republicans. From 1932 to 1980, the Democrats became the dominant party once again.

Political dominance does not mean you control the presidency, both parties in Congress and the Supreme Court. We know, for example, that Eisenhower and Nixon were Republican presidents during the era of Democratic dominance. But they were pulled to the center by the Democratic tide. Neither Eisenhower nor Nixon sought to undo the New Deal, nor could they have done so had they wanted to. In a way, Eisenhower solidified the New Deal, and Nixon parts of the Great Society, by acquiescing to them.

Since 1980, however, American politics has been a draw. Neither party has enjoyed real dominance. Reagan was president for two terms in the eighties, but he mostly had a Democratic Congress. Then Clinton was president for two terms in the nineties, but the GOP swept the Congress in 1994. George W. Bush and Barack Obama both initially had congressional majorities in both houses but couldn't hold them, forcing them to deal with rival party obstruction in their second terms.

Then, in 2016, everything came up for grabs. The Democrats saw a chance to make their plantation permanent. If Hillary won the presidency and Democrats rode her coattails to make strong gains in the House and the Senate, Democrats would have not only the presidency and the Congress but also the chance to lock the Supreme Court into a 6–3 Democratic majority. This would spell the beginning of the end for Republicans, sending them the way of the Whigs.

Then the Democrats could open the gates to massive illegal immigration, while at the same time granting amnesty to the illegals already here. By adding several million new voters to the rolls—mostly but not exclusively Latino—Democrats could expand their Latino plantation and also tip the balance of American votes, now precariously divided between the parties, decisively in their favor. This would give Democrats the kind of control that would last indefinitely into the future.

We've seen it happen in California, which was once Nixon country and Reagan country. As James Q. Wilson argued decades ago in the essay "Reagan Country," California once embodied the American dream of owning a piece of paradise with two cars in front and a pool in the backyard.[4] But illegal immigration has changed the demographic composition of the state. The Republican Party is no longer competitive at the state level, and Democrats can safely count on Californians to vote for whomever they nominate in a presidential year.

I moved to California in 2000. Much as I liked the sun, the palm trees and the ocean, over time I saw what it means to live in a progressive one-party state. Eventually I grew weary of the confiscatory taxation, the absurd regulations, the preposterous edicts making it illegal to report illegals and granting children the right to decide their own gender. This, I realized, is progressive utopia, and I didn't want to subsidize it anymore, so Debbie and I moved to her home state of Texas. For progressive Democrats, however, California is the model, and their hope is that as California goes, so goes the nation.

But the American people, speaking through the same relatively narrow electoral majority that elected Lincoln, decided otherwise. By electing Trump and preserving Republican majorities in the House and, much more narrowly, the Senate, Americans gave the GOP the dominance that Democrats aspired to. In his first few months, Trump saved the Court by shepherding Neil Gorsuch's nomination to confirmation. One more appointee and the Court—which is now leaning GOP—will be out of Democratic hands.

So this explains the dismay and horror of the Democrats at Trump's presence in the White House. For them, in the words of progressive critic Walter Kirn, "the unimaginable has become the historical." Trump's election "gave me the impression that time was warping." It was a "trick of the gods to remind us cocky mortals that we are not in control of our affairs." It was a "total eclipse . . . cutting a spooky swath of darkness across the republic," giving Kirn himself a "sense of temporal displacement."[5] This quasi-religious vocabulary gives you a sense of how big the stakes were for Kirn and others like him.

Then there is Trump's Olympian vigor, which must only add to the left's dismay. Not only is Trump in there but he is a fighter, and he fights on both the political and cultural fronts. He is the most politically incorrect president in American history. And as the tax bill, the Gorsuch nomination and progress on peace in Korea and in the fight against ISIS showed, Trump has the ability to get things done. Having dismissed him as a buffoon and a moron, the progressive left is now deathly scared of him.

THE WOLF AND THE LAMB

The similarities between Lincoln's day and our own go far beyond the surface resemblance between the 1860 and 2016 elections. Today, too, we have a Democratic plantation, not just black this time, but populated with dependent and subjugated minority populations. Today, as well, we have a befuddled Republican Party tempted to make peace with the plantation and in search of a leader who might have Lincoln's prescience and fortitude. Today Republicans have a chance, as Lincoln did, to topple the Democratic plantation, perhaps this time even beyond the possibility of salvage and rehabilitation.

Let's begin with the perversion of language, a problem as familiar in Lincoln's time as it is in our own. Then, as now, enslavement was justified by the Democrats through an appeal to obfuscation and deception. Lincoln did not hesitate to point this out. In an 1864 address at a Baltimore fair, Lincoln said, "We all declare for liberty, but in using the same word we do not all mean the same thing. With some the word liberty may mean for each man to do as he pleases with himself, and the product of his labor; while with others the same word may mean for some men to do as they please with other men, and the product of other men's labor."

Continuing in his characteristic manner of being both homespun and deep, Lincoln added, "The shepherd drives the wolf from the sheep's throat, for which the sheep thanks the shepherd as a liberator, while the wolf denounces him for the same act as the destroyer of liberty. Plainly the sheep and the wolf are not agreed upon a definition of the word liberty, and precisely the same difference prevails today among us human creatures, even in the North, and all professing to love liberty."[6]

Even in the North. Lincoln recognized that the Northern and Southern Democrats were in it together, and that the Democrats were the party of the wolf, invoking liberty for themselves even as they suppressed and choked the liberty of others and stole the fruits of their labor. For all the vicissitudes of history, some things remain the same. Vulpine extortion and theft have defined the Democratic plantation from the outset, and they continue to define the Democratic plantation even now.

This is not to say that the plantation in the twenty-first century is unchanged from what it was in the nineteenth. In a partial vindication of both Parmenides and Heraclitus, we see that history is an account of both continuities and discontinuities. In the movie *The Godfather*, the Corleone family moved its operations from New York to Las Vegas. Why? Because their opportunities in New York grew thin. Thus they moved from labor rackets involving control of the unions and bootlegging to the more fertile territory of casino gambling.

The move to Vegas showed creative improvisation, the ability to start afresh and build from the ground up, and yet the Corleones remained the Corleones. The crime family itself did not change, even when it changed location and tactics. Theft and extortion continued as the heart of the operation. In New York it was camouflaged as the olive oil business; in Vegas it was hidden behind the operation of casinos. In both places, however, the Corleones used their power to forcibly extract money from others.

In some respect, the Democrats are like the Corleones. And just like that large and varied family, the Democrats over time have shown themselves to be a mixed bunch. Some are thoughtful, like Calhoun and Fitzhugh; others are dull, like Pierce and Buchanan. Some are swashbuckling, like Van Buren, Boss Tweed and LBJ; others are drearily pedantic, like Woodrow Wilson and Obama. Some are straight-laced, like Taney and Jimmy Carter; others are con artists, like Andrew Jackson, FDR and Bill and Hillary Clinton. What unites this political family through time, however, is the commitment of its leaders to the plantation in its various guises and phases.

The old Democrats made a gallant attempt to make an open public defense of the slave plantation. Today's Democrats, however, recognize that their new urban plantations are indefensible. In this respect, we can liken the Democrats to today's neo-Nazis. The old Nazis were open about their anti-Semitism, and they attempted to justify their horrific treatment of Jews. Hitler repeatedly warned that the Jews deserved what was coming to them, and so on. But after the Holocaust, things changed.

Today's neo-Nazis don't try to defend the Holocaust; they deny it even happened. In a similar vein, today's Democrats don't claim credit for the conditions of their urban plantations. Even though those places are one-party systems, run exclusively by Democrats, they attempt to foist the blame for their unlivable conditions on white racism, on Republicans, on America in general, on anyone except the group that created those plantations and has governed them over the half century from their formation to the present.

TWO BIG LIES

The progressive account of American history—which is basically a narrative designed to cover up the plantation—is defined by two big lies. The first big lie is that fascism is a phenomenon of the right. The second is that racism is a defining characteristic of conservatives and of the Republican Party. Both lies work together to distort American history and to project the blame for Democratic atrocities onto the very people who sought, with varying degrees of success, to stop them.

In reality, as I have shown in this book, fascism is a phenomenon of the left, and racism is the defining characteristic of progressives and the Democratic Party. This is true not merely of the origins or the history of progressives and Democrats; it is also true of the ideology and practice of progressive Democrats today. So they are the real fascists; they are the real racists. Only when these big lies are fully exposed can we clearly see the plantation in full view and recognize who is responsible for it.

We need to look closely because the Democratic plantation is a kind of amoeba; it evolves over time. In this book I have shown five distinct plantation phases, bringing us up to the present. The first phase was the old rural slave plantation, 1828 to 1860. Here the Democratic planter class became rich and lazy by directly stealing the labor and liberty of the slaves. The Democrats became prosperous by ripping off the poorest of the poor.

We should not think of this as a purely private racket. The state played a role as well, through an elaborate structure of laws that upheld the plantation. The state also employed slave patrols to protect what it viewed as the property of the plantation. It was a good racket while it lasted, but unfortunately for the Democrats, it was ruined by Lincoln and the Republicans and finally came to an end at Appomattox in 1865.

The second phase was Van Buren's Northern urban machine, 1836-1932, itself modified from the rural plantation. Here the Democrats figured out how to exploit not blacks but ethnic immigrant populations, recognizing them to be as fearful, vulnerable and insecure as the slaves. Democrats bought the votes of these groups through goodies appropriated from the city treasury; essentially they perverted the founders' constitutional scheme by turning politics into a crooked game of looting the taxpayer to fund an ethnically based patronage system of government employment and government handouts designed to keep the crooks perpetually in power.

The third phase was the national progressive plantation, which we can also term the fascist plantation. I date this from 1932 to 1964. Here Wilson in theory and FDR in practice converted the local and state ethnic machines of the nineteenth and early twentieth centuries into a single machine. The federal government became the Big House, controlling the private sector and, increasingly, the ordinary lives of citizens. FDR's plantation overseers were not city ward operatives but rather labor union organizers and strongmen who drew on the muscle of the federal government to force into compliance employers and also fellow workers.

While importing ideas from Mussolini's Italy and Hitler's Germany, FDR created in America a distinctive democratic brand of fascism, which is to say, fascism that courted popular support in order to sustain FDR in office. Yet notwithstanding his appreciation for Mussolini, FDR's fascist plantation more closely resembled Nazism than Italian fascism in that it had a strongly racist component, facilitating segregation, lynching and racial terrorism against African Americans.

The fourth phase was LBJ's plantation, which can be officially dated 1964 to 1980, although a good bit of it continues to the present day. LBJ realized that after World War II, racism had declined sharply and therefore the Democratic Party could no longer count on the white racist vote, even in the South. The problem was that Americans were simply not racist enough! So in a historic turn, LBJ decided that Democrats thereafter should go after the black vote.

He reconstituted FDR's plantation by, in effect, turning blacks from a group directly oppressed and exploited by the Democrats into a group only indirectly exploited because now they were an ethnic constituency, as for example the Irish had been in the past. Unlike the old plantation, where the slaves worked and produced things, LBJ's plantation was designed to produce nothing and prevent its inhabitants from working. Self-control was replaced by government control, and the idle, uneducated, irresponsible citizen became LBJ's model citizen. The Big House now existed to take care of such people.

LBJ's plantation was responsible for the cultural pathologies of the inner city, in some cases doing even more harm to the African

American community than had been done by earlier generations of Democrats through slavery. Slavery, for example, disabled but did not permanently destroy the black family; somehow LBJ's welfare state managed to do what even slavery could not do. Democrats, although rhetorically inconsolable about the plight of the black underclass, have no intention of changing it because they want to keep this population fully dependent on them.

Finally, there is today's multicultural plantation, which includes LBJ's plantation but can more accurately be termed Obama's plantation. Thus we can date it from the 1980s through today. Notice that Obama himself did very little for blacks. He rarely visited the inner city. He did nothing to address the issues of crime, gangs or broken families. All he did was to expand welfare benefits and food stamps. Clearly blacks are a group that Democrats now take for granted. Even America's first African American president didn't feel the need to address their plight, other than to keep the benefits flowing to ensure their total dependency on the Democratic Party.

Obama's "remaking" of America seems to have focused more on what may be termed the frontier of the Democratic plantation. Obama fought hard to legalize and normalize gay marriage, and he introduced the DACA policy of refusing to deport the children of illegal immigrants who have grown up in the United States. In this respect Obama may be considered a plantation recruiter, seeking to draw new groups—homosexual activists and illegals—to join blacks in relying on the federal government for their security and advancement.

Obama, like Bill Clinton, was part of the project to expand the Democratic plantation beyond blacks to include Latino barrios and Native American reservations. Each group was recruited into a project of delivering votes as part of an ethnic collective, in exchange for which each group was maintained in a state of stupefied subjugation. So powerful was this parasitism that groups became dependent and servile and, despite their miseries, constantly voted to sustain in power the party that was subjugating them.

Even Asian Americans would have enclaves if the Democrats could figure out how to lock them into ethnic Chinatowns and Koreatowns. Of all minorities, Democrats have had the least success with this group. The Asian American plantation seems to have only overseers, very few inhabitants. Democrats, however, are hoping to change that. As an Asian American myself, I can only wish them failure with this exploitative project.

PLANTATION CONTROL

Only whites—even whites undergoing economic hardship and plagued by cultural dysfunction—have so far resisted succumbing to the lure of the Democratic plantation. What makes this hard for the Democrats to take is that whites used to be on the plantation, both the poor whites of the South and the ethnic whites who were once part of the Northern urban machines. Van Buren had them, Wilson had them, FDR had them, but now the Democrats have lost them.

What happened? The problem is that whites assimilated. The Irish became Americans and ceased to think of themselves as Irish. They were once Irish Americans; now they are Americans of Irish descent. One may say that ethnic identity became an American identity. The affirmation of American identity is one of the hallmarks of the Republican Party. Thus when the immigrants assimilated, the Democrats lost them as a group to the GOP. This is the main reason why Democrats don't want Latinos to learn English and assimilate, because that might mean Latinos would follow the example of the Irish and escape the political captivity of the Democratic Party.

Plantation control is a very serious business. These are terrible places that no one is supposed to leave, or even want to leave. The happiest people on the plantation are the overseers, who siphon off large amounts of money reserved for the poor and the destitute while also enjoying their task of lording it over the plantation's hapless inhabitants. Conscious of this, the Democrats have anointed a vast multicultural overseer class to patrol their new ethnic plantations.

One of the main tasks of the overseers is to ensure that few people depart the plantation. The overseers do this not merely through working to establish the complete dependency of their subject populations. They also do it by vilifying anyone—especially blacks or other minorities—who seek to criticize or reform the Democratic plantation. In the mode of Du Bois vilifying Booker T. Washington, today's overseer class bashes black and Hispanic conservatives and independents, accusing them of being accessories to minority oppression.

What makes these accusations downright insane is that the Democratic plantation is the greatest force for oppression and racist subjugation in American history. Nowhere is racist exploitation today more obvious than on the Democrats' multicultural plantations. Even so, we have the strange phenomenon of plantation administrators and accessories—the real Uncle Toms—accusing free-thinking and freedom-loving minorities of being Uncle Toms. The vehemence of these accusations shows how much the Democratic plantation class has always hated runaways.

The only prospect scarier for a Democrat than a plantation runaway is the dismantling of the plantation system itself. The Democrats currently have no intention of dismantling it. The only way they would consider that would be if the plantation ceased to pay off politically for them. In that case, they might give it up. But that would spell the end of the Democratic Party as it is now constituted. The Democrats, in that case, would have to go straight or, what seems more likely given the party's history, find themselves a new scam.

A GLORIOUS HISTORY

There is only one group that can shut down the plantation: Trump and the Republican Party. Both have a direct stake in doing this, because the plantation is antithetical to what Trump believes and to what Republicans have stood for and stand for today. While many Republicans have no idea how to defeat the plantation—some are in fact wasting their energies fighting against Trump—they can and must learn. Only Trump and the GOP together can save American nationalism and avert the death of the nation.

To a degree never recognized, Lincoln and the Republicans are the founders of modern American nationalism. Wait a minute, you say. Shouldn't we credit the American founders for that? Not really. It is true, as Samuel Huntington writes, that only in the founding era "did the British settlers on the Atlantic coast begin to identify themselves not only as residents of their individual colonies but also as Americans." Ben Franklin, who called himself a "Briton" prior to 1776, began to consider himself an American following the Revolution.

Even so, Huntington recognizes, it was not until the conclusion of the Civil War that America's identity as a single nation was securely established. Prior to the Civil War we were the United States, plural; only after Appomattox did we become the United States, singular. "Since the Civil War," Huntington writes, "Americans have been a flag-oriented people. The Stars and Stripes has the status of a religious icon and is a more central symbol of national identity for Americans than their flags are for people of other nations." Memorial Day was also commemorated for the first time following the Civil War.[7]

Today's progressive Democrats, just like their Democratic forbears, loathe American nationalism because it advances a unifying vision that poses a mortal threat to their politics of ethnic mobilization and to the Democratic plantation itself. "I never use the word 'Nation' in speaking of the United States," John C. Calhoun declared in 1849. "We are not a Nation but a . . . Confederacy of equal and sovereign States."[8]

If Calhoun reviled American nationalism in the name of states' rights, today's Democrats do so in the name of internationalism or ethnic diversity. Progressive philosopher Martha Nussbaum denounces "patriotic pride" as "morally dangerous" and urges Americans to give their "allegiance" to the "worldwide community of human beings." Political scientist Amy Gutmann insists it is "repugnant" for Americans to regard themselves "above all as citizens of the United States." And invoking the ethnic diversity in this country, Elizabeth Bruenig recently wrote in the *Washington Post* that nationalism is a chimera because the American nation itself is a chimera. "Such a thing does not exist."[9]

The Republican Party is well equipped to fight the plantation because it has a glorious history of fighting against racism and white supremacy. This is hardly known, even in the precincts of the GOP. Here we can identify the great battles fought by the GOP. First, Republicans mobilized the armies of the North to defeat the combined efforts— military and political—of the Democratic Party to save slavery and make it permanent.

Second, Republicans shut down the Ku Klux Klan for a period and fought vigorously, though not successfully, to curb Democratic efforts to promote segregation and racial terrorism. Third, Republicans spearheaded the civil rights revolution of the 1860s—the revolution that produced the Thirteenth, Fourteen and Fifteenth Amendments—as well as Reconstruction, the first attempt to build a multiracial democracy in America, which was sadly thwarted by the Democrats. Fourth, a century later, Republicans were indispensable to the passage of the civil rights laws, including the Civil Rights Act of 1964 that made those original Republican amendments a practical reality.

Republicans are also the original formulators of the doctrine of color-blindness that is often credited to Martin Luther King Jr. When King said he dreamt of living in a nation where we are judged by the content of our character, not the color of our skin, he was echoing the GOP ideal first enunciated a hundred years earlier by Frederick Douglass. King deserves appreciation, of course, for reaffirming the principle, but he should have given credit to Douglass for coming up with it.

Progressives privately loathe Douglass, and in public they dishonor him by ignoring him. Douglass, not King, is America's greatest black leader—I suspect King would have acknowledged this—yet progressives fawn over King while spurning Douglass. This silent treatment is not merely because Douglass was a Republican. It is also because Douglass, speaking to the Massachusetts Anti-Slavery Society just days before the Civil War ended, uttered what is from the progressive point of view the ultimate heresy.

Douglass raised the question: what must be "done" for the former slaves? He answered, "Do nothing with us! Your *doing* with us has already played the mischief with us. Do nothing with us! If the Negro cannot stand on his own legs, let him fall! . . . All I ask is, give him a chance to stand on his own legs also! Let him alone! . . . If you will only untie his hands and give him a chance, I think he will live."[10]

Ouch! What could be a starker repudiation of the Democratic plantation? Douglass can be heard speaking across the span of time to that conniving bigot LBJ, telling the corrupt old Democrat that he sees right through him and wants none of his condescending patronage. Progressive Democrats can forgive Douglass his tirades against the old slave plantation—at least publicly, that is their position also—but they cannot forgive the scorn he presciently heaped on their current one.

PARTY OF LINCOLN

Douglass embodied who the Republicans are, the party of individual rights and upward striving and what Douglass himself called the "self-made" man. These were also, as we have seen, Lincoln's ideals. Today there are many Republicans who blame Trump for the de-Reaganization of the Republican Party and wistfully pine for the 1980s era of gentleman's politics. This is, by and large, the main source of anxiety about Trump in some Republican quarters, and it is also the driving momentum of the so-called Never Trump movement.

I came of age in the Reagan area, and I too prefer a more civil political climate. But that is not the America we live in now. Reagan's policies and style were calibrated to deal with the specific problems and specific political environment of the late 1970s. Today, however, a good deal of Reaganism is dated. Not only has stagflation—that toxic combination of slow growth combined with runaway inflation—disappeared and the Soviet Union collapsed, but Reagan himself would be a fish out of water in the dark, roiled currents of today.

But Lincoln wouldn't. His political environment was even more roiled than the one we have now. And Lincoln would have seen that, in this environment, an environment made by a gangster clan of Democrats like Obama and Hillary, you don't get very far with Reagan's courtly style. In short, Trump is the man of the hour, not Reagan. Trump has the chance to do what Reagan never even dreamed about, taking a page from Lincoln and smashing the Democratic plantation.

When we consider Trump's two big Republican "heresies"—his positions on trade and immigration—we can see that they might be heresies from Reagan's point of view, but they were not heresies from Lincoln's point of view. As Gabor Boritt shows in *Lincoln and the Economics of the American Dream*, Lincoln's GOP was unabashedly protectionist and viewed tariffs as a necessary and valid economic strategy to protect American workers and American industry from mercantilist competition from European powers. And while many progressives as well as conservatives insist that tariffs have never worked, Boritt shows that America had tariffs from Hamilton's time through the end of the nineteenth century, and it was during this period that America grew most rapidly and became the largest economy in the world, surpassing Great Britain.[11]

On immigration, too, Trump and Lincoln can be seen as generally aligned. This point is hardly obvious, but we get a vital clue about how Lincoln would have thought about today's immigration debate by considering the position Lincoln actually took on extending civil rights—the right to full citizenship, the right to vote, the right to serve on juries—to blacks. Lincoln basically held that it was wrong for any people, anywhere, to enslave another people, because slavery was wrong or, to put it philosophically, against natural right.

But natural rights are not the same as civil rights. Civil rights are the product of living in a particular community. The community is a social compact between the citizens who have formed that community. These existing citizens have the right to decide who gets to be a member of their club, and on what terms. For this reason, Lincoln insisted that opposition to slavery and the extension of civil protections to blacks were two separate issues. Before the war Lincoln was committed to fighting only for the former; only after the war did he move tentatively in the direction of the latter.

It follows from this that Lincoln would have agreed with Trump that the interests of natives must be considered prior to those of potential new immigrants, and that natives are the ones who get to decide who is allowed to immigrate, and in what number, and on what conditions. This, by the way, applies to decisions about legal and illegal immigration. But hold it, the progressive will say, "America is a nation of immigrants. Immigrants are the ones who made America."

Actually, this is only a partial truth. As the founders and Lincoln all recognized, the first Americans were not immigrants. They were settlers. There's a difference. Immigrants are people who come individually, in families or in small groups to a country that has already been created and established. Immigrants, one may say, are people who apply to be members of a club whose rules appeal to them. Settlers, however, are the original group that forms that community in the first place and charts out its basic rules or constitution. This settler label would apply both to the Pilgrims and the American founders.

Trump somehow knows all this, either through learning or just intuitively. And ironically Trump, in adopting the policies of Lincoln rather than those of Reagan, is proving that he is the first Republican since Reagan to win the support of the group once known as the "Reagan Democrats." Since Reagan, the GOP has unsuccessfully wooed these voters by anodyne appeals to abortion and other social issues. Trump is the first one to appeal to them both on economic and social issues, and that is why the descendants of the Reagan Democrats now have a new name: Trumpsters.

Trump is the only Republican on the scene today who actually has a chance to launch the final defeat of the Democratic plantation. Trump can realize Lincoln's goal of a country that lifts "artificial weights from all shoulders" and affords its citizens "an unfettered start" in the race of life.[12] To do this he must re-Lincolnize the GOP.

First, this means going further than opposing racial preferences and affirmative action. He must eliminate racial categories from the census and promote a new civil rights act that outlaws using those categories to discriminate against any ethnic group, black, white, brown or yellow. Republicans have been talking color-blindness for a long time; it's time to implement it.

Second, Trump must invade the Democratic plantation with creative policies that restore entrepreneurship, jobs and opportunity to America's barrios, ghettos and Native American reservations. Surely there are blacks, Latinos and Native Americans in these communities who would welcome a chance to learn, to improve themselves and to prosper there. Trump and the GOP can help this process through a bold combination of tax incentives, deregulation and arm-twisting of the kind that Trump specializes in, as well as the suspension of destructive family and social policies that encourage illegitimacy, crime and civic breakdown. The GOP already has the formula; what's needed now are the spine and the nerve to put it into effect.

It won't be easy. Trump needs the Republicans behind him on this because the Democrats, who are already in a fevered mode, are going to go berserk. We are likely to see a Democratic uproar echo through the halls of Congress, reverberate through the media, cause fainting spells in Hollywood and crack the tectonic plates of the culture. Trump and the Republicans—united, calm and collected—should show the same resolve that Lincoln said, in effect, to the Democratic planters of his time: bring it on.

To be clear, the long-term goal for Trump and the GOP is not merely to improve life on the plantation. The goal, rather, is its shutdown, the panic-filled dispersion of the overseers, in short, total emancipation. Once these hellholes are permanently transformed, no longer will America be plagued by the wretched politics of white supremacy and ethnic exploitation. Whites, blacks and browns can all dream the American dream and pursue happiness, not so much as whites, blacks, Latinos or whatever, but rather as individuals, as families and as Americans.

Finally, we need the cleansing antidote of truth. Democrats today are not content with promoting lies; they are insistent that we collaborate and bow down to their lies. This is not a new demand. "The question recurs," Lincoln said of the Democrats in his Cooper Union speech in February 1860, "what will satisfy them?" And Lincoln answered, "this and only this: cease to call slavery wrong and join them in calling it right . . . Silence will not be tolerated—we must place ourselves avowedly with them."[13] The enforcement of political correctness has been a Democratic strategy from Lincoln's day to our own.

For too long conservatives and Republicans have allowed big lies to take over the culture and, in some cases, their minds. This progressive cultural hegemony has polluted our education system and our media with fake narratives and fake history. It has also created a kind of Stockholm syndrome among conservative intellectuals. "In our hearts we know we're wrong." But we're not wrong. We've been lied to. It's time for us to stop apologizing—we have nothing to apologize for—and go on the offensive. Truth is our deadliest weapon, if we will deploy it.

The defeat of the plantation would make Trump the first great president of the twenty-first century and the GOP the worthy custodian of American ideals. With our support, Trump can bring to an end the vicious train of exploitation that the Democratic Party has wrought for nearly two hundred years. What better way to rescue the principles of the founders and to vindicate the philosophical statesmanship of Lincoln than to sweep away this blight on the American experiment, this nightmarish interruption of the American dream?

"The fiery trial through which we pass," Lincoln said in his Annual Message to Congress in 1862, "will light us down, in honor or dishonor, to the latest generation." The point, he had already stated in his Peoria speech several years earlier, was not merely to save the union. Rather, "If we do this, we shall not only have saved the Union; but we shall have so saved it as to make, and to keep it, forever worthy of the saving." This America worth saving is the object of our striving; it is what Lincoln termed "the last best hope on earth."[14]

NOTES

PREFACE

1. Edmund Burke, *Reflections on the Revolution in France* (New York: Penguin, 1982), p. 172.
2. Benedict Anderson, *Imagined Communities* (London: Verso, 2016), p. 6–7, 144.
3. Abraham Lincoln, Lyceum Address, January 27, 1838, abrahamlincolnonline.org.

INTRODUCTION

1. Thomas Jefferson, *Notes on the State of Virginia* (New York: W. W. Norton, 1982), p. 165.
2. "Full Text of Donald Trump's Speech in Poland," July 6, 2017, nbcnews.com.
3. Sarah Wildman, "Trump's Speech in Poland Sounded Like an Alt-Right Manifesto," July 6, 2017, vox.com; Jake Johnson, "Disturbing Undertones Detected in Trump's Bizarre Poland Speech," July 6, 2017, commondreams.org; Peter Beinart, "The Racial and Religious Paranoia of Trump's Warsaw Speech," July 6, 2017, theatlantic.com.
4. Jack Goldsmith, "Will Donald Trump Destroy the Presidency?" October 2017, theatlantic.com; Conor Lynch, "Donald Trump Is Destroying America's Standing in the World and May End Up Destroying the World," June 8, 2017, salon.com; Edward McCarey McDonnell, "Donald Trump Is Killing American Ideals," January 31, 2017, baltimoresun.com; Yascha Mounk, "The Past Week Proves That Trump Is Destroying Our Democracy," August 1, 2017, nytimes.com; Ryu Spaeth, "Donald Trump Is Killing Us," August 14, 2017, newrepublic.com; Dana Milbank, "President Trump Is Killing Me. Really," September 15, 2017, washingtonpost.com.
5. Laurence Tribe, "Trump Must Be Impeached. Here's Why," May 13, 2017, washingtonpost.com.

6. Noah Millman, "Will Trump's Loose Lips Lead to a Military Coup?" May 16, 2017, theweek.com.

7. Kate Sheridan, "Trump Could Destroy the Entire Human Species Says Yale Psychiatrist Who Warned Congress Members," January 6, 2018, newsweek.com.

8. Jacqueline Thomsen, "Warren: Trump Is a 'Racist Bully,'" January 16, 2018, thehill .com; Tom Tillison, "Joy Reid Blows Up on MSNBC: Trump Has 'Blatantly Bigoted Views,' He's 'Unabashedly White Nationalist,'" December 23, 2017, bizpacreview.com; Jay Pearson, "Donald Trump Is a Textbook Racist," October 4, 2017, rollingstone.com; Frank Rich, "Nothing's Shocking Anymore with Trump," August 17, 2017, nymag .com; Jesse Berney, "Trump's Long History of Racism," August 15, 2017, rollingstone .com.

9. Toni Morrison, "Mourning for Whiteness," November 21, 2016, newyorker.com.

10. Cited by Timothy P. Carney, "Racial Politics: Democrats Brought the Coals, Trump Fanned the Flames," October 9, 2007, aei.org; Rich, "Nothing's Shocking Anymore with Trump"; Chauncey DeVega, "Congratulations, America—You Did It! An Actual Fascist Is Now Your Official President," January 21, 2017, salon.com; Michael Starr Hopkins, "Republicans and Their Identity Politics Are Destroying America," September 6, 2017, the hill.com.

11. "How White Supremacy Became the Alt-Right," transcript, *The Rachel Maddow Show,* September 4, 2017, msnbc.com.

12. "Hillary Clinton on Whether President Trump Is Racist," September 15, 2017, pbs.org; Berney, "Trump's Long History of Racism."

13. Paul Krugman, "Fascism, American Style," August 28, 2017, nytimes.com; Isaac Chotiner, "Too Close for Comfort," February 10, 2017, slate.com; Timothy Snyder, "Donald Trump and the New Dawn of Tyranny," March 3, 2017, time.com.

14. Charles Blow, "Trump Isn't Hitler. But the Lying . . . ," October 19, 2017, nytimes.com; Andrew O'Hehir, "Donald Trump: Not Exactly Hitler! But His 'Nazi Germany' Comments Conceal a Dark Parallel Pattern," January 14, 2017, salon.com; Larry Elliott, "Joseph Stiglitz: 'Trump Has Fascist Tendencies,'" November 16, 2017, theguardian.com; "Historian of Fascism: Why Trump Firing FBI Director Comey amid Russia Probe Is So Worrisome," May 11, 2017, democracynow.org.

15. Chris Hedges, "Trump and the Christian Fascists," July 24, 2017, commondreams.org; Matthew MacWilliams, "The One Weird Trait That Predicts Whether You're a Trump Supporter," January 17, 2016, politico.com; Charles Blow, "The Other Inconvenient Truth," August 17, 2017, nytimes.com.

16. Kirk Noden, "Why Do Working-Class People Vote Against Their Interests?" November 17, 2016, thenation.com.

17. For the subsequent account see Ta-Nehisi Coates, *Between the World and Me* (New York: Spiegel and Grau, 2015), p. 6–7, 10; Ta-Nehisi Coates, *We Were Eight Years in Power* (New York: One World, 2017), p. xvi, 164, 180, 182, 189, 211–12, 341–42, 344, 362, 346–47; Ta-Nehisi Coates, "Nathan Bedford Forrest Has Beautiful Eyes," June 17, 2009, theatlantic.com; Amy Goodman, "Full Interview: Ta-Nehisi Coates on Charlottesville, Trump, the Confederacy, Reparations & More," August 15, 2017, democracynow .org.

18. Michael Omni and Howard Winant, *Racial Formation in the United States* (New York: Routledge & Kegan Paul, 1986), p. 72.

19. David Brion Davis, *Inhuman Bondage* (New York: Oxford University Press, 1986), p. 197; Harry V. Jaffa, *A New Birth of Freedom* (New York: Rowman & Littlefield, 2004), p. 177.

20. House Divided speech, June 16, 1858, in Abraham Lincoln, *Selected Speeches and Writings* (New York: Vintage, 1992), p. 131.

21. George Fitzhugh, *Sociology for the South* (Richmond: A. Morris, 1854), p. 94.

22. Cited by Eugene Genovese, *Roll, Jordan, Roll* (New York: Vintage, 1974), p. 81.

23. Mary Boykin Chesnut, *Mary Chesnut's Diary* (New York: Penguin, 2011), p. 81–82.

24. Jefferson, *Notes on the State of Virginia*, p. 163.
25. Cited by Daniel Walker Howe, *What Hath God Wrought* (New York: Oxford University Press, 2009), p. 524.
26. Cited by Lewis Lehrman, *Lincoln at Peoria: The Turning Point* (New York: Stackpole Books, 2008), p. 155.
27. Burton W. Folsom, *New Deal or Raw Deal?* (New York: Threshold Editions, 2008), p. 145, 269; see also Mark Leff, *The Limits of Symbolic Reform: The New Deal and Taxation* (New York: Cambridge University Press, 1984), p. vi.
28. Jim Hoft, "JFK Files: Documents Show Democrat President Lyndon Johnson Was KKK Member," October 29, 2017, thegatewaypundit.com; Michael Miller, "Strippers, Surveillance and Assassination Plots: The Wildest JFK Files," October 27, 2017, washington post.com.
29. Cited by Mario Cuomo and Harold Holzer, *Lincoln on Democracy* (New York: Harper-Collins, 1990), p. 3.
30. Kenneth Stampp, *The Peculiar Institution* (New York: Vintage, 1984).
31. Dave Weigel, "Racialists Are Cheered by Trump's Latest Strategy," August 20, 2016, washingtonpost.com.
32. Cited by Arlie Russell Hochschild, *Strangers in Their Own Land* (New York: The New Press, 2016), p. 224.

2. DILEMMA OF THE PLANTATION

1. Thomas Jefferson, letter to John Holmes, April 22, 1820, in Merrill D. Peterson, ed., *The Portable Thomas Jefferson* (New York: Penguin, 1985), p. 568.
2. Steve Wyche, "Colin Kaepernick Explains Why He Sat during National Anthem," August 27, 2016, nfl.com.
3. Eric Reid, "Why Colin Kaepernick and I Decided to Take a Knee," September 25, 2017, nytimes.com.
4. Noel Ransome, "Colin Kaepernick Took a Knee for All of Us," October 2, 2017, vice .com.
5. Dennis Farney, "As America Triumphs, Americans Are Awash in Doubt," *Wall Street Journal,* July 27, 1992, p. A-1.
6. John Hope Franklin, "The Moral Legacy of the Founding Fathers," *University of Chicago Magazine,* Summer 1975, p. 10–13.
7. Carl Skutsch, "The History of White Supremacy in America," August 19, 2017, rolling stone.com.
8. Edmund S. Morgan, *American Slavery, American Freedom* (New York: W. W. Norton, 1975), p. 4; James Boswell, *Life of Samuel Johnson* (New York: Charles Scribner, 1945), p. 353.
9. *Dred Scott v. Sandford,* 60 U.S. 393 (1857).
10. Harry V. Jaffa, *A New Birth of Freedom* (New York: Rowman & Littlefield, 2004), p. 289.
11. Abraham Lincoln, *Selected Speeches and Writings* (New York: Vintage, 1992), p. 177, 241; Harry V. Jaffa, *Crisis of the House Divided* (Chicago: University of Chicago Press, 2009), p. 314.
12. Cited by David Herbert Donald, *Lincoln* (New York: Simon & Schuster, 1995), p. 201.
13. Garry Wills, *Lincoln at Gettysburg* (New York: Simon & Schuster, 1992), p. 38.
14. Lincoln, *Selected Speeches and Writings,* p. 99, 221, 243.
15. Harold Holzer, *Lincoln at Cooper Union* (New York: Simon & Schuster, 2005), p. 126–28.
16. Cited by Lewis Lehrman, *Lincoln at Peoria* (New York: Stackpole Books, 2008), p. 291.
17. See, e.g., Conor Cruise O'Brien, "Thomas Jefferson: Radical and Racist," October 1996, theatlantic.com.
18. George Washington, letter to Robert Morris, April 12, 1786, in W. B. Allen, ed., *George Washington: A Collection* (Indianapolis: Liberty Press, 1989), p. 319; James Madison, speech at Constitutional Convention, June 6, 1787, in Max Farrand, ed., *The Records*

of the Federal Convention of 1787 (New Haven: Yale University Press, 1937), vol. 1, p. 135; John Adams to Robert Evans, June 8, 1819, in Adrienne Koch and William Peden, *Selected Writings of John and John Quincy Adams* (New York: Knopf, 1946), p. 209; Benjamin Franklin, "An Address to the Public from the Pennsylvania Society for Promoting the Abolition of Slavery," in J. A. Leo Lemay, ed., *Writings* (New York: Library of America, 1987), p. 1154.

19. Thomas Jefferson, *Notes on the State of Virginia* (New York: W. W. Norton, 1982), p. 140, 143.
20. Thomas Jefferson, letter to Benjamin Banneker, August 30, 1791, in Peterson, *Portable Thomas Jefferson,* p. 454.
21. Jefferson, *Notes on the State of Virginia,* p. 138.
22. Winthrop Jordan, *White Over Black* (New York: W. W. Norton, 1977), p. 28–29, 32.
23. Peterson, *Portable Thomas Jefferson,* p. 517.
24. Jefferson, *Notes on the State of Virginia,* p. 163.
25. Cited by David Brion Davis, *Inhuman Bondage* (New York: Oxford University Press, 2006), p. 146.
26. Ibid., p. 125.
27. Peterson, *Portable Thomas Jefferson,* p. 14.
28. Jefferson, *Notes on the State of Virginia,* p. 138.
29. Lincoln, *Selected Speeches and Writings,* p. 95.
30. Cited by Forrest McDonald, *Novus Ordo Seclorum* (Lawrence: University Press of Kansas, 1985), p. 160.
31. Michelle Alexander, *The New Jim Crow* (New York: The New Press, 2012), p. 26.
32. Davis, *Inhuman Bondage,* p. 17.
33. Frederick Douglass, "The Constitution of the United States: Is It Proslavery or Antislavery?" (1860) in Philip S. Foner, ed., *The Life and Writings of Frederick Douglass* (New York: International Publishers, 1950), vol. 2, p. 478.
34. Cited by Donald, *Lincoln,* p. 176.
35. Cited by Jaffa, *New Birth of Freedom,* p. 77.
36. Lincoln, *Selected Speeches and Writings,* p. 120.
37. Orlando Patterson, *Slavery and Social Death* (Cambridge, MA: Harvard University Press, 1982), p. vii.
38. Davis, *Inhuman* Bondage, p. 153; Gordon Wood, *The Radicalism of the American Revolution* (New York: Vintage, 1991), p. 186–87.

3. PARTY OF ENSLAVEMENT

1. George Fitzhugh, *Sociology for the South* (Richmond: A. Morris, 1854), p. 48.
2. "Confederate Monuments Are Coming Down across the United States," August 28, 2017, nytimes.com.
3. Matt Vespa, "Progressives Gone Wild? Abraham Lincoln Statue Vandalized in Chicago," August 18, 2017, townhall.com.
4. Joshua Zeitz, "Why There Are No Nazi Statues in Germany," August 20, 2017, politico .com.
5. "Robert E. Lee's Opinion Regarding Slavery," letter dated December 27, 1856, civilwar home.com.
6. Cited by Harry V. Jaffa, *Crisis of the House Divided* (Chicago: University of Chicago Press, 2009), p. 312–13, 339; cited by David Herbert Donald, *Lincoln* (New York: Simon & Schuster, 1995), p. 210.
7. Cited by David M. Potter, *The Impending Crisis* (New York: HarperPerennial, 1976), p. 347.
8. Elizabeth Fox-Genovese and Eugene Genovese, *The Mind of the Master Class* (New York: Cambridge University Press, 2005), p. 73; Winthrop Jordan, *White Over Black* (New York: W. W. Norton, 1977), p. 346.

9. Cited by Douglas Blackmon, *Slavery by Another Name* (New York: Anchor Books, 2008), p. vii; cited by Bernard Bailyn, *The Ideological Origins of the American Revolution* (Cambridge, MA: Harvard University Press, 1992), p. 236.

10. John Blassingame, *The Slave Community* (New York: Oxford University Press, 1979), p. 77; Fox-Genovese and Genovese, *Mind of the Master Class*, p. 231; Stanley Elkins, *Slavery* (Chicago: University of Chicago Press, 1976), p. 209.

11. Blassingame, *Slave Community*, p. 80–81.

12. Drew Gilpin Faust, *The Ideology of Slavery* (Baton Rouge: Louisiana State University Press, 1981), p. 4–5; Eugene D. Genovese, *The World the Slaveholders Made* (Middletown: Wesleyan University Press, 1988), p. 131.

13. James Henry Hammond, "Speech on Receiving Petitions for the Abolition of Slavery in the District of Columbia," cited by Fox-Genovese and Genovese, *Mind of the Master Class*, p. 11.

14. John C. Calhoun, speech on the Oregon Bill, 1848, cited in Harry V. Jaffa, *A New Birth of Freedom* (New York: Rowman & Littlefield, 2004), p. 212; John C. Calhoun, Senate speech of January 10, 1838, in Eric McKitrick, ed., *Slavery Defended* (Englewood Cliffs: Prentice-Hall, 1963), p. 18.

15. Potter, *Impending Crisis*, p. 27, 29.

16. Frederick Law Olmsted, *The Cotton Kingdom* (Bedford: Applewood Books, 1861), p. 16; Kenneth Stampp, *The Peculiar Institution* (New York: Vintage, 1984), p. 146.

17. Booker T. Washington, *Up from Slavery* (New York: Barnes & Noble, 2003), p. 10.

18. Cited by Bruce Levine, *Half Slave and Half Free* (New York: Hill and Wang, 2005), p. 17–18.

19. Gordon Wood, *The Radicalism of the American Revolution* (New York: Vintage Books, 1991), p. 115–16.

20. Kenneth S. Greenberg, *Honor and Slavery* (Princeton: Princeton University Press, 1997), p. 7–9, 11–14, 74, 137.

21. Mary Boykin Chesnut, *Mary Chesnut's Diary* (New York: Penguin, 2011), p. 99; Eugene Genovese, *Roll, Jordan, Roll* (New York: Vintage, 1974), p. 426.

22. Drew Gilpin Faust, *James Henry Hammond and the Old South* (Baton Rouge: Louisiana State University Press, 1982), p. 87.

23. Chesnut, *Mary Chesnut's Diary*, p. 338.

24. Samuel Cartwright, *De Bow's Review*, XI (1851), p. 331–34.

25. Frederick Douglass, *Narrative of the Life of Frederick Douglass, an American Slave* (New York: Penguin, 2014), p. 67.

26. Ad placed by Andrew Jackson in the Nashville *Tennessee Gazette*, September 26, 1804, cited in Daniel Walker Howe, *What God Hath Wrought* (New York: Oxford University Press, 2009), p. 329.

27. W. E. B. Du Bois, *Black Reconstruction* (New York: S. A. Russell, 1935), p. 9.

28. Genovese, *World the Slaveholders Made*, p. 129.

29. Junius Rodriguez, *Slavery in the United States* (New York: ABC-CLIO, 2007), vol. 1, p. 286.

30. The subsequent account draws mainly from Fitzhugh's two best-known books, *Sociology for the South* and *Cannibals All!*, as well as the Fitzhugh writings excerpted in Drew Gilpin Faust's collection *The Ideology of Slavery*. See esp. Fitzhugh, *Sociology for the South*, p. 22–28, 45, 48, 83, 93, 179, 201, 291, 294, 302; George Fitzhugh, *Cannibals All!* (Cambridge, MA: Harvard University Press, 1988), p. 15–18, 30, 32, 52, 69, 94 199, 212, 247, 249; Faust, *Ideology of Slavery*, p. 274, 277, 283, 289, 295.

31. C. Vann Woodward, "Introduction," in Fitzhugh, *Cannibals All!*, p. xxxviii.

32. Abraham Lincoln, First Debate with Stephen Douglas at Ottawa, August 21, 1858, mason.gmu.edu.

33. Abraham Lincoln, "Speech to One Hundred Fortieth Indiana Regiment," March 17, 1865, quod.lib.umich.edu; Abraham Lincoln, fragment on slavery, undated, in Abraham Lincoln, *Selected Speeches and Writings* (New York: Vintage, 1992), p. 175–76.

34. Cited by Jaffa, *Crisis of the House Divided,* p. 35; Potter, *Impending Crisis,* p. 341.
35. Stephen Douglas, "Popular Sovereignty in the Territories," September 1859, harpers
    .org; Kenneth Stampp, ed., *The Causes of the Civil War* (New York: Touchstone, 1991),
    p. 108.
36. Cited by Jaffa, *Crisis of the House Divided,* p. 311.
37. Ibid., p. 48.
38. Lincoln, *Selected Speeches and Writings,* p. 194.
39. Cited by Potter, *Impending Crisis,* p. 342; cited by Jaffa, *New Birth of Freedom,* p. 326;
    cited by Lord Charnwood, *Abraham Lincoln* (Mineola: Dover Publications, 1997), p.
    131.
40. Cited by Potter, *Impending Crisis,* p. 349; cited by John Channing Briggs, *Lincoln's
    Speeches Reconsidered* (Baltimore: Johns Hopkins University Press, 2005), p. 147; Ma-
    rio Cuomo and Harold Holzer, eds., *Lincoln on Democracy* (New York: HarperCollins,
    1990), p. 158.

4. URBAN PLANTATION

1. George Washington Plunkitt, *Plunkitt of Tammany Hall* (New York: Timeless Classic
   Books, 2010), p. 1.
2. Peter Beinart, "How the Democrats Lost Their Way on Immigration," July–August
   2017, theatlantic.com.
3. Jared Sichel, "Six Insane California Laws That Go Into Effect Monday," December 29,
   2017, dailywire.com; Adam Shaw, "Oakland Mayor Consulted with Illegal-Immigration
   Activists Before Tipping Off ICE Raid," March 16, 2018, foxnews.com.
4. Vivian Wang, "In Rebuke to Trump, Cuomo Pardons 18 Immigrants," December 27,
   2017, mobile.nytimes.com.
5. John McCormack, "Obama to Latinos: 'Punish' Your 'Enemies' in the Voting Booth,"
   October 25, 2010, weeklystandard.com.
6. Thomas B. Edsall, "The Democrats' Immigration Problem," February 6, 2017, nytimes
   .com.
7. Terry Golway, "The Forgotten Virtues of Tammany Hall," *New York Times,* January 17,
   2014, nytimes.com; "The Case for Tammany Hall Being on the Right Side of History,"
   March 5, 2014, npr.org.
8. Ted Widmer, *Martin Van Buren* (New York: Times Books, 2005), p. 6–8.
9. Kevin Baker, "The Soul of a New Machine," August 17, 2016, newrepublic.com.
10. Chester Collins Maxey, "A Little History of Pork," *National Municipal Review* (1919), p.
    693.
11. Widmer, *Martin Van Buren,* p. xvii, 58, 68; Robert Remini, *Martin Van Buren and the
    Making of the Democratic Party* (New York: W. W. Norton, 1970), p. 1.
12. Widmer, *Martin Van Buren,* p. 4, 57; Daniel Walker Howe, *What Hath God Wrought*
    (New York: Oxford University Press, 2009), p. 483.
13. Remini, *Martin Van Buren and the Making of the Democratic Party,* p. 38.
14. Ibid., p. 129–30.
15. Martin Van Buren, Letter to Thomas Ritchie, 1827, Oxford University Press, global
    .oup.com.
16. Remini, *Martin Van Buren and the Making of the Democratic Party,* p. 132.
17. Ibid., p. 196.
18. Oscar Handlin, *The Uprooted* (New York: Little, Brown and Company, 1979), p. 31–33.
19. Ibid., p. 56–57.
20. Widmer, *Martin Van Buren,* p. 65.
21. Cited by Remini, *Martin Van Buren and the Making of the Democratic Party,* p. 11.
22. Cited by Richard Hofstadter, *The Idea of a Party System* (Berkeley: University of Cali-
    fornia Press, 1970), p. 250.
23. Cited by Terry Golway, *Machine Made: Tammany Hall and the Creation of Modern
    American Politics* (New York: Liveright Publishing, 2014), p. 84, 92, 100.
24. Ibid., p. 156.

25. Ibid., p. 176.
26. Alexander Hamilton, James Madison and John Jay, *The Federalist* (New York: Barnes & Noble, 2006), p. 14.
27. Abraham Lincoln, speech at Chicago, July 10, 1858, in Abraham Lincoln, *Selected Speeches and Writings* (New York: Vintage, 1992), p. 145.
28. James Madison, Book 10, in Hamilton, Madison and Jay, *Federalist*, p. 51–59.
29. Jay Cost, *A Republic No More* (New York: Encounter Books, 2015), p. xiii.
30. Plunkitt, *Plunkitt of Tammany Hall*, p. 67.

5. THE PLANTATION IN CRISIS

1. Cited by A. J. Langguth, *After Lincoln* (New York: Simon & Schuster, 2014), p. 61.
2. George Fredrickson, *Big Enough to Be Inconsistent* (Cambridge, MA: Harvard University Press, 2008); Fred Kaplan, *Lincoln and the Abolitionists* (New York: Harper, 2017); Tanya D. Marsh, "Abraham Lincoln Was a Racist and Other Hard Truths from Our Messy Past," August 16, 2017, huffingtonpost.com.
3. Lerone Bennett, *Forced Into Glory* (New York: Johnson Publishing, 2000).
4. "Civil War Historian Eric Foner on the Radical Possibilities of Reconstruction," March 11, 2015, democracynow.org.
5. Eric Foner, *Reconstruction* (New York: HarperPerennial, 2014), p. 228, 321, 604.
6. Cited by Bruce Levine, *Half Slave and Half Free* (New York: Hill and Wang, 2005), p. 227.
7. Cited by Foner, *Reconstruction*, p. xxi–xxii.
8. Cited by David Potter, *The Impending Crisis* (New York: HarperPerennial, 1976), p. 475.
9. Abraham Lincoln to Alexander H. Stephens, December 22, 1860, in Abraham Lincoln, *Selected Speeches and Writings* (New York: Vintage, 1992), p. 275–76.
10. Ibid., p. 159–60, 184–86, 190–91.
11. Kenneth Stampp, *And the War Came* (Baton Rouge: Louisiana State University Press, 1970), p. xi; Kenneth Stampp, *The Imperiled Union* (New York: Oxford University Press, 1981), p. 117.
12. Cited by Eric Foner, *Free Soil, Free Labor, Free Men* (New York: Oxford University Press, 1995), p. 264; James McPherson, *Battle Cry of Freedom* (New York: Oxford University Press, 2013), p. 224.
13. Abraham Lincoln, speech on the *Dred Scott* decision, June 20, 1857, in Lincoln, *Selected Speeches and Writings*, p. 120.
14. Mario Cuomo and Harold Holzer, eds., *Lincoln on Democracy* (New York: HarperCollins, 1990), p. 126.
15. Cited by Jennifer Weber, *Copperheads* (New York: Oxford University Press, 2006), p. 106; "Robert E. Lee's Decision to Invade the North in September 1862," civilwar.org.
16. Cited by McPherson, *Battle Cry of Freedom*, p. 591.
17. Ibid., p. 592.
18. David Herbert Donald, *Lincoln* (New York: Simon & Schuster, 1995), p. 313.
19. Ibid., p. 368.
20. Ibid., p. 415, 459; David Brion Davis, *Inhuman Bondage* (New York: Oxford University Press, 2006), p. 305.
21. Jefferson Davis, Message to the Confederate Congress, April 29, 1861, cited by Kenneth M. Stampp, ed., *The Causes of the Civil War* (New York: Touchstone, 1991), p. 153–54.
22. Cited by Harry V. Jaffa, *A New Birth of Freedom* (Lanham: Rowman & Littlefield, 2004), p. 216–17, 222.
23. Weber, *Copperheads*, p. 8.
24. McPherson, *Battle Cry of Freedom*, p. 595; Julia Golia, "The Emancipation Proclamation: Copperheads Respond," Brooklyn Historical Society, February 25, 2014, brooklyn history.org.
25. Cited by Donald, *Lincoln*, p. 513, 537.

26. Cited by Lord Charnwood, *Abraham Lincoln* (Mineola: Dover Publications, 1997), p. 416; cited by Donald, *Lincoln*, p. 527.
27. Cited by Donald, *Lincoln*, p. 596.
28. Ibid., p. 549.
29. McPherson, *Battle Cry of Freedom*, p. 852.
30. Cited by Donald, *Lincoln*, p. 470.
31. Foner, *Reconstruction*, p. 180.
32. Ibid., p. 425; David Chalmers, *Hooded Americanism* (Durham: Duke University Press, 1987), p. 10.
33. Joel Williamson, *The Crucible of Race* (New York: Oxford University Press, 1984), p. 339.

6. PROGRESSIVE PLANTATION

1. Woodrow Wilson, *History of the American People,* cited by Nathaniel Weyl and William Marina, *American Statesmen on Slavery and the Negro* (New Rochelle: Arlington House, 1971), p. 325–26.
2. Woodrow Wilson, *The State* (Boston: D.C. Heath & Co., 1889), see esp. p. 526–27.
3. Woodrow Wilson, "The Reconstruction of the Southern States," *Atlantic Monthly,* January 1901, p. 1–15.
4. Cited by Weyl and Marina, *American Statesmen on Slavery and the Negro,* p. 325–26.
5. Cited by Robert Norrell, *Up from History* (Cambridge: Harvard University Press, 2009), p. 243.
6. Dewey W. Grantham, "Dinner at the White House: Theodore Roosevelt, Booker T. Washington and the South," *Tennessee Historical Quarterly* 18 (June 1958), p. 112–30.
7. Jonah Goldberg, "Woodrow Wilson's Progressive Racism," November 21, 2015, national review.com.
8. Norrell, *Up from History,* p. 83, 392, 406.
9. W. E. B. Du Bois, *Crisis,* August 1912, p. 181.
10. Raymond Wolters, *Du Bois and His Rivals* (Columbia: University of Missouri Press, 2002), p. 245–46; W. E. B. Du Bois, "On Stalin," *National Guardian,* March 16, 1953, marxlsts.org; Werner Sollors, "W.E.B. Du Bois in Nazi Germany," *Chronicle of Higher Education,* November 12, 1999, p. B-4, 5.
11. Stanley Payne, *A History of Fascism* (Madison: University of Wisconsin Press, 1995), p. 127; A. James Gregor, *The Ideology of Fascism* (New York: Free Press, 1969), p. 355.
12. David Greenberg, "The Do-Gooder," July 26, 2010, newrepublic.com.
13. Abraham Lincoln, *Selected Speeches and Writings* (New York: Vintage, 1992), p. 379.
14. Edward Alsworth Ross, *Social Control* (New York: Macmillan, 1918), p. 74, 82.
15. David Brion Davis, *Inhuman Bondage* (New York: Oxford University Press, 2006), p. 298.
16. Eric Foner, *Reconstruction* (New York: HarperPerennial, 2014), p. 129.
17. Ibid., p. 131.
18. Ibid., p. 173.
19. C. R. Boxer, *Race Relations in the Colonial Portuguese Empire* (New York: Oxford University Press, 1963), p. 56.
20. George Fredrickson, *Racism: A Short History* (Princeton: Princeton University Press, 2002), p. 81.
21. Cited in Drew Gilpin Faust, ed., *The Ideology of Slavery* (Baton Rouge: Louisiana State University Press, 1981), p. 58.
22. Anthony Slide, *American Racist: The Life and Films of Thomas Dixon* (Lexington: University Press of Kentucky, 2004), p. 14, 130; see also David Stricklin, "Ours Is a Century of Light: Dixon's Strange Consistency," in Michele K. Gillespie and Randal L. Hall, *Thomas Dixon Jr. and the Birth of Modern America* (Baton Rouge: Louisiana State University Press, 2006), p. 81, 83.
23. Thomas Dixon Jr., *The Clansman* (Lexington: University Press of Kentucky, 1970), p. xi, 351–52.

24. Thomas Cripps, *Slow Fade to Black: The Negro in American Film, 1900–1942* (New York: Oxford University Press, 1977), p. 41–69; Donald Bogle, *Toms, Coons, Mulattoes, Mammies, and Bucks: An Interpretive History of Blacks in American Films* (New York: Bloomsbury, 2001), p. 3–10.

25. Letter from Thomas Dixon to Joseph Tumulty, secretary to the president, May 1, 1915, cited by Weyl and Marina, *American Statesmen on Slavery and the Negro*, p. 336–37; also cited by Norrell, *Up from History*, p. 413.

26. See, e.g., David M. Chalmers, *Hooded Americanism: The History of the Ku Klux Klan* (Durham: Duke University Press, 1987), p. 3.

27. Carol Anderson, *White Rage* (New York: Bloomsbury, 2016), p. 43.

28. Thomas D. Clark, "Introduction," in Dixon, *The Clansman*, p. xvii–xviii.

29. W. E. B. Du Bois, "Another Open Letter to Woodrow Wilson," *The Crisis*, September 1913, teachingamericanhistory.org.

30. Edwin Black, *The War Against the Weak* (Washington, DC: Dialog Press, 2013), p. 133; Thomas Leonard, *Illiberal Reformers* (Princeton: Princeton University Press, 2016), p. 116.

31. Black, *The War Against the Weak*, p. 192.

32. Leonard, *Illiberal Reformers*, p. 137.

33. Woodrow Wilson, *History of the American People* (New York: Harper and Bros., 1903), vol. 5, p. 212–13.

34. Adolf Hitler, *Mein Kampf* (Boston: Houghton Mifflin, 1999), p. 286, 439–40.

35. James Whitman, *Hitler's American Model* (Princeton: Princeton University Press, 2017), p. 1.

36. Ibid., p. 145; James Whitman, "When the Nazis Wrote the Nuremberg Laws, They Looked to Racist American Statutes," February 22, 2017, latimes.com.

37. Stefan Kuhl, *The Nazi Connection* (New York: Oxford University Press, 1994), p. 27, 36.

7. THE STATE AS BIG HOUSE

1. Mike Wallace, interview with Ronald Reagan, *60 Minutes*, CBS, December 14, 1975.

2. Ira Katznelson, *Fear Itself* (New York: Liveright Publishing, 2013), p. 282.

3. Timothy Snyder, *Bloodlands* (New York: Basic Books, 2010), p. 382; Alexander Von Plato, Almut Leh and Christoph Thonfeld, eds., *Hitler's Slaves* (New York: Berghahn Books, 2010); Marc Buggeln, *Slave Labor in Nazi Concentration Camps* (New York: Oxford University Press, 2014).

4. Wolfgang Sofsky, *The Order of Terror: The Concentration Camp* (Princeton: Princeton University Press, 1993), p. 76, 118, 171–72.

5. Stanley Elkins, *Slavery: A Problem in American Institutional and Intellectual Life* (Chicago: University of Chicago Press, 1976), p. 122–23.

6. Cited by James Whitman, *Hitler's American Model* (Princeton: Princeton University Press, 2017), p. 9–10.

7. Snyder, *Bloodlands*, p. 160.

8. Cited by Andrew Nagorski, *Hitlerland* (New York: Simon & Schuster, 2012), p. 41.

9. AP, "Truman's Racist Talk Cited by Historian," *Seattle Times*, November 3, 1991; William Lee Miller, *Two Americans: Truman, Eisenhower and a Dangerous World* (New York: Vintage, 2012), p. 353.

10. Katznelson, *Fear Itself*, p. 84–88.

11. Cited by C. Dwight McDorough, *Mr. Sam* (New York: Random House, 1962), p. 191.

12. David M. Chalmers, *Hooded Americanism* (Durham: Duke University Press, 1987), p. 80; Roger Newman, *Hugo Black* (New York: Pantheon, 1994), p. 98.

13. Eric Zimmerman, "Clinton says Byrd Joined KKK to Help Him Get Elected," July 2, 2010, thehill.com.

14. Robert Dallek, *Franklin D. Roosevelt* (New York: Viking, 2017), p. 278.

15. Howard Ball, *Hugo L. Black* (New York: Oxford University Press, 1996), p. 98–99.

16. Arthur Schlesinger Jr., *The Politics of Hope* (Boston: Houghton Mifflin, 1962), p. 124–25.

17. Cited by Wolfgang Schivelbusch, *Three New Deals* (New York: Picador, 2006), p. 27.
18. A. James Gregor, *Young Mussolini and the Intellectual Origins of Fascism* (Berkeley: University of California Press, 1979), p. 98, 125.
19. Stanley G. Payne, *A History of Fascism, 1914–1945* (Madison: University of Wisconsin Press, 1995), p. 230.
20. John P. Diggins, *Mussolini and Fascism* (Princeton: Princeton University Press, 1972), p. 165; Schivelbusch, *Three New Deals* (New York: Picador, 2006), p. 23.
21. Cited by Schivelbusch, *Three New Deals*, p. 18–19.
22. Franklin D. Roosevelt, "Message to Congress on the Concentration of Economic Power," April 29, 1938, publicpolicy.pepperdine.edu.
23. Henry Scott Wallace, "American Fascism in 1944 and Today," May 12, 2017, nytimes.com.
24. A. James Gregor, *Giovanni Gentile: Philosopher of Fascism* (New Brunswick: Transaction, 2008), p. 63; Giovanni Gentile, *Origins and Doctrine of Fascism* (New Brunswick: Transaction, 2009), p. 31.
25. Cited by A. James Gregor, *The Ideology of Fascism* (New York: Free Press, 1969), p. 185.
26. Roger Griffin, *Fascism* (New York: Oxford University Press, 1995), p. 4; Roger Griffin, *The Nature of Fascism* (New York: Routledge, 1993), p. 47.
27. Zeev Sternhell, *The Birth of Fascist Ideology* (Princeton: Princeton University Press, 1994), p. 201, 204.
28. Gentile, *Origins and Doctrine of Fascism*, p. 25.
29. Gotz Aly, *Hitler's Beneficiaries* (New York: Metropolitan Books, 2006), p. 8, 21–23, 30, 314.
30. Cited by Diggins, *Mussolini and Fascism*, p. 279.
31. Ibid., p. 226–28, 287.
32. Cited by Schivelbusch, *Three New Deals*, p. 32.
33. Katznelson, *Fear Itself*, p. 235.
34. Diggins, *Mussolini and Fascism*, p. 280; Jonah Goldberg, *Liberal Fascism* (New York: Doubleday, 2007), p. 156.
35. Katznelson, *Fear Itself*, p. 22.
36. Ira Katznelson, *When Affirmative Action Was White* (New York: W. W. Norton, 2005), p. 22.
37. Ibid., p. 82.
38. Cited by Earl Black and Merle Black, *The Rise of Southern Republicans* (Cambridge: Harvard University Press, 2002), p. 52.
39. Katznelson, *Fear Itself*, p. 168.
40. Ibid., p. 9, 486.
41. Franklin D. Roosevelt, Inaugural Address, March 4, 1933, presidency.ucsb.edu; Franklin D. Roosevelt, Address at Madison Square Garden, October 31, 1936, presidency.ucsb.edu.
42. Cited by Kevin Phillips, *The Emerging Republican Majority* (Princeton: Princeton University Press, 2015), p. 51.
43. Terry Golway, *Machine Made: Tammany Hall and the Creation of Modern American Politics* (New York: Liveright Publishing, 2014), p. 294; Jay Cost, *A Republic No More* (New York: Encounter Books, 2015), p. 52–54.
44. Burton W. Folsom, *New Deal or Raw Deal?* (New York: Threshold Editions, 2008), p. 120–21.
45. Cost, *Republic No More*, p. 175–76.

8. CIVIL RIGHTS AND WRONGS

1. Lyndon Johnson, statement to Missouri Democratic senator John Stennis during debate on the Civil Rights Act of 1957, cited by Robert Caro, *The Years of Lyndon Johnson: Master of the Senate* (New York: Vintage, 2003), p. 954.

2. James W. Muller, "A Kind of Dignity and Even Nobility: Winston Churchill's *Thoughts and Adventures*," August 10, 2013, theimaginativeconservative.org.

3. Cited by Robert P. Jones, "How Trump Remixed the Republican Southern Strategy," August 14, 2016, theatlantic.com.

4. Jeet Heer, "How the Southern Strategy Made Donald Trump Possible," February 18, 2016, newrepublic.com.

5. Ben Fountain, "Reagan, Trump and the Devil Down South," March 5, 2016, theguardian.com.

6. Jones, "How Trump Remixed the Republican Southern Strategy."

7. Daniel Denvir, "Why Republicans Blaming Democrats for the KKK Are Profoundly Wrong," March 4, 2016, salon.com.

8. Earl Black and Merle Black, *The Rise of Southern Republicans* (Cambridge: Harvard University Press, 2002); Dan T. Carter, *From George Wallace to Newt Gingrich: Race in the Conservative Counterrevolution* (Baton Rouge: Louisiana State University Press, 1999); Kevin M. Kruse, *White Flight: Atlanta and the Making of Modern Conservatism* (Princeton: Princeton University Press, 2007).

9. Robert Dallek, *Flawed Giant* (New York: Oxford University Press, 1999); Marshall Frady, "The Big Guy" November 7, 2002, nybooks.com.

10. Michael Oreskes, "Civil Rights Act Leaves Deep Mark on the American Political Landscape," July 2, 1989, nytimes.com.

11. Robert Caro, *Lyndon Johnson: The Path to Power* (New York: Vintage, 1990), p. xix; Doris Kearns Goodwin, *Lyndon Johnson and the American Dream* (New York: New American Library, 1977), p. 14.

12. MacAoidh, "From the JFK Assassination Files: Was Lyndon Johnson a Klansman?" October 27, 2017, thehayride.com.

13. Lyndon Johnson, Howard University Address, June 4, 1965, reprinted in Lee Rainwater and William L. Yancey, *The Moynihan Report and the Politics of Controversy* (Cambridge: MIT Press, 1967), p. 126.

14. Dallek, *Flawed Giant*, p. 222.

15. Ira Katznelson, *When Affirmative Action Was White* (New York: W. W. Norton, 2005), p. 18–19.

16. Michael Shelden, "A Lewd, Crude Master," August 10, 2002, telegraph.co.uk; Jan Jarboe Russell, "Alone Together," August 1999, texasmonthly.com.

17. Shelden, "Lewd, Crude Master."

18. Cited by Dallek, *Flawed Giant*, p. 441.

19. Ibid.

20. Ibid., p. 223.

21. Caro, *Years of Lyndon Johnson*, p. 717.

22. Cited by Goodwin, *Lyndon Johnson and the American Dream*, p. 155.

23. Cited by Ronald Kessler, *Inside the White House* (New York: Simon & Schuster, 1996), p. 33.

24. Snopes, "Civil Wrongs," July 2016, snopes.com.

25. Howard Schuman, Charlotte Steeh, Lawrence Bobo and Maria Krysan, *Racial Attitudes in America* (Cambridge, MA: Harvard University Press, 1998); Maria Krysan, "Trends in Racial Attitudes," University of Illinois Institute of Government and Public Affairs, 2016, igpa.uillinois.edu.

26. George Fredrickson, *Racism: A Short History* (Princeton: Princeton University Press, 2002), p. 5.

27. Isabel Wilkerson, *The Warmth of Other Suns* (New York: Vintage, 2010), p. 9, 27, 536.

28. Cited by Eugene Genovese, *Roll, Jordan, Roll* (New York: Vintage, 1974), p. 126, 142–143.

29. Dallek, *Flawed Giant*, p. 75.

30. Shelby Steele, *A Dream Deferred* (New York: HarperCollins, 1998), p. 65.

31. Wilkerson, *Warmth of Other Suns*, p. 304.

32. Frederick Douglass, "The Nation's Problem," in Howard Brotz, ed., *Negro Social and Political Thought, 1850–1920* (New York: Basic Books, 1966), p. 316–17; Frederick Douglass, "The Destiny of Colored Americans," *The North Star*, November 16, 1849.

33. Mona Charen, "Whitewashing the Democratic Party's History," June 25, 2015, ricochet .com; Tal Kopan, "Hayes: Sorry for Wallace Party Label," June 12, 2013, prospect.org.

34. Harry Enten, "Were the Republicans Really the Party of Civil Rights in the 1960s?" August 28, 2013, theguardian.com.

35. Abraham Lincoln, *Selected Speeches and Writings* (New York: Vintage, 1992), p. 111–12, 146, 193, 235; see also Eric Foner, *Free Soil, Free Labor, Free Men* (New York: Oxford University Press, 1995), p. 20; David Herbert Donald, *Lincoln* (New York: Simon & Schuster, 1995), p. 110; Allen Guelzo, *Abraham Lincoln: Redeemer President* (Grand Rapids: William B. Eerdmans, 1999), p. 188; James McPherson, *Battle Cry of Freedom* (New York: Oxford University Press, 2003), p. 28; Harry V. Jaffa, *A New Birth of Freedom* (Lanham: Rowman & Littlefield, 2004), p. 300.

36. Abraham Lincoln, letter to his stepbrother, December 24, 1848, in Mario Cuomo and Harold Holzer, eds., *Lincoln on Democracy* (New York: HarperCollins, 1990), p. 41–42.

37. Matthew Rees, *From the Deck to the Sea: Blacks and the Republican Party* (Wakefield, NH: Longwood Academic, 1991), p. 1.

38. Jamelle Bouie, "Rand Paul at Howard," April 11, 2013, thedailybeast.com.

39. Katznelson, *When Affirmative Action Was White*, p. 32–36; Ira Katznelson, *Fear Itself* (New York: Liveright Publishing, 2013), p. 176.

40. Rob Stein, "New Nixon Tapes Reveal Anti-Semitic, Racist Remarks," December 12, 2010, washingtonpost.com.

41. Kruse, *White Flight*, p. 251.

42. Cited by George Packer, "Hillary Clinton and the Populist Revolt," October 24, 2016, newyorker.com.

43. Cited by George P. Shultz, "How a Republican Desegregated the South's Schools," January 8, 2003, nytimes.com.

44. Neal Devins, "Philadelphia Plan," Faculty Publications Paper 1637, William and Mary Law School, 1994, scholarship.law.wm.edu.

45. See, e.g., Howard Gillette, "Philadelphia Plan," 2013, philadelphiaencyclopedia.org.

46. Kevin Phillips, *The Emerging Republican Majority* (Princeton: Princeton University Press, 2015); Steven Conn, "A Quick Political History of White Supremacy," August 8, 2007, huffingtonpost.com; Carter, *From George Wallace to Newt Gingrich*, p. 42.

47. Phillips, *Emerging Republican Majority*, p. xix.

48. Ibid., p. 272.

49. The subsequent account is summarized from Byron Shafer and Richard Johnston, *The End of Southern Exceptionalism* (Cambridge, MA: Harvard University Press, 2006).

50. Kruse, *White Flight*, p. 261.

9. MULTICULTURAL PLANTATIONS

1. Shelby Steele, *A Dream Deferred: The Second Betrayal of Black Freedom in America* (New York: HarperCollins, 1998), p. 125–26.

2. Dinesh D'Souza, *The End of Racism* (New York: Free Press, 1995).

3. Ta-Nehisi Coates, *Between the World and Me* (New York: Spiegel & Grau, 2015), p. 14–17, 20, 23–24.

4. Ta-Nehisi Coates, *We Were Eight Years in Power* (New York: One World, 2017), p. 86.

5. Elijah Anderson, *Code of the Street* (New York: W. W. Norton, 1999), p. 33, 75, 92, 97, 140–41, 150–51, 156; Elijah Anderson, *Streetwise* (Chicago: University of Chicago Press, 1990), p. 92–93, 103, 112–14, 124, 126.

6. Eugene Rivers, "On the Responsibility of Intellectuals in the Age of Crack," September–October 1992, bostonreview.net.

7. Michelle Alexander, *The New Jim Crow* (New York: The New Press, 2012), p. 9.

8. E. Franklin Frazier, *The Negro Family in the United States* (Chicago: University of Chicago Press, 1966); Daniel P. Moynihan, "The Negro Family: The Case for National

Action," in Lee Rainwater and William Yancey, eds., *The Moynihan Report and the Politics of Controversy* (Cambridge, MA: MIT Press, 1967).

9. W. E. B. Du Bois, *The Negro American Family* (Cambridge, MA: MIT Press, 1970); Herbert Gutman, *The Black Family in Slavery and Freedom* (New York: Pantheon, 1976); Malinowski cited by Charles Murray, *Coming Apart* (New York: Crown Forum, 2013), p. 164.

10. See, e.g., Margaret Mead, *Male and Female* (New York: HarperPerennial, 2001).

11. Jeanette L. Nolan, "Learned Helplessness," britannica.com; Kendra Cherry, "What Is Learned Helplessness and Why Does It Happen?" June 24, 2017, verywell.com; Maria Konnikova, "Trying to Cure Depression, but Inspiring Torture Instead," January 14 2015, newyorker.com.

12. Paul Kane and Ben Pershing, "Democrat Rangel Charged with 13 Ethics Violations," July 30, 2010, washingtonpost.com; Josh Bresnahan, "Rangel Guilty on 11 Ethics Charges," November 16, 2010, politico.com.

13. Jaweed Kaleem, Cindy Chang and Jenny Jarvie, "At Two of the Nation's Most Historic Black Churches, Sermons Reflect on Martin Luther King and Take Sharp Aim at Trump," January 14, 2018, latimes.com.

14. Chris Fuchs, "Asian-American Advocates Blast Trump Decision to End DACA Program," September 5, 2017, nbcnews.com.

15. David Treuer, *Rez Life* (New York: Grove Press, 2012), p. 5, 27–29, 55, 187.

16. Sarah Hines, "The Bracero Program: 1942–1964," April 21, 2006, counterpunch.org.

17. Renato Rosaldo, *Culture and Truth: The Remaking of Social Analysis* (Boston: Beacon Press, 1993), p. 196.

18. Jens Manuel Krogstad and Mark Hugo Lopez, "Hillary Clinton Won Latino Vote but Fell Below 2012 Support for Obama," November 29, 2016, Pew Research Center, pewresearch.org.

19. Isabel Valle, *Fields of Toil* (Pullman: Washington State University Press, 1994), p. 5, 50, 158, 219.

10. HOLDOUTS

1. Wtf1958, blog post response to Stephanie Coontz, "How Clinton Lost the White Working Class," November 10, 2016, cnn.com.

2. Clarisse Loughrey, "Charlottesville: Van Jones Left in Tears Over Donald Trump's Press Conference Remarks," August 16, 2017, independent.co.uk.

3. Peter Holley, "KKK Official Newspaper Supports Donald Trump for President," November 2, 2016, washingtonpost.com.

4. Chris Reeves, "Jorge Ramos: Republicans Want to Make America White Again," February 12, 2018, townhall.com.

5. Ta-Nehisi Coates, "The First White President," October 2017, theatlantic.com.

6. Kiron Skinner, *Reagan: A Life in Letters* (New York: Free Press, 2004), p. 171.

7. Cited by Harry V. Jaffa, *Crisis of the House Divided* (Chicago: University of Chicago Press, 2009), p. 74.

8. Abraham Lincoln, letter to Joshua F. Speed, August 24, 1855, in Mario M. Cuomo and Harold Holzer, eds., *Lincoln on Democracy* (New York: HarperCollins, 1990), p. 83.

9. Frederick Douglass, "The Reason for Our Troubles," cited by Jill Lepore, "Wars Within," November 21, 2016, newyorker.com; Eric Foner, *Free Soil, Free Labor, Free Men* (New York: Oxford University Press, 1995), p. 233, 237.

10. Edward Carmines, Michael J. Ensley and Michael W. Wagner, "Ideological Heterogeneity and the Rise of Donald Trump," December 2016, researchgate.net; Daniel Cox, Rachel Lienesch and Robert P. Jones, "Beyond Economics: Fears of Cultural Displacement Pushed the White Working Class to Trump," May 9, 2017, prri.org; Emma Green, "It Was Cultural Anxiety That Drove White Working-Class Voters to Trump," May 9, 2017, theatlantic.com; Alex Roarty, "Report: Obama-Turned-Trump Voters Cost Hillary Election," May 1, 2017, seattletimes.com; Nate Cohn, "The Obama-Trump Voters Are Real. Here's What They Think," August 15, 2017, nytimes.com.

11. Paul Sracic, "Why Trump Gets Backing of White Working Class Voters," September 6, 2016, cnn.com.
12. David Wasserman, "The One County in America That Voted in a Landslide for Both Trump and Obama," November 9, 2017, fivethirtyeight.com.
13. Tim Hains, "CNN's Van Jones Speaks with Obama Voters Who Switched to Trump," December 7, 2016, realclearpolitics.com.
14. David Brion Davis, *Inhuman Bondage* (New York: Oxford University Press, 2006), p. 49.
15. Nancy Isenberg, *White Trash* (New York: Viking, 2016), p. 13.
16. Don Jordan and Michael Walsh, *White Cargo: The Forgotten History of Britain's White Slaves in America* (New York: New York University Press, 2008), p. 15.
17. Davis, *Inhuman Bondage,* p. 127.
18. Anne Case and Angus Deaton, "Mortality and Morbidity in the Twenty-First Century," March 2017, brookings.edu.
19. J. D. Vance, *Hillbilly Elegy* (New York: HarperCollins, 2016), p. 43–44, 173.
20. Justin Haskins, "Trump Keeps His Promise: Blacks and Hispanics Do Better with Him Than Obama," January 6, 2018, foxnews.com.
21. David Chalmbers, *Hooded Americanism* (Durham: Duke University Press, 1987), p. xii.
22. "Hugh Hewitt, Van Jones Spar Over White Supremacy," December 2, 2016, dailycaller .com; William Saletan, "What Trump Supporters Really Believe," August 29, 2017, slate .com.
23. "Jason Kessler," Southern Poverty Law Center profile, splcenter.org.
24. Chris Suarez, "Kessler Described as One-Time Wannabe Liberal Activist," August 17, 2017, dailyprogress.com.
25. Richard Fausset, "A Voice of Hate in America's Heartland," November 25, 2017, nytimes.com.
26. Michael Edison Hayden, "Neo-Nazi Who Calls for 'Slaughter' of Jewish Children Is of Jewish Descent, His Mom Says," January 3, 2018, newsweek.com.
27. Luke O'Brien, "The Making of an American Nazi," December 2017, theatlantic.com.
28. Jason Wilson, "The Races Are Not Equal: Meet the Alt-Right Leader in Clinton's Campaign Ad," August 26, 2016, theguardian.com.
29. Carol Swain, *The New White Nationalism in America* (Cambridge: Cambridge University Press, 2004), p. 21–24; Carol Swain and Russ Nieli, eds., *Contemporary Voices of White Nationalism in America* (Cambridge: Cambridge University Press, 2003), p. 102, 167–68, 254.
30. Blake Neff, "Meet Some of the Literal Fascists Attending the RNC," July 18, 2016, daily caller.com.
31. Swain, *New White Nationalism in America,* p. 29; see also "Sam Francis," Southern Poverty Law Center profile, splcenter.org.
32. Cited by George Packer, "Hillary Clinton and the Populist Revolt," October 31, 2016, newyorker.com.
33. Jared Taylor, *White Identity: Racial Consciousness in the Twenty First Century* (New Century Books, 2011), p. 233.
34. Ibid.
35. Bob Moser, "Richard Spencer Wins Again," October 20, 2017; Graeme Wood, "His Kampf," June 2017, theatlantic.com.

11. EMANCIPATION

1. Abraham Lincoln, "Address at Gettysburg, Pennsylvania," November 19, 1863, in Abraham Lincoln, *Selected Speeches and Writings* (New York: Vintage, 1992), p. 405.
2. Ibid., p. 273, 288, 314–15, 405; see also David M. Potter, *The Impending Crisis* (New York: HarperPerennial, 1976), p. 558; Harry V. Jaffa, *A New Birth of Freedom* (Lanham: Rowman & Littlefield, 2004), p. 245.
3. Jaffa, *A New Birth of Freedom,* p. 297.

4. James Q. Wilson, "A Guide to Reagan Country," May 1967, commentarymagazine .com.
5. Walter Kirn, "Easy Chair," *Harper's,* February 2018, p. 5.
6. Lincoln, *Selected Speeches and Writings,* p. 422–23.
7. Samuel Huntington, *Who Are We? The Challenges to America's National Identity* (New York: Simon & Schuster, 2004), p. xv, 3, 109, 126.
8. John C. Calhoun, letter to Oliver Dyer, January 1, 1849, cited in ibid., p. 114.
9. Martha Nussbaum, "Patriotism and Cosmopolitanism," in Martha C. Nussbaum et al., *For Love of Country* (Boston: Beacon Press, 1996). p. 4–9; Amy Gutmann, "Democratic Citizenship," in ibid., p. 68–69; Elizabeth Bruenig, "Trump's Solution to America's Crisis: Nationalism," January 30, 2018, washingtonpost.com.
10. Frederick Douglass, "What the Black Man Wants," speech to the annual meeting of the Massachusetts Anti-Slavery Society, Boston, April 1865, lib.rochester.edu.
11. Gabor Boritt, *Lincoln and the Economics of the American Dream* (Carbondale: University of Illinois Press, 1978).
12. Cited in Allen C. Guelzo, *Abraham Lincoln: Redeemer President* (Grand Rapids: William B. Eerdmans, 1999), p. 284.
13. Cited in Jaffa, *A New Birth of Freedom,* p. 171.
14. Lincoln, *Selected Speeches and Writings,* p. 99, 364.

INDEX